SPAIN AT WAR

Also Published by Bloomsbury

A Short History of the Spanish Civil War (2012), Julian Casanova
Right-Wing Spain in the Civil War Era (2012), Alejandro Quiroga and
Miguel Ángel del Arco Blanco
Spain: Inventing the Nation (2014), Carsten Humlebæk
The History of Modern Spain (2017), Adrian Shubert and José Alvarez Junco
The Modern Spain Sourcebook (2018), Aurora G. Morcillo, María Asunción Gómez,
Paula De La Cruz-Fernández and José Manuel Morcillo-Gómez
Antiauthoritarian Youth Culture in Francoist Spain (2018),
Louie Dean Valencia-García

SPAIN AT WAR

Society, Culture and Mobilization, 1936–44

Edited by James Matthews

BLOOMSBURY ACADEMIC
LONDON • NEW YORK • OXFORD • NEW DELHI • SYDNEY

Bloomsbury Academic
Bloomsbury Publishing Plc
50 Bedford Square, London, WC1B 3DP, UK
1385 Broadway, New York, NY 10018, USA

BLOOMSBURY, BLOOMSBURY ACADEMIC and the Diana logo are trademarks of
Bloomsbury Publishing Plc

First published in Great Britain 2019

A catalogue record for this book is available from the British Library.

A catalog record for this book is available from the Library of Congress.

ISBN: HB: 978-1-3500-3012-1
ePDF: 978-1-3500-3010-7
eBook: 978-1-3500-3011-4

Typeset by Deanta Global Publishing Services, Chennai, India

To find out more about our authors and books visit www.bloomsbury.com
and sign up for our newsletters.

CONTENTS

LIST OF ILLUSTRATIONS

ACKNOWLEDGEMENTS

My greatest thanks are to the contributors to this edited volume. It has been a pleasure to collaborate with such a talented group of historians and their translators, and to have many rich exchanges on their varied areas of expertise. I am pleased to have worked with two people in particular: the first is my chapter co-author, Michael Alpert, a mentor who first inspired my interest in the military aspects of the Spanish Civil War and from whom I have learnt so much over the years. The second is my father, Alan Matthews, a professionally qualified translator who generously translated two chapters in this volume and proofread a further two. I am also grateful to Robert Gerwarth, director of University College Dublin's Centre for War Studies, for his feedback on the initial book proposal. The project was conceived at his centre in Ireland, where I held a Marie Curie Intra-European Fellowship during 2012–14, and largely produced during the time I worked as a delegate for the International Committee of the Red Cross in Colombia, Democratic Republic of the Congo and Iraq. I am also grateful to the editors, contributors, and translators for their understanding when I was sometimes not easily contactable for extended periods of time; and to Mary Vincent and the anonymous reviewers who provided incisive constructive feedback. It has also been a pleasure to work with the editorial team at Bloomsbury Academic: Sophie Campbell, Dan Hutchins, Beatriz López, and Monica Sukumar. As always, my greatest source of support has been my family: my parents, Carol and Alan, and my sister (and now colleague!), Hannah.

James Matthews
Baghdad, April 2018

LIST OF CONTRIBUTORS

Ángel Alcalde is a lecturer at the University of Melbourne. He holds a PhD in History and Civilization from the European University Institute (Florence, Italy). He is a specialist in the social and cultural history of war in the twentieth century, with a focus on war veterans. His latest monograph is *War Veterans and Fascism in Interwar Europe* (Cambridge: Cambridge University Press; 2017).

Michael Alpert is Emeritus Professor of the History of Spain at the University of Westminster. He is the author of many publications on the government's armed forces including the widely acclaimed *The Republican Army in the Spanish Civil War, 1936–1939* (Cambridge: Cambridge University Press; 2013).

Ali Al Tuma is a Japan Society for the Promotion of Science postdoctoral fellow at the UN University in Tokyo. He holds a PhD from the University of Leiden. His research interests cover the Moroccan participation in the Nationalist forces during the Spanish Civil War and in the French army during the Second World War. He is the author of *Guns, Culture and Moors: Racial Perceptions, Cultural Impact and the Moroccan Participation in the Spanish Civil War (1936–1939)* (Abingdon: Routledge, 2018).

Ángela Cenarro is Professor of Contemporary History at the University of Saragossa. She has published widely on fascism, Francoism, and political violence during and after the Spanish Civil War. She is the author of *La sonrisa de Falange. Auxilio Social en la guerra civil y la posguerra* (Barcelona: Crítica, 2006), which examined Nationalist social care policies.

Pedro Corral is a journalist and independent researcher. He is the author of numerous books and articles on the Spanish Civil War that have focused on the social and military dimension of the conflict, including *Desertores: La Guerra Civil que nadie quiere contar* (Barcelona: Debate, 2006) and republished as *Desertores: Los españoles que no quisieron la Guerra Civil* (Cordoba: Almuzara, 2017).

Suzanne Dunai is a PhD candidate at the University of California, San Diego. Her dissertation research examines the social consequences of food shortages for urban women during the Spanish Civil War and the early Franco dictatorship. Her previous publication explored the changes in public opinion towards the consumption of offal during the 1940s in Madrid and Barcelona.

James Matthews is an unaffiliated researcher currently working with the International Committee of the Red Cross in Iraq and a former Marie Curie fellow at University College Dublin's Centre for War Studies. He is the author of *Reluctant Warriors: Republican Popular Army and Nationalist Army Conscripts in the Spanish Civil War 1936–1939* (Oxford: Oxford University Press, 2012) and editor of the analytical anthology *Voces de la trinchera. Cartas de combatientes republicanos en la Guerra Civil española* (Madrid: Alianza, 2015).

Xosé M. Núñez Seixas is acting chair of Modern History at the University of Santiago de Compostela. His research interests include regional and national identities in modern Europe and cultural history of war and violence, with particular reference to the Spanish Civil War and the Eastern Front during the Second World War. He is the author of *Camarada invierno: Experiencia y memoria de la División Azul* (Barcelona: Crítica, 2016; German version, Münster: Aschendorff, 2016), and has co-edited the collection *War Veterans and the World after 1945* (London: Routledge, 2018).

Mercedes Peñalba-Sotorrío is a senior lecturer at Manchester Metropolitan University. Her research interests are the impact of war on neutral countries, the history of Francoism, transnational fascism with a specific interest in relations between fascist parties, their use of cultural diplomacy, and the analysis of their propaganda and its relation to policy-making and the spread of violence. She is the author of *La Secretaría General del Movimiento. Construcción, coordinación y estabilización del régimen franquista* (Madrid: Centro de Estudios Políticos y Constitucionales, 2015) and is currently working on a monograph on the development of Nazi propaganda campaigns in Spain and Spanish-German relations during the Second World War.

Hernán Rodríguez Velasco holds a doctorate from the University of Salamanca and has written about the Republican military intelligence services, including the repressive SIM. He is the author of *Una derrota prevista. El espionaje militar republicano en la Guerra Civil española (1936–1939)* (Granada: Comares, 2012).

Michael Seidman is Professor of History at the University of North Carolina, Wilmington. His research specialty is Modern European Social/Individual History. His latest book is *Transatlantic Antifascisms: From the Spanish Civil War to the End of World War II* (Cambridge: Cambridge University Press, 2017). He has also written *The Victorious Counterrevolution: The Nationalist Effort in the Spanish Civil War* (Madison, WI: University of Wisconsin Press, 2011) and *Republic of Egos: A Social History of the Spanish Civil War* (Madison, WI: University of Wisconsin Press, 2002).

Verónica Sierra Blas is Professor of History of Written Culture at the University of Alcalá, where she coordinates the *Seminario Interdisciplinar de Estudios sobre Cultura Escrita* (SIECE) and the research group *Lectura, Escritura, Alfabetización*

(LEA). She is a specialist in the study of contemporary personal documents, specifically letters, and is the author of *Palabras huérfanas. Los niños y la Guerra Civil* (Madrid: Taurus, 2009; French version, Rennes: Presses Universitaires de Rennes, 2016) and *Cartas presas. La correspondencia carcelaria en la Guerra Civil y el Franquismo* (Madrid: Marcial Pons, 2016).

Ian Winchester holds a PhD from the University of New Mexico, where he researched masculinity and military service during the Franco dictatorship of 1939 to 1975. He has presented his work at numerous conferences, including the Association for Spanish and Portuguese Historical Studies.

Chapter 1

THE WARTIME MOBILIZATION OF SPANISH SOCIETY, 1936–44: AN INTRODUCTION

James Matthews

On the first day of 1937 we challenged the enemy to a football match. We arranged a time, emerged from the trenches and built goalposts from branches that we jammed into the ground: the match began. We beat them six goals to two. When we were on our way back and about to reach our trenches, they opened fire; I don't think they did so because we were Reds and they were Nationalists, but because we had scored six goals against them. That's what pissed them off.

> Memoirs of Miguel Gila[1]
> Humourist and Spanish Civil War veteran

A 'New' Military History

In spite of the unabated flood of books on the Spanish armed forces and their battles, historians of Spain in the twentieth century have focused relatively little on the interaction of society, culture, and the armed forces, even in the period that has overwhelmingly attracted most attention: the Spanish Civil War of 1936–9.

Existing military histories of Spain have tended instead to analyse the organizational and political aspects of the country's different armies,[2] as well as the precise details of their wide-ranging military campaigns[3] and the biographies of their leaders.[4] The literature based on these analytical frameworks has produced outstanding results and has substantially improved our knowledge of Spanish armies at war. But it is only in the last few decades that historians have examined and prioritized the study of the experience and motivations of low-ranking individuals in their work on Spanish societies at war.[5] As such, the divisions between social and cultural historians and traditional military ones have remained relatively impermeable.

By the second decade of the twenty-first century, so-called new military history is by no means new any longer. Writing in the early 1990s, Peter Paret identified the label of 'new' military history from at least as far back as the late 1960s and defined it as a

> partial turning away from the great captains, and from weapons, tactics, and operations as the main concerns of the historical study of war. Instead we are asked to pay greater attention to the interaction of war with society, economics, politics, and culture.[6]

The argument that a social and cultural approach to warfare and violence enriches our understanding of causality, experience, and consequences is widely accepted.[7] It has also helped highlight the 'variety and change that have typified military institutions, thought, and practice over the ages'.[8] A broader definition of military history and a move away from a battlefield perspective has provided opportunities to ask new questions about societies and people at war, particularly when it also employs comparative and transnational analysis. More recent methodological approaches to warfare have focused on the phenomenology and logic of violence,[9] which are largely absent from traditional military history, and novel re-evaluations have most notably transformed the study of the First World War. In this case, the dialogue between military history and social and cultural history has been effective in challenging traditional political and nation-centric interpretations of that conflict, and even its spatial and temporal boundaries.[10] In doing so, it has enabled a more complex and nuanced understanding of the First World War by incorporating a history of wartime experience and representations, and just as importantly, their legacies in the post-war world. These approaches have not yet been applied as extensively to the Second World War, although recent studies have also produced remarkable new insights into participants' preoccupations and motivations.[11]

This volume aims to develop similar dialogue between military history and social and cultural history in the Spanish case, and has two principal objectives. The first is to advance recent groundbreaking research on the relationship between the Spanish armed forces and society and culture. The principal thread that runs through this book is the impact of wartime mobilization on individuals' lives and the ambition to reintroduce this non-elite group experience into the structural history of the period. Low-ranking participants in both the armed forces and the rearguard are treated as people with a degree of agency, rather than as pawns within rigid organizational systems in which only those in positions of command take decisions and influence outcomes.[12] The underlying notion is that the daily exercise of choice by subalterns, even within narrow limits, can significantly affect the course and our understanding of historical processes. This analytical focus also sheds important light on the particularities of the Spanish wartime experience and which include the way the conflict was framed by the two sides' embellished narratives, as well as the mechanisms for mobilizing populations en masse.[13] The second objective is to make available a cross section of leading Spanish-language historiography on this theme that is not otherwise available in English.

The chapters complement – and, at times, challenge – traditional, political historiography via an emphasis on the grassroots perspective of the experience of war and mobilization between 1936 and 1944. The dates have been chosen to incorporate the period in which Spanish society underwent the most intense period of wartime 'cultural mobilization' during the twentieth century.[14] This happened not only during the civil war itself, but also during the Second World War, when General Francisco Franco's regime asserted itself through continued mobilization against its Republican enemies in peacetime and remained on a continued war footing because of the raging global conflict.[15] This edition focuses significantly on the Spanish Civil War for the double reason that it was the period during which most Spaniards, soldiers and civilians alike, were directly affected by war and that has subsequently attracted most attention from historians working on its social and cultural dimensions. It has also concentrated on the army, rather than the navy or air force, as the largest, most influential of the three branches in which Spaniards served or with which they had contact. The air war, however, is considered through the profound effect that sustained bombing campaigns had on the civilian experience of conflict. Finally, it has also engaged with the human and experiential aspects of 'new' military history and attempted to cover a broad cross section of Spanish (and colonial) society. However, it leaves out excellent work on, for example, the financing of Spanish war efforts and international fighters' participation, as well as war and memory.[16]

Politics and the Military

For most of the twentieth century, Spanish politics and the military were significantly intertwined, even though an increasingly impoverished Spain had ceased to be a major European military power by the start of the nineteenth century and obsolete equipment, low pay, and inadequate training frequently beset its forces. Despite having been associated with liberal reform and progress in the nineteenth century, during the majority of the twentieth century the armed forces became, with a few prominent exceptions,[17] largely synonymous with conservatism and reactionary politics.

On the eve of the twentieth century, the Spanish military reeled from the loss of the remnants of the country's overseas empire, principally Cuba, the Philippines, and Puerto Rico, in 1898. Its biggest challenges were maintaining its relevance and dignity following catastrophic defeats at the hands of the United States. As a result, over the next decades the armed forces channelled their colonial ambitions into a series of interconnected wars in Morocco with small-scale and expansionistic 'pacification' campaigns in between. The Melilla War of 1909–10 and the Rif War of the early to mid-1920s extended Spain's control in North Africa, but not without bloody and humiliating setbacks, including the 1909 defeat at the so-called *Barranco del Lobo*, or Wolf's Ravine, and the rout of Annual in 1921 in which Rif Berbers killed about 10,000 mainly conscript Spaniards.

These events had direct effects on mainland politics. In 1909 Catalan reservists due to be embarked for Morocco revolted and sparked the 'Tragic Week' strikes and a wave of anticlerical church burnings; the Annual 'disaster', as it was termed in Spain, led to the collapse of the government of the day under Manuel Allendesalazar and encouraged General Miguel Primo de Rivera's takeover in 1923, in part to avoid the military facing a full enquiry and assuming responsibility for the defeat. It has also been argued convincingly that officers' experience of conflict in Morocco resulted in the use of colonial methods against the labour movement in metropolitan Spain. This was particularly the case during the Asturian miners' revolution of October 1934 and later during the Spanish Civil War.[18]

During the immediate post-1898 period the armed forces also refined their self-perceived role as the safeguard of the traditional Spanish nation and its existing social and economic hierarchies. This manifested itself as the prerogative to identify and repress 'internal enemies' such as Catalan and Basque separatists and working-class political organizations, including socialists, anarchists, and communists, as well as their trade unions, that aimed to push mass political suffrage and land reform.[19] The praetorian proclivity, marked by officers' *pronunciamientos*, or takeovers, was particularly notable during the 1923 to 1930 Primo dictatorship, as well as during the July 1936 uprising that directly triggered the Spanish Civil War, and during the long years of the Franco dictatorship. Officers who served in Morocco (*africanistas*, as opposed to *peninsulares*, who served on the mainland) especially identified with the call to defend traditional Spain and they were prominent among the initial civil war insurgents. There were, however, also widespread calls for a military takeover in 1919 during the height of widespread strikes that provoked an anti-Bolshevik 'Red Scare', as well as a failed military coup in 1932 led by General José Sanjurjo against the Republican-Socialist government during the Second Republic. This tendency was encouraged by the blurred lines between the military and forces of public order, which often included the secondment of officers between the two. Indeed, the armed forces were instrumental in quashing potentially revolutionary uprisings both during the 1917 socialist- and anarchist-organized industrial action and the 1934 Asturian miners' strike. Moreover, between 1906 and 1931 the armed forces retained judicial jurisdiction over Spanish civilians that offended the 'honour' of the military or the *Patria*, the fatherland.[20]

Neither 1914 nor 1945 were the major turning points for Spanish political or military history, unlike for the majority of the European continent. In both world wars, Spain remained officially neutral even though the conflicts generated internal political divisions. In the First World War, tensions between those who supported the Entente – generally Liberals and socialists – and those who backed the Central Powers – conservatives, the army, and the aristocracy – have been described as a bitter 'civil war of words'.[21] During the early to mid-stages of the Second World War, hard-line Falangists urged Franco to join the Axis powers and fulfil their expansionistic ambitions for Spain, including into Portugal and French North Africa. While Spain did not formally enter the war, in part because its military was critically underfunded and underequipped despite being hypertrophied from the civil war, it sent units of volunteers, known as the Blue Division (army) and Blue Squadron (air force), to participate in Germany's war against the Soviet Union and communism in the East.

Mobilizing for Civil War and World War

Spanish military history follows a significantly different timeframe from Europe's major powers. The country's principal and most devastating war during the twentieth century was, unusually for most of the continent, an internecine conflict in which two sides fought to impose their version of Spanish identity and the right to shape the country's future. And while the Spanish armed forces were frequently engaged in combat during the period covered by this book, they did not at any point take part in full-blown international war. Although this collection is primarily concerned with individuals, it would be impossible to write a history of Spain and Spaniards at war without outlining the course of the military campaigns fought during the period and how the chapters in this volume fit into that timeline.

The Civil War of 17 July 1936 was triggered when factions of the army in the Moroccan Protectorate rose up against the Republican government and brought to a head a number of different and superimposed conflicts – between centrists and regionalists, traditionalists and reformers, religious believers and secularizers, cosmopolitan urbanites and rural traditionalists, and different classes and political ideologies – which had wracked Spain and led to social conflict and often violence. The plotters were motivated by their common fear of the Spanish left, which they believed to be gaining ground and which they associated with separatism, social revolution, secularization, and the breakdown of public order. The Spanish Second Republic, particularly under the Popular Front government elected in February 1936, was perceived to embody this assault on traditional Spain and was seen as the force behind escalating street violence and strikes. While the military plotters expected a quick victory, the relative balance of forces enabled a violent three-year civil war that also embroiled Nazi Germany and Fascist Italy on the Nationalist side against the Soviet Union on the Republican.[22] Their actions against the government also unleashed the social revolution from which they wanted to defend Spain.

During the initially blurry division of Spain into two camps, both sides scrambled to seek armed support and legitimacy for their ambitions. On 18 July 1936, numerous mainland military units followed the example in Morocco, taking control of considerable swathes of territory: the entirety of Old Castile, León, Galicia, and Navarre; the western parts of Aragon and Andalusia, as well as Cáceres, the northern province of Extremadura. These included areas with notable levels of leftist activism, including Seville and Saragossa, and in three prominent cities, Oviedo, Toledo, and Granada, the rebellious military garrisons were isolated amid a hostile local population until relieved. Forces loyal to the government retained control over the remaining Spanish territory, including the main population centres of Madrid, Barcelona, and Valencia; the northern territories, however, comprising Asturias, Santander, and the majority of the Basque Country, were cut off from the main Republican block. This was also the period of most widespread repression in the two zones' rearguards and the violence on both sides claimed almost as many lives in the Spanish Civil War as the actual fighting. It had multifaceted causes that can be traced to considerably before the civil war and mobilized many thousands in the killing sprees that were most intense in the immediate aftermath of the uprising.

On both sides ad hoc militia units and mobile columns composed of political militants and members of the armed and security forces fought each other for control of the cities and strategic positions, including for example the mountain passes north of Madrid. On the government side, socialists, anarchists, and the growing Communist Party mobilized their militants and unions, who believed they were taking part in a great sociopolitical revolutionary civil war. They also raised militia columns that were the backbone of the Republic's improvised and desperate initial defence against the rebels, even if they did not always cooperate effectively between each other. This is the subject of Michael Alpert and James Matthews's contribution, which examines the period before the formal creation of the Republican Popular Army in October 1936 and elucidates how a partially successful military uprising met sufficient resistance to allow it to develop into a lengthy conventional war. On the Nationalist side, the militias were mainly drawn from the Falange and the Carlists, as well as from supporters of the *Confederación Española de Derechas Autónomas* (CEDA), or Spanish Confederation of the Autonomous Right. These first two, the Falangist and Carlist militias, are the subjects of Mercedes Peñalba-Sotorrío's chapter. While they too were a key part of the Nationalists' early mobilization, they were quickly united into a political identity subordinate to the rebels' military leadership. This caused significant friction between the two organizations that was also reflected by militia fighters in the front lines, even if the divisions in the Nationalist camp were not as acute as those faced by their enemies.

While the pre-war Spanish army was roughly equally split between the two camps, on the Nationalist side it remained largely organizationally intact, in stark contrast with the Republican side, where units dispersed amid the social revolution. In this period, both sides also looked to procure international support. While German and Italian aircraft helped ferry the élite Army of Africa to Seville to start their vertiginous advance on Madrid, Soviet Russian military aid and the first International Brigades reached the Republic in time to take part in the successful defence of the capital. In many ways, the failure of the rebels to take Madrid – a situation in which the balance of forces was such that no one side could fully prevail – signalled the transition from partially successful coup to a full-blown civil war. This shift was also accompanied by militarization and organization in the Republican camp, most notably with the creation of the Popular Army and its political commissariat. Both sides also implemented mass conscription – the Nationalists automatically and the Republicans more hesitantly, for political reasons – and over three years almost three million men received mobilization orders to serve in the two armies. James Matthews examines the creation and management of the conscript armies in the two zones in the context of 'total war', as well as the specifically Spanish experience of the men forced to fight in comparison to other contemporary European wars.[23] While the Nationalists inherited the greater part of the pre-war army's structures and traditions, the Republicans created a new model of an armed force that emerged from its militia components.

In the next stage of the conflict, two sizeable armies faced off around Madrid, without either being able to break the deadlock, and the Nationalists managed to successfully recapture the isolated strip of northern Republican territory. Twice the Nationalists attempted to encircle the capital, once in the south in the Jarama valley (February 1937) and again in the north, advancing with their Italian allies, the *Corpo Truppe Volontarie* (CTV), or Corps of Volunteer Troops, on Guadalajara in March. And twice the Republicans repelled them at great cost to both sides. The Republicans counter-attacked in Brunete, in July, but their offensive failed to gain traction too. In the north, however, it was a different story and the rebels' advance steadily crushed Basque ambitions for independence, capturing Bilbao in June and advancing onto Irún, near the border with France in August. By the end of September 1937, the northern Republican zone had effectively been subdued. During this period, communist and anarchist factions within the Republican camp fought each other in street battles in Barcelona in May 1937, triggering the government crisis that forced Prime Minister Largo Caballero's resignation. His successor, Dr Juan Negrín, was a socialist, but closer to the communist position. He was also committed to keeping revolution out of the government, consolidating government power over worker organizations, and was able to introduce more traditional discipline in the Republican army.

Despite a massive influx of men into the two armed forces and the large-scale acquisition of war materiel, neither side had the capacity to field more than one main operational army at any given time during the entire conflict. The two armies also faced the considerable challenge of keeping fighters committed to the cause, as Pedro Corral examines in his study of desertion. However, it was the Republic that faced especially acute problems with unauthorized absences, particularly towards the end of the war when supplies – and as a result, combatants' morale – were often desperately low. The Nationalists' attempt to create an effective fighting force also involved the mobilization of an unprecedented number of Moroccan soldiers both from Spain and France's protectorates. Almost 70,000 Moroccan men with a fearsome military reputation fought with the rebels in Spain, and Ali Al Tuma analyses their experiences, motivations, and interactions with the Spanish population. The two sides also sought an effective understanding of the enemy's movements and morale. In a chapter that employs 'new' combat history, Hernán Rodríguez Velasco traces the grassroots functioning of the government's information and espionage services through an examination of front-line agents and their civilian contacts in rebel territory. Neither side, however, significantly made use of guerrilla forces during the conflict, in part because the leaders were distrustful of the political independence that this could entail.

From Madrid, the Nationalists turned their attention to the centre-east of the country, advancing into Aragon. The Republic still wielded a large and powerful army, but it gradually lost territory to its enemies. It was, however, capable of two last major offensives in the war. The first was aimed at Teruel, the only provincial capital recaptured by the government during the entire war, and that fell to Republican troops in December 1937. The victory, however, in the end proved hollow, as the Nationalist counter-attack retook the city in freezing winter conditions in February 1938 and pushed on to split Republican territory once more in two, reaching the Mediterranean coast in April. This Republican defeat in Teruel in the winter of 1937/8 is traditionally seen as the military turning point of the war. From here onwards, the government was increasingly short of men and supplies, stripping the countryside bare before the end of the conflict to feed its population and obliging reluctant men as young as sixteen and as old as forty-five to join front-line units. The second Republican offensive, launched across the Ebro River in July 1938, was again initially successful and surprised the Nationalist military command. But, like during the Brunete campaign, the Republican infantry became pinned down and rebel relief forces steadily pushed them back to their starting point by November. From here onwards the Republican military retreated in disarray and the Nationalists advanced rapidly into the northeast of the country. The city of Barcelona fell on 26 January 1939 triggering a massive exodus of refugees towards France. On the international stage, Britain and France signed the Munich Agreement in September 1938 with Nazi Germany and Fascist Italy – both openly assisting Franco militarily in Spain since the start of the conflict – and undermined the Republican leadership's hope that the outbreak of a European-wide conflict would force the two democracies to intervene on their side in Spain.[24]

It was during the civil war that Spanish civilians were for the first time exposed to the effects of 'total war' and neither gender, age, nor non-combatant status kept them from its direct consequences. This included the violent rearguard repression described above, as well as bombing, disease and the widespread and critical shortages, especially of food, that particularly shackled the Republican war effort and starved and demoralized its citizens, many of whom were refugees. In his chapter, Michael Seidman provides a comparative analysis of the two warring sides' economies, arguing that the rebels were more effective in establishing economic controls and supplying their zone with basic necessities – a factor that was crucial in their victory. But civilians also entered into contact with the military during the civil war and in the later period through other means: as families and partners of drafted soldiers, and in nursing and other non-combatant roles, as well as through the expanded number of women working as prostitutes. In this context, Ángela Cenarro examines social work during the war and the significant and politicized mobilization of women to tend to the elderly, refugees and women and children. In her chapter, Verónica Sierra Blas examines children's experience of the war not just as victims of the fighting, but also as historical agents in their own right. In this sense, they were both the source and the targets of wartime mobilizing narratives. Suzanne Dunai provides a case study of wartime Republican cities and focuses on eating and the increasingly dire situation of food provisioning, which were quotidian concerns for all Spaniards in that zone regardless of age, gender, or political affiliation.

In the final stage of the civil war, the Republic was again divided on whether to continue resistance at all costs or to try and negotiate with the Nationalists. These divisions eventually led to the coup within the civil war in Madrid that pitted communists against other political groups within the government that in March 1939 rose up against the Negrín premiership. The second bout of street fighting definitively demoralized the Republic's remaining defenders, and on 28 March 1939 Madrid fell to the Nationalists' troops without hardly any resistance. Days later, on 1 April 1939, Franco declared the civil war over and the Republic defeated.

Nationalist Spain, however, did not abandon its war footing or demobilize its forces immediately. Quite the opposite: the victors' embellished narratives and the repression of former Republicans transitioned seamlessly into the immediate post-war period in which a general European conflict loomed. As Ángel Alcalde shows, a cultural repression of the defeated was crucial in the early construction and consolidation of the Franco regime, which excluded former Republicans from national life and left many in abject poverty. While the state simultaneously provided benefits for victorious veterans, such as preferential civil service employment opportunities, many also faced hardships in the post-war period, as this examination demonstrates. The Nationalists' virulent anti-communist narratives also endured in a wartime setting during Spain's limited but vicious conflict with the Soviet Union, as Xosé M. Núñez Seixas explores in his chapter on the Blue Division and its Eastern deployment between 1941 and 1944 with the Nazi German Wehrmacht. Numerically speaking, however, the mobilization for Russia was relatively small in comparison to that which continued within Spain in the early period of the Second World War and where the bloated armed forces also fought communist-organized guerrillas that aimed to overthrow Franco. The armed forces were a central pillar of the Franco regime, alongside the Catholic Church and, as Ian Winchester examines in his chapter, the Francoist authorities used compulsory and widespread peacetime military service to impose its vision of normative masculinity on a large number of Spanish men through its military discourse, education, and culture. It also employed an extended four-year period of military service as a means to punish men who had fought with the Republic during the civil war and maintain a pre-emptively large standing army during the Second World War.

In sum, the chapters that follow seek to recover the individual from the political history of 1939 to 1944 and use an expansive set of lenses to examine the experience of conflict and mobilization in a setting of 'total war'. In doing so, it reconsiders a crucial human facet of twentieth-century Spanish history.

Further Reading

Graham, Helen. *The Spanish Civil War: A Very Short Introduction*. Oxford: Oxford University Press, 2005.

Lannon, Frances. *The Spanish Civil War 1936-1939*. Oxford: Osprey, 2002.

Thomas, Hugh. *The Spanish Civil War*. London: Penguin, 2003.

Vincent, Mary. *Spain, 1833-2002, People and State*. Oxford: Oxford University Press, 2007.

Notes

1   Miguel Gila, *Y entonces nací yo. Memorias para desmemoriados* (Madrid: Temas de Hoy, 1995), 181.

2   The best overview of the Spanish military is *A Military History of Modern Spain. From the Napoleonic Era to the International War on Terror*, ed. Wayne H. Bowen and José E. Álvarez (Westport, CT: Praeger, 2007). See also Fernando Puell de la Villa, *Historia del Ejército en España* (Madrid: Alianza, 2009), as well as Michael Alpert's excellent *The Republican Army in the Spanish Civil War, 1936 1939* (Cambridge: Cambridge University Press, 2013) (1st edition, in Spanish, 1978; the English version has a new chapter on 'experiences of individuals', which reflects recent historiographical interests); and José Semprún, *Del Hacho al Pirineo: El Ejército Nacional en la guerra de España* (Madrid: Actas, 2004).

3   The most prolific writer of detailed campaign histories has been José Manuel Martínez Bande, *Monografías de la guerra de España*, i–xviii (Madrid: San Martín, 1964–79).

4   The most well-known biography, with a remit far beyond traditional military history, is Paul Preston's magisterial *Franco: A Biography* (London: HarperCollins, 1993). See also, for example, José Andrés Rojo, *Vicente Rojo. Retrato de un general republicano* (Barcelona: Tusquets, 2005).

5   Particularly notable among these are Pedro Corral, *Desertores: La guerra civil que nadie quiere contar* (Barcelona: Debate, 2006); José Hinojosa Durán, *Tropas en un frente olvidado. El ejército republicano en Extremadura durante la Guerra Civil* (Mérida: Editora Regional Extremadura, 2009); and Michael Seidman's two books, *Republic of Egos: A Social History of the Spanish Civil War* (Madison, WI: University of Wisconsin Press, 2002) and *The Victorious Counterrevolution: The Nationalist Effort in the Spanish Civil War* (Madison, WI: University of Wisconsin Press, 2011). My own *Reluctant Warriors. Republican Popular Army and Nationalist Army Conscripts in the Spanish Civil War 1936-1939* (Oxford: Oxford University Press, 2012) develops this interest. In the 1970s Rafael Abella first published two vivid accounts of the Nationalist and Republican rearguards during the civil war, but unfortunately did not footnote his sources: *La vida cotidiana durante la guerra civil: La España Nacional* (Barcelona: Planeta, 2006) and *La vida cotidiana durante la guerra civil: La España Republicana* (Barcelona: Planeta, 2004). Most of these works emphasize the role of 'self-interested' individuals not living up to their expected ideological commitments. For an alternative view of the Republican side, that argues that a syncretic, but genuine and popular 'antifascist culture … was certainly in the making in Spain', see Hugo García, 'Was There an Antifascist Culture in Spain during the 1930s?', in *Rethinking Antifascism: History, Memory and Politics, 1922 to the Present*, ed. Hugo García et al. (New York: Berghahn, 2016), 92–113.

6   Peter Paret, 'The New Military History', in *Parameters*, The US Army War College Quarterly (Autumn 1991): 10–11.

7   Mark Moyar, 'The Current State of Military History', in *The Historical Journal* 50 (2007): 225–40. See also, Jeremy Black, *Rethinking Military History* (Oxford: Routledge, 2004). Critics have argued, however, that the pendulum may have swung too far the other way leading to a 'reduced role of combat within analytical narratives' in 'new' military history. See William P. Tatum III, 'Challenging the New Military History: The Case of Eighteenth-Century British Army Studies', *History Compass*, 5/1 (2007): 80. The essays in *Warfare and Culture in World History*, ed. Wayne E. Lee

(New York: New York University Press, 2011) also advocate a 'return to the battlefield' but with an examination of the role of culture.

8   John A. Lynn, *Battle. A History of Combat and Culture* (New York: Westview, 2003), xiv.

9   See especially Joanna Bourke, *An Intimate History of Killing: Face-to-Face Killing in Twentieth-Century Warfare* (London: Granta, 1999); Dave Grossman, *On Killing: The Psychological Cost of Learning to Kill in War and Society* (New York: Back Bay, 2009) and Stathis N. Kalyvas, *The Logic of Violence in Civil War* (Cambridge: Cambridge University Press, 2006).

10 For a ground-breaking recent example of comparative and transnational history that expands the very concept of the First World War, see *War in Peace. Paramilitary Violence in Europe after the Great War* ed. Robert Gerwarth and John Horne (Oxford: Oxford University Press, 2012).

11 On individuals' motivation see, for example, Sönke Neitzel and Harald Welzer, *Soldaten: On Fighting, Killing and Dying* (London: Simon & Schuster, 2012). For front-line experience see Omer Bartov, *The Eastern Front, 1941–1945, German Troops and the Barbarisation of Warfare*, 2nd edn. (Basingstoke: Springer, 2001).

12 For a theoretical approach to historical agency, see Alex Callinicos, *Making History: Agency, Structure, and Change in Social Theory* (Leiden: Brill, 2004).

13 This is a move away from what Lynn calls the concept of the 'universal soldier', which does not account sufficiently for cultural variations when examining different societies at war, and which by extension could also, in the age of 'total war', be extended to include an equally flawed concept of a 'universal civilian'. See Lynn, *Battle*, xiii–xvii. In this context, embellished narratives are understood to be what synthesized and characterized the fundamental meanings of the conflict for its participants. See, for example, Samuel Hynes, 'Personal Narratives and Commemoration', in *War and Remembrance in the Twentieth Century*, ed. Jay Winter and Emmanuel Sivan (Cambridge: Cambridge University Press, 1999), 207.

14 The term 'cultural mobilization' is from John Horne, 'Introduction: Mobilizing for "Total War", 1914-1918', in *State, Society and Mobilization in Europe during the First World War*, ed. John Horne (Cambridge: Cambridge University Press, 2002), 1–18.

15 The argument that the civil war did not end after the fighting is most closely associated with Michael Richards, *A Time of Silence: Civil War and the Culture of Repression in Franco's Spain* (Cambridge: Cambridge University Press, 1998). The Franco regime only began to demobilize during the Second World War. See Ismael Saz Campos, 'El primer franquismo', *Ayer*, 36 (1999): 201–22.

16 See, for example, José Ángel Sánchez Asiaín's meticulous, *La financiación de la Guerra Civil española. Una aproximación histórica* (Barcelona: Planeta, 2012); Richard Baxell, *British Volunteers in the Spanish Civil War: The British Battalion in the International Brigades 1936-1939* (London: Routledge, 2004) and Paloma Aguilar, *Memoria y olvido de la guerra civil española* (Madrid: Alianza, 1996).

17 For example, Fermín Galán was executed in 1930 for leading a Republican and anti-Monarchist military uprising in Jaca. During the Second Republic, left-wing officers joined the secret *Unión Militar Republicana Antifascista* (UMRA), or Republican Antifascist Military Union.

18 Sebastian Balfour, *Deadly Embrace. Morocco and the Road to the Spanish Civil War* (Oxford: Oxford University Press, 2002).

19 For the classic studies of politics and the military during this period, see Stanley G. Payne, *Politics and the Military in Modern Spain* (Stanford: Stanford University Press,

1967) and Carolyn Boyd, *Praetorian Politics in Liberal Spain* (Chapel Hill: University of North Carolina Press, 1979).

20 Manuel Ballbé, *Orden público y militarismo en la España constitucional 1812–1983* (Madrid: Alianza, 1983).

21 Gerald H. Meaker, "'A Civil War of Words": The Ideological Impact of the First World War in Spain', in *Neutral Europe between War and Revolution 1917-23*, ed. Hans A. Schmitt (Charlottesville: University of Virginia Press, 1988), 1–66.

22 'Nationalist' and 'Republican' are used throughout this volume simply as terms to identify the two warring camps.

23 The definition of 'total war' is contested, especially as to whether the First World War or the Second World War should be considered the model type. See Roger Chickering and Stig Förster, 'Are We There Yet? World War II and the Theory of Total War', in *A World at Total War: Global Conflict and the Politics of Destruction*, ed. Roger Chickering, Stig Förster and Bernd Greiner (Cambridge: Cambridge University Press, 2005). For the Spanish case, see Roger Chickering, 'The Spanish Civil War in the Age of Total War', in *'If You Tolerate This...': The Spanish Civil War in the Age of Total War*, ed. Martin Baumeister and Stefanie Schüler-Springorum (Frankfurt: Verlag, 2008), 28–46.

24 Michael Alpert, *A New International History of the Spanish Civil War*, 2nd ed. (Basingstoke: Palgrave Macmillan, 2004), 165–70. The policy of resistance was particularly associated with Prime Minister Juan Negrín.

Part One

INITIAL MOBILIZATION

Chapter 2

'WITH NOTHING BUT OUR BARED CHESTS': REPUBLICAN ARMED COLUMNS IN THE MILITIA PHASE OF THE SPANISH CIVIL WAR

Michael Alpert and James Matthews

The partially successful right-wing military uprising on 17 July 1936 triggered a rapid response from the Spanish left, which mobilized to oppose the insurgent faction of the army. The groups that fought for the Republic immediately after the coup were an uncoordinated and diverse combination of union- and party-organized volunteer militia. Socialists, anarchists, and communists, whose organizations intended to advance their own political agendas – including social revolution – while fighting for the government, raised columns and armed their militants with the help of the authorities to quell the insurrection. They were reinforced and at times also led by members of the security and armed forces.[1] These men, and to a lesser extent women, were the Republic's first line of defence against the insurgents after the pre-war regular Spanish army disintegrated – even in areas where the military rising had failed – and revolution generally prevailed.[2]

The Republican militia phase of the Spanish Civil War captured the imagination of contemporaries and subsequent observers, and the image of popular mobilization has persisted as a major reference point in the conflict to this day. Indeed, the militia forces have tended to eclipse other Republican participants in popular memory of the war, with perhaps the exception of the famed International Brigades. The process began early in the conflict and was driven by both Spaniards and foreigners, often with an ideological objective. Politicized accounts of fighting in Spain and orchestrated propaganda photographs of militiamen and women greatly contributed to this development.[3] One of the principal reasons was that the image of popular mobilization benefited the Republican government and its supporters because it was associated with widespread support and a sense of legitimacy in the conflict. It was also politically expedient because the militia were largely raised from among Spain's industrial workers and agricultural labourers.

Yet despite the militia's exalted position in the pantheon of the Republic's defence during the civil war, its early defenders have been relatively understudied.[4] This chapter is an attempt to fill this gap and it makes extensive use of primary sources to examine the Republican militia period of the Spanish Civil War in the central zone of the conflict.[5] Most of these sources are from the Republican military hierarchy itself, which tend to reflect the obvious discomfort of professional officers trying to command undisciplined and untrained militia, and need to be balanced against other, less voluminous material. To do so, the chapter looks at militia make-up, equipment and recruitment, as well as organization and effectiveness on the battlefield. A study of the Republic's militia forces is important to comprehend how a partially successful military uprising met sufficient resistance to develop into a three-year-long conventional war. It also helps explain the Republic's need to militarize and regularize its forces, establishing its control over disparate units, and the creation of the Republican Popular Army within three months of the insurgents' uprising.[6] This chapter also examines the reasons why the Republican militia came to be considered a liability, to be controlled and regimented, unlike in the Nationalist zone where the Falangist and Carlist militia were militarized from the beginning of the conflict and considered a valuable asset on the battlefield (as examined in Chapter 3).

Mobilization, Make-Up, and Equipment of the Militia Columns

Historians generally now acknowledge that Republican militia were made up of politicized militants, and were not the product of widespread popular mobilization. As such, the militia 'cannot be described as "the nation in arms"'.[7] Madrid and its surrounding metropolitan area had a population of approximately 1.5 million and yet only supplied 10,000 volunteers, according to one estimate.[8] The number of volunteers was also low in Valencia and Catalonia, the other two important Republican population centres.[9] One estimate for Barcelona tallied as few as 5,000 men in militia units and argued there were fewer volunteers than there were arms.[10] Franz Borkenau, a contemporary observer, described a similar situation in the countryside, where there was 'practically no volunteering … in the villages'.[11] Militia enrolment figures remained low despite forceful press campaigns and sustained social pressure to enlist, and highlighted the limitations of voluntary recruitment via political parties and unions.[12] Indeed, widespread popular mobilization was not forthcoming for either side.[13]

For both Republicans and Nationalists, it was therefore largely the most politicized militants who volunteered, while the masses were only later genuinely mobilized by conscription. Estimates for the total number of Republican militia fighters vary, but the figure is generally about 100,000.[14] From records produced by the *Comandancia General de Milicias*, the General Command of Militias, an organization charged with coordinating the volunteer fighters, it is 'plausible' that there were 89,391 men in arms in the central zone during October 1936.[15] Another estimate, by military historians Ramón y Jesús María Salas Larrazábal, estimates 120,000 Republican volunteers in the first months of the conflict.[16]

Before the Republic instituted obligatory military service, however, it attempted to establish control over its forces by creating two different organizations. These were the *Inspección General de Milicias*, the Inspectorate General of Militias, and its successor named above, the *Comandancia*.[17] Both were intended to create a disciplined and reliable fighting force for the Republic and used techniques such as refusing to pay and supply badly organized battalions in order to encourage compliance. Indeed, militia supplies and pay were not centralized or regularized until the institution of the *Inspección*.[18] However, as analysed below, the two bodies' jurisdiction and authority were frequently contested.

In response to the military coup, initial Republican militia units were hastily assembled and the make-up of their combatants was therefore highly heterogeneous. They were an ad hoc mix of party and union militants, as well as military and security forces personnel who had remained loyal to the Republic in the face of their colleagues' attempted coup d'état. The column commanded by General Bernal holding the Somosierra mountain pass north of Madrid at the end of July 1936, less than a fortnight after the uprising, exemplifies this diversity. His total forces numbered 2,166 people, including 764 civilian volunteers (possibly including women, although their gender and political affiliation do not appear on the roster), 458 infantrymen from the pre-war Spanish army, 138 cavalrymen, 125 civil guards (the militarized rural police force), 80 Assault Guards (the urban police force set up during the Second Republic), and 62 Carabineers (the border police). The remainder were from the military's pre-war artillery, sapper, medical, and communications units.[19] Other militia columns show a similarly broad variety of combatant origins[20] (see Figure 2.1).

Figure 2.1 Heterogeneously equipped Republican militia forces ready themselves to oppose the military uprising. España. Ministerio de Defensa. Archivo General Militar de Ávila (AGMAV), F.11, 3/3.

The early stages of the conflict were confusing not only as both sides scrambled to gather armed support, but also as the lines between the two camps became established. Militia reports give an indication of the tense days in the period before making contact with the enemy. For example, the Navacerrada Column reported in early August that their limited intelligence on the enemy columns' movements including questioning a 'friend of the interior minister' who summered in the village of Valsaín, north of Madrid, and whose information was corroborated by two women who were also holidaying there and had walked to the mountain pass with their sons.[21]

Militia weaponry was generally heterogeneous and made supply and maintenance difficult because of the number of different parts and calibres needed. One unnamed unit, for example, had just more than 2,500 rifles originating from five different countries and required ammunition of three different calibres.[22] Other units lacked the variety, but suffered shortages and unreliable equipment. A particular problem was the maintenance of more complex weapons, such as artillery pieces and machine guns, and the Guadarrama Column, holding a position north of Madrid, reported that only 'two of the five machine guns belonging to the Assault Guards functioned, albeit deficiently, because of the lack of armourers to undertake repairs'.[23] The quality of the ammunition was not much better and, in September 1936, the column also calculated that an extra 25 per cent was needed to 'replace those [bullets] which might not work'.[24] Militia columns also fought without uniforms and many fighters only had their civilian clothes or uniforms from the pre-war army and security forces, including ones looted from barracks' stores after the military uprising and which sometimes even included German-style steel helmets. In August 1936, for example, the same Guadarrama unit reported the 'urgent' need for changes of clothing, including 2,000 uniforms and 4,000 sets of overalls.[25]

Militia commanders faced shortages of trained officers and men, highlighting the Republic's manpower problems.[26] The scarcity of professional officers was particularly critical in technical units. For example, the artillery detachment of the Guadarrama Column described above requested in September 1936 two captains, seven lieutenants, and six second-lieutenants (*alféreces*) to fully man the unit's batteries.[27] The general staff of the central area of operation, around Madrid, acknowledged the problem when it wrote to the commander of the Gallo Column to say that a 'complete complement of officers is exceptional in today's circumstances', particularly those with 'technical guarantees', meaning those that were sufficiently trained.[28]

Other columns expressed shortages of militia fighters, who were required to cover a 2000-kilometre-long series of fronts throughout Spain.[29] Militia commanders stationed in Cercedilla, north of Madrid, in mid-August 1936 speculated that the reason their forces had not been overrun was that the enemy Nationalist columns attacking Madrid from the north were similarly undermanned:

The Sierra front has stabilized for the fundamental reason that neither the enemy nor we have sufficient numbers to create a manoeuvring force to attack in one or more locations or to attempt an encircling operation. Whichever side first obtains a manoeuvrable force of about five or six thousand men … will have every probability of prevailing on this front.[30]

The Bueno Column, for example, reported in an undated document that it did not have the resources to link up with the units around them and that these would have to send out combatants themselves to create a solid front.[31] Recruiting units also had trouble enlisting men. For example, in October 1936 the 2nd Martínez Barrio Battalion was recommended for disbandment by the *Comandancia* because they had been 'in the process of organization for the entire month of October and ha[d] not obtained in all that time more than 147 recruits'.[32] There is also evidence of resentment between men fighting in the forward positions and those who enrolled in the militia and remained in the rearguard while receiving their pay. For example, in August 1936, militia commanders in Cercedilla reported how 'unfair' it was that many 'strong militiamen … prefer tasks in the rearguard'.[33]

Even when the number of volunteers was sufficient, however, there was no guarantee that they would prove to be dependable combatants. The commander of the Rosal Column, for example, reported in September 1936 that he had been obliged to 'disarm half of his reinforcements' arrived from Santa Olalla, in New Castile.[34] Many professional officers regarded the militia as highly unreliable, especially before they had been exposed to combat. For example, the commander of the Barceló Column wrote in November 1936 that the 'troops that have arrived from Boadilla del Monte [west of Madrid] … have not been fire tested and do not know how to handle their weapons'.[35]

The Republicans' own statistical records provide a good cross section of volunteers in the Republican militia. In July 1937, the *Comandancia General de Milicias* compiled information on 3,300 militia fighters who had 'died, disappeared, or received invalidating wounds' before 31 December 1936. While these figures are the most complete set of data on militia fighters, it is possible that they may not represent the militia average. Men included in this analysis may, for example, have been both more likely to expose themselves to danger (and hence be killed, missing in action, or receive serious injuries), or, on the other hand, more likely to desert from their unit (and hence disappear). Nevertheless, the data provide useful information on the militia columns.

The average militia fighter was young, with over a quarter of the sample twenty years old or younger. Over 60 per cent were twenty-six years old or younger. At the other end of the scale, three men from the sample were more than sixty-one years old.[36] Fifty per cent of the fighters were single and had no children, while 26 per cent were both married and had children.[37] Unsurprisingly, the large majority, 92 per cent, were affiliated to either a party or a union.[38] However, most militiamen were only affiliated to a union, rather than a party: 75 per cent were not affiliated to a political party. By far and away the largest affiliation was to the socialist *Unión General de Trabajadores* (UGT), or General Union of Workers, at 62 per cent, followed by the anarchist *Confederación Nacional del Trabajo* (CNT), or National Confederation of Labour, at 22 per cent.[39] Only 23 per cent earned a pre-recruitment wage above 10 pesetas per day, the standardized militia pay, while the remainder earned less or were unemployed.[40] Finally, the most common profession was that of agricultural labourer, at 36 per cent, while builders (10 per cent), shop assistants (5 per cent), and mechanics (4 per cent) were also among the most represented. Many skilled, urban-based professions, such as bakers and carpenters were also present, but because the breakdown was so specific, each individual category was not a high percentage.[41]

In general, therefore, militants were young and many had not completed peacetime military service under the Second Republic, which recruited at the age of twenty-one. They were also unionized and principally either agricultural workers or skilled urban professionals. This profile is consistent with anarchism and socialism in Spain, which were strong in rural areas and industrial urban ones respectively. It is noteworthy that most militiamen experienced a wage increase by volunteering to fight, and this raises the question of whether some were motivated by financial gain, rather than politics. This certainly seems to have been the case at times, and George Orwell wrote of 15-year-old boys being signed up by their parents for their own economic benefit.[42] The evidence, however, is inconclusive because those who had most to gain from left-wing politicization were also those who earned the lowest wages under the exploitative labour system in place in Spain's fields and factories. Politics and better conditions were therefore not necessarily separable in the motivations of volunteer fighters.

Leadership and Approaches to Discipline

The logistical problem of securing men for the front and tracking their location was a complicated task, made all the more so because of the dislocation of the uprising and the initial collapse of central authority within the Republican zone. The anarchist militia of the central zone of the conflict admitted that in the early days of the war they could not keep track of casualties 'to inform the relatives of our militiamen'. One of the problems was the 'circumstance of volunteers being admitted to militia units directly'.[43] While this solved immediate manpower needs, it created difficulties for the rational allocation of available combatants. To counter this tendency, the *Comandancia* established a recruitment department to administer and regularize the task, where previously different parties and unions had recruited independently.[44] The main purpose was to 'ensure the loyalty of selected men, as well as their physical ability'. It also allowed the central command to create new units from recent recruits.[45]

There were recurrent clashes between professional military officers, who frequently led columns, and their militia charges. Part of the reason was that politicized volunteers mistrusted officers because the latter's former colleagues were directly behind the military uprising. Moreover, most union and party militants disliked militarized regulation, with the notable exception of the communist-organized units, which set them apart from other Republican militias and will be examined below. Anarchists in particular resisted the incursions on personal freedom that the army and traditional discipline represented, so much so that they refused to use standard organizational terms and called their companies *centurias*, or centuries, instead.[46] On 9 August 1936, for example, the civil governor of Guadalajara province wrote to the local commander after visiting the socialist militia forces under Jesús Martínez de Aragón in Sigüenza village. In a report that reflected a traditional view of authority, he described an 'extremely violent scene in which we feared an attack on Martínez de Aragón [by his own militia forces]'. The governor added that the professional officers were in a 'truly frightful situation ... they live in infernal conditions'.[47] A second-lieutenant who reported from Majadahonda, north-west of Madrid, described how the militiamen 'blamed everything [setbacks and shortages] that happened on all those with stars [i.e. officers]'. The officer added that he was challenged by the militiamen and had to make them see that their attitude was 'neither reasonable, nor fair'.[48]

Perhaps more damagingly for the Republic, militiamen did not always obey their commanders. A report from Colonel Jiménez Orge stationed on the Guadalajara front in October 1936 described how the 'CNT militia's lack of compliance to the authority of the command ... led these to occupy the town of Sigüenza against the express orders of the column's senior officer'. As a result of the unauthorized advance, the column had to defend a longer front of 70 kilometres with only 3,800 men and 3 machine guns. 'Our line, if it can be called such', the unit reported, 'is limited to isolated and undermanned detachments'.[49] Militiamen were considered undependable combatants and some refused to spend the night at the front and returned home to their families after a day's soldiering. 'The militiamen abandon their positions with thousands of excuses', according to a Rosal Column report from 15 September 1936.[50] The commander of the Oropesa Column, Colonel Mariano Salafranca, wrote in the same month that men from the largely anarchist *Aguilas* (Eagles) militia stationed on the main road to Madrid would 'leave their positions to go and eat in Talavera'.[51]

The language Republican militia commanders used shows that discipline was a considerable problem. The *Milicias Populares Antifascistas*, or Popular Anti-Fascist Militias, another name for the Communist Fifth Regiment discussed below, called for the 'establishment of a rigid, iron-like discipline that everyone will adhere to'.[52] Part of the problem in dealing with indiscipline was the necessity to conform to revolutionary practices, which emphasized convincing and co-opting participants instead of employing traditional military methods perceived to be arbitrary and insensitive. The thin line that militia commanders and professional officers were forced to navigate was exigent. In November 1936, for example, the commander of the Fifth Regiment's Lenin Battalion detailed the following condemnation of his militiamen's acts. Their indiscipline included

> abandonment of the lines in the face of the enemy, leaving the front without authorization, insubordination with certain detachment commanders, resistance to obey the orders of the command and discussion of these orders.[53]

Even when soldiers did not directly leave the battlefield, there is evidence that petty crime and indiscipline were widespread. The following article, for example, was included in the undated penal code issued to the Fifth Regiment and reveals other infractions:

> Any militiaman who takes advantage of his position of authority to commit theft ... who performs arbitrary arrests, commits arbitrary acts of violence against people or property, or who destroys without reason works of art, museums, or aqueducts will be punished with a posting to a disciplinary battalion for an unlimited period of time.[54]

Nevertheless, some militia commanders behaved like warlords and their columns took advantage of their position of strength. The CNT's Iron Column, for example, was infamous in Valencia for its expropriations and clashes with the re-established security forces.[55]

The Militia Forces in Combat: Performance and Politics

The militia's military and organizational weaknesses quickly became apparent in actual combat. Ad hoc units were often successful during the initial uncertainty of the uprising, such as the celebrated storming of the Montaña barracks in Madrid on 19 July 1936. However, they were little match for trained soldiers, and militia columns were easily scattered by the Foreign Legion and Moroccan *Regulares*. The experience of the Army of Africa was too much for the often courageous but inexperienced Republican volunteers. For example, on 18 September 1936 the commander of the Pedro Rubio battalion noted the 'frequency of great troop disintegrations [*desbandadas*] that occur without apparent reason and that cause the loss of extremely important positions'. He identified the causes of the 'panic' as the 'effect of aviation above all', as well as the 'inevitable privations of war: hunger, thirst and cold'.[56] The Mangada Column, for example, issued an order in August 1936 that prohibited militiamen from uttering 'exclamations such as, "There they are!"; "Run!"' in the presence of enemy aircraft because of the 'childish fear' it was considered to produce. The orders also reminded militiamen that enemy bombs were often jerry-built from 'tin cans that had once held chorizo sausage'.[57] Fighting for an ideological objective in a highly motivated manner did not enhance military competence – leadership and training could have shown militiamen that they could easily take cover from a single insurgent biplane dropping bombs – and neither did it compensate for a lack of equipment. Republican professional officers complained of militia fighters' unpredictability and frequently lacked the influence to control them.

The insufficiency of militia columns as military forces was particularly highlighted in the late summer of 1936, as Nationalist columns advanced on Madrid from the southwest. Militia forces abandoned both Talavera de la Reina and Santa Olalla without putting up hardly any resistance, and despite having constructed reasonable defensive positions. Colonel Salafranca, who commanded the Oropesa Column on this sector, wrote on 7 September a detailed and damning report of the military operations:

> The militiamen generally look to blame their retreats on the lack of commanders without any justification at all. Their retreats are the result of the militia's military structure and the heterogeneity of their units. These are a disorganized mix of men of noble spirits, brave and impassioned defenders of the cause, and men who are the complete opposite. This amorphous mass includes those who, according to the circumstances, will decide to follow one or other leader, and who do not have a conscience of their own; those who in a difficult and dangerous situation will egotistically seek the easiest path to protect their own lives and who forget their duties as militiamen and Republicans.[58]

Salafranca, who wrote with a perspective of a military traditionalist and a career officer, also described the chaotic battlefield, in which he was unable to contain the militia *desbandada* even though he was 'threatened with rifles' for trying to do so.[59] But it is also noteworthy that even in Aragon, where the Republican militias did not face the aggressive advance of professional troops, they were equally incapable of tackling the mix of Nationalist conscripts and militia they faced, who operated under the immediate imposition of military discipline and the willing acceptance of it. A particularly poignant example of the sheer incompetence of Republican militia in another theatre is the failure of the militia landings on Majorca in August 1936, which had disastrous consequences for the Republic's land and sea war efforts.[60]

From officers' reports, it is apparent that many militia units would dissolve in combat and then be reformed in the rear and brought back into the front line for new engagement with the Nationalists.[61] As a result, there was a cyclical and disruptive movement of Republican combatants. For example, in December 1936 the Villalba militia 'convinced militiamen from the Railroad [workers'] regiment to return to the Guadarrama front after a brief rest'.[62] However, the *Inspección General de Milicias* had to give multiple orders to disarm militia units because of their 'state of indiscipline' and often had to refuse these men's entry into Madrid.[63] Political publications often advocated greater punishments for militiamen who deserted (as examined in Chapter 5 of this volume). Different parties and unions also published copious editions of newspapers intended to motivate and instruct their militia combatants, and attempt to make up for an almost total lack of training for civilian volunteers. The first issue of *Milicia Popular*, for example, the Fifth Regiment's publication, was printed fewer than ten days after the military uprising. The publication included a call to arms and highlighted a sense of duty – 'Everyone must join the fight for true democracy!' – as well as list, for instance, 'hygienic rules' intended to reduce the spread of disease in the field.[64]

On the other hand, professional officers loyal to the Republic were frequently out of their depth and commanded units larger than those for which they were trained, further hampering the war effort. All military personnel who remained with the Republic after the July 1936 coup were rewarded with one loyalty promotion. This was a necessary step because of a lack of experienced commanders, but exacerbated the leadership problem, especially when some officers were granted 'two or more promotions'.[65] For example, in November 1936, the commander of the Carabanchel section of the front, southwest of Madrid, issued detailed instructions for unit commanders that included elements routine for experienced officers. Among these were orders to report daily status updates, including unit rosters and casualties, as well as 'short and clear' summaries of any combat and the unit's tactical situation.[66]

Further reasons for militia disorganization in combat were political loyalty to a particular party or union, and a heavily fragmented command structure. Rival organizations frequently refused to cooperate and even competed for scant resources on the battlefield. One anarchist veteran described how rival Trotskyite militiamen (from the *Partido Obrero de Unificación Marxista* (POUM), or Workers' Party of Marxist Unification) just watched, and even laughed, as his unit went into action against the Nationalists on the Aragon front.[67] In addition, politicized militia leaders were often more dependent on instructions from party or union central committees than they were on the Republican government.[68] Political differences between militia units of the various left-wing political parties and unions also created difficulties for the Republic's organization. This was recognized by the government and, with the formal creation of the Popular Army, new battalions were 'numbered correlatively, without any [politicized] sobriquet' as most of the initial columns had adopted.[69]

Political divisions within the Republican camp raise the question of whether some party or union militia were more effective than others. The *Partido Comunista de España* (PCE), or Communist Party of Spain rapidly gained strength and members during the civil war, and its militia, the Fifth Regiment, was particularly successful in projecting an image of high morale and dependability in its propaganda.[70] As argued above, however, day-to-day orders suggest that the Fifth Regiment suffered similar indiscipline to other militia groups. Their principal contribution to the Republican war effort may have stemmed more from their recognition of the need for military hierarchy and discipline than their ability to enforce these conditions. They also helped recruit and train as many as 25,000 combatants for the Republic, which was significant, even if PCE leaders often claimed almost three times that number.[71] While communists might not have been better combatants in battle, they differentiated themselves in this way from anarchists, who most heavily resisted militarization.[72] As a result, when the Republic instituted the Popular Army in the autumn of 1936, it used numerous Fifth Regiment units as the foundation for the new armed forces.[73]

Despite the anarchists' rejection of militarism, they too organized a considerable number of units. For example, the anarchist militia of the central zone created a total of nineteen operational battalions of militiamen. They reported recruiting an eventual 32,000 men who, with the militarization decrees, were organized into Popular Army Mixed Brigades, fighting both in Madrid and later in Teruel province.[74] This number, however, is self-reported and in all likelihood also inflated because of the pressure to be seen to keep pace with other parties and unions.[75]

Not all militiamen fought ineffectually, however, and some columns were able to hold up the Nationalists, even if briefly, such as in the defence of both Badajoz and Toledo, particularly when they had reasonable defensive positions and did not have to face the Moroccan-led advances in open country.[76] A militia unit surprised the Nationalists with its dogged resistance four miles south of Mérida using the natural barrier of the river Guadiana.[77] At Almendralejo, Río Tinto, and Sigüenza militiamen also fought to the death.[78] General Vicente Rojo later summed up his assessment of militia fighters:

> [They] were able to resist sporadically in some places where the energy of commanders prevailed, but this did not prevent the majority being routed without let-up and retreats that lacked any order, even though there were many acts of bravery in combat.[79]

To professional officers it was clear Republican militia units needed training and discipline in order to become an effective fighting force. As Colonel Salafranca wrote:

> If trenches are difficult defensive positions for disciplined regular forces, then it is rash to station militia troops in these positions. Militiamen do not thrive in trenches; they want scrubland, rocks and trees, but flee the parapet when it is punished by machine guns or aeroplanes.[80]

It is therefore plausible that militia fighters could have resisted the Nationalists more frequently had they been deployed as far as possible in adequate defensive positions.[81] This was the case when Republican militias successfully defended Madrid in November and December 1936, although by this time the nascent Popular Army was in formation and the Republic received moral and material assistance from the arrival at the front of International Brigade volunteers and Soviet-supplied heavy weaponry, including T-26 tanks.[82]

The Beginnings of Militarization and the Popular Army

The dissolution of the regular pre-war army created substantial logistical problems for the Republic, which had to institute new systems to manage and supply their impromptu defenders. An inspection of the Guadarrama front from 29 July 1936, less than a fortnight after the uprising, reported that the militia were 'supplying themselves with meat' by hunting down bulls in the mountains.[83] The column lacked brandy, coffee, and eggs, the only provisions mentioned specifically and, revealingly, in that order. In August 1936, for example, the Republican military forces unified the pay scale for all combatants, establishing it at the initially generous 10 pesetas per day for privates.[84] Individual militia paymasters were ordered to cease their activities by the end of the month.[85] At the beginning of October 1936, however, militia units and the defence ministry scuffled over rosters and the pay that columns were owed.[86] An order from August 1936 stated that the 'spectacle of badly dressed and undisciplined militia forces in the provincial capitals ... must cease'. The same order stated that the militiamen were 'living at the expense of merchants and industry, and using chits for items not absolutely necessary'.[87] On the other hand, supply officers who refused unwarranted demands were accused of being 'crypto-rebels'.[88] One syndicalist leader described the situation as a 'perpetual mass revolt demanding foodstuffs'.[89] Socialist leader Julián Zugazagoitia, who later became interior minister, wrote that the 'Republic [was] fighting a war without recourse to laws'.[90] The Fifth Regiment summed up the problems the Republic faced in its organization in August 1936:

> [The difficulties in preparing for war] are caused by the profusion of committees that function without the necessary communication between them. Apart from those established by the state, each union has its own ones with influence over everything. All of these undoubtedly function with the aim of serving the cause, but as their actions are not coordinated or regulated by a single body, the efforts of different groups for the most part counteract each other and the work of all of them is neutralized; effective management [of resources] is lost and both money and time are wasted.[91]

One of the measures intended to counter this duplication was the government's September 1936 requirement for local militia units, which guarded villages and roads in the rearguard, to be 'legalized'. This ensured that the units were formally included in the government payroll, but they were also obliged to detail their number of men and arms to the authorities.[92] A report from October 1936 stated that the previous system meant the government had been paying three or even four men a daily 10-peseta wage for every available weapon in the rearguard, which was considered too expensive and gave a false impression of militia strength.[93] Other men who fled from front-line units tried to enrol in the local militia to keep their benefits, demonstrating their 'egotistic desire for comfort, fear of danger at the front and desire to enjoy the two *duros* [10 pesetas; a *duro* was a colloquialism for five pesetas] daily wage and the food allowance'.[94]

There is evidence, however, of militia fighters' needs being accommodated by their columns. For example, the organization of the Fifth Regiment, written in August 1936, detailed the establishment of 'political representatives' who were to 'look after the needs and ensure good treatment of the militia fighters': the forerunners of political commissars.[95] The representatives' job was to act as mediators both between the volunteer combatants and professional officers, whose relationship could be tense, and between the Republican government and the various parties and unions that raised militia. Other dispensations were made too. In an undated order, for example, the Rovira Column established a postal service so combatants could communicate with rearguard areas.[96] The anarchist militia of the central zone reported that they had 'commandeered a luxury hotel [in the centre of Madrid]' to use as a hospital and even set up a dental clinic for their fighters.[97] Enrique Líster, the communist commander, later wrote that the Fifth Regiment held education and entertainment in high regard, and organized reading and writing classes, as well as cinema screenings.[98] Likewise, not all units suffered continuous shortages and the Suárez Column reported in early December 1936 that the unit had 'hot food every day' on the Madrid front.[99]

Conclusions

The militia, as improvised emergency defence forces, were insufficient when the failed coup became a drawn-out affair. The party and union's columns were largely unsuccessful in battle and were unable to adequately provision and organize their atomized forces. It was also hard for both the government and their officers to control them. By September 1936 the Republic ran the serious risk of losing the war. The militia forces south of Madrid were in full retreat, and little stood in the Nationalists' path to the capital. A sturdy defensive line was desperately needed, as well as disciplined and reliable fighting forces. In this context, politicized and revolutionary approaches to fighting a war were forcefully subjugated to the reality of the military situation, and the government created the Republican Popular Army.

The militia affected the course of the Spanish Civil War in crucial ways, however. First, ad hoc combatants helped defend the Republican government at a sensitive period in which the coup could have quickly succeeded had it not been opposed with arms. The role of loyalist groups of former armed forces and security personnel was central, but political militants made a contribution to preventing a rapid takeover by the insurrectionary army. This was particularly crucial, as regular army units had disintegrated in the Republican zone following the 17 July 1936 uprising, unlike in the Nationalist zone where the insurgents quickly harnessed them.

Second, the militia columns, which included former soldiers and policemen, allowed the Republic time to reorganize its forces into the more conventional Republican Popular Army that was able to resist the Nationalist forces for three years of civil war. There is also evidence that the militia forces became increasingly more organized during the militia period of the Spanish Civil War. In comparison to the unregulated militia groups of July 1936, the organizational capabilities of the *Comandancia* and its supply system were a considerable improvement. With these mechanisms, the Republic had a reasonable grasp of the men and weapons at its disposal, and growing authority over them. The militia was itself also the foundation for the Popular Army and fighting columns were amalgamated into the government's new Mixed Brigades as from October 1936. The creation of the Republican Popular Army and the institution of conscription was tacit acceptance by the government that it could not fight the burgeoning war with militia forces alone.

Finally, militia fighters helped establish the mythologized manner in which the Republic conceived its struggle. The armed units of the first hour became central and powerful points of reference in both Republican propaganda and subsequent mobilization campaigns, which, in part, accounts for their enduring influence in popular imagery of the civil war. The nature of militia units, however, also had lasting influence on the emerging Popular Army, and both the political commissariat and unit trench newspapers, for example, can be traced back to the earliest period of the war. The Republican columns were not intended to fight a protracted conflict, but the legacies of the militia phase of the Spanish Civil War were both organizational and conceptual, and have endured considerably beyond the extent of the government's resistance against the Nationalist forces.

Further Reading

Alpert, Michael. *The Republican Army in the Spanish Civil War 1936-1939*. Cambridge: Cambridge University Press, 2013.

Matthews, James, *Reluctant Warriors. Republican Popular Army and Nationalist Army Conscripts in the Spanish Civil War 1936-1939*. Oxford: Oxford University Press, 2012.

Miralles Bravo, Rafael, *Memorias de un comandante rojo*. Madrid: San Martín, 1975.

Paz, Abel, *Buenaventura Durruti 1896-1936*. Paris: Max Chaleil, 2000.

Salas Larrazábal Ramón. *Historia del Ejército Popular de la República*, 4 vols. Madrid: Editora Nacional, 1973.

Seidman, Michael. *Republic of Egos: A Social History of the Spanish Civil War*. Madison, WI: University of Wisconsin Press, 2002.

Notes

1 For the importance of the security forces, see Manuel Ballbé, *Orden público y militarismo en la España constitucional 1812–1983* (Madrid: Alianza, 1983), 393–4. The July 1936 uprising's leaders were often more concerned about the reaction of the local, professional security forces than the garrisons, because the former were better armed and trained than conscripts.

2 Prime Minister José Giral handed out government weapons to unions and parties on 19 July 1936. See Santiago Álvarez, *Memorias II. La guerra civil de 1936/1939. Yo fui Comisario Político del Ejército Popular* (La Coruña: Ediciós do Castro, 1993), 29–30. The day before, Giral's predecessor, Santiago Casares Quiroga, disbanded army units that joined the rebellion, but the decree affected loyalist units too, and they ceased to be at the government's disposal for its defence. *Gaceta de Madrid. Diario Oficial de la República*, 19 July 1936. The Catholic and nationalist Basque Country was the only prominent region in government-controlled Spain not to experience revolution.

3 See, for example, the first issue of *Milicia Popular. Diario del 5° Regimiento de Milicias Populares*, 26 July 1936, which referred to the militia comprising the 'most engaged [*más sano*] sectors of the working class and of the popular masses'. George Orwell, *Homage to Catalonia* (New York: Harvest, 1980) (originally London, 1938) and Ernest Hemingway, *For Whom the Bell Tolls* (New York: Charles Scribner's Sons, 1940) were

particularly influential outside Spain. See also, *Land and Freedom*, dir. Ken Loach, 1995 and *Libertarias*, dir. Vicente Aranda, 1996.

4 More has been written specifically about women in militia columns, for example, even though they comprised a lower proportion of fighters, than about the militia columns themselves. In general three categories of women were involved: the politically militant, such as the ones portrayed in the film *Libertarias*; those who went to cook, wash, and support their menfolk; and the prostitutes, who contributed to the spread of venereal disease. See, for example, Mary Nash, 'Women in War: *Milicianas* and Armed Combat in Revolutionary Spain, 1936–1939', *The International History Review*, 15/2 (May 1993): 269–82; and Lisa Lines, 'Female Combatants in the Spanish Civil War: *Milicianas* on the Front Lines and in the Rearguard', *Journal of International Women's Studies*, 10/4 (May 2009): 168–87. The number of women in some militia units was significant. For example, on 5 September 1936, the Sigüenza Column reported 30 women in a 560-strong unit. Archivo General Militar, Ávila (AGMAV), Zona Roja [*sic*] (ZR), Armario (A.) 94, Legajo (L.) 1334, Carpeta (C.) 2, Documento (D.) 2/2.

5 This principally includes Madrid and the surrounding regions of New Castile and Old Castile (modern-day Castilla-La Mancha and Castilla y León respectively). For reasons of space, the specificities of militia columns from Catalonia and the Basque Country will not be considered here.

6 *Gaceta de Madrid*, 16 October 1936. Most militia units in the central zone had been incorporated into the Popular Army by January 1937; elsewhere, the process took longer. See Pedro Corral, *Desertores: La guerra civil que nadie quiere contar* (Barcelona: Debate, 2006), 99.

7 Michael Alpert, *The Republican Army in the Spanish Civil War 1936-1939* (Cambridge: Cambridge University Press, 2013), 56–8. See also Corral, *Desertores*, 81–5.

8 Ramón Salas Larrazábal, *Historia del Ejército Popular de la República* vol. I (Madrid: Editora Nacional, 1973), 423. As a former Nationalist officer, his estimates for Madrid and for Barcelona below are possibly on the low side as a way to minimize the scale of Republican volunteer mobilization. This professional background also leads him to view unfavourably not only the revolutionary ideals of Republican combatants, but also their antimilitarist lack of discipline and training.

9 Michael Seidman, *Republic of Egos: A Social History of the Spanish Civil War* (Madison, WI: University of Wisconsin Press, 2002), 38–9.

10 Ramón Salas Larrazábal and Jesús María Salas Larrazábal, *Historia General de la Guerra de España* (Madrid: Rialp, 1986), 121.

11 Franz Borkenau, *The Spanish Cockpit: An Eyewitness Account of the Spanish Civil War* (London: Weidenfeld and Nicholson, 2000), 206.

12 One anarchist group described their 'intense propaganda campaign to enlist volunteers'. AGMAV, ZR, A.94, L.1334, C.11, D.1/3. The government also emphasized the quality of the rations volunteers received, as an added incentive. Corral, *Desertores*, 87–8.

13 Seidman, *Republic of Egos*, 38.

14 Compare this to the twenty-eight reserve classes and estimated 1.7 million men conscripted by the Republic before the end of the conflict. Summarized in Seidman, *Republic of Egos*, 40. The relationship between volunteer militiamen and pre-war paramilitary forces has not been sufficiently explored, even though the question has been formulated. Julio Aróstegui, 'Sociedad y milicias en la Guerra Civil Española: Una reflexión metodológica', in *Estudios de historia de España: Homenaje a Manuel Tuñón de Lara* vol. II, ed. Santiago Castillo et al. (Madrid: UIMP, 1981), 307–25.

15 Alpert, *The Republican Army*, 36.
16 Salas Larrazábal and Salas Larrazábal, *Historia General*, 124. This figure includes militia units in Aragon and Levant, so differs less from Alpert's figure than may initially seem.
17 *Gaceta de Madrid*, 20 October 1936.
18 Alpert, *The Republican Army*, 30–1. The *Comandancia*'s accounting was 'scrupulous'. Alpert, *The Republican Army*, 36.
19 AGMAV, ZR, A.97, L.966, C.5, D.1/1.
20 See, for example, the report dated 7 October 1936 from the column commanded by Lieutenant Colonel Burillo and stationed south of Madrid in Aranjuez. AGMAV, ZR, A.97, L.966, C.7, D.2/3.
21 AGMAV, ZR, A.97, L.966, C.7, D.6/1. The front lines did not become defined until early August 1936. Anthony Beevor, *The Battle for Spain: The Spanish Civil War 1936-1939* (London: Phoenix, 2006), 79.
22 AGMAV, ZR, A.97, L.966, C.3, D.2/14.
23 AGMAV, ZR, A.97, L.967, C.20, D.2/12.
24 AGMAV, ZR, A.97, L.967, C.1, D.1/2.
25 AGMAV, ZR, A.97, L.967, C.21, D.1/17.
26 Although the 15,400 professional army officers on the 1936 active list were approximately evenly divided between Nationalist and Republican zones after the coup, only a small proportion were sufficiently trusted by the Republic. Many professional officers in the Republican zone went into hiding, or were imprisoned or murdered. Alpert, *The Republican Army*, 86–91.
27 AGMAV, ZR, A.97, L.967, C.1, D.1/1-3. The Guadarrama Column submitted an earlier petition for officers in August 1936. See AGMAV, ZR, A.97, L.967, C.21, D.1/17.
28 AGMAV, ZR, A.97, L.966, C.10, D.1/1-2.
29 Although the front lines were not initially continuous in Spain, this was approximately three times longer than the First World War's Western Front.
30 AGMAV, ZR, A.97, L.966, C.20, D.3/1. They were from the communist *Octubre* (October) and *Acero* (Steel) Battalions, as well as local Cercedilla militia.
31 AGMAV, ZR, A.97, L.966, C.6, D.4/4.
32 AGMAV, ZR, A.94, L.1334, C.10, D.3/18.
33 AGMAV, ZR, A.97, L.966, C.20, D.3/1-2.
34 AGMAV, ZR, A.97, L.967, C.26, D.1/2.
35 AGMAV, ZR, A.97, L.966, C.4, D.4/1.
36 AGMAV, ZR, A.94, L.1334, C.3, D.1/2.
37 AGMAV, ZR, A.94, L.1334, C.3, D.2/2.
38 AGMAV, ZR, A.94, L.1334, C.4, D.1/2. This table also presents information on the dates of affiliation and whether this was before or after the uprising. The large majority, however, 87 per cent, were listed as 'with unknown date'.
39 AGMAV, ZR, A.94, L.1334, C.4, D.3/2.
40 AGMAV, ZR, A.94, L.1334, C.6, D.1/2. This was the wage of a skilled labourer.
41 AGMAV, ZR, A.94, L.1334, C.7, D.2/2-3.
42 Orwell, *Homage to Catalonia*, 12. Better pay saw a rise in volunteerism, particularly in rural areas. Salas Larrazábal, *Historia del Ejército Popular* I, 420.
43 AGMAV, ZR, A.94, L.1334, C.11, D.1/4.
44 Alpert, *The Republican Army*, 35. Many men were organized by their profession, including, for example, *Artes Blancas*, a bakers' battalion, and *Artes Gráficas*, a

printers' battalion. For a socialist recruitment announcement, see AGMAV, ZR, A.94, L.1334, C.10, D.1/8-9.

45 AGMAV, ZR, A.94, L.1334, C.9, D.2/13.

46 'Discipline was almost a crime', later wrote anarchist leader Diego Abad de Santillán. Quoted in Beevor, *The Battle for Spain*, 125. Although some of its content is tendentious, there are vivid descriptions of the disorder in anarchist columns in Rafael Miralles Bravo, *Memorias de un comandante rojo* (Madrid: San Martín, 1975).

47 AGMAV, ZR, A.97, L.966, C.12, D.1/16-20.

48 AGMAV, ZR, A.94, L.1334, C.12, D.1/42-3.

49 AGMAV, ZR, A.97, L.966, C.13, D.3/1.

50 AGMAV, ZR, A.97, L.967, C.26, D.1/2.

51 AGMAV, ZR, A.97, L.967, C.12/4.

52 AGMAV, ZR, A.94, L.1334, C.10, D.1/5.

53 AGMAV, ZR, A.97, L.967, C.11, D.1/3.

54 AGMAV, ZR, A.94, L.1334, C.10, D.1/6.

55 Helen Graham, *The Spanish Republic at War 1936–1939* (Cambridge: Cambridge University Press, 2002), 88.

56 AGMAV, ZR, A.97, L.966, C.14, D.2/2-3.

57 AGMAV, ZR, A.97, L.967, C.4, D.1/1.

58 AGMAV, ZR, A.97, L.967, C.12/5.

59 AGMAV, ZR, A.97, L.967, C.12/1-2.

60 For the campaign, see Josep Massot i Muntaner, *La guerra civil a Mallorca* (Barcelona: Abadía de Montserrat, 1977).

61 See, for example, AGMAV, ZR, A.97, L.966, C.4, D.2/5.

62 AGMAV, ZR, A.94, L.1334, C.11, D.3/1. See also AGMAV, ZR, A.94, L.1334, C.12, D.1/13.

63 AGMAV, ZR, A.94, L.1334, C.12, D.1/2-62.

64 *Milicia Popular*, 26 July 1936. These included regularly brushing teeth and changing underwear.

65 AGMAV, ZR, A.94, L.1334, C.10, D.1/2.

66 AGMAV, ZR, A.97, L.967, C.6, D.2/12.

67 Quoted in George Esenwein and Adrian Schubert, *Spain at War: The Spanish Civil War in Context 1931–1939* (Harlow: Longman, 1995), 144–5.

68 R. D. Richardson, 'Foreign Fighters in Spanish Militias: The Spanish Civil War 1936–1939', *Military Affairs*, 40/1 (February 1976): 8.

69 *Gaceta de Madrid*, 20 October 1936.

70 See, for example, *Milicia Popular*, 30 July 1936. One article in this edition described the machinegun section as 'full of youthful enthusiasm, with physical presence and a burning love of freedom'.

71 Alpert, *The Republican Army*, 45.

72 One of the Republic's important challenges was organizing an army while rejecting the rebels' militarism. Gabriel Cardona, *España 1936-1939. La guerra militar: La batalla de Madrid* (Madrid: Historia 16, 1996), 69.

73 Cardona, *La batalla de Madrid*, 90–1.

74 AGMAV, ZR, A.94, L.1334, C.11, D.1/12.

75 Alpert, *The Republican Army*, 50.

76 One commentator ascribes all militia success to their professional military and security forces components. See Salas Larrazábal, *Historia del Ejército Popular* I, 479.

77   Hugh Thomas, *The Spanish Civil War* (London: Hamish Hamilton, 1977), 373. Thomas refers to this battle as the first contest of the war.

78   Alpert, *The Republican Army*, 52–3. Surrender was not an alternative as captured militiamen were executed in the early stages of the conflict. Paul Preston, *The Spanish Civil War 1936–39* (London: Weidenfeld and Nicolson, 1986), 62.

79   Vicente Rojo, *Así fue la defensa de Madrid: Aportación a la historia de la Guerra de España, 1936–1939* (Madrid: Comunidad de Madrid, 1987), 60.

80   AGMAV, ZR, A.97, L.967, C.12/5.

81   Alpert, *The Republican Army*, 52. See also Beevor, *The Battle for Spain*, 116.

82   Beevor, *The Battle for Spain*, 166–85.

83   AGMAV, ZR, A.97, L.967, C.20, D.2/2-5.

84   *Gaceta de Madrid*, 16 August 1936.

85   AGMAV, ZR, A.97, L.967, C.17, D.1/3.

86   See, for example, AGMAV, ZR, A.94, L.1334, C.10, D.3/24. In this case, the Communist Fifth Regiment claimed it was drawing pay for missing and wounded men in case they returned to the unit.

87   AGMAV, ZR, A.94, L.1334, C.10, D.1/1-2. See also Salas Larrazábal, *Historia del Ejército Popular* I, 416.

88   Graham, *The Spanish Republic at War*, 83.

89   Quoted in Graham, *The Spanish Republic at War*, 100.

90   Julián Zugazagoitia, *Guerra y vicisitudes de los españoles* (Barcelona: Tusquets, 2001), 240.

91   AGMAV, ZR, A.94, L.1334, C.10, D.1/3.

92   See, for example, AGMAV, ZR, A.94, L.1334, C.10, D.2/1.

93   AGMAV, ZR, A.94, L.1334, C.10, D.3/10.

94   AGMAV, ZR, A.94, L.1334, C.10, D.3/11.

95   AGMAV, ZR, A.94, L.1334, C.10, D.1/1. For the institution of the political commissariat within the Popular Army, see *Gaceta de Madrid*, 16 October 1936.

96   AGMAV, ZR, A.97, L.967, C.28, D.3/1-2.

97   AGMAV, ZR, A.94, L.1334, C.11, D.1/6-7.

98   Enrique Líster, *Nuestra guerra: Aportaciones para una historia de la guerra nacional revolucionaria del pueblo español 1936–1939* (Paris: Librairie du Globe, 1966), 61–7.

99   AGMAV, ZR, A.97, L.967, C.30, D.1/1.

Chapter 3

RED BERETS, BLUE SHIRTS: NATIONALIST MILITIA FORCES IN THE SPANISH CIVIL WAR*

Mercedes Peñalba-Sotorrío

Immediately after the 18 July 1936 military uprising, Carlists and Falangists mobilized to support the Nationalist war effort, becoming the two largest militia components of the rebel army. Soon enough, the rebels received further military support from Germany and Italy. In December 1936, a contingent of fascist volunteers arrived in Cadiz. Eager to join the rebel forces, they were quick to ask for red berets – an unmistakably Carlist symbol – as proof of their bonding and fraternity with the Spanish volunteers. The apparently inconsequential gesture soon provoked tensions within the rebel militias. Some Falangist women, urged on by their comrades, took upon themselves to falsely inform the Italian volunteers of the Republican symbolism of the red beret, associating its colour with the enemies of Mussolini and Franco. The Italians immediately threw the berets on the floor and trampled all over them, provoking the Carlist militia (the *requetés*) delegate to bring his complaints to the attention of the local Falangist head.[1] Such incident not only reflects the rivalry between Falangists and Carlists, but also illustrates the importance of symbolic language in shaping the image of the combatants and the relationship between them. In fact, the red beret would be at the centre of many frictions among Falangists and Carlists during the conflict, particularly after the Unification Decree of April 1937 fused both groups into a single and politically emasculated entity.

An Uneasy Collaboration against a Common Enemy

As historian Javier Rodrigo has stated, civil wars are not only total war conflicts, but also multi-layered ones. They are, at the same time, national and international, regular and irregular, against armies and the people, resulting in particularly violent events.[2] Because civil wars involve a fight about the essence of the nation and the shaping of a frequently utopian future society, conflicts within fighting coalitions are key to understanding them. Tensions between Falange and Carlism are a good example. United in their fight against the Republic, Falangist and Carlist fighters were comrades-in-arms at the front, but were divided over many issues: their leaders competed for the New State's top political positions, and their grassroots supporters clashed over different modes of interpreting the war and its objectives. Although united by a common goal and their opposition to liberalism, communism, and parliamentarism,[3] they were opposed regarding key elements of their cosmologies. For Falange and its leader, José Antonio Primo de Rivera, Carlism was an uncompromising, obstinate, and obnoxious movement,[4] whose ideas of corporatism and obsession with the monarchy could neither solve Spain's problems nor obliterate the class struggle. For Carlism, Falange's syndicalism seemed a socialist deviation, which paired with their centralism and statist proposals for the country, endangered their more regional, *foralista* – that is, the observance of the traditional laws and institutions of the regions and the rejection of liberal centralism – and on-paper anti-statist approach to government. These suspicions, however, did not prevent their youth organizations from pursuing joint street actions during the last months of the Republic. As Martin Blinkhorn stated in his seminal work on Carlism, the gap between them was 'wide at some points and at others almost non-existent'.[5] Consequently, their relationship was complex, and displays of comradeship and loyalty were frequently accompanied by clashes.

Carlism, a cultural phenomenon rooted in a highly traditionalist notion of Spain, found it problematic to align itself with the fascist, modernizing and at times pagan nature of the Falange. Traditional and political historiography has focused on this conflict, particularly for the area of Navarre and the Basque Country, showing how these clashes among volunteers reflected the political struggle at the top of both organizations.[6] However, even though this is true to an extent, more important motivations than political rivalry lay at the core of these tensions. Frictions among grassroots volunteers were born only partially out of political rivalry. More often than not, issues of identity, mentality, and cultural models rather than specific aspects of their ideology or programmatic objectives shaped the individual war experience of these fighters. This would be particularly true of Carlism, whose rebellion against the Republic, as Javier Ugarte argues, can be better understood through the symbolism of its language, its myths, and its liturgy, than as a well-crafted ideology. Carlism was an essentialist phenomenon more than a systematic political philosophy. Its ideas were simple and easily summarized in the slogan God, Country, and King – and as the Carlist Jaime del Burgo points out, the 'common folk' were unable to dig deeper than that.[7] The majority of their volunteers interpreted the civil war as a continuation of a century-long mission to restore the traditional monarchy and protect their traditional way of life, not as a struggle for personal political power. Of course, this was not true of the higher echelons of the party, who did, indeed, pursue political power, but stood divided in their approach to the emerging Francoist regime and the role that Carlism was to play within it. In this sense, divisions between the Navarre leadership and the presidency of the *Comunión Tradicionalista*, held by the Andalusian Manuel Fal Conde since 1934,[8] added a new layer of complexity that also touched upon the experience of grassroots combatants.

The image that current historiography and primary sources offer of Falangist fighters is quite different. Whether motivated by a heartfelt fascism, hatred for the Republic and communism, a desire to gain some (social, political or economic) power, or survival, they tended to be more attracted by the social aspects of the Falangist ideology and its modern ethos, than by the Carlist world view. A young *margarita*, that is a Carlist woman, captured the difference between both organizations in a simple, yet powerful way: 'The Falangist woman is made, the Carlist woman is born.'[9] Other testimony highlights how newcomers could be easily 'made' into Falangists: 'My girlfriends and I joined Falange, which was the best known, although there were other groups like the *requetés* and the one with Gil-Robles, *Acción Popular* I believe it was called.'[10] Falange's proselytism and novelty resulted in an almost meteoric growth that the party would most probably not have experienced without the war. Not to say that Carlism did not grow as well. Thanks to the skilled leadership of Manuel Fal Conde, the *requeté*, the Carlist militia, grew particularly in Andalusia, where it took on more radical notes than northern Carlism.[11] However, although broadly represented throughout the Peninsula, it grew almost exclusively thanks to its own traditional militancy and, once the war was over, lost its newfound members as quickly as it had acquired them.[12]

Falange and Carlism were the only organizations with proper militias on the rebel side before the outbreak of the conflict, whose unparalleled growth, constituting around the 90 per cent of all rebel militias,[13] propelled them to the forefront of the political struggle within the emergent state. Falange established 116 battalions or *banderas*, which numbered just over 200,000 men, while the *requeté* constituted 35 *tercios*, also battalion-sized, which in total numbered 60,000–65,000 men.[14] However, overall numbers are hard to establish, not least because the organizations themselves tended to artificially inflate them in order to exalt their own importance.[15] Nevertheless, their role in the early days of the uprising, where they constituted a significant proportion of the most dedicated of pro-coup supporters, should not be understated. Once under full military jurisdiction, militia units fought alongside regular army units throughout the Spanish Peninsula, and were often entrusted with the most dangerous and sensitive positions during military operations alongside the Nationalists' other elite units, the Moroccans and the Spanish Legion.

In this context, the militias were key, not only because of their contribution to the war effort, but because their actions could be used to justify the ideological predominance of each organization. This was particularly true of the Falange, whose militia had a key political function. For the Spanish fascist party, the militia was an integral section of the party, destined to secure the conquest of the state and maintain the party in power. Post-war attempts to recover direct control over it and transform it into a political police force attest to this reality.[16] The *requeté* was equally central to the Carlist movement. The nostalgia for war and the hope of another that acted as mobilizing myths during peacetime[17] transformed the *requeté* into an instrument for both political and military mobilization. It constituted the only properly paramilitary organization in the pre-war period, although it was conceived as an auxiliary force, an insurrectional instrument, soon to be demobilized after victory.[18] In this, they differed greatly from the Falangist volunteers, many of whom expected political compensation after the war, or even during it. This factor, paired with the Falange's considerably larger membership, would foster clashes with the *requetés* from the very beginning.

Furthermore, the relationship between both movements had been characterized by a dynamic of rapprochement/rejection since the beginning. Following Falange's foundation, Carlist leaders made it clear that Falangism was not at all new, and not even necessary. As one of them would note, even if the fascists were the sons of Traditionalism, 'let us agree that they are degenerate sons'.[19] These assessments did not preclude the leaders of both organizations from pursuing an agreement and further collaboration to topple the Republic, and even consider a fusion when it became apparent that Franco wanted a unified party. In fact, once the failed coup gave way to a civil war, reluctance to cooperate transformed into professions of friendship. As early as September 1936, Araúz de Robles, a member of the Carlist *junta*, declared there was no opposition between their programmes; their Catholicism as well as the universal character of their politics would preclude any potential conflicts between the statism of Falange and the anti-statism of Carlism.[20] While making obvious its disgust at the fascist and foreign character of Falange, the Carlist news outlet, *El Pensamiento Navarro* (Navarrese Thought), proclaimed as well the lack of fundamental incompatibilities between both movements.[21] The same outlet saw, in 1936, a proliferation of reciprocal greetings between Carlist and Falangist fighters, which attempted to symbolize their blood brotherhood. This was apparently confirmed by the Unification Decree, for which they said they had been yearning for so long.[22] Nonetheless, professions of friendship could not hide the fight for precedence that was taking place between them. While stating their brotherhood in arms, Falangist and Carlist publications continued to present themselves as the vanguard of the developing war.

In practice, their relationship during wartime was marked not only by a question of precedence but numbers. As the Spanish Civil War was a performative process in which the transformation of society was being decided,[23] they both saw it as an opportunity to impose their view of Spain within the rebel coalition. For Falange, bolstering its numbers was key to this process, reflecting in turn its fascist desire to integrate as much of society as it could into its project. This attitude provoked constant complaints. In Arcos de la Frontera, in Andalusia, fighters who had transferred from Falange to the *requeté* were said to have been detained and punished by Falangist authorities.[24] Others were denied their discharge in order to prevent them from joining the Carlists.[25] In Malaga, according to Fal Conde, Falange tried to take advantage of the militarization of the militias to bolster its numbers, even threatening to shoot the secretary of the Carlist *Junta* if any Falangist attempted to transfer to the *requeté*.[26] Similar threats apparently followed from Morocco to Galicia. In Navarre, Carlists reported on the fascist party's recruitment tactics, from conscripting leftists in return for their lives, to enlisting people without their knowledge, or poaching *requetés*.[27] The Youth sections experienced clashes as well. In Morón de la Frontera, also in Andalusia, Falange accused Carlists of paying Falangist cadets to transfer to their organization. A Falangist reacted by stripping one of the boys who had transferred of his red beret and defecating inside.[28] As proven by multiple examples, Falangist fighters were quick to notice that insulting the red beret was the most effective way of humiliating Carlists.

Insults and crossed accusations were also common between militias, with desertion and the presence of *emboscados*, or shirkers, in the rearguard being a favourite topic when it came to proving who fought better or was more reliable. Carlists accused Falangists of remaining in the rearguard to occupy political positions, a practice corroborated by the reports of the single party.[29] In Lumbier, in Navarre, the head of the *requeté* complained bitterly: 'When those in the Lumbier Falange go to the front lines, spilling their blood and giving their lives in the service of God and Country, as the *requetés* have done, purifying their shady, dark and anti-patriotic past conduct, only then will be time for us to live together as equals in merit, but not before.'[30] Further complaints on the behaviour of rearguard Falangists arrived from other villages in Navarre. In Aibar, the local head of the *requeté* complained because his daughter had been temporarily detained by the head of a passing Falangist squad, for saying that they should be at the front and not in the rearguard.[31] The diary of a *requeté* talked even of the desertion of a whole Falangist company at the front line.[32] A phenomenon that was at least partly explained by the number of leftists they had recruited, and a less common, but not unheard of occurrence among the *requeté*.[33] However, Carlists were not notoriously disciplined either. Particularly before the militarization of the militias, it was common for *requetés* to give themselves the unilateral right to leave, especially after major victories or to engage in agricultural labours back home. They eventually returned to the front, and were punished for their actions, but this did not seem to end the practice completely.[34]

Complaints about Falangist repression were also commonplace, and sometimes provoked fear even among its own members.[35] For many, these actions were proof of the radical and uncontrollable character of Falange, as well as of its status as a refuge for leftists and 'reds'. But others, like Dolores Baleztena, were not ignorant of the connivance between the 'few Falangist assassins' and the military, who did nothing to prevent the repression.[36] However, this created the false appearance of a non-repressive Carlism, which was certainly untrue, particularly in Navarre, where they enjoyed powers akin to those of a state.[37] These actions, however, were not denounced by the Falange, either because it did not find them problematic or because they were committed in a Carlist stronghold. But while repression might not have posed concerns, *requetés*' behaviour towards Falangists did in some cases. Falangist Juan Francisco Bermejo remembers how *requetés* went 'on the hunt for Falangists' at sunset: 'They were very brave, they were always first and the best we had in Spain … but that could not stand, because they not only attacked the reds, but also their own comrades as well.'[38]

A Half-Hearted Fusion

Although not important enough to endanger the war effort, these incidents grew considerably after the Unification Decree of April 1937. While the militarization of the militias had quashed attempts on the part of Carlists to increase their military presence and prompted Fal Conde's banishment, the new decree put an end to the internecine struggles within Falange's leadership.[39] The decree also thwarted Fal Conde's aspirations of absorbing Falange[40] and came to facilitate the opposite. The new measure consolidated Falange's influence over the new single party by adopting its program, while professing the utmost respect for the military tradition and contribution of the Carlists and including a vague reference to the restoration of the monarchy. But while both issues fostered clashes among the leaders of both organizations, it was the fusion of uniforms, rituals, and sections, which truly created unrest among grassroots volunteers.

On the higher echelons of power, despite Fal Conde's protests, the Carlist delegation from Navarre accepted Franco's decision with ease, while on Falange's side, the incarceration of Manuel Hedilla, Falange's provisional head, was followed by the acceptance of the new status quo by the so-called legitimist group. Although frictions between both groups would ensue, as they attempted to secure and expand their spheres of influence within the single party, they ceased to openly question the Unification. Many, in fact, accepted it as a necessary measure,[41] but there were still some significant incidents among grassroots volunteers. There was, for example, talk of leaving the front in some Carlist *tercios*. A company of the America regiment on the Guadalajara front burnt the blue shirts issued as a composite uniform, which also included a red beret, and when a *requeté* was arrested for opposing Unification the rest of the unit refused to go on the attack until he was released. It was also not uncommon for Carlists and Falangists to cross rival shouts of 'Franco and King' versus 'Franco and Falange', at official events.[42]

These frictions demonstrate how the front (see Figure 3.1) and the rearguard were closely interlinked, not only because of the constant transfer of troops but because the rearguard came to be a front line in its own right, marked by the dynamics of power relations and ideological struggles.[43] Contrary to self-interested versions and romanticized narratives that painted a cohesive and brotherly picture of the *Frontsgemeinschaft* (front-line community), where militias accepted the Unification Decree with ease, as opposed to a rearguard where scheming aspirational politicians provoked incidents and rejected the forced political amalgamation, reality was more complex.[44] The front and the rearguard were not watertight compartments, and many times incidents in the rearguard involved fighters recently returned from the front, passing through or temporarily stationed there. Even if experience of front-line fighting and tight cooperation under military discipline left little space to politics, volunteers were still affected by the ideological struggle that was taking place in the rearguard and interacted with it.

Events in the rearguard caught up with the situation in the front lines as talk started about the unavoidable fusion of the militias. The Unification Decree merged them into one, allowing them to maintain at least some of their symbols and uniforms.[45] Nonetheless, the integration process that followed threatened to alter this situation and to replace their independent identities with a new overarching Francoist identity, which in practice meant the adoption of the Falangist symbols and politics. Given the importance of the militias and their political value, the

Figure 3.1 Nationalist militiamen of the María de Molina Carlist *tercio* (battalion) share a meal in the proximity of the Tagus front. AGMAV, F.419, 21/21.

newly appointed Political Secretariat, mostly populated by Falangists, proceeded to dictate norms to secure their seamless incorporation to the single party. They were ordered to serve in merged headquarters, to report only to the new appointed authorities, and to cease using their old name, which sparked multiple incidents regarding the use of their different uniforms and symbols. Additionally, political advisers were appointed to mediate between the political and military authorities to which they had to answer. While the overall military authority was not being questioned, all militiamen had to report to the local party authority whenever they were off active military duty.[46] Confusion surrounding this issue prompted local authorities to request further clarification, and provoked a number of clashes between the *requeté* and the single party.

Carlists were uneasy about the fact that orders from the single party could override Franco's Unification Decree regarding the regulation of the militias. Consequently, in Jerez, Andalusia, during a period of inactivity over the summer of 1937, the *Tercio de Nuestra Señora de la Merced* (Our Lady of Mercy) resisted the attempts of the local secretary of the party to inspect the troops, seeing it as a challenge to the military authority. Further clashes saw the detention of one of their *requetés* for not performing the fascist greeting while off duty. Unable to successfully put an end to the situation, José García y Barroso, ex-delegate of the *requeté*, decided to bring his complaints to Franco. He referred, quite accurately, both to the Unification Decree and to the recently approved party by-laws, which not only preserved their uniforms and symbols, but also stated that the militia should follow specific regulations, not yet approved. They should, therefore, answer exclusively to the military, and not to the political secretary. He asked to be able to live and die bearing the Carlist badge, 'honoured by a purity of conduct and an unfailing loyalty, glorified by the blood of heroes and sanctified by the lives and deaths of so many martyrs'.[47]

Incidents between the militias were not uncommon. In Tauste, Aragon, Falange's insistence in pushing forward their programme at a gathering organized to discuss agrarian matters resulted in direct confrontation with the *requetés*. As the military authorities sided with Falange, the volunteers from Navarre decided to leave without permission, returning home and eventually joining different units elsewhere.[48] Similar incidents happened on the front lines, as young *requeté* Manuel Sánchez Forcada narrated in his diary. In Vallfogona, in Catalonia, he wrote, Falange tried to incite the defection of enemy soldiers by addressing them through the radio, ending the broadcast with the Falangist hymn *Cara al Sol*. This prompted the Republican fighters to ask provocatively, over the lines, why they did not play the *Oriamendi*, the Carlist anthem, as well. Falange's refusal almost ended in open confrontation with the traditionalists. Only playing it three times in a row, provoking Republican applause, put an end to the incident.[49] All these clashes reflected how the *requeté* not only refused to place itself under the political authority of a latecomer like Falange, but that it would not tolerate the elimination of its traditions, pride, and identity.

Falange's imposing attitude was even more noticeable regarding the merging of all other sections within the party. The Political Secretariat decided that, to facilitate the fusion of headquarters and sections, whenever one of the two parties did not constitute at least a 5 per cent of the membership, it should submit to the authority of the other one.[50] No matter how many times the secretariat was reminded of the Falangist habit of recruiting leftists or even counting Moroccans as members, the rule remained unchanged.[51] Furthermore, only Carlists were required to present a declaration signed by three different people to prove their right to membership, which reduced considerably their presence in the single party. In Lérida, for example, the local authorities suggested extending the window for admissions to foster the entry of more Carlists, but this seems to have been the exception, not the rule.[52] This meant that, in the long run, while Navarre continued to function as the stronghold of the *Comunión Tradicionalista*, prompting the complaints of the Falangists affected,[53] most regions and sections easily fell under Falange's control.

Falange's strength in numbers allowed it to remain in charge of most party delegations, while Carlists tried their best to halt or at least defer the co-option of their Youth and Women's sections.[54] In this context, conflicts between workers and particularly students from both organizations were frequent. Eventually, the Carlist workers' organization disappeared with the imposition of the vertical unions, but the Association of Traditionalist Students continued to exist in the shadows.[55] It is, therefore, not surprising that the *Comunión Tradicionalista* thought of restraining the political, if not the military, collaboration of their volunteers. Only Franco's will to foster the Carlist influence within the party in order to restrain Falange's fascism and prevent the latter's aggressive centralism from strengthening separatist movements in the country would assuage the former's fears. The Carlists' did not want a reversal of the Unification, but aspired to control the Basque Country, Navarre, Catalonia, and Valencia, as well as to preserve their symbols, and exert influence over the party in matters of religion and corporatism.[56] None of it, except for control of Navarre and the preservation of certain traditions and symbols, would happen. Still, attempts to establish a second Carlist stronghold in the Catalonian and Valencian areas encountered fierce opposition from Falange, who claimed that administrative devolution was no more than a cover for peripheral nationalisms. In fact, the strongest complaint about Carlists avoiding the front and staying in the rearguard concerned Catalonia, where it was said hundreds of *requetés* had shirked their military obligations.[57] Carlism was also painted as a refuge for the *Lliga Regionalista*, a Catalan conservative party, whose regionalism was seen by Falange as a covert separatism.[58] This confrontation highlighted how qualitatively different Falangist and Carlist nationalisms were. Whereas Falangist nationalism was more centralist and oriented towards the restoration of the empire, Carlist nationalism tended to legitimate the status quo, placing high importance in the role of the provinces and the harmonizing role of Catholicism.[59]

The role of religion and the Catholic Church was indeed another point of confrontation. Although united in their Catholicism and their *Crusade* against the Republic, they differed considerably in their religious views. The Catholic unity of Spain was key to the Carlist ideology, as it was understood as the only way to guarantee political unity.[60] Falange, however, conceived the church in a position subordinate to the state, placing fatherland above God, and the pursuit of the revolution over the idea of the *Crusade*.[61] No matter how frequent their professions of Catholicism were[62] this fostered suspicions of atheism and paganism among the Carlist leaders, who already frowned upon Falange's fascist nature. As a result, Carlists refused to swear the oath imposed by the single party to its members, which not only placed Country above God, but also demanded members to give their lives in the service of Falange and submit completely to its authorities.[63]

Symbolic Language and Identity Building

In any case, the majority of rank-and-file Carlists did not seem to be concerned with highly ideological questions. This did not, however, mean they were at ease with the new situation. The way they experienced and understood their militancy determined, in no small way, their reactions to the dominant and at times aggressive attitude of Falange. Most of them had been born into Carlism and grown up listening to stories of the Carlist wars. They were part of a lineage; a community that, in the majority of cases, had welcomed them into their fold since birth.[64] Several testimonies attest to how they perceived their Carlist identity as something they had been born with: 'My father is a Carlist, my grandfather is a Carlist, we are Carlists! Huh! Then I am a Carlist!' Therefore, as Carlist families grew, so did the reach of Carlist militancy. However, although initial socialization was carried out within the family, in due time, their Carlism was reinforced by a complex associative framework and individual study.[65] In this way, Carlism might be received but it had to be willingly maintained.

A sense of belonging was further ensured through a rich symbolic language, in which rituals and traditions played an important part. Both the role of the family and this symbolic framework helped transform Carlist thought into a narrative easily transmitted through generations,[66] and further reinforced through commemoration. The importance of commemorations, however, was not exclusive to Carlism. Since the beginning of the conflict, widely understood on the rebel side as a *Crusade* against liberalism and irreligion, the celebration of funerals, for example, took on a special symbolic meaning. These events not only transformed their dead into martyrs, integrating families and friends still deeper into the war effort, but also staged the cooperation and shared sacrifice of the volunteers through professions of camaraderie and the interpretation of both anthems.[67]

Furthermore, the progressive consolidation of Francoism throughout the country saw the adoption of Falangist festivities, particularly the commemoration of the party's foundation and the death of Matías Montero – their first martyr, who was killed in 1934 while distributing the Falangist newspaper – as well as the adoption of the Carlist feast of the Martyrs of Tradition. The festival commemorated the death of the first king of the Carlist dynasty and constituted the most important festivity in their calendar. As a result, the emerging regime was quick to adopt it as an official celebration. However, the first time the single party came to be in charge of it, they publicized the event so little that its impact was minimal. Eventually, Carlists decided to continue to celebrate the festivity independently, resulting in a symbolic struggle between the official Francoist event and the unofficial but more intimate Carlist one.[68] The apparently homogenous nature of Francoism, with its rhetoric of victory and complex symbolic framework, hid in plain sight, but only to an extent, the heterogeneous nature of the rebel coalition.

If rituals and commemorations played an important role in maintaining the cohesion of the group, symbols, banners, and uniforms played an even more important one in reinforcing the individual identity of the low-ranking volunteers. Symbols and icons were fundamental to their sense of belonging and identity, as they allowed for them to link their individual experience to that of the group, helping them to recognize themselves in the experience of others. Particularly for Carlists, bearing these symbols and participating in their shared traditions served as validation of the path they had chosen.[69] Merging symbols and uniforms was, therefore, key to the construction of a new unified party. Eventually, Carlist and Falangist identities were supposed to give way to their combined identity as Francoists. Given their long-standing struggle to impose their values and ideological frameworks onto the new utopian society they believed to be building, it is not surprising that both would take the matter particularly seriously. While Carlists, like their fathers and grandfathers, were 'driven by the same religious and patriotic ideals, arms at the ready to defend our eternal and absolute rights over people's consciences and over society'.[70] Falangists, believing themselves to have been the first to bring the fight to the Republic and determined to create a new fascist state, did their best to impose their emblems, uniforms, and denomination over any others, a behaviour that preceded the Unification Decree.

This symbolic struggle provoked the largest number of complaints by members of all ranks of both organizations, especially Carlists. Most Falangist objections actually reflect the resistance of the *requeté* to their perceived overbearing attitude, and very few mention mockery of their symbols, basically to the fascist salute.[71] Only in Navarre it is easy to find a significant number of complaints of the imposing attitude of the *Comunión Tradicionalista*: mostly of Carlists monopolizing all positions of power and acting as if the Unification had not happened. Still, there were also reports of Carlists avoiding the celebration of the funerals for José Antonio Primo de Rivera, or priests slapping children in the street for singing *Cara al Sol*.[72] In contrast, it is hard to find a Carlist complaint on any topic that does not refer as well to some act of disrespect against the beret, the *Oriamendi*, or another symbol. In Prado del Rey, Cadiz, Falangists were said to deny entry to town to anyone bearing the beret. In Pamplona, youth were detained for singing Carlist songs; in Elizondo, a Falangist stripped a *margarita* of her emblem and spat on it; and in Vigo, Falangists' response to Carlist monarchist shouts was to attempt an attack on their headquarters.[73] As a local Falangist head affirmed, there was only 'one prophet, José Antonio; one caudillo, Franco; one national-syndicalist shield; and to hell with all others'.[74]

Stripping them of the beret, throwing it on the floor, mocking their anthem, arresting them for not performing the fascist salute, and forcing them to wear the Falangist uniform or sing the *Cara al Sol* were quite common.[75] But Falange's aggressive attitude was sometimes contested with defiance. In Tolosa, Guipuzkoa, a Carlist refused to wear the *Auxilio Social* (Social Aid; the welfare organization established by Falange and inspired by the Nazi *Winterhilfe*) badge unless they sung their anthems, and placed their flags and portraits where they were supposed to be. In Huelva, as the single party had finally adopted the red beret as part of the composite uniform, *requetés* instead were seen wearing the black beret decorated with the royal crown.[76] The red beret represented an element of continuity, a link to their ancestors and their history. It was, therefore, a garment of great sentimental value: 'Above my beret, only God.'[77] For some, finding it co-opted by the single party was an offence, for others it was the fact that so many Falangists refused to wear the beret.

The struggle for the identity of the single party caused so many clashes that the Political Secretariat had to constantly remind members of the obligation to use the new combined denomination for the party, now called *Falange Española Tradicionalista y de las Juntas de Ofensiva Nacional Socialista* (FET y de las JONS), or Traditionalist Spanish Falange of the Committees of the National Syndicalist Offensive. Furthermore, the avalanche of complaints, regarding the anthem and banners of the Carlists, prompted a change to the rule that compelled all local heads to place portraits of José Antonio and Franco in their headquarters, to further include a portrait of at least one Carlist figure.[78] The measure had been badly received by a movement that considered itself a big family where the patriarch (the king) and his family were constantly present via the celebration of their birthdays and the hanging of their portraits in Carlists' homes.[79] If they could not shape the programme of the party, they could at least ensure their presence was not completely erased from it. Still, the Carlist presence within the single party eventually became residual, not even having a role within the organization for veterans. The *Delegación Nacional de Ex-Combatientes* (DNE), or National Delegation of Ex-combatants, tightly controlled by the single party, required the veterans' full compliance with the political system as a precondition for assistance, something that did not sit well with many Carlists. In their eyes, the organization seemed to be an exclusive Falangist organization. This feeling of exclusion was further reinforced when, in the context of the Cold War, the DNE decided to exclude from the benefits schemes ex-combatants who were not members of the party.[80] The Carlist presence in the single party was reduced to their Navarre stronghold, from where they could not threaten the consolidation and development of the Francoist regime.

Conclusions

The wartime experience of both low-ranking Carlist and Falangist militiamen was marked by this dualistic dynamic of hostility and cooperation, which ended in the residual integration of Carlism into the single party. Most rank-and-file Carlists seemed more attracted to actual fighting than party politics. In fact, many were not even interested in becoming official members of the Francoist party. However, the aggressive and imposing attitude of Falange must have surely played a significant role in this matter. Carlists accepted their necessary submission to the military in the service of the fatherland and their values, but could not accept a complete submission to a newcomer that failed to show them the respect they perceived to be due. The strongly cultural and essentialist character of Carlism fused identity and politics and made any disrespect of their symbols and traditions highly offensive, as it also meant disrespect of their dead, their ancestors, and their history. Many felt they were being robbed of their identity after having sacrificed so much for victory. Exclusion from the veteran organization only reinforced this perception.

Carlists might have offered fewer volunteers, but their forces were strategically decisive.[81] As a result, the little compensation they received, and the treatment they suffered during the integration process, drove many to eventually return home or continue to collaborate with Fal Conde in hiding.[82] Falange was not overly content with the new situation: in fact, a number of Falangists came to feel betrayed by Franco and his co-optation of their movement. However, it is impossible to deny that it emerged from the war as a victor. The single party would never complete the conquest of the state or control the majority of the cabinet, but the conflict allowed it to obtain ample political power, and to expand its reach over society through the control of instruments and spaces of socialization, in a way that would not have otherwise been possible. Meanwhile, Carlists were at least partially excluded from public commemorations of the Spanish Civil War, as Falangist symbols took precedence. This, however, did not erase their individual and collective war experience, which they saw as a continuation of the Carlist wars of the 1800s and a reaffirmation of their personal identity. Even as Carlism kept evolving under Francoism, at times clashing with the regime, the Spanish Civil War continued to play a pivotal role in the history of the movement.

Further Reading

Blinkhorn, Martin. *Carlism and Crisis in Spain 1931-1939*. Cambridge: Cambridge University Press, 1975.

Canal, Jordi. *Banderas blancas, boinas rojas: una historia política del carlismo, 1876-1939*. Madrid: Marcial Pons Historia, 2006.

Caspistegui, Francisco Javier. "'Spain's Vendée', Carlist Identity in Navarre as a Mobilising Model'. In *The Splintering of Spain: Cultural History and the Spanish Civil War, 1936–1939*, edited by Chris Ealham and Michael Richards, 177–96. Cambridge: Cambridge University Press, 2005.

Fraser, Ronald. *Blood of Spain. The Experience of Civil War, 1936-1939*. London: Allen Lane, 1979.

Payne, Stanley G. *Falange. A History of Spanish Fascism*. Stanford: Stanford University Press, 1961.

Seidman, Michael. *The Victorious Counterrevolution. The Nationalist Effort in the Spanish Civil War*. Madison: University of Wisconsin Press, 2011.

Thomas, Joan Maria. *Lo que fue la Falange: la Falange y los falangistas de José Antonio, Hedilla y la Unificación*. Barcelona: Península, 1999.

Ugarte, Javier. *La nueva Covadonga insurgente: orígenes sociales y culturales de la sublevación de 1936*. Madrid: Biblioteca Nueva, 1998.

Notes

[*] Part of this research was funded by the Government of Navarre.

1 The *Requetés'* delegate to the local head of Falange, Cadiz, 23 December 1936, *Archivo General de la Universidad de Navarra* (AGUN)/Manuel Fal Conde (MFC)/187.

2 Javier Rodrigo, *Una historia de violencia. Historiografías del terror en la Europa del siglo XX* (Barcelona: Anthropos, 2017), 71.

3 José Luis Zamanillo, close collaborator of Manuel Fal Conde, highlighted these common values as proof of their harmonic collaboration with Falange at the beginning of the war, Manuel J. Fal Conde, Fernando M. Noriega, and Juan Pujol, *Fal Conde y el requeté juzgados por el extranjero. Crónicas de prensa* (Burgos: Requeté, 1937), 175–6.

4 Indalecio Prieto, *Convulsiones de España: pequeños detalles de grandes sucesos* (México: Oasis, 1968), vol. I, 138–42.

5 Martin Blinkhorn, *Carlism and Crisis in Spain 1931-1939* (Cambridge: Cambridge University Press, 1975), 80–5, 181; see as well: Juan Vázquez de Mella y Fanjul, *Ideario de la Comunión Tradicionalista* (Pamplona, 1937).

6 Manuel Martorell, 'Navarra 1937-1939: el fiasco de la Unificación', *Príncipe de Viana* 69, no. 244 (2008): 429–58; Francisco Javier Caspistegui, 'Navarra y lo carlista. Símbolos y

mitos', in *Signos de identidad histórica para Navarra*, eds. A. Martín and J. M. Aguirre (Pamplona: Caja de Ahorros de Navarra, 1996), 355–70. References to tensions surrounding the Unification Decree are common in the main works on Falange: Joan Maria Thomas, *Lo que fue la Falange: la Falange y los falangistas de José Antonio, Hedilla y la Unificación* (Barcelona: Plaza & Janés, 1999); Stanley G. Payne, *Falange: A History of Spanish Fascism* (Stanford: Stanford University Press, 1961); Sheellagh M. Ellwood, *Prietas las filas: historia de Falange Española (1933-1983)* (Barcelona: Crítica, 1984).

7   Javier Ugarte, *La nueva Covadonga insurgente: orígenes sociales y culturales de la sublevación de 1936* (Madrid: Biblioteca Nueva, 1998), 408–9, 420.

8   See Blinkhorn, *Carlism and Crisis*; Javier Ugarte, 'El carlismo en la guerra del 36: la formación de un cuasi-estado nacional-corporativo y foral en la zona vasco-navarra', *Historia Contemporánea*, 28 (2009): 49–87; Jordi Canal, *Banderas blancas, boinas rojas: una historia política del carlismo, 1876-1939* (Madrid: Marcial Pons, 2006); Aurora Villanueva, *El carlismo navarro durante el primer franquismo, 1937-1951* (Madrid: Actas, 1998).

9   Canal, *Banderas blancas, boinas rojas*, 248.

10 Alfonso Bullón de Mendoza and Álvaro de Diego, *Historias orales de la guerra civil* (Barcelona: Ariel, 2000), 91.

11 Blinkhorn, *Carlism and* crisis, 71, 78; Julio Aróstegui, *Los combatientes requetés en la Guerra Civil Española* (Madrid: La Esfera, 2013), 75.

12 Julio Aróstegui, *Los combatientes carlistas en la Guerra Civil española, 1936-1939* (Madrid: Aportes XIX, 1991), 59; Blinkhorn, *Carlism and crisis*, 88; Josep C. Clemente, *Breviario de historia del carlismo* (Brenes: Muñoz Moya, 2000), 42.

13 Alberto Reig Tapia, 'Falangistas y Requetés en guerra', in *La guerra civil española*, ed. Manuel Tuñón de Lara (Folio, 1996), 85.

14 Milicias Nacionales. Falange y Requetés. Archivo General Militar de Ávila, Censo-Guía de Archivo de España e Iberoamérica. http://censoarchivos.mcu.es/CensoGuia/fondoDetail.htm?id=577090 (accessed 31 December 2017).

15 Historians continue to debate the accuracy of overall numbers of militants in both organizations, a task further complicated by their fusion into a single entity in 1937. The most recent data on the debate can be consulted in Alfonso Lazo Díaz and José Antonio Parejo Fernández, 'La militancia falangista en el suroeste español: Sevilla', *Ayer*, 52 (2003): 237–43. Lazo numbered the Falangist militancy in five of the eight Andalusian provinces as 169,500 members in 1937; Alfonso Lazo Díaz, *Una familia mal avenida: Falange, Iglesia y Ejército* (Madrid: Síntesis, 2008), 49. This data makes statements by Falangist newspaper *Arriba* of 350,000 members in January 1937, more believable; Payne, *Falange: A History*, 146.

16 Draft for the reorganization of FET y de las JONS, Archivo General de la Administración (AGA) 9 (17.02) 51/18956.

17 Canal, *Banderas blancas, boinas rojas*, 273.

18 Aróstegui, *Los combatientes requetés*, 57-77.

19 Blinkhorn, *Banderas blancas, boinas rojas*, 166–7.

20 Fal Conde, Noriega and Pujol, *Fal Conde y el requeté*, 72.

21 Román Oyarzun, 'Una idea Requeté y Fascio', *El Pensamiento Navarro*, 19 December 1936.

22 *El Pensamiento Navarro*, 25 April 1937, 28–29 July 1936.

23 Rodrigo, *Una historia de violencia*, 73.

24 Report outlining several incidents in Arcos de la Frontera, 21 December 1936, AGUN/MFC/187.

25 Provincial *Requeté* delegate to the chief inspector of Militia forces, Jerez, 21 January 1937, AGUN/MFC/187.

26 Manuel Fal Conde to the General-in-Chief of the Army of the South, 17 December 1936, AGUN/MFC/187.

27 Report on Falange's recruitment tactics, Junta Central Carlista de Guerra, 8 March 1937, *Archivo General de Navarra* (AGN)/*Diputación Foral de Navarra* (DFN)/ C20301. Local Carlist Junta in Arguedas to the Junta Central Carlista de Guerra de Navarra (JCCGN), 18 December 1936, AGN/DFN/20301. Report, JCCGN, 1936, AGN/DFN/C20304-1; Meeting of the JCCGN, 19 January 1937, AGN/DFN/C51189-1.

28 Internal report of the *Comunión Tradicionalista*, 9 April 1937, AGUN/MFC/188.

29 Some examples in AGA 9 (17.10) 51/20538, 20519.

30 Local head of the *Requeté* to the JCCGN, Lumbier, 17 February 1937, AGN/DFN/ C51189-3.

31 Local head of the *Requeté* to the JCCGN, 24 December 1936, AGN/DFN/C20301.

32 *A Requeté's Campaign Diary*, Documentation Centre, *Museo del Carlismo*.

33 Michael Seidman, *The Victorious Counterrevolution. The Nationalist Effort in the Spanish Civil War* (Madison: University of Wisconsin Press, 2011), 237–41; Michael Seidman, *Republic of Egos: A Social History of the Spanish Civil War* (Madison: University of Wisconsin Press, 2002), 149; Francisco J. Caspistegui, '"Spain's Vendée", Carlist Identity in Navarre as a Mobilising Model', in *The Splintering of Spain. Cultural History and the Spanish Civil War, 1936–1939*, ed. Chris Ealham and Michael Richards (Cambridge: Cambridge University Press, 2005), 187; James Matthews, '"Our Red Soldiers": The Nationalist Army's Management of its Left-Wing Conscripts in the Spanish Civil War 1936-9', *Journal of Contemporary History* 45, no. 2 (2010): 344–63.

34 Seidman, *The Victorious Counterrevolution*, 237; Aróstegui, *Los combatientes carlistas*, 53.

35 Bullón de Mendoza and de Diego, *Historias orales*, 182; Ronald Fraser, *Blood of Spain. The Experience of Civil War, 1936-1939* (London: Allen Lane, 1979), 165, 319.

36 Fraser, *Blood of Spain*, 169.

37 On Carlist repression, Ugarte, 'El carlismo en la guerra', 64–5; Manuel Martorell and Josep Miralles Climent, *Carlismo y represión 'franquista' tres estudios sobre la Guerra Civil y la posguerra* (Madrid: Arcos, 2009). More recently, Mikelarena has provided sufficient detail to justify the need for further exploration of Carlist repression, and suggested the existence of collaboration between Falange and the *requeté*. Fernando Mikelarena, 'Estructura, cadena de mando y ejecutores de la represión de boina roja en Navarra en 1936', *Historia Contemporánea*, 53 (2016): 593–621.

38 Bullón de Mendoza and de Diego, *Historias orales*, 49.

39 Javier Tusell, *Franco en la Guerra Civil: una biografía política* (Barcelona: Tusquets, 1992), 72–3; Joan M. Thomàs, *El gran golpe: el 'caso Hedilla' o cómo Franco se quedó con Falange* (Barcelona: Debate, 2014).

40 *El Siglo Futuro*, 4 January 1934.

41 Fraser, *Blood of Spain*, 320; Bullón de Mendoza and de Diego, *Historias orales*, 35.

42 Martorell, 'Navarra 1937-1939', 429–58; Fraser, *Blood of Spain*, 319. On the Falangist resistance to Unification, see Thomàs, *El gran golpe*.

43 Javier Rodrigo, 'Retaguardia: un espacio de transformación', *Ayer*, 76, *Retaguardia y cultura de guerra, 1936-1939* (2009): 15.

44 Salvador Torrijos Berges, *Mis memorias de la guerra* (Saragossa: Tip. M. Serrano, 1939). Sometimes incidents in the rearguard were automatically blamed on leftist

recruits and undercover agents, AGN/DFN/C20300, AGUN/MFC/190. Although this could explain some clashes, it does not discredit the existence of genuine incidents between volunteers.

45 Unification Decree, *Boletín Oficial del Estado*, no. 182, 20 April 1937.

46 Memo 5, 15 June 1937, AGA 9 (17.12) 51/21102; Memo 11, 7 July 1937, AGA 9 (17.12) 51/21102.

47 Correspondence regarding the *Tercio de Nuestra Señora de la Merced*, June to October 1937, AGUN/MFC/187. On the history of the *Tercio*: Aróstegui, *Los combatientes requetés*, 726–49. A similar complaint was logged in with the provincial delegate of Justice and Law, Malaga, 8 October 1938, AGA 9 (17.10) 52/2961.

48 Aróstegui, *Los combatientes carlistas*, 321.

49 Manuel Sánchez Forcada, 'Diario de campaña de un requeté pamplonés, 1936-1939', *Príncipe de Viana* 64, no. 230 (2003): 674.

50 Memo 1, 7 May 1937, AGA 9 (17.12) 51/21102.

51 AGUN/MFC/189, 257, 191, 192.

52 Manuel Fal Conde to Raimundo Fernández Cuesta, 2 March 1938, AGUN/MFC/178; Local head of the party to the general secretary, Lérida, 23 September 1939, AGA 9 (17.10) 51/20868.

53 Archivo Fundación Nacional Francisco Franco (AFNFF), Doc. 6280, 6285.

54 In Navarre they tried to prevent their youth from joining the single party by counting them as militiamen. They also tried to ensure the *margaritas*' cooperation with the *Delegación Nacional de Asistencia a Frentes y Hospitales*, led by the Carlist María Rosa Urraca Pastor, instead of the Women's Section under the rule of José Antonio's sister, Pilar Primo de Rivera. Attempts by the latter to bring all women under her control resulted, in some places, in the immediate and massive defection of the *margaritas*. AGA 9 (17.02) 51/19174, 20532; Luis Doreste to the Political Secretariat, 3 July 1937, AGUN/MFC/189. See also Chapter 9 of this volume.

55 23 October 1937, *Boletín del Movimiento*, 83–5; Manuel de Santa Cruz, *Apuntes y documentos para la historia del tradicionalismo español: 1939-1966* (Madrid: Gráficas Gonther, 1979), vol. I, 166.

56 AGUN/MFC/133/258.

57 *Report on Catalonia*, June 1937, AGA 9 (17.10) 51/20525.

58 Falangist Report, San Sebastian, June 1937, AGA 9 (17.10) 51/20525.

59 Ugarte, *La nueva Covadonga*, 313–9; Blinkhorn, *Carlism and Crisis*, 67.

60 Vázquez de Mella y Fanjul, *Ideario de la Comunión*; Francisco J. Caspistegui and Gemma Pierola, 'Entre la ideología y lo cotidiano: la familia en el Carlismo y el Tradicionalismo (1940-1975)', *Vasconia: Cuadernos de historia – geografía*, 28 (1999): 46. AGUN/MFC/258.

61 For example, 'To Caesar what is of Caesar and to God what is of God', 7 February 1937, Imperio, AGUN/MFC/259.

62 'Falange', *Arriba España*, 14 February 1937. 'Our civil war is inspired by the morality, the religion of Christ, the National-Syndicalism that God wants to return to Imperial Spain', Torrijos Berges, *Mis memorias*, 21. The Falangist Alberto Pastor described the national-syndicalist revolution as 'pure evangelism, the doctrine of Jesus Christ that everyone should live better, not that some should be well-off and others poor'; Fraser, *Blood of Spain*, 87.

63 'Falange and Religion', AGUN/MFC/259; Falangist Report, 21 December 1938, AGA 9 (17.10) 52/2961.

64 Canal, *Banderas blancas, boinas rojas*, 242–8; Caspistegui and Pierola, 'Entre la ideología', 45–56. Not every Carlist was born one, some approached Carlism later in life and others saw it as part of a wider traditionalist identity, with which they primarily identified. Javier Ugarte, 'El carlismo hacia los años treinta del sigio XX. Un fenómeno señal', *Ayer*, 38 (2000): 182.

65 Caspistegui and Pierola, 'Entre la ideología', 52–5.

66 Ugarte, *La nueva Covadonga*, 409–10.

67 Francisco J. Caspistegui, 'El proceso de secularización de las fiestas carlistas', *Zainak*, 26 (2004): 793–4. Mary Vincent, 'The Martyrs and the Saints: Masculinity and the Construction of the Francoist Crusade', *History Workshop Journal*, 47 (1999): 90.

68 Zira Box, *España, año cero la construcción simbólica del franquismo* (Madrid: Alianza, 2010), 153, 158.

69 Caspistegui, 'El proceso de secularización', 789.

70 Quoted in Caspistegui, '"Spain's Vendée"', 181.

71 People making the fascist salute were said to have a headache or to want to go for a swim. Their mockery was not witty, but it still sparked a reaction by the single party in some cases, AGUN/MFC/187, 260.

72 See these and other complaints from Navarre in AGA 9 (17.10) 52/2961.

73 *Requeté* delegate to the chief inspector of Militia forces in Cadiz province, 21 January 1937, AGUN/MFC/187; president of the San Martín de Unx Circle to the JCCGN, 8 January 1937, AGN/DFN/C20301; Report on Falange's actions in Navarre, 8 March 1937, AGN/DFN/C20301; Report on the situation in Vigo, 25 November 1937, AGUN/MFC/191.

74 Complaint of a *requeté* to the general secretary, Aranda de Duero, 11 September 1939, AGA 9 (17.10) 52/2961.

75 Report on Falange's actions in Navarre, 8 March 1937, AGN/DFN/C20301. Other complaints stemming from numerous provinces can be found in AGUN/MFC/187, 188, 190, 191, 192.

76 Falangist Report, Tolosa, 30 October 1938, AGA 9 (17.10) 51/20517; Falangist Report, Huelva, 31 October 1939, AGA 9 (17.10) 51/20502.

77 Caspistegui, 'Spain's Vendée', 191.

78 Memo 6, June 1937, AGA 9 (17.12) 51/21102; Telegram 33, 7 July 1937, Telegram 36, 10 July 1937, *Boletín del Movimiento*, 10-11; Telegram 3, May 1937, *Boletín del Movimiento*, 6; Telegram 11, *Boletín del Movimiento*, 8; the general secretary, Raimundo Fernández Cuesta, confirmed in a letter to the Count of Rodezno that he received several complaints regarding disrespectful attitudes towards Carlist symbols, AGA 9 (17.10) 51/20497.

79 Canal, *Banderas blancas, boinas rojas*, 267, 367.

80 Ángel Alcalde, 'War Veterans and Fascism during the Franco Dictatorship in Spain (1936-1959)', *European History Quarterly* 47, no. 1 (2017): 78–98; AFNFF, doc. 64. For more on this veterans' organization, see Chapter 12 of this volume.

81 Aróstegui, *Los combatientes requetés*.

82 Manuel Martorell, 'Carlismo, historia oral y las "zonas oscuras" de la Guerra Civil', *Gerónimo de Uztariz*, 23–4 (2008): 221; Martorell, 'Navarra 1937-1939', 430. In the early 1940s, reports on clandestine Carlist circles and meeting places outside the single party's control were fairly common in some areas, as I have studied elsewhere: Mercedes Peñalba, *Entre la boina roja y la camisa azul: la integracion del carlismo en Falange Española Tradicionalista y de las JONS (1936-1942)* (Pamplona: Gobierno de Navarra, 2013).

Part Two

MOBILIZING FOR TOTAL WAR

Chapter 4

FOOT SOLDIERS FOR THE TWO SPAINS: CONSCRIPT EXPERIENCE DURING THE SPANISH CIVIL WAR

James Matthews

Neither side expected what is now known as the Spanish Civil War of 1936 to 1939 to involve conscription. The faction of the army that rose up against the government on 17 July 1936 anticipated a swift and overwhelming takeover of the state and its apparatus. Republican officials hoped that the rebels would be quashed as efficiently as their predecessors had been in 1932 when General José Sanjurjo staged a short-lived uprising. Both sides, however, were wrong in their initial optimism and the relative balance of forces enabled a partially successful coup to develop into a long and bloody civil war. The turning point, when both sides realized that they would need to mobilize as many resources as possible, came after the initial weeks when neither could rapidly defeat the other. It was compounded by the Nationalists' failure to take Madrid in the winter of 1936 and thereby secure a swift victory over the government.[1] For the Francoist rebels this decision to forcibly recruit was automatic and almost immediate,[2] whereas for some political groups loyal to the Republic – notably the anarchists – the associated militarism of a forced call-up was anathema to their political views.[3] As a result, the government's decision to militarize the militias, implement martial discipline, and conscript was only brought to a head by the real risk of defeat at the hands of the insurgents.[4]

This chapter seeks to examine the conscript experience during the Spanish conflict in a comparative light. Fewer than one in ten combatants on both sides were volunteers, despite the enduring image of voluntary and popular mobilization, notably within the Republican zone (and examined in Chapter 2). And without resorting to obligatory military service, neither side would have been able to conduct a three-year-long war or mobilize its male population in anywhere near the numbers necessary for 'total war'. It looks to examine what made the experience of the Spanish Civil War unique in comparison to other armies in comparable twentieth-century conflicts. In analysing this question, the chapter considers the mechanisms of conscript recruitment on both sides and examines the conceptual frameworks and embellished narratives – including nationalism – used to explain the conflict to the conscripted men, who themselves had different experiences depending on where they were recruited and their age during the Spanish Civil War. Finally, it considers day-to-day living conditions in the often-static front lines and the different approaches to discipline that the two sides employed in the attempt to create a reliable and motivated fighting force. Desertion and loss of morale are not considered in detail because they form the bulk of Chapter 5 in this volume. It is important to note here that while conscripts made up the majority of both sides' combatants they were by no means the only type of soldier in the two armies. Other than their initial volunteers, the Nationalists' land forces also comprised the crack troops of the *Africanistas* – the Legion (a highly professional force made up of Spaniards) and the *Regulares* (combat-experienced Moroccan mercenaries whose overall numbers rose to 70,000 by 1939, and examined in Chapter 6) – and large numbers of Italian troops, as well as a small contingent of Portuguese. The government forces, meanwhile, drew on the motivated and communist-organized volunteers that fought in Spain as the International Brigades. In this sense, this chapter only examines a part of the forces – albeit the largest category by numbers – that both sides deployed during the conflict.[5]

Implementing Conscription

Once the two sides had decided that they would need to call up the manpower reserves at their disposal, they implemented their conscription basing themselves on the peacetime systems already in place and that relied on the civilian *ayuntamientos*, or town halls, which held essential records on Spanish men. In this sense, both Republicans and Nationalists set out from a common framework onto which they grafted new systems. Essentially Spanish men would receive call-up instructions to gather at the nation's town halls where they would undergo medical assessment and, if classed fit for service or fit for auxiliary services, they would be drafted into the army.[6] Using these systems, the Republic mobilized twenty-eight reserve classes by the end of the war, amounting to a theoretical total of 1.7 million men between the ages of sixteen and forty-five (1915–42 cohorts), and an attempt to use every last available male body for the war effort. In turn, and by their victory in April 1939, the Nationalists had mobilized fourteen and a half age groups, totalling 1.26 million men between the ages of eighteen and thirty-three (1927–41 cohorts): a much younger maximum recruitment age than in the government's Popular Army.[7]

To aid the mass mobilization, both sides created organizations with the mandate to oversee this vital function. The Republic set up specialized centres known as the *Centros de Reclutamiento, Instrucción y Movilización* (CRIM), or Recruitment, Training and Mobilization Centres.[8] The Nationalists, in turn, gave the issue greater institutional importance and established the *Dirección General de Movilización, Instrucción y Recuperación*, or the Directorate General of Mobilization, Training and Recovery, also known as MIR, and responsible for the army's mobilization, training, and manpower.[9] Training on both sides was generally rudimentary, but the Nationalists were able to grant the matter greater priority and established systems in which units prepared for the front in a sustained and relatively lengthy fashion. They were able, for example, to take advantage of their possession of Spanish Morocco to train up large units together, away from the front line, giving the officers and men time to create the cohesion that is so important for military effectiveness.[10] However, in times of operational need, both sides rushed soldiers to the front with scarcely any preparation and expected them to learn from the veterans. Republican soldiers were, for example, sometimes only allowed to fire five practice shots before a front-line posting and each training company only had five working rifles[11] (see Figure 4.1).

The systems of recruitment were thus not radically different to those that would have been activated in the case of Spain fighting an international war. And, like in nationwide mobilization elsewhere, both sides also attempted to exempt society's most vulnerable from the call-up, including the sons of poor widows in the Republican zone and the third brother from the same family in the Nationalist.[12] Both sides also attempted to assign the most arduous posts to the younger, single men where possible.[13] The distaste held by some groups within the Republican camp for conscription is reminiscent of that reluctance in First World War Britain – where Prime Minister H. H. Asquith had introduced the 'Bachelors' Bill' in 1916 under the guise of shunning a move towards general conscription[14] – albeit for different, largely antimilitarist reasons. And while the Republic readied its mixed

Figure 4.1 Republican conscripts heading to the front wave goodbye to their families. AGMAV, F.16, 19/19.

brigades – newly created units of 3,000–4,000 men – as individual entities within the territory it controlled,[15] the Nationalists, in contrast, used the British-inspired regiment as the building block for creating 700-man battalions that were then assigned to operate independently of the mother regiment.[16]

Historians writing about the experience of warfare have rejected the concept of the 'universal soldier', which tacitly has sustained that military experience has a fundamental universality regardless of the temporal and geographical specificities of a conflict.[17] Yet this is undoubtedly a framework for understanding conflict that many participants have at times relied on to describe their experiences. In the Spanish case, George Orwell, who fought with the anarchist *Partido Obrero de Unificación Marxista* (POUM), or Workers' Party of Marxist Unification militia on the Aragon front in the early months of the war, traced a common thread with other conflicts by invoking injuries and death, fear, the smell of battle, and exposure to the elements:

> The picture of war set forth in books like *All Quiet on the Western Front* is substantially true. Bullets hurt, corpses stink, men under fire are often so frightened that they wet their trousers. … (People forget that a soldier anywhere near the front line is usually too hungry, or frightened, or cold, or, above all, too tired to bother about the political origins of the war). But the laws of nature are not suspended for a 'red' army any more than for a 'white' one. A louse is a louse and a bomb is a bomb, even though the cause you are fighting for happens to be just.[18]

But, as John Lynn argues, a focus that is overly materialistic and corporal does not account sufficiently for cultural variations when examining different societies at war,[19] and no doubt Orwell would have agreed, given his close observation of revolutionary Spain during the early stages of the conflict. It is argued here that while the most significant differences between the two sides' experiences involved the political messages that explained and summarized the conflict, it is impossible to examine the experience of the civil war without examining the differences in the material conditions of the two sides' troops. It is to these that the analysis now turns, before examining their ideological lines.

Material Conditions and Mundane Needs in the Front Lines

It has been widely documented that the Nationalist Army was generally better at supplying its conscripts with material goods, a factor that certainly influenced crucial differences in the experience of war for the men called up on the two sides. This includes what Michael Seidman has termed the 'corporal experiences of solids and liquids', including food, drink, and clothing.[20] In this domain, the Nationalists controlled their rearguard areas more effectively, limiting inflation, boosting production and, crucially, limiting peasant hoarding. The contrast with the Republican zone was stark, and in that zone prices soared and producers distrusted government paper money, preferring instead to keep their produce for themselves (aspects that are explored in detail in Chapter 8 of this volume). This, in turn, meant that, on average, Nationalist soldiers were better fed than their Republican counterparts, and they suffered fewer acute supply shortages in the front line. The rebels were also able to put on shows of generosity for their soldiers at special occasions, including a Christmas bonus in the form of extra supplies or cash.[21]

Moreover, the differences with the government zone became more critical as the war progressed. The Nationalists captured ever more territory and resources from the government, and eventually the Republic and its soldiers experienced defeat, its associated humiliation, and sometimes exile: experiences that Nationalist combatants did not of course encounter. Other benefits were also more adroitly administered by the Nationalist Army, including pay, which while initially less generous than in the Popular Army was issued on time and was not undermined by inflation, which rapidly eroded the initially extremely generous 10-peseta daily wage that government soldiers received at the outset. Nationalist soldiers' families in the rearguard were also adequately provided for by so-called combatants' subsidies, which effectively meant soldiers did not have to worry about the material provisions for their loved ones in the rearguard. As has been examined elsewhere, satisfaction of these mundane daily needs, such as adequate food, sufficient and prompt pay, and the fair allocation of leave played a fundamental role in capturing and maintaining the troops' loyalty. And when they were neglected, men on both sides quickly became demoralized (as explored in Chapter 5).[22] A poignant example from the Republican side is the case of a delivery of horsemeat for rations; already such animal protein was considered to be culturally questionable by Spanish soldiers, but far worse was that it was so rotten that it had to be buried, untouched by the hungry men.[23]

Other factors that affect the experience of soldiering are the tools available for the task, which most obviously involves adequate weaponry, but also sufficient equipment for the climatic conditions in which men are forced to fight. In this too, unsurprisingly, the Nationalists had the upper hand and Republican soldiers often fought with equipment that was unreliable and in a bad condition. For example, a particular problem that plagued the Popular Army was the use of recycled bullets – spent cases that were collected and sent to ammunition factories for refilling. In March 1937, a commissar (a supervisory political officer; examined below in more detail) of the 31st Mixed Brigade noted the 'real danger' that faced soldiers firing recycled bullets. He also expressed the importance of keeping 'good ammunition' for the 'moments of action against the enemy'.[24] Other shortages often saw Republican soldiers fighting without access to blankets and in woefully inadequate rope sandals in the depths of winter. This can be seen from the numerous winter campaigns in the Republican rearguard in which the authorities collected warm clothes for the front.[25] For example, one soldier, Rafael Gomia of the 80th Mixed Brigade, described his unit as 'without clothes' in a letter home.[26] Meanwhile, men in the 96th Mixed Brigade, who were not even issued rope sandals, had to protect their feet with rags and towels until they could find alternatives.[27]

That is not to say, however, that Nationalist troops were luxuriously supplied and had a comfortable existence in comparison to Republican soldiers. There are plenty of examples of rebel soldiers facing shortages and having to forage for food, particularly when offensives meant that units were often far ahead of their supply corps,[28] or of soldiers fighting without blankets and footwear.[29] What it does mean, however, is that the Nationalists were largely able to avoid the acute crises that the Republic faced and that contributed to their soldiers losing trust in the legitimacy and credibility of their recruiting authorities – and, by extension, in the government and its representatives.[30] Some of the most extreme examples of these shortages and that incited a dramatic loss of morale include a soldier who developed painful mouth ulcers and symptoms similar to scurvy from lack of food;[31] another claimed in a letter home to have lost thirty kilograms while stationed on the Madrid front.[32]

On a physical level, the main difference between the two sides was therefore the ability to consistently and adequately supply and equip a fighting force. In this sense, and in general terms, the Nationalist Army was closer to militaries in which soldiers generally felt they could rely on basic provisioning, such as in the British, French, and German (until late 1918) armies of the First World War. That is not to say that these armies did not have their exceptional and serious issues, such as the French army mutinies of spring 1917. These were clearly linked to the perceived futility and bloodiness of the failed April Nivelle offensive, but they can also be interpreted as political actions, comparable to labour strikes, in which soldiers demanded better attention to food and the allocation of leave.[33] But in these armies the average soldier was not consistently neglected to the extent of undermining the fundamental legitimacy of his recruiting authorities. The Republic, in contrast, was more similar to armies where the ability to provide basic necessities and equipment was frequently questioned. Perhaps at the outset of the conflict the Popular Army was similar to the Italian Army in the First World War, which was capable of mounting a war effort, albeit one that was frequently disjointed and underprovided. On the fronts of northern Italy, the armies suffered a 'wretched lack of adequate equipment' and supplies in the snow-capped mountains were frequently poor and unreliable.[34] In the last year of the conflict in Spain, a more apt comparison might be made between the Republican Popular Army and the Tsarist Russian army before the February Revolution, where logistical disarray and material scarcity was the norm and clearly contributed to a fundamental loss of confidence in the ancien régime.[35] For example, on some Spanish fronts, such as during the chaotic retreat from Teruel in March 1938, the Popular Army suffered effective collapse for material and morale reasons, and ceased to present an effective front to the advancing Nationalist Army until it was able to regroup using the Ebro River as a natural defensive position.

A further influencing factor with regard to the experience of the war in Spain was the amount of combat and the level of engagement and exposure required from the two sides' conscripts. On both sides the most difficult operations were entrusted where possible to the elite troops detailed above, rather than conscripts.

This created an important dichotomy between the two types of soldiers, and conscripts were largely employed by both sides to hold the line on relatively static fronts where the greatest risk was the occasional aerial attack.[36] In many ways, the Spanish Civil War was a modern twentieth-century conflict in which men were marshalled en masse to fight on fronts far from their homes. Moreover, both armies also employed modern military technology, including state-of-the-art armoured vehicles and aviation often supplied by their international allies. However, at the same time, many combatants experienced the conflict in similar ways to the generations that fought in Spain's relatively small-scale and ill-fated earlier colonial wars, notably in the Philippines and Morocco. In this sense, many conscripts on both sides fought with obsolete firearms and woefully inadequate equipment. They were also required to march long distances on foot to the front, and their food and equipment were often transported by mule.

This is important when considering the conscript experience of war because many men were not directly involved in the fighting for months at a time. As one military historian has argued, the Spanish Civil War was a 'paupers' war', in which both sides could only deploy one significant operational army at any time, and 'important' activity only occurred on comparatively small sectors of the front.[37] In this context there was also a divide between the two sides. Whereas the Nationalists had relatively ample supplies of experienced soldiers, the Republic's availability dwindled rapidly, especially with the heavy casualties suffered by the International Brigades in the desperate defence of Madrid in late 1936. Consequently, the government increasingly demanded more sacrifices of its conscript soldiers than their enemies did, and expected them to bear the consequences of Popular Army material shortfalls.[38] In neither army, however, were the overall losses in any way comparable to the severe attrition rate of the Great War's Western Front, or that of the Nazi German army fighting in the East after 1942, where even the formation of vital primary groups between groups of soldiers was affected by the staggering casualty rate.[39]

A further factor when considering conscript experience on the two sides was the search for mundane, but psychologically important, comforts. This included aspects such as the provision of extra rations, the means to contact family and loved ones in the rearguard, and the availability of sex. For the first two, it was again the Nationalists who instituted more effective systems and one Nationalist veteran remembered that there was a thriving trade in the immediacy of the front and that it was easy to obtain basic goods. As there were 'so many servicemen, those who had a little business of this kind [near villages at the front] had good sales'. He also remembered that his comrades 'spent a good number of pesetas buying sweets and alcohol'.[40] The Nationalist high command also allowed certain Moroccan soldiers to work as military travelling salesmen stocking 'bottles of cognac, condensed milk, tobacco, razor blades, soap, envelopes and fountain pens'.[41] In contrast, Republican conscripts were more likely to scrounge or hunt between the front lines.[42] Both sides were able to institute postal services to connect combatants with the rearguard, but the Nationalists system was more efficient and they developed a system for delivering parcels to its soldiers at a relatively cheap cost to the sender, which was crucial for the morale of not only the front-line combatants, but also their families.[43]

As for the availability of sex, it is clear from sources on both sides that the civil war created a climate of greater permissiveness that reflected an unprecedented number of men in arms, and therefore away from their wives and regular partners. On the Nationalist side, the new reality made an appearance in jokes in the press, despite formal intolerance from the conservative and Catholic authorities, as the following example from combatants' newspaper *La Ametralladora* (*The Machine Gun*) shows. In a sketch titled 'The Prodigal Son', a child states: 'I am a precocious child.' 'Why?' he is answered. 'Have you directed an orchestra? Can you do calculus?' 'No', he replies, 'I was born before my parents were married.'[44] One chaplain remembered disapprovingly that an unnamed general was 'obsessed' with the motto: 'For my soldiers, women and wine.'[45] On the Republican side, anarchists in particular initially campaigned to redefine attitudes and de-stigmatize sexuality,[46] and the recurring warnings against contracting venereal disease in the military press and elsewhere underscore that sex, both consensual and transactional, as considered below, became increasingly available. Republican propaganda and public health posters accentuated the dichotomy between sexual pleasure on the one hand, and death on the other with the aim of reducing disease that undermined the war effort. One, for example, showed a beautiful, naked woman with her arm round a slumped soldier wearing a Popular Army helmet. She is all flesh apart from the hugging arm, which is that of a skeletal cadaver.[47]

The hardships and economic necessity caused by the Spanish Civil War also drove many women into prostitution.[48] The Nationalist Army was relatively tolerant of this activity, but wanted the practice to be inconspicuous and concealed from the general civilian population. As the commander of the I Army Corps stated in an order sent in December 1937 to the 107th Division: 'Prostitution must be regulated and … situated in easily controlled localities and places.' Women who worked as prostitutes were required to carry 'documentation that accredits them as such', and both they and the 'public houses' in which they worked had to 'submit to the hygiene controls established by the medical authorities'.[49] Prostitution in the Republican zone also became endemic, despite Popular Army rumours that their cognac was laced with gunpowder to reduce sexual urges.[50] Within the government zone the spread of venereal disease was particularly rampant, and can in part be attributed to a less rigid control of prostitution and initially generous salaries for Popular Army soldiers. For example, between August 1936 and March 1937 the Second Military Hospital, in charge of treating VD, recorded over 70,000 cases[51] in spite of the 175,000 leaflets distributed to the Republican Army of the Centre by the end of that time period.[52] On both sides, however, it was the women, rather than men, who were largely blamed for the spread of VD as a result of their 'sexual deviancy', and their customers were absolved of responsibility. This was an expected stance from the Nationalists, where control of VD among soldiers was more effective, but initially uncertain from the Republicans, where a revolutionary change in consensual sexual mores was a possibility.

The search for material comforts is a common trait of men at war and the differences between the two armies' experiences here are largely due to disparities in availability in the case of food and other material goods sold, bartered, or scavenged by soldiers in the front lines. Or, in the case of sexual encounters, the prevailing cultural mores; and in the case of transactional ones, the attitudes of the authorities with respect to their will and ability to control such activity and contain its potentially damaging side-effects.

Framing the Conflict: Mobilizing Discourses, Discipline, and Education

While the physical and material is clearly important in gauging conscript experience – and the important differences between the two sides – a fundamental factor was also the messages that attempted to explain the conflict to the drafted men. In many ways it was at this level that the experience of fighting in Spain acquired its distinctiveness in comparison to other early to mid-twentieth-century wars, which were predominantly fought between nations. In this sense, it was impossible to separate the civil war fighting experience from the fact that it was a conflict in which the two zones' authorities attempted to impose one vision of Spain over another with force of arms. This, in turn, defined their visions of, among others, the nation, discipline, and education, and how they attempted to instil them in conscripts in the two opposed armies.

The most important differences between the two sides were the distinctive versions that told the glorified story of what each was fighting for. These visions were created and then reinforced in different ways on both sides, including the two respective organizations charged with a similar function of motivating the troops and enforcing a degree of political orthodoxy and adhesion within the ranks. These were the political commissariat on the Republican side – with clear influence from, but not an imposition by, Soviet Russia – and the military chaplaincy on the Nationalist. Both sides also heavily relied on zealous junior officers for this role as well.[53] Popular Army soldiers, in particular, were subject to a barrage of information and in November 1937 an average battalion-sized unit's commissars delivered 174 monthly speeches, a rate of almost 6 per day.[54] The Republic additionally published an enormous quantity of good quality and professionally edited front-line newspapers. Units as small as battalions, with between 500 and 800 men, had their own multi-page newspaper with photos, drawings, and articles that were highly individualized; these were not mere leaflets. In addition, most Mixed Brigades (about 3,000–4,000 men), Divisions (10,000 men), and Army Corps (20,000 men) had their own publications.

Nationalist Spain relied on tradition as a central source of its strength, and particularly evoked an image of eternal Spain linked to the Catholic Church. Religious mobilization was effective even though there were important and uncomfortable exceptions, most notably the Catholic and anti-revolutionary *Partido Nacionalista Vasco* (PNV), or Basque Nationalist Party, in the Basque

Country that fought with the government. Religion was a powerful mobilizing tool because it infused the Nationalist project with a superior moral purpose and kindled emotional anti-Republican sentiment through frequent reminders of church burnings and the murder of clergy. Moreover, it encouraged the steely martial masculinity and sacrifice that readily bolstered the war effort and projected the 'warrior-monk' as an ideal combatant type.[55] Indeed, there is ample evidence that conscripts were exposed to religious revival in Nationalist Spain, and unit chaplains regularly delivered speeches to their charges. For example, in January 1939 the chaplain of the medical corps of the 75th Division lectured his soldiers on 'The Divine Origin of Christianity'.[56] As soldier Sebastián Hormiga Domínguez, also of the 75th Division, said in a speech in December 1938: 'Wars are won by soldiers in whose hearts beats a faith in God and a *Patria* [fatherland]'.[57]

The Republic, in contrast, developed a novel definition of what it meant to be a soldier, a man, and a citizen at war. Notions of appropriate masculine behaviour were modified by the Republic's need to distance itself from the Nationalist ultra-masculine stance. While Republican soldiers were clearly expected to show valour and dedication, they were also encouraged to show greater sophistication than the enemy, and also be literate, educated, and freethinking. This creation of a relaxed masculinity that rejected a virulently martial version is reminiscent of that cultivated in Britain during the Second World War in juxtaposition to the perceived attitudes of the Nazi German military forces.[58]

The two sides in Spain also attempted to create new loyal followers from the generally non-politicized conscripts that were called up for combat. The war provided both sides with an unprecedented opportunity to influence the men under their control and engage in state building, even if both camps had clearly contrasting notions of citizenship and participation in the war. This was another means to mobilize with the aim of creating new Republicans and Nationalists from previously uncommitted conscripts. As a result of the violence of the war, its duration, and the constant indoctrination of combatants in both sides' trenches, this was successful in some cases. Republican veteran Eduardo Pons Prades referred to this explicitly in his memoirs and wrote of conscripts who became 'convinced, resolute, and in many cases determined combatants'.[59]

With this objective in mind, both sides appealed to nationalism as a mobilizing discourse, with the nation of course interpreted in radically different ways, to broaden and strengthen their mobilization. One reason why both sides used nationalist discourse for their wartime mobilization was that it provided 'great strategic political profitability at a marginal expense in the short- to medium-term'.[60] Nationalism had potentially the broadest appeal among the men targeted by both sides' recruitment drives, and it cast a wider net than even anti-Marxism and anti-fascism. Nationalism appealed to isolated and apolitical peasants who in July 1936 were not members of either political parties or unions – and could therefore not be rallied via these – yet represented the largest proportion of Spain's adult male population subject to conscription. This is evidenced by the fact that many peasants neither became active volunteers for the Republican militia, nor resisted the government's call-up orders in 1937.[61] In this sense, the lowest common denominator of goals was the creation of combatants who provided a minimum level of effective service in uniform, rather than the creation of sophisticated political ideologues. The appeal to nationalism was therefore not vastly dissimilar to mobilizing narratives of nation states at war between themselves, and certainly underlines that the Nationalists did not monopolize nationalist discourse in the conflict. Perhaps the greatest difference in the Spanish case, compared to other national armies is that the nationalism was created in opposition to a markedly different narrative about the same nation. And both sides looked to discredit the competing version, in many cases by associating it with Machiavellian foreign powers, be it the Soviet Union for the Republic or Nazi Germany and Fascist Italy for the Nationalist camp.

The two sides' conscripts were also subject to two very different styles of discipline, which had a significant bearing on their experience in the ranks. In general, Nationalist discipline was traditional and rigid, and partially relied on very real threats and the application of punitive violence for those who did not conform. This is eminently visible from their readiness to execute in the front lines men who were considered loyal to the Republic without needing official sanction from the rearguard military authorities. For example, veteran chaplain Jaime Tovar remembered his unit being 'paraded in front of the bodies' of three executed deserters.[62] Nationalist discipline and their manner of ensuring conformity was more subtle, however, than relying on repression alone. They also tactically introduced a parallel system of rewards that encouraged a minimum level of effective service from their conscripts, even those with known left-wing political profiles. By serving adequately in the Nationalist Army, men were able to redeem their pasts, from a Francoist perspective, and protect their own lives, as well as those of their families. Their privileges, such as combatants' subsidies and campaign pay, were also safeguarded on the same condition. The army therefore actively sheltered those who were prepared to contribute to the war effort. In this way, the Nationalist Army avoided serious breaches of discipline and successfully retained thousands of men who were not initially loyal to the rebels' cause.[63] In many cases, they also managed to retain the paternalistic approach by officers towards their charges that many transnational studies of morale and discipline point to as a fundamental factor for effective military leadership.[64] This is seen, for example, in the attitude of the fatherly general quoted above who wanted his men to have access to the solaces of 'women and wine'.[65]

The Republican Popular Army, in contrast, frequently suffered from its conscientious decision to distance itself from the traditional, and therefore Nationalist, military model. A more relaxed and inclusive approach to discipline fitted the Republic's political and social image. For example, José Muñoz Ortega from the 55th Mixed Brigade rated highly his own unit's officers in late 1938 because 'here everyone is equal'.[66] However, claims about equality between men and officers also created serious disciplinary problems for the new army. Michael Alpert argues that the Republican Popular Army 'suffer[ed] from inefficiency which led to or stemmed from a lack of will and the breakdown of social authority'. This is evidenced by the disrespectful attitude that soldiers often displayed towards their officers and the fact that the Nationalists were more successful at officer training and had a better social base from which to recruit particularly junior officers.[67] For example, in March 1937 men of the Republican 31st Mixed Brigade used the 'lack of [officers'] presence at physical drills' as one of their main 'arguments' against taking part. Such a complaint would have been seriously punished in the Nationalist Army. However, it is significant that the proposed solution in this Mixed Brigade was to make the sessions obligatory for the officers as well.[68]

The counterpoint to this initially relaxed approach to discipline was the extreme measures considered necessary to re-establish control over Popular Army soldiers when these did not follow orders. Zealous political commissars often instigated these punishments, and perhaps one of the most poignant examples was the fate of fifty men of the 84th Mixed Brigade executed by Republican authorities during the Battle of Teruel in January 1938.[69] In many ways the two approaches were two sides of the same coin, and reflected a less constant relationship between the army and its soldiers than that which the Nationalist Army was able to achieve and enforce throughout the conflict. The incident also highlights the serious loss of morale that the Popular Army suffered increasingly acutely towards the end of the conflict.

In this sense, the Republican army was initially closer to militaries that were less class-bound in their hierarchy and there was a more informal relationship between officers and men. Traditional historiography draws out this kind of difference between, for example, the First World War Australian army in comparison to the more rigid and class-conscious British one, even if more recent works have played down some of the horizontality previously claimed for the antipodeans. But while Australian discipline did at times break down – for example famously at Étaples in France in the second half of 1916 – the exemplarity and severity of violence considered necessary to contain it was, however, never as fierce as that employed by the Spanish wartime Republic.[70]

A further divide between the two armies and their framing of the conflict was their approaches to education. The Republican army encouraged soldiers to participate in day-to-day cultural and educational activities with the stated goals of political emancipation and self-improvement, which were summed up by the front-line newspaper *Movilización* (*Mobilization*):

> We are fighting for culture: we fight for universal access to the temples of science and human knowledge; we fight so that we and our children can live happier lives; we fight so that after our victory we may drink our fill from the fount of knowledge.[71]

In this way, lowly conscripts were provided with a vested interest in the Republican cause and granted a voice of sorts within the military institution, even while the messages transmitted were heavily infused with propaganda.[72] This was partly achieved through the press, where soldiers could contribute material, and through the units' mural newspapers. It was also achieved through competitions in which the winners were given either sums of money or short periods of leave. For example, one newspaper offered a 25-peseta prize for the best essay on the topic:

'What Are You Fighting for?'[73] Additionally, Republican combatants were also encouraged to learn how to read and write through progressive literacy campaigns. For example, in October 1937, in the Army of the Centre alone, over 42,000 men regularly attended classes.[74] This was a real break with pre-war Spanish armies, where literacy was considered at best a marginal priority. In the Popular Army, the press was littered with encouragement and listed the achievements of these campaigns with evident pride.[75] In this sense, there is a clear link with the Soviet Red Army of the Russian Civil War, where the production of front-line newspapers was encouraged and soldiers motivated to participate, even if it sometimes meant 'illustrating the army's defects'.[76]

The Nationalist Army is often considered not to have placed any value at all on soldiers' education.[77] This is not entirely the case, and chaplains often performed some functions similar to the 'cultural militia', the militarized schoolteachers who taught Republican soldiers on the other side of the lines. And no doubt the Nationalists had a vested interest in creating a literate army because men who can read and write are more versatile soldiers and can, for instance, act on written instructions, rather than oral ones. As one veteran chaplain – named head of the 'illiterates' academy' working with four soldier-teachers – remembered, it was 'rough, but satisfactory work; satisfactory in its own right because of the lads' enthusiasm to learn, and also because of their great joy when they write home for the very first time'.[78] The lessons, like the Republican ones, were heavily politicized in their content: '"I" for Imperio [Empire] and Isabel'; '"F" for Falange and Franco'.[79] Units also set up 'mobile libraries' for their soldiers and bought the books using cash donations. In November 1938 the 107th Division set one up with some 900 volumes, a mix of 'works of a religious and patriotic nature, general culture, theatre and novels etc'.[80] What is true, however, is that the rebels did not accord the issue significant institutional priority and, perhaps more importantly, the objective was not political and emancipatory as it was in the Republican camp.

Conclusions

The experience of fighting the Spanish Civil War was therefore measurably different for the two sides' soldiers. The Nationalist soldier was more likely to be adequately fed and clothed, and have reasonably efficient military equipment, even if for the first half of the conflict these differences should not be too overstated. He was more likely to have professional or professionalized officers and a constant relationship with them that was hierarchical, paternalistic, and subject to potentially severe punishment for indiscipline. The Republican soldier, in contrast, was more likely to learn how to read and write in the trenches, and have access to a wider breadth of genuine educational opportunities. By the last year of the conflict, however, the average government conscript would face desperate shortages of both rations and equipment; he would be significantly older on average than his rebel counterparts; and he would be tasked with more difficult and dangerous operations on the battlefield as the number of elite troops available to the Popular Army declined. He may also have been subjected to more violent and arbitrary discipline as the military situation became increasingly desperate in the prelude to overall defeat. More importantly, however, the Republican conscript was bombarded with a veritable barrage of publications and speeches that sought to underline the version of Spain that the government was fighting for, and which conscientiously rejected the version projected by the Nationalists. Ultimately the Nationalist Army was more effective at managing its conscripts than the Republican Popular Army and frequently managed to coerce the unwilling, and sometimes even the actively hostile, into adequately completing their military service. This is a vital factor in understanding the outcome of the war.

Further Reading

Alpert, Michael. *The Republican Army in the Spanish Civil War 1936-1939*. Cambridge: Cambridge University Press, 2013.

Hinojosa Durán, José. *Tropas en un frente olvidado. El ejército republicano en Extremadura durante la Guerra Civil*. Mérida: Editora Regional Extremadura, 2009.

Matthews, James, *Reluctant Warriors. Republican Popular Army and Nationalist Army Conscripts in the Spanish Civil War 1936-1939*. Oxford: Oxford University Press, 2012.

Puell de la Villa, Fernando. *Historia del Ejército en España*. Madrid: Alianza, 2009.

Salas Larrazábal Ramón. *Historia del Ejército Popular de la República*, 4 vols. Madrid: Editora Nacional, 1973.

Seidman, Michael, 'The Soldiers' Experience of the Spanish Civil War' in *'If You Tolerate This...': The Spanish Civil War in the Age of Total War*, ed. Martin Baumeister and Stefanie Schüler-Springorum (Chicago: University of Chicago Press, 2009).

Semprún, José. *Del Hacho al Pirineo: El Ejército Nacional en la Guerra de España*. Madrid: Actas, 2004.

Notes

1 For reasons of space, this chapter focuses on conscripts fighting in the central regions of Spain and does not consider the particularities of recruitment specific to regions such as Galicia, the Basque Country, and Catalonia.

2 For example, as early as 31 July 1936, the mayor of Valladolid had drawn up a list of a potential 539 '*mozos* [young men of recruitment age] fit for military service'. Archivo Municipal, Valladolid (AMVA), Serie Quintas y Reemplazos, Carpeta (C.) 6469–2.

3 The last unit to accept militarization was the anarchosyndicalist column *Tierra y Libertad* (Land and Freedom).

4 For a summary of the issues the militia columns faced see Coronel Mariano Salafranca's report from the Talavera sector, south of Madrid, from 3 September 1936. Archivo General Militar Ávila (AGMAV), Zona Roja [*sic*] (ZR), Armario (A.) 97, Legajo (L.) 967, Carpeta (C.) 12/5. See also Chapter 2 of this volume.

5 For general histories of the Republican army, see Michael Alpert, *The Republican Army in the Spanish Civil War 1936-1939* (Cambridge: Cambridge University Press,

2013) and Ramón Salas Larrazábal, *Historia del Ejército Popular de la República* 4 vols (Madrid: Editora Nacional, 1973). For the Nationalist Army, see José Semprún, *Del Hacho al Pirineo: El Ejército Nacional en la Guerra de España* (Madrid: Actas, 2004).

6 For an example of Nationalist call-up orders see AMVA, Serie Quintas y Reemplazos, C. 6488–6; for the Republican side, see Archivo General de la Guerra Civil Epañola, Salamanca (AGGCE), Sección Militar (SM) 1908, File Francisco Garnacho Gutiérrez. A veteran described his Republican medical examination by doctors who 'auscultate, feel and inspect at full speed'. Lluís Montagut, *Yo fui soldado de la República* (Barcelona: Inèdita Editores, 2003), 12.

7 This is in contrast to the 120,000 and 100,000 volunteer combatants the Republicans and Nationalists could respectively muster. These numbers are summarized in Michael Seidman, *Republic of Egos: A Social History of the Spanish Civil War* (Madison, WI: University of Wisconsin Press, 2002), 40. Seidman adds that the Republican conscription figure may be inflated because of a significant number of draft evaders. However, the conscript-to-volunteer ratio remains firmly in favour of the former on both sides. A man's cohort in both armies was the year in which he turned 21.

8 For their organization, see *Diario Oficial del Ministerio de la Guerra*, 1 October 1936.

9 See *Boletín Oficial del Estado (BOE)*, 25 March 1937.

10 See, for example, AGMAV, Zona Nacional (ZN), A.35, L.1, C.6, Documento (D.) 1/57. In this case it was the 152nd Division created in June 1937 and which served with the Army of the South.

11 This example is from the Cuenca CRIM (no. 8) in January 1938. AGMAV, ZR, A.77, L.332, C.1, D.1/1.

12 For the Republic, see *Gaceta de la República*, 23 February 1937; for the Nationalists AGMAV, Cuartel General de Generalísimo (CGG), A.2, L.182, C.22, D.2/1.

13 See, for example, AGMAV, CGG, A.2, L.188, C.48/1 and 3.

14 Ilana R. Bet-El, *Conscripts: Lost Legions of the Great War* (London: Sutton, 1999), 12. For a consideration of the conscription issue in Britain see Ralph J. Q. Adams and Philip P. Poirier, *The Conscription Controversy in Great Britain*, 1900-18 (London: Macmillan, 1987).

15 Cardona, *España 1936–1939: La guerra militar* (Madrid: Historia 16, 1996), 89–90.

16 Semprún, *Del Hacho al Pirineo*, 30.

17 John A. Lynn, *Battle. A History of Combat and Culture* (New York: Westview, 2003), xiv.

18 George Orwell, 'Looking Back on the Spanish War', in *The Penguin Essays of George Orwell*, ed. George Orwell (London: Penguin, 1984), 223.

19 Lynn, *Battle*, xiii–xvii.

20 Michael Seidman, 'The Soldiers' Experience of the Spanish Civil War' in *'If You Tolerate This...': The Spanish Civil War in the Age of Total War*, ed. Martin Baumeister and Stefanie Schüler-Springorum (Chicago: University of Chicago Press, 2009), 186. Seidman also lists 'sex', and shall be considered below.

21 For the December 1937 bonus, see AGMAV, CGG, A.1, L.33, C.131, D.8/3.

22 James Matthews, *Reluctant Warriors. Republican Popular Army and Nationalist Army Conscripts in the Spanish Civil War 1936-1939* (Oxford: Oxford University Press, 2012), Chapters 4 and 5.

23 This was, for example, the case for the 24th Mixed Brigade on 17 and 18 November 1937. AGGCE, SM 2467, Parte, 19 November 1937.

24 AGMAV, ZR, A.74, L.1164, C.12, D.1/13.

25 One such campaign is described in *Moral del Combatiente*, 1 October 1938.

26 AGMAV, ZR, A.66, L.803, C.2, D.1/2.

27 Javier Pérez Gómez, *La brigada de los toreros: historia de la 96 Brigada Mixta del Ejército Popular* (Madrid: Almena, 2005), 57.

28 Enrique Cabrerizo Paredes, *Memorias de un cura en nuestra guerra civil* (Guadalajara: Ayuntamiento de Durón, 1992), 71.

29 AGMAV, ZN, A.37, L.10, C.6, D.5/9. In this case, it was the 107th Division in November 1938.

30 For the nature of the loss of credibility, see James Matthews, *Voces de la trinchera. Cartas de combatientes republicanos en la Guerra Civil española* (Madrid: Alianza, 2015).

31 AGMAV, ZR, A.60, L.701, C.7, D.6/3–4.

32 Antonio Bullón de Mendoza and Álvaro de Diego, *Historias orales de la guerra civil* (Barcelona: Ariel, 2000), 120.

33 Leonard V. Smith, 'War and "Politics": The French Army Mutinies of 1917', *War in History* (1995) 2/2: 180–201.

34 Mark Thompson, *The White War: Life and Death on the Italian Front, 1915-1919* (London: Faber & Faber, 2009), 204.

35 See, for example, Irina Davidian, 'The Russian Soldier's Morale from the Evidence of Tsarist Military Censorship', in *Facing Armageddon: The First World War Experienced*, ed. Hugh Cecil and Peter Liddle (London: Leo Cooper, 1996), 425–33.

36 Michael Seidman, 'Quiet Fronts in the Spanish Civil War', *The Historian* 61, no. 4 (1999): 821–42.

37 Semprún, *Del Hacho al Pirineo*, 311.

38 Pedro Corral, *Desertores: La guerra civil que nadie quiere contar* (Barcelona: Debate, 2006), 197.

39 Military psychology studies refer to 'primary group cohesion' as a fundamental factor affecting a unit's fighting abilities. Primary groups are the small, informal, and mutually supportive bands that soldiers within military structures form with their peers. See Omer Bartov, *Hitler's Army: Soldiers, Nazis and War in the Third Reich* (Oxford: Oxford University Press, 1991), Chapter 2.

40 José Llordés, *Al dejar el fusil* (Barcelona: Ariel, 1969), 95.

41 Ibid., 180.

42 See, for example, AGGCE, SM 2067, Orden General del 441 Batallón, 111 Brigada Mixta, 30 August 1938.

43 For the Republican postal service, see Matthews, *Voces de la trinchera*; for the Nationalist packages, *BOE*, 15 October 1936.

44 *La Ametralladora*, 6 February 1938.

45 Quoted in Jaime Tovar Patrón, *Los curas de la última cruzada* (Madrid: Fuerza Nueva, 2001), 204.

46 Mary Nash, *Defying Male Civilization: Women in the Spanish Civil War* (Denver, CO: Arden, 1995), 160–2.

47 Inmaculada Julián, 'La representación gráfica de la mujer', in *Las mujeres y la guerra civil española: III jornadas de estudios monográficos. Salamanca, octubre 1989* (Salamanca: Instituto de la Mujer, 1991), 356.

48 There were as many as 200,000 prostitutes by 1940, working both in brothels and independently. Mirta Núñez Díaz-Balarte, *Mujeres caídas: Prostitutas legales y clandestinas en el franquismo* (Madrid: Oberon, 2003), 23.

49 AGMAV, ZN, A.37, L.3, C.9, D.3/34.

50 Pérez Gómez, *La brigada de los toreros*, 54.
51 AGMAV, ZR, A.60, L.713, C.12, D.2/11.
52 AGMAV, ZR, A.60, L.713, C.12, D.2/1–9.
53 For a comparison between commissars and chaplains, see James Matthews, 'Comisarios y capellanes en la Guerra Civil: Una mirada comparativa', *Ayer* 94, no. 2 (2014): 175–99.
54 AGGCE, Estado Mayor (EM) (2) 2, C.19/62.
55 See especially, Mary Vincent, 'The Martyrs and the Saints: Masculinity and the Construction of the Francoist Crusade', *History Workshop Journal* 47 (1999): 68–98. For the 'warrior-monk', see Michael Richards, *A Time of Silence: Civil War and the Culture of Repression in Franco's Spain* (Cambridge: Cambridge University Press, 1998), 152–3.
56 AGMAV, ZN, A.38, L.7, C.15, D.8/114.
57 AGMAV, ZN, A.38, L.7, C.15, D.3/31.
58 Sonya O. Rose, 'Temperate Heroes: Concepts of Masculinity in Second World War Britain', in *Masculinities in Politics and War: Gendering Modern History*, ed. Stefan Dudink, Karen Hagemann, and John Tosh (Manchester: Manchester University Press, 2004), 177.
59 Eduardo Pons Prades, *Un soldado de la República: Memorias de la guerra civil española 1936–9* (Madrid: Guillermo del Toro, 1974), 172.
60 Xosé Manoel Núñez Seixas, *¡Fuera el invasor! Nacionalismos y movilización bélica durante la guerra civil española (1936–1939)* (Madrid: Marcial Pons, 2006), 23.
61 Franz Borkenau, *The Spanish Cockpit: An Eyewitness Account of the Spanish Civil War* (London: Weidenfeld & Nicholson, 2000), 206.
62 Javier Tovar Patrón, *Los curas de la última cruzada* (Madrid: F.N. Editorial, 2001), 208.
63 This dynamic is explored in detail in James Matthews, '"Our Red Soldiers": The Nationalist Army's Management of its Left-Wing Conscripts in the Spanish Civil War 1936–1939', *Journal of Contemporary History* 45, no. 2 (April 2010): 344–63.
64 'Competence, leadership skills, paternalism and courage' determined a British First world War officer's relationship with his men. Gary Sheffield, *Leadership in the Trenches: Officer-Man Relations, Morale and Discipline in the British Army in the Era of the First World War* (London: Macmillan, 2000), 114.
65 Quoted in Tovar Patrón, *Los curas*, 204.
66 AGMAV, ZR, A.66, L.803, C.2, D.1/17.
67 Michael Alpert, 'Soldiers, Politics and War', in *Revolution and War in Spain 1931–1939*, ed. Paul Preston (London: Routledge, 1984), 213.
68 AGMAV, ZR, A.74, L.1164, C.12, D.1/1.
69 For a history of the brigade, see Pedro Corral, *Si me quieres escribir: Gloria y castigo de la 84ª Brigada Mixta del Ejército Popular* (Barcelona: Random House Mondadori, 2004).
70 Sheffield, *Leadership in the Trenches*, 165–77.
71 *Movilización*, 10 October 1938.
72 For the educational project, see Christopher H. Cobb, *Los milicianos de la cultura* (Bilbao: Editorial de la Universidad del País Vasco, 1995).
73 *Balas Rojas*, 14 April 1937.
74 Alpert, *El Ejército Popular*, 208.
75 See, for example, *Avanzadilla: Órgano de la 36 Brigada Mixta*, 30 May 1938.
76 Francesco Benvenuti, *The Bolsheviks And The Red Army, 1918-1922* (Cambridge: Cambridge University Press, 1988), 142.

77 Sandie Holguín, *Creating Spaniards: Cultural and National Identity in Republican Spain* (Madison, WI: University of Wisconsin Press, 2002), 193.

78 Cabrerizo Paredes, *Memorias de un cura*, 32.

79 Holguín, *Creating Spaniards*, 193.

80 AGMAV, ZN, A.37, L.2, C.6, D.4/17.

Chapter 5

DESERTION AND SHIRKING IN THE SPANISH CIVIL WAR: MAN VERSUS PROPAGANDA

Pedro Corral
Translated by Carlos Yebra López and James Matthews

The manner in which the Spanish Civil War is remembered continues to be affected to this day by the extraordinary reach of the propaganda campaigns conducted by the two sides. Both the Nationalists and the Republicans had a vested interest in portraying their respective zones as fundamentally committed to the war effort, and particularly with regard to the enthusiasm of their combatants. But an examination of the reality of the struggle tells a significantly different story.

As early as 1957, a perceptive witness of the conflict, journalist Herbert L. Matthews, a correspondent for the *New York Times* in the Republican zone, penned a noteworthy criticism of the epic version of the civil war that projected a high level of engagement on both sides and that still makes an appearance in debates about the conflict today: 'Even during the Civil War I estimated that only about 20 percent of the Spanish people – ten on each side – provided the driving force to keep it going.'[1]

Observations such as this one by Matthews suggest a necessary reconsideration of the average Spaniard's commitment to participate willingly in the fratricidal conflict. In turn, this change of perspective opens up many related issues, including the important subject of wartime propaganda. The considerable effort made by both sides in the propaganda war, involving substantial artistic production, particularly on the Republican side, has often been understood as an outpouring of popular enthusiasm for the conflict. But, in reality, it was precisely the weak mobilization of Spanish society that elicited such a volume of propaganda in the first place. The efforts made on both sides to encourage social participation through slogans, speeches, posters, leaflets, and documentaries were enormous. What is more, it is evidence that they sought to galvanize by all means possible the martial spirit of a society that, for the most part, demonstrated lacklustre enthusiasm throughout the conflict.

The low effective social engagement in the conflict pointed out by Herbert L. Matthews reflects the fact that both sides' military forces consisted overwhelmingly of conscripts. These men were forced to take up arms for the sole reason of being old enough to do so (as is explored in Chapter 4 of this volume). The profusion of images featuring seasoned volunteer fighters that appeared in both zones during the early stages of the conflict disguised a more prosaic and less idealistic reality: the need for the two contending authorities to open recruiting offices and call up the manpower necessary to continue the fight.[2]

In comparison to other European conflicts, the topic of desertion has only relatively recently made an appearance in the historiography on the Spanish Civil War.[3] This is largely due to an enduring interest in the traditional political and ideological spheres of the conflict, as well as an approach to military history that favoured studies of wartime tactics and organization over the experience of individuals in battle. This was further compounded by the fact that neither side, including their political heirs, wanted to recognize that enthusiasm for their cause was not absolute.

In fact, the relative scarcity of military recruits was a serious concern in both zones from the beginning of the conflict. It is therefore not surprising that the recruitment of volunteers became, as of August 1936, a race in which both sides deployed a whole array of material offers to encourage enrolment, promising generous salaries and food rations, and even guaranteed jobs once the conflict was over. The most strident measure introduced on the Republican side was the establishment of a 10 pesetas-per-day wage to combatants, five times what soldiers earned before the outbreak of war.[4] For an approximate idea of the relative value of this salary, it is significant that three quarters of the militiamen killed in combat in the first six months of the war were unemployed or earned a daily wage of fewer than 10 pesetas before the conflict and suggests that the pay, at least in part, was responsible for their decision to enlist.[5] And yet, these incentives did not generate a widespread enthusiastic response among Spaniards. In the autumn of 1936, the number of volunteer soldiers in the governmental zone was not higher than 120,000 (as examined in Chapter 2), whereas in the rebel zone there were no more than 100,000.[6] In total, the number of Spaniards taking up arms voluntarily was about 220,000 in a country of just under 25 million inhabitants.

The First Warnings against Desertion

In addition to a lack of volunteers, the need to increase the military effectiveness of the militia units led both sides to rapidly impose militarization on their heterogeneous armed supporters. This also shows how professional military commanders on the Republican side mistrusted ad hoc militia units because of their lack of discipline and fighting capacity. Indeed, extremely early on in the conflict, direct threats were made so as to avoid desertions within the ranks of the Republican militia units, which suggests that the reality of combat rapidly undermined the morale of many initial volunteers. An example of these is the warning published on the cover of *El Socialista* newspaper, the mouthpiece of the *Partido Socialista Obrero Español* (PSOE), or Spanish Socialist Party, on 30 September 1936. Next to the figure of a militiaman shot dead from behind, the message is clear: 'Militiaman. Death penalty for the deserter who flees!'[7] (see Figure 5.1).

Figure 5.1 A printed warning in newspaper *El Socialista* reads, 'Death penalty for the deserter who flees!' José Bardasano, *El Socialista*, 30 September 1936. Fundación Pablo Iglesias, Madrid, Spain.

The low level of volunteer mobilization and their questionable effectiveness forced both sides to resort to conscription after a few weeks (as explored in Chapter 2). The mobilization potential of obligatory conscription during the war, with an average of 240,000 men per reserve class, amounted theoretically to a total of 5 million men. However, the actual number of Spaniards incorporated into the ranks on both sides did not exceed approximately 2.5 million: 1.3 million in the Republican Popular Army and just over 1.2 million in the National Army.[8] This means that a further 2.5 million Spaniards joined the ranks of an 'invisible army' that avoided military service altogether during the war despite belonging to mobilized reserve classes. This mass of men was made up of those considered unfit for service and those involved in industries crucial to the war effort, and who therefore legitimately avoided the call-up. But it also included those who ignored the mobilization orders, who sought exemptions on false grounds or who feigned illness and deployed a plethora of pretexts not to put on a uniform, take up arms, and head to the front. In total, this number of men was significant and approximately equal in number to the combined total of men serving in both sides' armies.

The above conclusion is backed up by the mobilization figures of the 1937 reserve class, which are the only complete ones to have survived in the archives. Franco's headquarters tallied 59,698 draftees in the 1937 reserve class call-up, whereas the Republican Ministry of Defence totalled 52,719, not taking into account the isolated northern provinces.[9] To the 112,417 draftees of the 1937 reserve class call-up that were effectively mobilized in both zones, approximately 5,000 from the Republican provinces of Vizcaya, Santander, and Asturias should be added, plus another 10,000 as a combined total of those who enlisted as volunteers on both sides. And yet, this gives a total of no more than 127,500 men under arms, a difference of 112,500 in comparison to the approximately 240,000 men that theoretically made up each reserve class. This means that 47 per cent of the 1937 recruits that should have joined the ranks on one or other side did not do so. Presumably a proportion of them had a legitimate reason not to, such as physical disability or working in a war-related industry, but a significant number risked punishment for disobeying their call-up orders.

The tepid warlike fervour shown by these conscripts is noteworthy because it was the first reserve class of those recruited in both zones not to have undertaken peacetime military service and therefore was not exposed to the enthusiasm-dampening trials of army life. This fact is even more remarkable given that this reserve class was mobilized on the Francoist side before the end of the first year of the war, and on the Republican side exactly one year after the start of conflict. This demonstrates that by mid-1937 a reluctance to go into battle had already become a serious problem that hampered both sides' mobilization efforts.

Thus, in the Spanish Civil War, thousands of potential conscripts ended up becoming deserters. There were considerable pockets of fugitives (known as *emboscados*; literally 'in hiding') in the mountain ranges of both zones. Despite the fact that the Francoist side labelled them as 'Marxist fugitives', the possibility that there were military deserters among them is highly probable, as frequently also happened in the Republican zone. The case of the escapees in the mountain ranges of Huelva and Seville is perhaps the most extensively documented in the rebel zone.[10] Numerous military operations took place in the rearguard of both areas in order to search for and capture these deserters, especially in Catalonia, Castilla-La Mancha, Levante, Andalusia, and Asturias. Sometimes such rearguard operations against the bands of fugitives and deserters consumed valuable resources and required considerable forces to leave the front, as in the case of a battalion of the Republican 134th Mixed Brigade. This unit carried out a sweep against those who had fled into the Sierra de Cadí, a mountainous region between Barcelona, Girona and Lérida, in October 1938, during the crucial Battle of the Ebro.[11]

An Amnesty for Fugitives from the Ranks

The phenomenon of the fugitives and *emboscados* was so considerable in the Republican zone that Juan Negrín's government was forced to issue a decree granting them amnesty in August 1938 in the hope that at least some would join the Popular Army; he promised a pardon to those who did so. Scared and hungry, thousands of deserters left their hideouts and joined military units at the end of the Battle of the Ebro: they were the so-called 'reserve class from the hills' (*quinta del monte*).[12] Moreover, a significant number of those amnestied joined the ranks of the former International Brigades so as to make up for those foreign volunteers repatriated in September 1938.[13]

In an analysis of desertions during the civil war there were two distinct stages. The first centred on the rebels, who until the end of 1937 were concerned about the alarming number of fugitives and deserters. The second phase began with the conquest of the northern Republican zone in October 1937 and was cemented with the collapse of the Aragon front and the division of the Republican zone, in March and April 1938 respectively. During this latter period, the concern about defections and the lack of enlistment became an issue almost exclusively for the Republican side.

One of the main goals of the propaganda wars in the trenches was to incite enemy soldiers to desert. The promises made by both sides to those deserting their respective armies included exorbitant amounts of money or even Christmas hampers, although ideological arguments generally prevailed among the Republican messages. An especially important incentive for deserters was to secure a good posting in the other zone or even to be exempted from joining a front-line unit. Both sides regularly promised not to re-enlist deserters if they belonged to a reserve class that had not yet been mobilized in their zone. This proved a convincing lure to change sides, especially when Republican conscription outpaced the Nationalist one, as evidenced by the following text from a Francoist pamphlet launched into the Republican trenches to encourage desertion:

> We are not asking you to come over to our side in order to expand our army. The proof of this is that the 1925, 1926, and 1927 reserve classes, as well as younger men, are peacefully in their homes. Militiaman, come over to our side so that you aren't exposed to death and killing, and to ensure that peace once more reigns among Spaniards.[14]

Moreover, since both contending armies distrusted the newcomers, they instructed defectors to join units in sectors other than those they came from. Thus, if the deserter in question had changed sides through an active front, he knew that he would probably be sent to a quieter one or even to rearguard services. This is confirmed by the fact that Francoist fugitives to the Republican side were often posted to rearguard battalions and entrusted, among other tasks, with watching over enemy prisoners.[15]

Indeed, sheer survival in the face of considerable material and training shortages was the dominant motivation of the large majority of deserters. In addition to the hardships of the conflict, recruits often lacked military training, a situation that was frequently condemned by both sides at the official level. Conscripts were sent into the front lines sometimes without even having undergone the most basic of training. This was reported in February 1938 by Lieutenant Colonel Luis Morales, of the Republican Levante Army (Eastern Spain), in a report on the defeat during the Battle of Teruel. He called for a radical change in system of training recruits, so that they were not sent to war 'without even having done a day's shooting practice and without having learned how to handle the regulation rifle'.[16]

The situation was not markedly different on the Francoist side, even though it has become commonplace to claim that Franco's troops were well trained in comparison. Between January and February 1938, for example, Franco's headquarters received a number of complaints from division commanders taking issue with the 'insufficient training of the new contingents sent to cover casualties'. These complaints were also echoed in the following month of June. Upon being asked to offer a permanent solution to this problem, the person in charge of mobilization and training at the Burgos headquarters, General Luis Orgaz, argued that the 'greediness of the fronts [i.e. manpower needs]' allowed for neither the deadlines nor the training programme to which recruits were theoretically subjected to be met.[17] Indeed, the situation did not appear to improve, and during the following August the commander of the Nationalist Army of the North, General Fidel Dávila, received a report on recruits from the Balearic Islands, who were said to have joined the front 'with very poor military training, to the extent that most do not know how to handle a rifle or a hand grenade'.[18]

Thus it could be argued that Spaniards forced to take up arms considered themselves to be little more than 'cannon fodder', and this exacerbated new recruits' low level of morale. This is evident, for example, in a report from the commissars of the 27th Mixed Brigade (deployed on the Madrid front) as from October 1938:

> Although the recruits that joined the ranks later on arrived with low morale, they improved thanks to the [propaganda] work carried out, even though there are still some who have yet to grasp the meaning of the war we are fighting; and so these continue to have a very low level of morale, almost the same as when they first arrived at the battalion.[19]

In addition to the lack of military training there was also insufficient food and of poor quality, as well as a shortage of appropriate clothing for the hardships in the trenches (as examined in Chapter 4). This contributed to the proliferation of diseases such as scabies, malaria, gangrene, typhoid, and scurvy. Not even a strict ideological and propagandistic indoctrination was enough to overcome the shortcomings of these basic needs. Moreover, the unfavourable course of the war for the Republican side exacerbated the shortages in its units. For example, in November 1938 sick leave in the Republican Army of Andalusia reached 94 per cent of the total number of absences granted: 2,432 sick men were evacuated, compared to 13 dead and 138 wounded by enemy fire.[20] In some of its units, as in the 147th Mixed Brigade, epidemics of scurvy occurred because of the absence of fresh fruit and vegetables in the troops' diet for months on end.[21]

A soldier assigned to the Andalusian front, Ángel Lomas, denounced this in a letter censored for being defeatist: 'The only disease I have is that I'm very hungry and I never eat my fill because they give us little to eat and very little bread, so I'm telling you, I'm hungrier than ever.'[22] Another of his companions, Jaime Romeo Súñer, made it abundantly clear in another letter to a friend that without adequate food there was no way to successfully endure the front lines:

> The most annoying thing for us here is the food, because they give us little and we are hungry, because, imagine: in the morning they give us some coffee, which

is dirty water, and at midday, a little soup with a piece of potato, [and] the dinner is the same, so imagine if you can hold out [on these levels of rations], because if it were broth, as long as they gave us enough, it would allow us to survive, but with this, there is no chance.[23]

The lack of footwear and clothing also undermined combatants' morale. The commissar of the 96th Mixed Brigade, Ernesto Rojas, was descriptive in denouncing the situation of his men in the autumn of 1938:

A whole battalion cover[s] their feet [with rags] due to a lack of footwear; and no matter how careful one tells them to be, their trousers wear out. Each year 400 trousers are given to the Brigade. Many soldiers are baring their testicles and not because of their carelessness.[24]

This shortage of food and clothing was the motivating factor in the desertion of many Republican soldiers who were woefully equipped for the difficult front-line tasks demanded of them.

On the pro-Franco side, the lack of adequate footwear and clothing was also a cause for desertion, even though these were more limited in the latter stages of the war when the Nationalists had established a solid rearguard economy (as explored in Chapter 8). For example, the soldier Francisco Castillo Ledesma was arrested in May 1938 for lacking a laissez-passer in the rearguard. He had escaped from his unit after appearing before a doctor with serious injuries caused by the lack of footwear. Since he 'could not keep up with the advanced [Nationalist] forces' he was sent to the kitchens to wait for a new shipment of boots to arrive, but he fled soon after.[25]

A further problem was a delay in the payment of salaries, which increased the fighters' concerns about the situation of their families in the rearguard, and again affected Republicans more seriously. This was denounced in August 1938 by Gil Roldán, an anarchist commissar of an Army Group in the Catalan zone, as the cause of desertions to the rear, including those of soldiers with 'great political backgrounds [i.e. left-wing pasts] and military experience': 'The soldier who does not collect his pay regularly and on time therefore cannot send money home, and is obliged to think incessantly about the possible tragedies that could befall his household.'[26]

The concerns experienced by men of military age at the prospect of leaving their families in the midst of wartime hardship was a further motivation to avoid recruitment. Juan Boix Badosa, a young farmer from San Feliú de Pallerols (Girona) who had supported his mother and his two sisters since the death of his father, was arrested while attempting to cross the border into France with other deserters disobeying their call-up. 'I did not want to know anything about the war. My concern was my family. How would it help my mother and my sisters if I got killed? At least from France I thought I could continue to help them', Boix told the author of this chapter when he recounted his experience.[27]

The life of the average combatant was, in short, significantly different from that featured in propaganda films. Mariano Ramos Pons, a veteran of the 85th Mixed Brigade, explained this to Valerio Torrijos, a young man from the Valencian town of Massanassa, who longed to be called up. It is a moving testimony with regard to the reaction of an individual to collective mobilization, and a portion of the letter was identified by the Republican censorship services for being demoralizing:

> I am happy and pleased that you want your reserve class to be called up so that you can join the army, but I have to give you a little warning: do not get caught up in the excitement just because you have seen the war movies and you have seen how suffering is portrayed in them, since the reality is something entirely different. It is very pleasant to witness war from a cinema seat … [but] if you happen to set foot in the trenches, do write to me again and I would be glad if at that point you still have the same degree of enthusiasm.[28]

The concern of both sides about the lack of warlike enthusiasm of their populations was confirmed when their respective authorities circulated regulations against the departure from Spain of men of military age. On the Republican side, on 29 October 1936, the government banned the departure of those over twenty years of age via a decree ordering the militarization of men between that age and forty-five. This made them available to the government, under the threat of being declared deserters, for any work or service carried out 'in the name of national defence'.[29] In the face of the numerous flights abroad, the Republican consulates were instructed to deny men of military age any support established for civilian refugees.[30] In 1937, the prohibition to leave Republican Spain was increased to those aged eighteen and over, because those draftees were expected to be eventually mobilized, as happened with the even younger 17-year-old so-called 'feeding-bottle' or 'pacifier' reserve class ('*quinta del biberón*' or '*quinta del chupete*').

In December 1936 Franco also banned via decree the possibility for men aged between eighteen and forty to travel abroad.[31] But then he made the measure even stricter. On 19 October 1937 he lowered the age to be permitted abroad to sixteen 'in view of the growing number of young people of seventeen years of age who are known to emigrate to America in order to avoid the of the fulfilment of their military obligations by this means'.[32]

It is no coincidence either that after eight months of war and in the face of evidence that many were avoiding their conscription, the two sides annulled all existing legal exemptions to undertaking wartime military service. And, as in so many other cases, both sides coincided in the dates of these dispositions. Franco suspended the exemptions on 20 February 1937.[33] The Republican authorities did so three days later, on 23 February, under Prime Minister Largo Caballero.[34]

The Two Spains against the Uncommitted Men

The two sides also announced on the same day, on 18 June 1937, that they would tighten the provisions concerning fugitives, deserters, and self-mutilation.[35] In an order dated that day, the Francoist authorities established that those who did not obey the call-up of their reserve class would be found guilty of the crime of 'simple desertion' and would be forced to undertake their military service with a four-year add-on in the Spanish Legion or with the *Regulares*, the Moroccan troops in the Nationalist Army. The rationale behind the punishment was clear: these were the shock brigades that traditionally suffered the highest number of casualties in combat.[36]

The 18th of June 1937 also brought bad news for the fugitives in the area under Popular Front control. Whether it was by chance or with foreknowledge, on the very day that Franco hardened reprisals against those who resisted recruitment, Negrín's government decided to equate 'simple desertion' for not obeying the call-up with 'desertion in the face of the enemy', a crime which was punished more harshly. A decree from the Ministry of National Defence, then led by the socialist Indalecio Prieto, established that fugitives would be punished with six to twenty years of internment in labour camps, and that they still had to undertake their wartime military service in front-line disciplinary battalions.[37] Ten months later, on 5 April 1938, Negrín also became Minister of Defence, following the collapse of the government forces after the Francoist offensive in Aragon, a manoeuvre which concluded on 15 April with the partition of the Republican zone in two. A week earlier, on 8 April, Negrín passed a new order, even harsher than the previous one, to the effect that those who had not obeyed the call-up be tried for the crime of high treason, and unless they showed up at the nearest recruitment offices within three days, be liable as a result for capital punishment. In addition, local authorities were required to report all men belonging to mobilized reserve classes who were in their villages and not serving in the Popular Army.[38]

The authorities on both sides were also wary of those declared 'unfit for military service' (*inútiles*), in the light of evidence that some of them had evaded the call of duty by faking disabilities or illness. Throughout the war, those classified as unfit for service were repeatedly recalled to review their cases, and under the threat of being considered deserters if they did not obey.

On the Republican side, even the victims of venereal disease were on the radar for evasion of duty, as they were suspected of deliberately infecting themselves. This is evidenced by an order issued by General Sebastián Pozas, head of the Army of the Centre, and dated 25 November 1937: 'It is necessary to pay close attention to the recovery of patients suffering from venereal disease, as it has been observed that in many cases this is a pretext to avoid serving in the trenches.'[39] In the Republican Army of the Ebro, before the decisive battle of the war and by means of an order dated 5 July 1938, rigorous instructions were issued against venereal disease, in view of the fact that the number of cases represented a 'risk of a significant reduction in the number of forces'. Soldiers were warned that those infected after the order would be subject to a month's arrest. If they became infected again, they would be assigned to the 'disciplinary company' (*compañía correccional*) for a month. And if they became infected a third time they would be tried and punished for self-inflicted injury.[40]

Another way of avoiding the front was the use of fraudulent official exemptions, which the Nationalist side described as a 'national vice'. To counter this, Franco issued numerous provisions, intended to end the 'special connections' enjoyed by Falange members who managed to remain in the rearguard in spite of having been mobilized via their reserve classes. General Queipo de Llano himself wrote to General Franco on 8 October 1937 requesting that the local leaders of the new single party be exempted from the recruitment of the 1929 reserve class, due to their 'very important organizational efforts in the rearguard'. Franco flatly refused to exclude them.[41]

In the Republican zone, different parties and unions retained the power to decree exemptions from military service until the middle of the war and they were almost always granted to members and sympathizers. In addition to being a major source of unjustified exemptions, parties and unions also became one of the surest ways to avoid military service. It is surprising, for example, that as late as March 1938 the *Unión General de Trabajadores* (UGT), or General Union of Workers, and the *Confederación Nacional del Trabajo* (CNT), or National Confederation of Labour, the socialist and anarchist unions respectively, included in joint instructions to their supporters the commitment to encourage 'all members to comply enthusiastically with the mobilization orders'.[42] The abuses reached such an extreme that on 21 October 1937 the Popular Front government was forced to issue a decree to stop the 'inadmissible intrusions from various entities and centres' when it came to granting exemptions to men called up, since this was the 'exclusive prerogative of the Ministry of National Defence'. According to the decree itself, the situation had ended up causing a 'litany of unjust privileges and irritating abuses that ought to be eliminated for the sake of equity'. In addition, and to underscore the fact that this decree challenged the power of parties and unions, the Republican government demanded that conscripts who 'had not [joined the ranks of the Popular Army] because of political and trade union activities' should do so.[43] The Republican authorities took this step remarkably late, and a whole year into the conflict. In addition, it was approved on the same day that the government definitively lost the Northern Front, following the fall of Gijón into Francoist hands.

The president of the Republic, Manuel Azaña, reflected in his journal on the difficulties experienced by Prieto to enact his decree against the exemptions and privileges that abounded in the rear. On the same day, 21 October 1937, Azaña wrote caustically:

> It seems that this decree has been discussed for three hours in the Council of Ministers, because the communists do not like some of the amendments. A few socialist ministers have also squealed a little. The Republicans and Negrín have endorsed Prieto's project. In former times, exemptions from military service were sought from the rich, the friars, and so on. Now the Minister of War is challenged [by parties and unions] in order to remove or maintain exemptions in favour of such or such workers. Did we talk about equality before the law? *C'est une vue de l'esprit* [It is nothing but an illusion].[44]

In both zones, war-related industries, official organizations, and rearguard services were also a safe haven for those who wanted to avoid their military duties, and who sought to be declared 'irreplaceable' in their posts, even if they were not genuinely so. Beginning in 1937, both sides established periodic revisions within the military factories so that bosses could vouch that men called up but mobilized 'in the workplace' were truly 'irreplaceable', and not avoiding military service.

Documents from the Nationalist zone demonstrate that the mobilization of an additional reserve class frequently prompted a flurry of men who previously worked in other sectors to join war-related industries. This is the reason why the Francoist authorities ordered that in these industries older men should replace younger workers, who could then be called up. At the time of mobilization, only the younger specialized workers who were able to prove that they had been working for at least a year could remain in their war-related factory posts.[45]

The abuse of the power to grant exemptions reached the highest ranks of the Republican side, as denounced shortly after the end of the conflict by General Vicente Rojo himself, head of the general staff of the Popular Army:

> In the rearguard, morale lacked solidity. The danger [posed by the enemy] was clear and rigorous measures were expected, because everyone considered them necessary, indispensable to keep the state afloat; however, the first provisions to flush out the shirkers from their hiding places met enormous resistance, rather than the needed support: high officials, even ministers, did not hesitate to conspire in order to obtain an exemption for relatives or friends, thus setting a deplorable example.[46]

Even during the war, General Rojo stated that the 'pursuit of shirkers in the rearguard', who numbered thousands of individuals, was an 'urgent and radical' necessity for the survival of the Republic. This was expressed in an analysis of the military situation he sent to President Negrín on 20 September 1938, on the eve of the Munich pact. This agreement, in which Britain and France effectively conceded to Nazi Germany's ambitions to annex a strategic portion of Czechoslovakia, also sealed the fate of the Republic, which was definitively abandoned to its fate by the democratic powers:

> There are many thousands of citizens who are capable of military service but do not undertake it because they are indispensable to the organizations where they work. Everyone can be indispensable in the task they exercise, but all tasks must be abandoned when a call to duty is made to citizens. This measure is considered urgent and radical because the leniency towards some creates an evident state of demoralization in those who do take up arms.[47]

High-ranking officers on both sides criticized the privileged situation of the numerous people exempted, although it was more evident on the Republican side. Julián Henríquez Caubín, chief of Staff of the Army of the Ebro, would bitterly admit five years after the defeat of the Republic to the ineffectiveness of the measures taken against the so-called irreplaceable men:

> The *Carabinero* units [responsible for coastal and border defence], the units responsible for public order, the ministries, the political and trade union organizations ... all these places were full of young people, probably in excess of

the numbers required to completely rebuild our [military] units. Ninety percent of the tasks these men undertook in such positions could have been carried out more responsibly by older men, and even by women or by the war-wounded.[48]

Justice Mechanisms and Repressive Measures against Deserters

The repressive measures carried out against deserters and fugitives in many ways demonstrate that they were a common enemy faced by both sides during the Spanish Civil War. So much so that Nationalists and Republicans reinforced with comparable vigour the judicial procedures and punishments for those who tried to unilaterally turn their backs on the war.

As for the deserters to the enemy – the defectors – those who were caught during their flight were often killed on the barbed wire in no man's land or executed following a summary trial. One poignant case, among the many that can be found among the wartime documents, is that of the soldier José González Fernández. A man from Bilbao assigned to the Republican 39th Mixed Brigade, he was riddled with bullets from his own trenches on 12 September 1937 as he attempted to flee to the Nationalists on the Casa de Campo front in Madrid. The command later found his farewell letter in the trench: 'I'm not a fascist. If I leave, it's because we have lost the war and since I'm no fool I don't want to become cannon fodder', he had written.[49]

The rebels imposed military rule in their zone from the first moment of the uprising, as a direct consequence of their declaration of a state of war. In the Republican zone, this did not happen until the 23 January 1939 so that the rebels were not recognized as formal belligerents and thus not legitimized as an enemy. And while the Francoists did not change the content of the Code of Military Justice, they did not wait long before introducing a system to ensure its rapid implementation, even on the front lines themselves. This had the effect of reinforcing the exemplariness of the different punishments. On 28 July 1936, the rebel National Defence Junta declared that all military crimes would be tried in summary hearings. In December 1936, the so-called *Consejos de trinchera*, or Trench Councils, were founded for rank-and-file soldiers and 'extremely serious cases that merit the death penalty', such as desertion to the enemy.[50] Once the sentence was handed down, the execution of the penalty was carried out without having to wait for a formal acknowledgement from Franco's headquarters.

The repressive conditions in the Francoist rearguard effectively ensured the arrest of many fugitives and deserters. Strict rules for obtaining a laissez-passer, which were granted by the military governors, made it difficult for deserters to travel between different provinces in that zone. These documents were issued only for trips of fewer than fifteen days, and were granted only for a longer period if the petitioners were deemed to be persons of 'absolute guarantee' in terms of their loyalty to the regime. In practice, Franco's side hardly changed the substance and form of military justice. This not only represented continuity with the pre-war army, but also demonstrated the confidence of the new regime in the evolution of the war and the effectiveness of its own repressive measures.[51]

In contrast, in the Republican zone military criminal laws were tightened up following significant military defeats and territorial losses as the war progressed. Thus, Republican military justice transitioned from a frustrated project for a revolutionary penal code, in accordance with the antimilitarist spirit of the militias (explored in Chapter 2 of this volume), to the imposition of strict military law.

At the beginning of the war, Republican military justice was exercised by so-called *Tribunales Populares*, or Popular Courts, established in August 1936 and whose jurisdiction was extended the following month to cover crimes committed by combatants. Nevertheless, its operational ability in relation to this type of crime was limited.[52] The first judicial structures that specifically encompassed military crimes on the Republican side were the *Tribunales Populares Especiales de Guerra*, or Special Popular War Courts, created by Largo Caballero's government on 16 February 1937.[53] These courts were replaced by the *Tribunales Populares de Guerra*, or Popular War Courts, in a 7 May decree. Once dictated, the sentence had to be unanimously approved by the auditor, the army chief, and the commissar general. Otherwise, it passed to the Supreme Court. If the penalty was death, it would not be applied until approved by the government.[54] Barely a month after taking office in May 1937, Juan Negrín's new cabinet, which was presented as the 'Victory Government', toughened military justice with a decree instituting summary trials for the 'culprits of flagrant military offences'. This decree, approved one day before the fall of Bilbao on 19 June 1937, allowed the immediate execution of the accused without approval from the government and, therefore, without the possibility of pardon, as was already the case under the Franco regime.[55]

The campaign against deserters reached further degrees of intensity on both sides. On the pro-Franco side the relatives of the deserter were detained and their property confiscated, and if his relatives had a left-wing past, they were likely to be shot.[56] Although on the Republican side these measures against families were already applied on the Northern Fronts, they were accentuated by an extraordinarily severe provision introduced by Juan Negrín: sending the deserter's father or brothers to directly replace them at the front. Negrín's order, signed on 2 June 1938, was sent to Republican units with instructions to limit its distribution and that it should not be given 'greater circulation' than it being read aloud to new recruits and repeated to the troops once a week.[57]

In addition to the deserters, there were also those who relied on self-mutilation as a way to escape the front. Self-inflicted injuries were so numerous that they came to be jokingly called 'contagious wounds' in both zones. The easiest method was to shoot oneself in the hands or feet, or to position the arms or legs above the parapet, waiting for an enemy bullet. Many of the self-mutilated were shot by both sides on the spot or left on the front line with no other treatment than a bandage, so that gangrene eventually killed them.[58]

The extent of this phenomenon, even in the first months of the conflict, forced the military authorities of both zones to increase the punishments for voluntary disablement. On the Republican side, the governments of Asturias and the Basque

Country established the death penalty for the crime of self-mutilation in two decrees of 12 March and 21 May 1937. The Negrín government took the same measures in June of that year, within the context of tightening punishments for military crimes.[59] On the Nationalist side, the penalties for self-mutilation were not made more severe, but it was established that a soldier who had shot himself could not leave his position on the front, and would be instead transferred into a disciplinary unit. Those who shot themselves in the legs were placed in advanced positions, so that they were the most exposed to the assaults of the enemy. If the self-injury had occurred in the arms, they were used as messengers relaying information between different positions during the course of combat. In cases in which the self-mutilated soldier had a leftist past, he could be accused of 'aiding the rebellion', a crime punishable by death.[60]

This chapter is a brief overview of the civil war that few people on either side wanted to reveal, at least in Spain. It exposes another side of a conflict in which hundreds of thousands of Spaniards did not associate with the causes and ideologies of the fratricidal struggle, and even many of those who did identify with a particular position tried to escape the brutal conditions in which they perceived themselves to be little more than pawns or 'cannon fodder'. Although they were traitors in the eyes of their side's propaganda, they demonstrated an unwavering loyalty to their own survival. And although they were branded as cowards, they set an example of extraordinary bravery in defending their individual freedom in the midst of a violent and fratricidal civil war.

Further Reading

Alpert, Michael. *The Republican Army in the Spanish Civil War 1936-1939*. Cambridge: Cambridge University Press, 2013.

Corral, Pedro. *Desertores. La Guerra Civil que nadie quiere contar*. Debate: Barcelona, 2006.

Matthews, James. *Reluctant Warriors. Republican Popular Army and Nationalist Army Conscripts in the Spanish Civil War 1936-1939*. Oxford: Oxford University Press, 2012.

Seidman Michael. *Republic of Egos. A Social History of the Spanish Civil War*. Madison, WI: University of Wisconsin Press, 2002.

Varios Autores. *La justicia en guerra. Jornadas sobre la Administración de Justicia en la Guerra Civil española*. Ministerio de Cultura: Madrid, 1990.

Notes

1 Herbert L. Matthews, *The Yoke and the Arrows: A Report on Spain* (New York: G. Braziller, 1957), 84.

2 Each zone had 200,000 combatants in September 1936, according to Ramón Salas Larrazábal, *Los datos exactos de la Guerra Civil* (Madrid: Ediciones Rioduero, 1980), 105. If we deduct the military and security forces available to both sides at the beginning of the conflict, according to the same author, the number of civilian volunteers who took up arms did not reach 100,000 for either side.

3   Notable among these are Pedro Corral, *Desertores. La Guerra Civil que nadie quiere contar* (Debate: Barcelona, 2006) and Michael Seidman, *Republic of Egos: A Social History of the Spanish Civil War* (Madison, WI: University of Wisconsin Press, 2002). For a more theoretical approach that uses data from the Spanish Civil War, see Theodor McLauchlin, 'Desertion, Terrain, and Control of the Home Front in Civil Wars', *Journal of Conflict Resolution* 58, no. 8 (December 2014), 1, 419–44. For classic studies of desertion in other wars, see Alan Forrest, *Conscripts and Deserters: The Army and French Society during the Revolution and Empire* (Oxford: Oxford University Press, 1989) and John Keegan, *The Face of Battle* (New York: Viking, 1976).

4   *Gaceta de la República*, 231, 18 August 1936.

5   Archivo General Militar de Ávila (henceforth AGMAV), Zona Roja [*sic*] (ZR), Comandancia General de Milicias, Legajo (L.) 1334, Carpeta (C.) 3, Documento (D.) 1.

6   Seidman, *Republic of Egos*, 64. See also: James Matthews, *Reluctant Warriors: Republican Popular Army and Nationalist Army Conscripts in the Spanish Civil War 1936-1939* (Oxford: Oxford University Press, 2012).

7   Fundación Pablo Iglesias, *El Socialista*, Madrid, 30 September 1936.

8   These are approximate calculations provided in my book *Desertores*, 529–35. I draw on the figures of Salas Larrazábal, starting from the estimate that each reserve class in practice contributed 80,000 men to each side. Salas Larrazábal, *Los datos exactos*, 288–9.

9   Nationalist figures are available in AGMAV, Zona Nacional (ZN), Cuartel General del Generalísimo (CGG), L.188, C.1, D.22. For the Republican figures, see AGMAV, ZR, Ministerio de Defensa Nacional, L.506, C. 8. D. 1.

10 Francisco Espinosa Mestre, *La guerra civil en Huelva* (Huelva: Diputación Provincial, 1996); y AGMAV, ZN, Ejército del Sur, L.21, 22, 23, 26, 27, 28 and 31.

11 Carlos Engel, *Historia de las Brigadas Mixtas del Ejército Popular* (Madrid: Almena, 1999), 118.

12 *Diario Oficial del Ministerio de Defensa Nacional*, 211, 19 August 1938.

13 Corral, *Desertores*, 312–13.

14 AGMAV, ZR, Prensa y Propaganda, L.84, C.3, D.1.

15 Corral, *Desertores*, 147.

16 AGMAV, ZR, Ejército de Levante, L.787, C.6.

17 AGMAV, ZN, CGG, L.144, C.69, D.32.

18 AGMAV, ZN, Cuerpo de Ejército del Turia, L.1, C.10, D.1.

19 AGMAV, ZR, 27 Brigada Mixta, L.1,158, C.14, D.1.

20 AGMAV, ZR, 27 Brigada Mixta, L.851, C.5, D.2.

21 Ibid.

22 AGMAV, ZR, Ejército de Andalucía, L.803, C.2, D.1.

23 Ibid.

24 Javier Pérez Gómez, *La Brigada de los toreros: Historia de la 96.ª Brigada Mixta del Ejército Popular* (Madrid: Almena, 2005), 91.

25 AGMAV, ZN, Cuerpo de Ejército del Maestrazgo, L.3, C.4, D.1.

26 José Peirats, *La CNT en la revolución española*, vol. 3 (Paris: Ruedo Ibérico, 1971), 170.

27 Author interview with Juan Boix Badosa, 30 August 2005.

28 AGMAV, ZR, Ejército de Andalucía, L.803, C.2, D.1.

29 *Gaceta de la República*, 224, 31 October 1936.

30 Archivo del Nacionalismo Vasco (Vergara), Gobierno de Euzkadi [*sic*] (GE), 36, 2.

31 AGMAV, ZN, CGG, L.41, C.23 and 26, D.1.

32 AGMAV, ZN, 105 División, L.1, C.1, D.5.

33 Instituto de Historia y Cultura Militar, Legislación del Nuevo Estado, vol. 2, 292.
34 *Diario Oficial del Ministerio de la Guerra*, 47, 23 February 1937.
35 The reforms of Republican military justice were published in *Gaceta de la República*,
    170, 19 June 1937. Among other measures, the reforms implemented summary trials
    for the 'culprits of flagrant military offences', plus not obeying the call-up was made
    equivalent to desertion in the face of the enemy.
36 *Boletín Oficial del Estado*, 241, 18 June 1937.
37 *Gaceta de la República*, 170, 19 June 1937.
38 *Diario Oficial del Ministerio de Defensa Nacional*, 86, 11 April 1938.
39 AGMAV, ZR, VI Cuerpo de Ejército, L.943, C.5, D.1.
40 AGMAV, ZR, Ejército del Ebro, L.795, C.1, D.1.
41 Instituto de Historia y Cultura Militar. Legislación del Nuevo Estado, vol. 1, 214, and
    vol. 4, 98. Queipo de Llano's letter and Franco's answer can be found in AGMAV,
    CGG, L.183, C.14, D.6.
42 Peirats, *La CNT en la revolución española*, vol. 3, 37.
43 *Gaceta de la República*, 296, 23 October 1937.
44 Manuel Azaña, *Diarios de guerra* (Barcelona: Planeta DeAgostini, 2005), 445.
45 AGMAV, ZN, CGG, L.183, C.11, D.83.
46 Vicente Rojo, *¡Alerta los pueblos!* (Buenos Aires: Aniceto López, 1939), 22.
47 Rojo, *¡Alerta los pueblos!*, 30.
48 Julián Henríquez Caubín, *La Batalla del Ebro* (Mexico City: Unda y García, 1944),
    345.
49 AGMAV, ZR, 39 Brigada Mixta, L.1,182, C.1.
50 AGMAV, ZR, 152 Division, L.1, C.11, D.1.
51 Franco himself established that a laissez-passer for leave to rearguard areas should be
    issued directly by the generals commanding divisions. *Boletín Oficial del Estado*, 355,
    10 October 1937.
52 Glicerio Sánchez Recio, 'Justicia ordinaria y Justicia popular durante la guerra civil', in
    *Justicia en Guerra. Jornadas sobre la Administración de Justicia durante la Guerra Civil
    española* (Madrid: Ministerio de Cultura, 1990), 105.
53 *Gaceta de la República*, 48, 17 February 1937.
54 *Diario Oficial del Ministerio de la Guerra*, 117, 14 May 1937.
55 *Gaceta de la República*, 170, 19 June 1937.
56 The most abundant documentation of these reprisals in the Nationalist zone is
    preserved in the Archivo General Militar de Ávila (AGMAV) and corresponds to the
    Cuerpo de Ejército de Aragón.
57 An example of Negrín's orders can be found in AGMAV, ZR, VIII Cuerpo de Ejército,
    L.952, C.7, D.1.
58 Manuel Picardo Castellón, 'Experiencia personal en un hospital quirúrgico de
    primera línea durante nuestra Guerra Civil', in *Los médicos y la medicina en la Guerra
    Civil* (Madrid: Sanidad Ediciones, 1986), 196.
59 Glicerio Sánchez Recio et al., *La justicia en guerra. Jornadas sobre la Administración de
    Justicia en la Guerra Civil española* (Madrid: Ministerio de Cultura, 1990). AGMAV,
    ZR, Ejército del Norte, L.854, C.8, D.17.
60 AGMAV, ZN, Cuerpo de Ejército de Aragón, L.2. C.2.

Chapter 6

THE REDS AND THE GREENS: ENCOUNTERS BETWEEN MOROCCAN AND REPUBLICAN ENEMIES DURING THE SPANISH CIVIL WAR*

Ali Al Tuma

The encounter between Moroccan troops and the Republicans during the Spanish Civil War was, generally, a vicious one. Unsurprisingly in this war, the views of one another were often negative and not infrequently such enmity translated into violent action that violated the laws of war. That the Moroccan troops played a crucial military role in the early days, weeks, and months of the Spanish Civil War is common knowledge to students of the Spanish conflict. Moroccan troops and the legionnaires of the Army of Africa occupied much of Andalusia and Extremadura, and defeated one Republican army after another until they reached the gates of Madrid by November 1936. Nationalists, besieged in the Alcazar of Toledo or in Oviedo, could not be relieved by rebel Peninsular units and had to hear spoken Arabic and see the red headgear of the *Regulares* to know that salvation was coming. The importance of the Moroccan troops certainly diminished as the civil war progressed and as the Spanish peninsular armies grew and foreign contingents and weapon technology were flown in. Yet, the Moroccans' role remained important during the whole period of the war. Perhaps Seidman does not exaggerate when he notes that 'the Moroccan army may well have been, as a number of perceptive observers have labelled it, "the decisive factor" of the war'.[1] Estimates of the total number of Moroccans that fought in the war vary between 75,000,[2] more than 78,000,[3] and around 80,000.[4] This represents fewer than 10 per cent of the total combatants who fought under General Franco between 1936 and 1939.[5]

The main source of recruitment was the Spanish Protectorate, where the *interventores* (military controllers) and local tribal chiefs played a significant role. Thanks to their work, recruitment efforts intensified in the Rif, in Jebala and in Gomara.[6] Many former leaders of the 1920s anti-Spanish armed rebellion in northern Morocco would join the Nationalist war effort along with ex-rebel combatants. Another source of recruitment was Ifni and the Sahara, although these less densely populated regions would provide smaller numbers of recruits compared to northern Spanish Morocco. Thousands also came from French

Morocco, despite the Sultan's decree prohibiting men from joining the war and the risk of imprisonment by the French of those who tried to cross the border into Spanish Morocco, or those who returned from Spain to their homes.[7] Their motives were, most historians agree, largely economic, although others argue that far from being the only motives, some Moroccans were driven by the spirit of adventure or even influenced by religious propaganda.[8] Military instruction, for recruits with no prior military experience, could vary between several months and as low as a couple of weeks (in some cases even less) before being shipped to Spain, depending on the situation of enemy pressure on the different fronts.[9] During the training period the recruits learnt to use rifles, hand grenades, machine guns, and mortars, like Spanish recruits to the Nationalist Army did.[10]

This chapter considers the attitudes of both Republicans and Moroccans towards each other and the actions that were taken by both based on these attitudes, which often determined the fate of the foot soldier, both Moroccan and Spanish, as well as direct communication between both sides. While focusing largely on the civil war itself, this chapter also delves into the post-war anti-Francoist guerrilla period, and relies significantly on underused first person testimony to do so.

Captives in the Gran Vía: Moroccans through the Eyes of Republican Spain

In 1937 the Spanish journalist Manuel Chaves Nogales published a collection of nine short stories in France called *A sangre y fuego*. Horrified by the cruelty of both parties to the war he exiled himself to France where he wrote about the ugly aspects of the conflict. Though classified as stories, he claimed each of his accounts had been 'extracted faithfully from a strictly true fact, every one of its heroes has a real existence and authentic personality that has been discreetly veiled only due to the proximity of the events'.[11] One of these stories – in fact two stories in one – deals with the fate of two captured Moroccan soldiers. The first one, being injured, was taken to a village called Monreal, where he was medically treated. The revolutionary committee discussed his fate, with anarchists favouring his release if he was to reject his past and commit to become a worthy citizen of a free Iberia. The communists suggested he should serve against the 'rebels' under a watchful eye, while the Republican delegates demanded he be sent to Madrid. But the 'people' demanded his death, and so it happened. After his successful treatment at the hospital, militiamen put him against the wall and shot him. The second was captured along with other Moroccans during the assault on the University City in Madrid. The Republicans paraded them in the main avenue of Gran Vía to a public that seemed less hostile, some of whom even believed the Moroccans had rebelled against Franco. But, at nightfall, the prisoners were taken to a quiet spot on the outskirts of the Spanish capital where they were shot dead.[12]

In addition to the assurances of the author, there is good reason to believe that Chaves Nogales's stories were merely dramatized versions of the truth. Archival material presents a similar case. In October 1936 the general staff of the Nationalist columns of the southern sector reported that in Madrid 'a captured legionnaire has been paraded, maltreated and later shot, a number of *Regulares* too who were photographed and later shot'.[13] Manuel Tagüeña, a prominent Republican commander in the war, wrote about how at the end of August 1936 in Peguerinos, his forces managed to repel a Nationalist attack and a number of prisoners, including 'Moors', fell into his troops' hands. The orders, according to him, were to shoot all prisoners, an instruction dutifully carried out. A lucky Moroccan was the last prisoner to fall into their hands, by which time the soldiers 'were tired of spilling blood'. The Moroccan turned out to be a veteran of the First World War battle of Verdun, and was sent to Madrid where 'he might save his life'.[14]

The early period of the war witnessed the execution of Moroccan troops with such frequency that even though there was no Republican governmental or military policy to sanction the killings, the chances of a Moroccan soldier surviving capture were low, a pattern that might have decreased with the progression of war but was still manifest from time to time. Historian Sánchez Ruano cites the American journalist Edward Knoblaugh, who reported that Republicans in the neighbourhood of El Escorial burnt captured Moroccans alive.[15] The well-known Republican and communist commander Valentín González, nicknamed *El Campesino*, or The Peasant, was reported to have had many of the captured Moroccan prisoners under his jurisdiction executed.[16] Some on the Republican side, generally outsiders, admitted the existence of the problem of executing the Moroccan prisoners and tried to remedy it. In October 1936, the French communist leader and International Brigade commander, André Marty, reported to the Comintern that

> our [communist] party took the right position vis-à-vis the Moroccans. All the [Spanish] papers were constantly cursing the Moroccans. We made the first attempt to win over the Moroccan people. With this goal in mind, we put on the radio an Arab public speaker. It is possible that the Moroccans did not understand him since he spoke in the literary language, which is different from the common Arabian language. But the first step was taken, and it had significant consequences. The anarchist organ began to write 'about our brothers, the Moroccan soldiers.' And we made it so that captured Moroccan soldiers could freely walk the streets of Madrid without risking their lives.[17]

Another foreigner who tried to tackle this issue was Najati Sidqi, a Palestinian communist whom the Comintern sent to Spain in October 1936 to encourage Moroccan soldiers to defect to the Republican side by writing pamphlets, in Moroccan Arabic, and even using a megaphone on the front lines.[18] While in Spain he assumed the alias of Mustafa bin Kala.[19] Though he started optimistically, the mission soon left him frustrated. The Spanish 'comrades' were always suspicious of any Moroccan, and while Sidqi struggled to convince Moroccan soldiers to surrender, he complained more than once about the execution of Moroccan prisoners of war at the hands of the Republicans who 'rarely showed mercy'.

According to him, the Spanish communist leaders showed indifference towards the executions and towards 'the Moroccan cause' in general. Sidqi 'started to feel, deep in [his] heart, that [his] mission was failing'.[20] He left Spain at the end of 1936 for Algeria to seek a more effective method of inciting the Moroccans to rebel against Franco by establishing a radio station. The 'Algerian project', however, never materialized and Sidqi never returned to Spain.[21]

The reasons for the frequency with which captured Moroccans were executed are diverse. Some Spanish soldiers complained to Sidqi about their distrust of Moroccan soldiers who on more than one occasion, the Spanish soldiers claimed, would feign surrender by raising their fists and shouting in broken Spanish 'yo estar rojo' (I being Red), only to then throw hand grenades.[22] The hostile attitude was undoubtedly linked to propaganda about the 'Moroccan savage' that leading Republican figures spread and the atrocities they attributed to the Moroccan soldiers. Facing the Moroccans led, not infrequently, to panic among the Republicans, especially in the summer and autumn of 1936, a period in which the advance of the Nationalist troops was called by some *avance a gritos* (advancing by shouting) in reference to the shrieks of the Moroccans that announced their presence, and prompted some Republican leaders to reprimand their troops and assure them that the Moors were 'men just like you'.[23] The massacres that accompanied the march of the Army of Africa in the first few months of 1936 must have greatly contributed to this fear. The Moroccans awed even members of the International Brigades: 'The worst blokes we ever came across were the Moors', remembers one of the British veterans. 'God they were vicious. ... They'd put the fear of God into you. They were death or glory blokes [who] thought they'd be going to heaven as soon as they were shot'.[24] Another British veteran stated, '[They] didn't sit around doing nothing. If they're in the line, they're in the line and they're always looking to kill someone'[25] (see Figure 6.1).

The Moors in Republican Myths and Fears

A particular act of savagery associated with the Moroccan troops, and which earned them the wrath of the Republicans, was rape. The female communist icon, Dolores Ibárruri, known as *La Pasionaria* famously decried, 'The savage Moors, drunken with sensuality who run amok raping our girls, our women in the villages that have been trampled by the fascist hooves. ... Moors, brought from the Moroccan *aduars* [Arab villages] from the most uncivilized of the Riffian settlements and rocks'.[26] Soon after the arrival of Moroccan troops in southern Spain stories of mass rape spread among the Republicans. In some cases such rapes were reported as witnessed first-hand by, for example, the American journalist John Whitaker who wrote how a Moroccan commander let forty Moroccan soldiers rape two Republican militia women.[27] Antonio Bahamonde, who was in 1936 the chief propagandist for General Queipo de Llano in Seville and who defected later to the Republic, wrote in 1938 how the Moroccans raped the women they found on their way and killed them later.[28] This reputation was enhanced by the traditional image of the 'Moor' as a lustful being and by Queipo de Llano's own radio transmissions

Figure 6.1 A *Tabor* (battalion) of Moroccan soldiers parades through the recently captured city of Vitoria, in the Basque Country, in 1937. AGMAV, F.363, 2, 255/255.

in which he tried to instil terror in the Republican spirits by announcing that 'women of the reds' have finally come to know 'real men' at the hands of members of the Spanish Legion and the Moroccan *Regulares*.[29] However, there are no statistics as to the scale of the rapes attributed to the Moroccans, so it has not been shown whether the victims number in the dozens, hundreds, or thousands. Francisco Sánchez Ruano notes that known atrocities by Moroccans, including rape, are confined to a few villages of Andalusia, Extremadura, the zone of Toledo, and around Madrid (in the early stages of the war), as well as in Catalonia (during the war's final stage), although he wonders whether this geographical limitation is due to lack of research.[30] Furthermore, rape was not exclusively committed by Moroccans, but also by Falangists,[31] and even by Republicans.[32] The Moroccan veterans, interviewed by this author and others, have either denied rapes taking place, or acknowledged them as individual incidents, adding that the perpetrators were executed, thus pointing out that such practices were not permitted.[33] It is very possible that these Moroccan interviewees are reliable when denying witnessing large-scale rapes, as most of them joined the war after the summer and autumn of 1936, when the mass rapes by Moroccan troops are generally thought to have taken place.[34] They also largely denied any other physical aggression against Spanish civilians though acknowledged that these feared them initially; the Moroccans sometimes also remembered friendly relations with the civilians.[35]

In addition to being a response to the perceived savagery of the Moroccans, the Republican hostile attitude was also the result of years of demonizing the Moroccan as a result of the Rif wars of the 1920s and a Spanish historical bias against them. The philosopher and writer Juan Goytisolo concludes that 'our Left, apart from some rare and honourable exceptions, has chosen the myth, the fantasy, the cliché' in dealing with the Moroccan aspect of the war. He states that the Spanish secularist bias against the Moroccan, deeply ingrained in the traditional collective discourse, obscured and voided 'the socio-economic opinions of our Marxists', and he describes the Republican attack on the Moroccans as 'xenophobic, openly racist'.[36] Madariaga agrees and considers that the old prejudices were so deeply rooted, not only in the popular classes, but also among many at the top of the Republican camp, that the Republicans had no well-defined ideas about how to orient their propaganda towards the Moroccans.[37] The Spanish Popular Front, in spite of 'many efforts to see them with different eyes and use a language more in accordance with leftist ideology', continued to consider the Moroccans as 'cruel' and 'savages'.[38] Certainly, an important factor was the leftist rebellion in Asturias in 1934, the legacy of which was that the left as a whole held the Foreign Legion and the Moroccan *Regulares* principally responsible for crushing the Asturian revolution, as well as for the repression, summary executions, and looting that followed.[39]

Moroccan Impressions of Capture

As seen above, the Republicans' hostile attitude was translated into a general Republican refusal to give quarter or accept the surrender of Moroccan troops.[40] The Moroccan soldiers were therefore aware of the grim fate that they faced, should the Republicans capture them. Jorge Vigón Suerodíaz, a Nationalist officer at the time of the war, wrote that in January 1938, during the Battle of Teruel, he witnessed a large formation of Republican prisoners marching past who were guarded by *Regulares* soldiers. One of the prisoners was in extremely bad condition and Vigón accompanied this 'poor young man' to the nearest first-aid post. But one Moroccan sergeant reacted with surprise to the officer's comment and responded: 'Poor no, my commander, poor is the Moor whom they take and kill, poor is the Moor whose feet the Reds burn. The Red is not poor, the Red is bad.'[41] One Moroccan veteran witnessed the body of a fellow soldier, cut-up and hung: 'We said to each other: look, look what the Reds do to the Muslims! And if we got one of them the same would happen, like the other'.[42] Another affirmed that 'the Reds, if they captured one [Moroccan] they would kill him and that is that'.[43] Or, as already mentioned, the execution could be postponed as 'at first they would parade them in the streets and then kill them'.[44] A few Moroccans who deserted back to French Morocco told their interrogators similar tales. Layachi o si Mohamed ould si Ali who constantly referred to the Republicans as 'Russians', stated that the Moroccans noticed that the '"Russians" would cut the throats of and shoot the prisoners they take whereas General Franco is merciful towards those his troops capture', an interesting account since this deserter does not seem sympathetic to the army or the war effort.[45] Another deserter, Mfeddel ben Taieb bel Hadj Ali, who spoke about low morale in the army, noted that despite the weak spirit among the troops, deserting to the enemy was not an option because 'their fate would be worse'.[46] This made the Moroccan soldiers generally more tenacious in fighting, and in large part accounts for the low numbers of soldiers willing to surrender to the enemy,[47] or accept the fate of a prisoner of war. Even among the few who deserted some were not to spend the entire war in the Republican camp and deserted back to the Nationalists.[48]

It is not known how many Moroccan prisoners of war were captured by the Republicans or how many Moroccan troops deserted to the enemy over the course of a three-year war. However, there is a document by the general staff of the Republican Army listing sixty-one Moroccan prisoners of war and deserters who came under Republican control between mid-1937 and mid-1938, among whom three were members of the socialist and anarchist trade unions: the *Unión General de Trabajadores* (UGT), or General Union of Workers, and the *Confederación Nacional del Trabajo* (CNT), or National Confederation of Labour, respectively.[49]

The fate of some of the prisoners who escaped execution demonstrates how discriminatory the Republicans were in dealing with the Moroccan soldiers. Madariaga mentions a trial, conducted by the Popular Tribunal on 26 October 1936 against four Nationalist soldiers, three Moroccans, and one Spaniard. Two of the Moroccans and the Spaniard belonged to a *Tabor* (battalion) of *Regulares* of Melilla, the third Moroccan belonging to the *Regulares* of Larache. The charge was 'aiding the fascist rebellion against the government of the Republic' and confronting the militias on the Toledo front. Surprisingly, the three Moroccans were found guilty and sentenced to life imprisonment, while the Spanish soldier was acquitted as the tribunal found that he had given 'unwitting support to fascism'.[50]

There is scattered evidence on individual Moroccans who became prisoners of war and survived to tell the tale. One of the few pieces of evidence concerns Mohamed ben Amar Illase, who claimed in 1941 that he went to Spain in 1937 along with the *Regulares* of Tetuan. While on the Toledo front, he asked permission to bathe and was seized by the Republicans who took him to a prison in Madrid, and later to one in Valencia and later still to Barcelona by boat. In Catalonia, while working close to the French border, he fled to France where he was detained for three months before being released. According to him, he demanded repatriation to Spain, which was only approved in February 1941, upon which he was detained by the Civil Guard.[51] However, this document does not provide information on whether there were other Moroccan prisoners and, if there were, whether they were treated differently or segregated, or whether Moroccans suffered any racially motivated maltreatment.

The Moroccans Encounter the 'Rojos'

Moroccan soldiers viewed their Republican opponents negatively on more than one level. On the religious plane, they certainly considered the Republicans to be on the wrong side as far as godly matters where concerned. Some Moroccans found that 'the *rojos* [Reds] killed the monks and destroyed the churches so they believed only in the hammer and sickle'. Another defined a *rojo* to be 'the enemy of Spain or the criminal who abandoned his religion'.[52] One veteran remembered that 'our *jefes* [officers] told us that the *rojos* have come from Russia and from

France to occupy Spain', and that the Moroccans were in Spain defending their own country 'for if the *rojos* would win, northern Morocco would be occupied by the *rojos*'.[53] The first impression the 'Reds' left upon the memory of another soldier was equally typical: 'When we went [to Spain] we found that the *rojos* were burning churches'.[54] It would therefore follow that if a Moroccan defected to the Reds 'he would die as an infidel'.[55]

But religion was not the only prism through which Moroccans viewed the Republicans. The general image that emerges from many testimonies of veterans is that of a violent and ruthless enemy, and not only towards the Moroccans themselves. One veteran remembered upon entering a captured city that 'we met Spanish women, clothed in black and weeping on their men and *novios* [boyfriends] and sons for they did not want to go with the *rojos*'.[56] As has already been examined, for many of the Moroccan veterans, the Republican soldiers were opponents who would give them no quarter. Not only would death follow falling into the hands of the enemy, but sometimes mutilation as well. Two veterans spoke of the bodies of Moroccans suffering mutilation, by being 'crucified',[57] their eyes gouged out, or the genitals cut off and put in their mouths.[58]

There are very few admissions by Moroccan interviewees of killing Republican prisoners, and whenever they did admit such actions they would frame it as a reaction to alleged Republican atrocities committed against Moroccan soldiers. The veteran who spoke about Moroccans being crucified explained how in return 'we burned them!'[59] Rather than literally setting enemy soldiers on fire, he probably meant killing a great number of them, although there was a system to this. 'We would kill a part of them and another part would be spared.' The ones that were killed, according to this veteran, were the 'genuine Reds' and not the ones 'taken by force'. How they would distinguish between the 'genuine' and 'forced' 'Reds' he partially explains by describing how he received the surrender of a Republican soldier. Speaking with admiration for the stubbornness of the 'Reds', he tells how he demanded of a Republican prisoner to shout:

> Viva España! [Long live Spain!] But the prisoner would say 'no'. I give him hell. He says 'Viva España'. I tell him 'Viva Franco!' [Long live Franco!] He would say 'No. Franco, no. I will not say viva. [Even if you] kill me I would not say Viva Franco'. We would get hold of him and would shoot him in the head and kill him and [still] he would not say 'Viva Franco'.[60]

As for spared Republican soldiers, some of them ended up in Morocco where they worked, long after the end of the war, on constructing roads and fortifications, 'while we [Moroccan soldiers] guarded them'.[61] If admissions to killing Republican prisoners were rare, it is even rarer and rather exceptional to find an admission in oral testimonies that unarmed combatants and even civilians were shot or otherwise harmed. For example, there is enough documentary evidence to show the shooting by Moroccan soldiers of Republican prisoners of war, by orders of their Spanish officers,[62] although this would not make them unique as both Spanish Nationalists and Republicans committed similar acts. But there are also some exceptional admissions in oral testimonies that unarmed people were shot. According to an ex-soldier of the *Regulares* of Larache, his unit captured two '*rojos*', one of them a doctor, both unarmed, and took them to the Spanish commander. When asked why they brought these prisoners, '[we] said that we found them and we brought them [to you]. He told us "next time kill them, wherever you find Reds kill them", so he called a corporal and told him to execute them.'[63] Another remembered that 'the commander would order whether they would kill them [prisoners]. They would bring them to the trenches and execute them, but the Spaniards would do the execution. We on the contrary had sympathy with them because they were like us, forced to participate in this war.'[64]

Speaking to the Republicans

When the Moroccans and Republicans were not trying to kill each other, there was some communication between the two sides when the fronts sometimes stabilized and opposing lines drew close to each other. This communication ranged from continuing the fight verbally to trying to entice the Moroccans to desert to the Republicans, and even, although rarely, conduct some mutually beneficial trade. As one veteran remembers, 'We talked to them in the front lines. We called them *rojos*, and they called us *gente verde* [green people].'[65] More prominent are the surviving Moroccan veterans' memories of some of the Republicans' attempts to induce them to surrender.

> In the trenches we would hear the Moroccan *darija* [Moroccan colloquial Arabic], they would bring them [Moroccans in the Republican camp] and they would talk using the megaphone. We did not know whether they had captured them or whether they were on their side. They would say 'we are in good health, we are well treated, we captured Tetuan, we captured Larache'. They only lied, it was but propaganda.[66]

One anecdote that would bring to mind the story of Najati Sidqi describes how 'the Reds put a megaphone on an olive tree and someone called in classical Arabic "You Rifian heroes, you freemen of Jebala. We appreciate your jihadi capabilities, which are not appreciated by Franco, who does not give you good food or money. Come to us and we will give you money and women and good food."'[67] One wonders whether the classical Arabic was spoken by a Spaniard, a non-Maghrebi Arab or even Sidqi himself, as neither the date nor the approximate period for this incident is given, nor does Sidqi himself mention promises of women to the Moroccan soldiers. According to yet another account, the voice of a Moroccan called Milud from Melilla was heard in Asturias calling on the Moroccans to desert to the Republicans for 'we have drink and food and women. Here, we are filled.' Those whom he called upon to desert would respond by insulting him and the Republicans with: 'You son of Jews' and 'You sons of dogs.'[68] Others responded to the invitation to surrender in return for money and women with the more obscene remarks of 'Hijo de Pasionaria, hijo [de] puta'.[69] Trading insults became a habit for many. 'They used to talk to us in Spanish, and we would respond in what Spanish we had. They would insult us and tell us what are you Muslims doing in our country, Spain?'[70] Interestingly one of the veterans told the Republicans that 'you came to our lands to fight us, so this is us coming to your lands to fight you'.[71] It is a remarkable comment from someone who was an ex-member of the Abdelkrim Al Khattabi's resistance movement and who later fought on the side of the very army that crushed the Abdelkrim rebellion of the 1920s in Morocco to which he was referring. It would have certainly been unwise to utter that statement where it could have been understood by the Spanish superiors or reported to them.

It is clear that since the Republicans who spoke to the Moroccans were convinced that the Moroccan volunteers in Franco's army came to Spain solely due to economic motives and to enjoy the loot, including women, it was more than natural that money and women were the main incentives used to try to attract Moroccans to desert. Archival evidence, at least on one occasion, corroborates the oral testimonies with regard to using the promise of women as incentives for Moroccan soldiers to desert. In February 1938, the second *Tabor* of the *Regulares* of Alhucemas, in the sector of Porcal (south of Madrid) sent an extract of a speech by the 'Reds' directed towards the 'natives' in which it was claimed that many 'Moors' were captured in Saragossa and were currently in Madrid and Barcelona. It invited the Moroccan soldiers to come over to their side as they would benefit from a 10-peseta daily wage (higher pay than in the Nationalist Army) and would have a 'happy life', reminding them that they, far from resting, 'live continuously in the trench where, unlike them [a clear reference to the Republican soldiers], they do not have women and other diversions'.[72]

For all the invitations to join the Republic, the Republican propaganda towards the Moroccans displayed on rare occasions other sentiments, as happened to a Moroccan unit that witnessed, while exiting a town in Extremadura, Republican planes dropping leaflets on which the Moroccans read the following xenophobic message: 'If you win we will rule, and if we win we will rule. We the Spanish are brothers. Out with the garbage.'[73] But the 'Moors' who fought against the Republic were not the only ones to suffer from a hostile attitude displayed by the Republic, for the same Republic displayed a similar attitude towards the North Africans who, in far lesser numbers, fought for the Republican cause.[74] This attitude towards pro-Republican 'Moors' serves to strengthen the opinion that the Republic's attitude towards the pro-Nationalist Moroccans was partially motivated by a long-standing anti-Moorish tradition.

Post-War Terror of the Moor

After the civil war, the Nationalists continued to employ Moroccan troops in Spain against remnants of the Republican army, composed of fighters who fled and refused to surrender and some civilians who joined them later and became known as *maquis*. In the early post-war period, mixed forces of Moroccan troops, forces of the Legion, civil guards, and Falangists were entrusted with finding and destroying the bands of anti-Franco resistance. These forces operated mainly in the regions of Cordoba, Asturias, Orense, León, Ciudad Real, and Valderrobres.[75] As the Spanish historian Secundino Serrano puts it, 'The relationship of these troops with the different populations followed the line of the behaviour of an occupation army: lootings were frequent and the number of deaths intensified.' Serrano cites two 1940 examples of this occupation army behaviour in the region of Cordoba. In the first, the '*Regulares* killed three neighbours', and in the second, 'colonial troops poured boiling oil into the ears' of the father of one of the anti-Francoist guerrilla fighters.[76] Despite these cases, the intensity of the violence was far lower compared to the active phase of the war and, after 1940, the role of the army diminished in fighting the guerrillas. The situation then changed again in 1943 to 1944 as guerrilla activities increased, and the defeat of friendly Nazi Germany loomed, which converted the guerrillas into a real threat that crystallized in the operation *Reconquista de España*, a failed invasion of northern Spain by 4,000 pro-Republican guerrillas. The regime dispatched the army, including companies of *Regulares* troops, to regions with concentrations of guerrillas or sensitive regions, using the Moroccans, for example, to guard the border with France,[77] or maintain order in Malaga and Granada.[78]

The post-war experience of the Spaniards with regard to Moroccan troops differed from place to place and from time to time, varying from violent experiences, as mentioned above to more benign ones, as was the case with an Asturian woman who was interviewed by Madariaga. During the 1940s, this interviewee, called Sole, witnessed Moroccan cavalrymen who were dispersed in villages, occupying requisitioned houses. 'They did not interfere with anyone and had good relations with people, but we all feared them.'[79] As Madariaga writes, the continued fear of the Moroccans is noteworthy given the correct behaviour of the troops. She considers it an instinctive rejection due to the inherited prejudices against the Moors, as well as their bad reputation as a result of horror tales.[80]

Some Moroccan veterans lived to talk about this episode in post-war fighting. Any violent act on their part towards the civilian population was almost totally absent from these memories, at least as they were revealed to their interviewers. Speaking about his memories in post-war Spain, Al Sebtaoui states that after the war, in which he had taken part, he was sent to Oviedo, the capital of Asturias where, 'we went to catch the chiefs of the *rojos* who were hidden there in the mountains, and would come down at night to commit crimes. We were on guard duty and we would hold their families captive to pressure them to surrender.'[81] This is a rare admission of repression towards civilians, though without inflicting actual physical violence. Abdelkader ben Mohamed was posted with his *Tabor*, after the end of the war, to Alcazarquivir in Morocco, only to be sent once again to Spain, to Asturias where he stayed for two years as 'we went around in the mountains looking for *rojos*'. The efforts were fruitful as 'we caught someone called Barrasco and his gang. That gang was roaming the mountains and they would go to their cousins [fellow Spaniards] and steal from them and drink there and stay in their houses and they would leave them nothing. Not one of them [i.e. the gang] was left. We caught them all and killed them.'[82] The presence of the Moroccan troops and more incidents of violence between them and (suspected) guerrillas would continue until the dwindling of the *maquis* movement and the subsequent withdrawal of Moroccan troops in 1951.

Conclusions

During the Spanish Civil War most of the Moroccan soldiers distrusted the Republicans and were not disposed to desert to their ranks, while the Republican soldiers distrusted Moroccans in general and displayed little sympathy or mercy towards those who surrendered. Republican attitudes reflected traditional Spanish negative views of the Moroccans, which were strengthened by the legacy of colonial wars and the more recent memory of the Asturias 1934 uprising, as well as the war crimes attributed to the Moroccans during the early stages of the conflict. Since the Republicans did not control Spanish Morocco nor any Moroccan units after the July 1936 uprising, they were unmotivated to encourage a less negative attitude towards Moroccans in general. Some foreign allies of the Republic were more sympathetic to the Moroccans and even considered it practical to display a positive attitude towards the Moroccans as individuals. But, despite occasional gestures of mercy, feelings of sympathy and reaching out, the divide was too marked to substantially change the basis of these largely violent Spanish-Moroccan encounters during the Spanish Civil War and its immediate aftermath.

Further Reading

De Madariaga, María Rosa. *Los moros que trajo Franco, La intervención de tropas coloniales en la Guerra Civil española*. Barcelona: Martínez Roca, 2002.
De Mesa, José Luis. *Los moros de la Guerra Civil española*. Madrid: Actas, 2004.
El Merroun, Mustapha. *Las tropas marroquíes en la Guerra Civil española*. Madrid: Almena, 2003.
Tuma, Ali Al. *Guns, Culture and Moors. Racial Perceptions, Cultural Impact and the Moroccan Participation in the* Spanish Civil War *(1936-1939)*. London and New York: Routledge, 2018.

Notes

*   'Reds' refers to the Spanish Republicans; *rojos* in Spanish. The Nationalists used the term derogatively to paint all the Republicans as communist agents of Moscow. 'Greens' here is a reference to the Moroccan soldiers, due to the association of the green colour with Islam, although the term was rarely used during the Spanish Civil

War to describe the Moroccans who were called, by all parties and almost always, *moros* or Moors.

1 Michael Seidman, *The Republic of Egos. A Social History of the Spanish Civil War* (Madison: University of Wisconsin Press, 2002), 43.

2 Thomas, *The Spanish Civil War* (New York: Modern Library, 2001), 944.

3 José María Gárate Córdoba, 'Las tropas de África en la Guerra Civil española', *Revista de historia militar,* no. 70 (1991): 56.

4 María Rosa de Madariaga, *Los moros que trajo Franco, La intervención de tropas coloniales en la Guerra Civil española* (Barcelona: Martínez Roca, 2002), 172.

5 Shannon E. Fleming, 'Spanish Morocco and the Alzamiento Nacional', *Journal of Contemporary History,* no. 18 (1983): 30.

6 María Rosa de Madariaga, *Marruecos. Ese gran desconocido. Breve historia del Protectorado Español* (Madrid: Alianza, 2013), 326–8; Mustapha El Merroun, *Las tropas marroquíes en la Guerra Civil española* (Madrid: Almena, 2003), 36–7.

7 Ali Al Tuma, *Guns, Culture and Moors: Racial Perceptions, Cultural Impact and the Moroccan Participation in the Spanish Civil War (1936-1939)* (New York and London: Routledge, 2018), 35.

8 Ibid., 11–12. Ali Al Tuma, 'Moros y Cristianos. Religious Aspects of the Participation of Moroccan soldiers in the Spanish Civil War', in *Muslims in Interwar Europe. A Transcultural Historical Perspective,* ed. Bekim Agai, Umar Ryad and Mehdi Sajid (Leiden: Brill, 2015), 159–63.

9 Different interrogations, by French officers, of Moroccan deserters from the Spanish army. Service Historique de la Défense (SHD), 3 H 266; Merroun, *Las tropas marroquíes,* 45; Gárate Córdoba, 'Las tropas de África en la Guerra Civil', 40, 50.

10 Merroun, *Las tropas marroquíes,* 45.

11 Manuel Chaves Nogales, *A sangre y fuego: Héroes, bestias y mártires de España* (Madrid: Austral, 2001), 33. In English as: *Heroes and Beasts of Spain* (New York: Doubleday, 1937).

12 Nogales, *A sangre y fuego,* 165–86.

13 Archivo Histórico Municipal de Cádiz (AHMC), Varela, 68/419.

14 Manuel Tagüeña Lacorte, *Testimonio de dos guerras* (Barcelona: Planeta DeAgostini, 2005), 130.

15 Francisco Sánchez Ruano, *Islam y Guerra Civil española. Moros con Franco y con la República* (Madrid: La Esfera de los Libros, 2004), 279–80.

16 Thomas, *The Spanish Civil War,* 696. A whole *Tabor* is supposed to have been captured and slaughtered. I doubt this particular incident or at least its magnitude, since no single Tabor was ever annihilated or disbanded as a result of heavy casualties. But it illustrates at least what the Republican media thought should happen to Moroccan prisoners.

17 Ronald Radosh, Mary R. Habeck, and Gregory Sevostianov eds., *Spain Betrayed: The Soviet Union in the Spanish Civil War* (New Haven, CT: Yale University Press, 2001), 49.

18 Najati Sidqi, *Mudhakkarat Najati Sidqi* (Beirut: Institute for Palestine Studies, 2001), 122, 137. The Spanish Arabist Nieves Paradela was the first Western researcher to uncover Sidqi's participation in the Spanish conflict having studied, in the 1980s, the then unpublished manuscript of his memoirs. See her 'Acción política y estancia española de Nayati Sidqi', *Temas Árabes,* no. 2 (1982): 121–42.

19 The Soviet correspondent for *Pravda* Mijail Koltsov noticed this Mustafa, whom he described as trying to induce Moroccan soldiers to desert, as well as trying to organize Moroccan units to fight for the Republic. He was presented as being of North African

origin, rather than a Palestinian. Mijail Koltsov, *Diario de la guerra de España,* trans. José Fernández Sánchez (Madrid: Akal, 1978), 106.

20 Sidqi, *Mudhakkarat,* 147, 152, 153.

21 Ibid., 148–51.

22 Ibid., 139.

23 Sánchez Ruano, *Islam y Guerra Civil española,* 247.

24 Quoted in: Ben Hughes, *They Shall not Pass! The British Battalion at Jarama* (Oxford: Osprey, 2011), 76–7.

25 Ibid.

26 See Miguel Martín, *El colonialismo español en Marruecos (1860–1956)* (Paris: Ruedo Ibérico, 1973), 181.

27 Ali Al Tuma, 'Victims, Wives and Concubines. The Spanish Civil War and Relations between Moroccan Troops and Spanish Women', in *Transnational Islam in Interwar Europe. Muslim Activists and Thinkers,* ed. Götz Nordbruch and Umar Ryad (New York: Palgrave Macmillan, 2014), 212–13.

28 Ibid., 213.

29 Ian Gibson, *Queipo de Llano. Sevilla, verano de 1936 (Con las charlas radiofónicas completas)* (Barcelona: Grijalbo, 1986), 84, 431.

30 Sánchez Ruano, *Islam y Guerra Civil,* 378–9.

31 Tuma, 'Victims, Wives, and Concubines', 213.

32 Sánchez Ruano, *Islam y Guerra Civil,* 378.

33 Tuma, 'Victims, Wives, and Concubines', 214–16. Despite this reputation there was no shortage of voluntary sexual and romantic relationships between Moroccan troops and Spanish women, many leading to marriages. The Nationalist authorities experienced this as detrimental to the mission of the Spanish Protectorate, to Spanish prestige and to the interests of the Spanish women, and tried to prevent such liaisons. Ibid., 216–23.

34 For opposing views by a number of historians on the large-scale rape charge against the Moroccan troops see Tuma, *Guns, Culture and Moors,* 59–60, 110–14.

35 Tuma, *Guns, Culture and Moors,* 63–4.

36 Juan Goytisolo, *Crónicas sarracinas* (Barcelona: Ruedo Ibérico, 1981), 37–9.

37 Madariaga, *Los moros que trajo Franco,* 400.

38 Ibid., 403.

39 José E. Álvarez, 'The Spanish Foreign Legion During the Asturian Uprising of October 1934', *War in History,* no. 18 (2011): 223–4.

40 José Luis de Mesa, *Los moros de la Guerra Civil española* (Madrid: Actas, 2004), 169.

41 Jorge Vigón Suerodíaz, *Cuadernos de guerra y notas de paz* (Oviedo: Instituto de Estudios Asturianos, 1970), 200. To this, Vigón responded '*But the Moor is good – I tell him – and will take this soldier to the first aid post* [Italics in the Spanish original]. The sergeant manages to shut up the guards, whose gibberish must be worrying these men.'

42 In the documentary *El laberinto marroquí* by Julio Sánchez Veiga, Icarius Films, New York 2009.

43 Testimony of Al Siddiq Al Kumaili, Tetuan, 24 September 1996, Mustapha El Merroun archive. El Merroun granted this author special access to his personal archive of transcripts of interviews he conducted with Moroccan veterans of the Spanish Civil War.

44 Testimony of Mohammed Al Ayyashi Al Bakouri, Tetuan, 4 July 1994, El Merroun archive.

45 Interrogation of Layachi o si Mohamed ouldsi Ali. SHD, 3 H 266.

46 Mfeddel ben Taieb bel Hadj Ali. SHD, 3 H 266.

47 Pedro Corral, *Desertores: La Guerra Civil que nadie quiere contar* (Barcelona: Debate, 2006), 446.

48 Corral, *Desertores*, 444.

49 Archivo General de la Guerra Civil, EM (2), 59/ 8.7.

50 Madariaga, *Los moros que trajo Franco*, 403–5.

51 Declaration by Mohamed ben Amar Illase. Archivo General de la Administración, Af, 81.1117.

52 Testimony of Al Buyekra, 21 April 1996, Fnideq, El Merroun archive.

53 Testimony of Abdelkader Al Shaoui, Tetuan, 3 December 1992, El Merroun archive.

54 Testimony of Al Ayyashi, Tetuan, 11 November 1993, El Merroun archive.

55 Testimony of Masoud, Tetuan, 25 April 1994. El Merroun archive.

56 Testimony of Abdelkader Al Shaoui, Tetuan, 3 December 1992, El Merroun archive.

57 Author interview with Mohammed ben Al Ayyashi Al Zerki, Ceuta, 30 June 2011.

58 Author interview with Abdesselam Mohammed Al Amrani, Ceuta, 30 June 2011.

59 Author interview with Mohammed ben Al Ayyashi Al Zerki, Ceuta, 30 June 2011.

60 Ibid.

61 Ibid.

62 Take, for example, the engagement at Seseña (between Toledo and Madrid) on 29 October 1936, where after repelling a Republican attack twelve Republican soldiers were captured. The report of the commander of the Moroccan unit that captured them explained that since these prisoners were captured with arms in their hands they were executed. The text gives the impression that this was a standard practice. AHMC, Varela, 69/429.

63 Testimony of Al Buyekra, 21 April 1996, Tetuan, El Merroun archive.

64 Testimony of Al Sebtaoui, Tetuan, 24 June 1994, El Merroun archive.

65 Testimony of Bushta ben Abdellah Zeruali, Tetuan, 27 February 1996, El Merroun archive.

66 Testimony of Al Buyekra, Fnideq, 21 April 1996, El Merroun archive.

67 Testimony of an unnamed member of the Association of Former Combatants and Victims of War, Tetuan, 2 December 1993, El Merroun archive.

68 Testimony of Ahmad ben Abdullah Al Omari, Tetuan, 12 April 1994, El Merroun archive.

69 'Son of Pasionaria, son of a whore'. Testimony of Mohamed ben Amar ben Al Hashmi, Tetuan, 24 June 1994, El Merroun archive.

70 Author interview with Abdelkader ben Mohammed, Alcazarquivir, 21 February 2011.

71 Testimony of Mhauesh, Tetuan, 23 March 1995, El Merroun archive.

72 Archivo General Militar de Ávila (AGMAV), caja 2494, carpeta 12/34.

73 Testimony of Bachir, Tetuan, 26 September 1996, El Merroun archive.

74 Abdelatif Ben Salem, 'La partipación de los voluntarios árabes en las Brigadas Internacionales. Una memoria rescatada', in *Marroquíes en la Guerra Civil española. Campos equívocos,* ed. J. A. González Alcantud (Granada: Anthropos, 2003), 117; Paul Nothomb, *Malraux en Espagne* (Paris: Phébus, 1999), 132.

75 Secundino Serrano, *Maquis. Historia de la guerrilla antifranquista* (Madrid: Temas de Hoy, 2001), 79. According to General Varela's documents, the Spanish army's Asturias Column that was organized in August 1939 to capture or kill the *huidos*, or those who fled to the mountains, was composed of sixteen Moroccan *Tabors*, and which were the overwhelming majority of the infantry units of this column. AHMC, Varela, 95/251–252.

76 Secundino Serrano, *Maquis,* 79.

77 Ibid., 140.

78 Jorge Marco Carretero, 'Resistencia armada en la posguerra. Andalucía oriental, 1939–1952' (PhD diss. Universidad Complutense de Madrid, Madrid, 2011), 104.

79 Madariaga, *Los moros que trajo Franco,* 378.

80 Ibid. In Sole's same rural municipality there used to be a Spanish military commander who terrorized the whole population and who was therefore called 'Moro Juan'. Asked by Madariaga why he was thus called, she answered: 'Because he was very bad.'

81 Testimony of Al Sebtaoui, Tetuan, 24 June 1994, El Merroun archive.

82 Author interview with Abdelkader ben Mohammed, Alcazarquivir, 21 February 2011.

Chapter 7

REPUBLICAN SPIES AND THEIR CIVILIAN INFORMERS IN THE NATIONALIST REARGUARD DURING THE SPANISH CIVIL WAR

Hernán Rodríguez Velasco
Translated by Alan Matthews

According to her Nationalist interrogators Faustina García Otaola was not a pretty woman, but at the age of twenty-six she displayed a 'truly exceptional integrity and strength of character'. At the end of 1938 the enemy arrested her near Segovia. Her crime? To have volunteered to work as a spy because she was 'sympathetic to the Reds' cause'. In fact, she was considered the 'core of the [spy] network', yet no sooner had she been detained, she had no qualms about informing on other agents or betraying the system that had been set up.[1]

During the Spanish Civil War hundreds of people, just like Faustina, worked as secret agents or informers. They helped obtain information or provided cover for the Republican spies who crossed the front line in search of details about the enemy zone. A considerable number of soldiers also risked their lives by crossing into enemy territory to gauge the strength of the foe and their intentions.

The training these agents received, their motivation, their types of missions, and their wages were a far cry from those of professionalized spies in twentieth-century international wars, or indeed those from the world of fiction. Nevertheless, the work they carried out has not been properly recognized nor sufficiently well studied, and it is important to understand the loyalist efforts to reduce the growing material, logistical, and manpower imbalance caused by military defeats. Republican espionage has certainly not featured prominently in the historiography of the conflict. Apart from Domingo Pastor Petit's research from the 1970s, which provided an overview of both sides' espionage services, studies of this topic in the Spanish Civil War have focused on the Nationalist side, on operations in France, or on the cryptography employed. But until recently no study had examined Republican espionage from a military perspective.[2] The aim of this chapter is to shed light on the efforts made by men and women, professionals and amateurs, who used the most precarious of means to obtain scraps of information about the Nationalist enemy.

For the most part, the documents consulted are from the Nationalist zone. These are primarily reports of the apprehension and interrogation of Republican agents and, while largely factual in nature, they often dissect the lives of the captives in detail. Republican documents, in contrast, tend to be instructional and lay out the actions required of the spies. Yet other sources are from the participants themselves, who recounted their experiences after the events, and sometimes in a self-serving manner, as in the case of the agent Ramón Rufat. His words sum up the less than romantic military intelligence work he undertook, and underline the prosaic nature of the contents of this chapter. He summed up his take on Republican espionage as follows: 'The reader must not expect to find in this book examples of edifying behaviour or plots worthy of fiction. ... In almost every case, the mystery and secrecy surrounding agents' work is in reality nothing more than their day-to-day adaptation to the circumstances in which they worked.'[3]

Building a Network from Scratch (July 1936–September 1937)

At the outbreak of the civil war, organized military espionage hardly existed on either side. There are two reasons for this: first, Spain had remained neutral in the First World War which prevented the development of secret services as happened in other countries; and second, the long-standing tendency in Spain of focusing espionage efforts on internal enemies with 'extremist' ideological beliefs, especially the communists, rather than external threats.

The only manual on espionage that the Spanish army had available – the 1935 'Regulations for a Wartime Espionage Service' – was considered by the officer who later ran the Information Services of the Republican Popular Army, to be an 'inadequate set of regulations, full of mistakes and shortcomings'.[4] In mid-1936 no more than a dozen officers were aware of its existence and its value was practically nil.

This inauspicious foundation was compounded by the disjointed state in which the Republicans found themselves after the July 1936 coup d'état – including the massive demobilization of regular pre-war military units and a severe distrust of professional soldiers by workers' organizations – and ensured that the collection and distribution of military information was not standardized. Worse still, the body that processed the heterogeneous reports up until September 1936, the Information Section of the General Staff of the Ministry of War, was largely incapable of exerting its authority, even in the areas supposedly under its control.

Because of a shortage of agents with a military background, the recently created Republican Popular Army recruited the majority of its agents and informers from civilian ranks. The dispatches received by the Ministry of War in Madrid came not only from organized militia columns but also from trade union organizations and from different types of civilians, ranging from civil governors to shepherds. Why was this? 'Because of the lack of confidence in army officers and the security forces still loyal to the government'[5] and also because the role of specialized secret agents had not yet been created within the army itself.

The Republican espionage effort was first developed on the Catalan and Aragonese fronts as a result of the porousness of the lines. For example, in the Alcubierre mountain range, in Aragon, units of partisans would cross the blurred front lines to sabotage enemy positions and at the same time gather information about the enemy forces.

Ramón Rufat recounts that Colonel Villalba, the officer in charge of the Aragonese zone, entrusted the organization and collection of information to seven foreign volunteers from the Maciá-Companys column considered to be exceptionally daring. From a lookout post on the top of a hill they would monitor enemy territory into which they would cross at night in search of targets to sabotage.[6] This was the start of a modus operandi which would slowly take shape during the conflict, but which only enjoyed limited success. The main reason for this is that most of the information gathered did not get beyond the head of each individual column and would rarely even reach the Catalan government's defence department[7] (see Figure 7.1).

As the war progressed, new espionage techniques were developed which enabled information to be gathered not only by crossing into enemy territory but also by exploiting different resources already in the enemy rearguard. Thus railway workers from Santander were able to communicate with their counterparts in Burgos with the 'help of the women who operated level-crossings', sending letters

Figure 7.1 Republican intelligence personnel monitor the front lines to gather information on the Nationalist enemy. AGMAV, F.44, 7.

from one zone to the other.[8] Likewise, taking advantage of rail transport, in the region of Cáceres and Salamanca, some women would station themselves on the 'outskirts of towns and ask for a ride to anywhere nearby, deliberately targeting vehicles in which military personnel were travelling'. Their aim was to pick up information if the occupants spoke indiscreetly. These women were considered a real risk and months later the enemy continued to highlight the existence of an 'important network of young, attractive, well-dressed female spies with lots of money and laissez-passer documents' whose mission was to cross the front lines and spy.[9]

Similarly, at the beginning of 1937, the Nationalists denounced the existence of spies in some of the hospitals on the Madrid front, especially in Griñón,[10] or the existence of other information gathering points in their own rearguard.[11] Meanwhile in Algeciras half a dozen border guards were arrested; these had been in contact with refugees from Gibraltar.[12] In the south, near Cordoba, reflectors were used to 'send signals from hill tops' seemingly to 'exchange messages with another reflector located on a city centre roof terrace'.[13] Whereas in the north of the country a group of Basque nationalists based in the south of France made use of two strategies: first, 'Spanish fishermen from Cantabrian ports who were out at sea would communicate at night while working with fishermen from the French coast'; and second, they would also contact 'people who lived up in the mountains near the border' to find out about events in San Sebastian.[14]

In Mallorca, the enemy recognized that spying on behalf of the Reds was 'fairly efficiently organized' since they realized that the 'plans to bomb Menorca and a floatplane reconnaissance mission were known in detail and well in advance'.[15] Indeed, a man by the name of Guri, who had been a policeman, communicated 'with the Reds in Barcelona' and was able to warn them in advance of the 'bombings of Barcelona' some forty-five minutes before they took place.[16]

Elsewhere, spies in Palencia prepared ambushes of Falangist forces,[17] and in Saragossa agents managed to infiltrate themselves slowly into this fascist organization and even reach mid-ranking officer level. Every week two railway workers belonging to the anarchist CNT and FAI would travel from Barcelona to Saragossa through an unguarded tunnel 'disguised as Falangists and make their way to [a bar called] Gambrinus. They also help[ed] people escape from Saragossa, also dressed as Falangists'.[18] The Aragonese capital was a source of considerable concern to the pro-Franco supporters as they had evidence that up until the end of September 'spies continually passed through and had set up a formidable spy network there'.[19] The porousness of the Aragonese front line encouraged people to cross and the Nationalists suspected that some militiamen who had joined their ranks had done so 'with the sole aim of spying'.[20]

During the first year of the war – as remembered by the man responsible for the Information Services – Republican espionage had slowly but surely taken shape 'from personal experiences rather than through the development of a detailed doctrine or the sharing of knowledge that affected the gathering of information'.[21] Audacious soldiers and daring but discrete civilians had carried out some impressive work relying on informers located in enemy territory and these people risked their lives by passing information to the Republic. This was the case, for example, of a 'lame woman who [sold] engravings and medals and who also frequent[ed] the bar Gambrinus and who [was] well-known in Saragossa.'[22]

In spite of everything, what stood out in this first phase were the good intentions rather than the level of organization. What is more, the intelligence reports did not always meet commanders' needs. In the summer of 1937 the Republic's own officers calculated that its intelligence gathering efforts in 'collecting information about the enemy and its locations and plans, can be considered to be of little or no value,'[23] its main source of useable information being Nationalist deserters.[24]

Professionalizing the Espionage Services (October 1937–October 1938)

Faced with such a situation it was clear that a more sophisticated secret service needed to be developed. The recently appointed head of the Information Service of the Republican Army's general staff, Manuel Estrada, concentrated his efforts on improving its operations, giving greater importance to espionage and the creation of some special-purpose sections. Among these, the *Servicio de Información Especial Periférico* (SIEP), or the Special Peripheral Information Service, was established. Its mission was to 'inform on the enemy's immediate rearguard – up to a maximum of 80-100 kilometres behind the front lines' – including 'examining the morale and political will of the troops and of the civil population in territory occupied by the enemy' in addition to 'enlisting and infiltrating secret agents into army headquarters, arsenals, aerodromes, naval bases and military factories.'[25]

The first steps were taken in August 1937 but its incorporation into the Popular Army's structure was initially patchy. At first a mere 1,500 pesetas was budgeted, a ridiculous amount which, although increased progressively, was always a reflection of the scant importance given to this service.[26] Most of the money was for agents' wages but this lack of funds was not the biggest problem; not only was there a shortage of technical know-how but also of specialized personnel and instructors for the agents.[27]

The 'Professional' Agents

With the aim of 'setting up new groups and further training those already in operation', the first spy school was formed. It is noteworthy that it was carried out with 'hardly any support from the General Staff'. From 12 to 25 September 1937 the first course was given 'for a group of 23 students, all from Popular Front organizations, and including 6 officers'.[28] Subsequently the number of schools multiplied and a sergeant was responsible for giving daily classes on 'accounting, map reading, road signs, railway signals, and shorthand (consisting mainly of writing words with only the first and final two letters)'.[29] Among other subjects taught was night-time orienteering. The spies were trained 'mainly by completing exercises to help them commit phrases and ideas to memory'.[30]

A soldier, Domicilio Fuertes, remembered being taught 'map reading, the ranks in the Nationalist Army and the organisation of the espionage services' whereas, in the Rocafort-Bétera school in the province of Valencia, Francisco Rodríguez was instructed in 'how to handle carrier pigeons'.[31] Later in this same school the students were put through a fortnight's course before an active duty posting. The course included 'studying how to add a telephone to the network and listen in to calls; also photography and how to take photos of aircraft, the build-up of tanks and how to recognize their markings, etc'.[32]

In the Castillo de Viñuelas school, in the province of Madrid, classes were given in 'horse riding, driving, technical drawing, mathematics, geography, Morse code and map-reading'. Talks were also organized on appropriate behaviour behind enemy lines, including the differences they needed to observe between impersonating a soldier, a sergeant, or an officer. They were also taught how to sing Nationalist hymns.[33] In Madrid a school 'taught Italian, Nationalist military discipline, patriotic songs and how to smoke a pipe. The students practised saying "Goodbye and long live Spain" [as a farewell; *Adiós y Arriba España*]. The students also received instruction on appropriate etiquette'.[34]

The courses lasted 'from 60 to 90 days at the end of which the new agents were transferred to the SIEP headquarters of the Army of the Centre' located in Madrid. From here they were posted to a smaller, front-line unit, which comprised a commanding officer, an adjutant, an assistant, two guides acquainted with the region and between six and ten agents.[35]

Those trained at the school were known either as mobile agents or agents in reserve. The latter were only employed to obtain detailed information about a specific sector or location, but essentially played the same role as their mobile colleagues who crossed the enemy lines and spent no more than a few days carrying out their assignments. These were given all the necessary documentation and were instructed in the work they were required to do. This type of agent was invariably a soldier specially recruited by the SIEP. If possible 'preference was given to candidates who already had some military knowledge, however basic',[36] although the soldier's disposition was key to his being signed up on the recommendation or order of an officer. One enemy report maintained that 'agents were recruited by asking different Brigade commanders to report back on the soldiers who inspired most confidence and who showed most determination and courage'.[37] This was the case of José Palomeque del Campo, an anarchist peasant, who was spotted by the political commissar of his battalion; likewise of Julio Montesinos López and Gonzalo Torres López, both farm labourers and affiliated to the Spanish Communist Party, and recruited by their officers.[38]

In other cases agents would volunteer. Two main reasons explain why there was never a shortage of these: first, agents would earn a higher wage and, second, they would also distance themselves from front-line fighting.

It was certainly money that attracted Bernardo Ballesteros, a butcher by trade and a 19-year-old volunteer from Talavera de la Reina, in the province of Toledo.[39] Spies received extra pay and enjoyed privileges compared with the common soldier. Generally speaking they would receive the same amount as militiamen, 10 pesetas a day, but would be paid an extra 500 pesetas, thus considerably increasing their wage to 800 pesetas a month. Furthermore, they were granted one month's leave for each assignment plus a bonus of 1,000 pesetas.[40] However, other sources claim that bonuses were less generous and varied between only 100 and 200 pesetas for each assignment to which was added three to ten days' leave.[41] In some reports it is stated that a 'car was made available for their work whenever they wanted' which seems a rather unlikely claim.[42]

What attracted the soldier, Ángel García, was not only the promise made to him by the captain of his company to give him 400 Nationalist pesetas there and then and another 5,000 on his return, but also the reward of being sent to the rearguard once his assignment was completed.[43] Francisco Navalón also acknowledged that he was drawn into espionage by undertaking courses on military observation on which he enrolled to 'avoid being sent to the front lines'. After his arrest he stated that it was on account of the propaganda and the ideas imparted by his teachers that he slowly came to realize that the whole purpose of the school was to 'persuade people to go into espionage work'. They convinced him by saying that the Nationalist enemy was in the sway of foreigners, an argument that appealed to his patriotism and pushed him into accepting. Nevertheless, intimidation also played a part: it was said that 'if they did not accept, they were advised to watch their backs from then on to avoid being the victim of some kind of unspecified accident'.[44]

The Nationalists were under the impression that Republican agents needed to meet the following requirements: '1. to be a deserter from the Nationalist Army; 2. to be accused of crimes and murders; 3. to have an unquestionable Marxist background, and 4. to be well acquainted with the region in which they were going to operate'.[45] The first three were little more than fanciful but the fourth made sense. Indeed, another report confirmed that the agents working in the central zone were 'recruited preferably from among people living in towns and villages in the provinces of Toledo and Madrid, regions under the control of our troops where our officers are trusted and have better relations with families who stay put in their home villages; people who, moreover, were already acquainted with the territory'.[46]

The average age of the SIEP agents was around twenty-five compared with over thirty for the officers and NCOs.[47] No one particularly stood out by the level of their education. The agents included labourers, farm workers, office employees, and students; what counted most were their skills and their commitment to the cause. Indeed, once they had signed up, it was difficult for them to get out as 'if for whatever reason they want to leave the Service, they are threatened with not continuing to enjoy a quiet life, given that they know certain things that are unwise to spread around'.

Agents were not always expected to start work immediately after finishing their training. After being recruited, they were taken, normally in groups of no more than six, to a holding location where they would live and where they would have very little contact with the local population. Even the post sent to them was addressed to the lieutenant who monitored it. While they waited for an operation, they were not given any news of their colleagues. They were told only, for example, that their colleagues had gone to the hospital and only when they returned from their assignment was the truth revealed, but 'deliberately exaggerating the quality of the work undertaken and the ease with which it was done, aiming thus to instil them with confidence and motivation'. It was claimed that 'three days before leaving on an assignment they were handed instructions for their preparatory study. On the day of the assignment itself they were given their false documents.'

A spy's personal belongings were usually quite modest. If they were to cross over into enemy territory, they had to be dressed in enemy uniform, usually of the 'worn and old' kind, and on their feet they would wear simple rope sandals. Other than their documents or safe-conducts valid for enemy territory, they also carried concealable weapons, including a 9 mm calibre pistol, a dagger, and hand grenades that they often secreted in their crotch.[48] As for equipment, statements made by one agent show that when he was captured his haversack contained 'two hunks of fresh bread – less than a day old – 10 bars of chocolate, 3 first-aid packets and a pair of khaki gloves';[49] a light set of supplies to facilitate speedy work.

Agents would almost always cross the front line after midnight accompanied by other spies or guides who would direct them to their destinations. To make the crossing in relative safety they would use passwords such as *Arriba Franco!* (Long Live Franco!); or they would throw three stones into the river or whistle twice on the river bank to alert someone to ferry them across; or when they arrived at a road the guides would say 'twenty three' and the agent had to reply 'thirty three'.[50] Some agents simply pretended to be deserters from the Republican side so as to 'undertake espionage tasks in the Nationalist rearguard'.[51]

After crossing the front line they would take the opportunity to rest until dawn in shepherd's huts, straw lofts, or in ruined or uninhabited houses, and then in the morning they would begin to 'go about a normal life in the nearby towns and villages'.[52] They might work alone or in pairs but that would depend on the nature of the assignment and what it required, and also on the character of the agents involved. In enemy territory they normally 'spoke to soldiers at checkpoints, in bars and so on, anywhere connected with the armed forces'[53] and would 'often go to farm houses and places that sold tobacco which they would buy in considerable quantity'.[54] Furthermore, the most daring even crossed the lines with a false membership card of the Spanish Falange. They then tried to pass themselves off as deserters with the aim of 'entering a Military Academy and obtaining a military rank, hoping thereby to be posted to the Southern, Central or Eastern Sectors, all of which had direct contact with the Red zone'.[55]

Once in enemy territory they tried not only to 'acquaint themselves with every detail of the situation' regarding the enemy forces and their deployment on the front, but they also had to identify different people in various places 'with the idea of designating them as potential informers'.[56] They would reward them 'generously, and leave them with the detailed information they had to gather before their next meeting'.[57]

Over the course of a mission it was often necessary to put up with considerable hardship so as to avoid capture, such as that faced by the soldier, Bernardo Ballesteros. After crossing the enemy lines and mixing with enemy soldiers and with civil guards, he had to spend the next two days in hiding in a pine grove without anything to eat.[58] On other occasions the informer let them down, as happened to Ángel García and Francisco Arribas. These two did not know each other previously and having crossed the front line together after a four-hour walk, they were abandoned by their guides in a cave somewhere near Segovia; on finally reaching their destination, they discovered that their contact, an ironmonger, had already been detained.[59]

At most, missions typically lasted a couple of days and were conducted in very specific geographical locations. Information would be gathered about any concentrations of troops and weapons in the locality.[60] In some specific cases highly accurate data were collected, causing some alarm in the enemy, but mostly the information assembled was not properly used to the Republicans' advantage.[61] The enemy's intentions were much harder to predict; and in this task the SIEP agents always faced the greatest of difficulties.[62]

When agents returned to Republican lines from a mission, they would head for a specific outpost and pretend to be deserters from the Nationalist lines; they would not reveal their real identities, but rather ask to see the commanding officer of the Division, the only person who knew of SIEP's existence.[63]

Civilian Informers

Agents officially known as residential were all civilians; they lived permanently in enemy territory and blended in with the local inhabitants. They worked as informers, gave shelter to mobile agents and helped them on their way through. Their work was a commonplace feature from the very start of the conflict. In San Martín de la Vega, in Madrid, the soldiers were 'in regular contact with a local washerwoman'[64] while in Algeciras 'railway workers and bus drivers' helped the Republican cause.[65] Most of the informers were male,[66] but the Nationalists had suspicions about 'one of the female German translators on Radio Salamanca' and about numerous women who 'worked for *Socorro Blanco* [White Aid; a conservative relief organization] in Madrid.'[67]

Civilians supported the Republican cause for a variety of reasons. 'Generally speaking, people with family in the Red zone were most sought after or people who shared their [leftist] ideology.'[68] Curiously, in most of the examples analysed personal or family motives predominated over ideological reasons. Some informers were women whose husbands were imprisoned or had fled the country, such as Cándida Zaldúa Amas, the wife of Ignacio Bengoechea, who had escaped to France; or María Belén Porcel from Alvargonzález whose husband was in prison in Ondarreta in San Sebastian province.[69] Antonio Rodríguez, a 'tall man from Seville, a primary school teacher or still undergoing teacher training, and the son of an employee of the Seville Town Hall', worked as an informer in an espionage network in Melilla because he was romantically involved with the sister of the Salas brothers, soldiers fighting on the Nationalist side but considered to be 'obviously red'.[70]

Typically most agents of this kind came from a humble background, a fact that sometimes surprised the enemy. In an operation conducted in Segovia province with thirty arrests, the enemy were astonished not only at the 'very humble background of most of those arrested' but also at 'the extraordinary skill they had shown in setting up a most efficient information network despite their lowly origins, their lack of education, their lack of training and the absence of other resources'.[71] The man in charge of the organization was a milkman from Hontoria in the province of Segovia by the name of Francisco Yagüe who 'in the course of his daily work visited every house of those involved without ever arousing suspicion'.[72]

However, by no means did every informer come from such low social origins. The spy network working on the Aragonese front was 'supported and sustained by a number of freemasons … including some of prominent social status and considered to be above suspicion'.[73] Among the informers working for the spy network in San Sebastian were Rosario Aguirre, an educated woman who ran a dental clinic in Beasain, and in cooperation with José Sarasola, the director of the local Guipuzcoano Bank.[74]

A particular feature of the Spanish Civil War was the amount of foreign involvement. Some soldiers from other countries worked as spies on the Republican side[75] and some foreign civilians also took part. Some Moroccans agreed to transmit messages to and from the French in Targuist in Morocco regarding what was happening in the Spanish Protectorate.[76] In an enemy report, the presence of a Russian woman in Barcelona during the Teruel offensive was highlighted; she 'entered the Nationalist zone carrying German documents and spoke perfect German'. It seems she was far from being the only one as similar women were known to live in Salamanca, Burgos, and Saragossa, 'all of them professionals reporting to Moscow'.[77]

The proximity of France encouraged many French nationals to become involved in espionage assignments. For instance, Dr Boissnière, a member of the French Socialist Party, was considered one of the leaders of Republican espionage in Toulouse.[78] On French soil itself, Republican émigrés and smugglers carried out spying 'with the help of gendarmes and customs officers, mostly belonging to the French Popular Front and all well acquainted with the border crossings'. Even members of the French administration helped in these efforts, for example, the French Embassy's naval attaché, Mr Moulec, 'smuggled weapons across the border'.[79] Diplomats like the Spanish consul in Bayonne, a man named Lecuona, and the consul in Tarbes,[80] also did their bit for the cause, as did the British vice-consul in San Sebastian, a Mr Golding, who acted as a link between Spanish Republicans exiled in France. With the help of some of his consular and embassy colleagues this British civil servant used the diplomatic pouch and consular cars to take information across the border without fear of being searched.[81]

Civilian spies had various ways of working. On fronts as porous and as nearby as the Madrid one, news was passed from one side to the other through 'the boundaries of El Pardo which gave on to those of Las Rozas'. In Palma de Mallorca a network of spies would put advertisements in newspapers.[82] In Malaga carrier pigeons were used to send messages over to Nemour in Algeria.[83] Many spies were 'supplied with false documents and travelled via France' before entering the enemy zone 'pretending to be business travellers' sympathetic to the Francoist cause while carrying 'passports issued by South American countries'.[84] In other cases, the best pretence was simply to behave as normal. For example, a lady in Malaga would pick up news about the front lines by going to a 'bar in the Plaza de los Capuchinos just opposite the barracks' frequented by military personnel. Afterwards she would pass on the information she obtained to drivers working for a transport company.[85]

One of the most common tasks that informers were expected to do was to recruit new spies. After crossing the enemy front line, Isidro García Otaola requested the collaboration of his sisters and they 'set out to look for new spies until they had successfully formed a whole network which provided news of the enemy almost every single day'.[86] On other occasions, missions did not focus exclusively on collecting information but also on 'smuggling people into France and delivering messages in both directions'. This is what a landowner by the name of José used to do; he lived near the French border in Navarre province and worked in collusion with the local parish priest.[87]

Backs to the Wall (October 1938–March 1939)

The enemy concluded that the SIEP was 'not performing well and that the agents' morale was no better than average'; they also maintained that the Republicans did not attach the same 'importance to them as they did to organizing guerrilla forces'.[88] The mission of these irregular combatants was to carry out acts of sabotage and attempt to bring about uprisings in the enemy zone, even if in practice units were hardly developed during the conflict.[89] The Nationalists also affirmed that Republican sources, soldiers and peasants, supplied 'information of little military value and almost always of zero use'; from this they deduced 'a lack of organisation, bad leadership by the officers in charge and difficulty in finding … informers capable of providing information of interest'.[90]

It was indeed true that the Republican espionage efforts had faltered. For this reason, towards the end of summer 1938 the commanders of the different Divisions and Army Corps were asked to evaluate the usefulness of the SIEP. Most were in favour of maintaining its operations, but others criticized with increasing vigour the 'shortage of personnel' and the lack of 'necessary means with which to do their job properly'. Up until this point, the head of the general staff of the Army of the Centre was of the opinion that information on the position, activities, and aims of the enemy was 'very scarce' and he considered it to be 'essential to reinforce the SIEP with highly qualified personnel of total loyalty and proven courage'.[91]

During the last six months of the conflict, efforts were made to improve the successes of espionage in general and of the SIEP in particular by recruiting agents who were better motivated, but this coincided with growing disillusionment within the Republican ranks. Perhaps as a result of trying to tackle the almost insurmountable human and material advantage that the Nationalist Army possessed at this juncture in the civil war, the Popular Army launched more espionage missions and deployed more informers. Nevertheless, this desperate attempt by the Republic only resulted in the loss of more agents. In fact, towards the end of 1938 and at the start of 1939 the Nationalist Army had succeeded in tracking down most of the Republican spies and their networks.[92] Franco's agents confirmed that, at least to the south of the River Tagus, the Republicans had lost informers and had cut back on sending agents into enemy territory 'not only because they obtain little information in this way, themselves being of limited intelligence, but also because a large number of them have been arrested'.[93]

The Most Common Espionage Failures

The reason for so many arrests was not only better security and effectiveness on the part of the Nationalists but also a range of mistakes the agents themselves made. Often they overlooked basic details and this gave them away almost immediately when they crossed into enemy territory. For example, Ramón Soronellas and Felipe Savarich, both from a village in the province of Tarragona, were stopped for carrying false safe-conducts, a fact which might have gone unnoticed had they not had a strong Catalan accent which stood out a mile in the depths of Castile – a more exceptional mistake than the lack of documents. Soronellas and Savarich were picked up when they were coming out of a tobacconist's in Sigüenza in Guadalajara.[94] Another two spies were captured when disguised as members of the Spanish Foreign Legion because they were not wearing standard-issue footwear.[95] On other occasions improperly forged documentation was specifically the problem: on the safe-conduct carried by one spy the individual number in the top left-hand corner was missing.[96]

Another common error was related to the spy's own incompetence. On one occasion, agents were sent into a zone carrying documentation appropriate for a Division that was no longer stationed there; it had already moved to another sector of the front.[97] Francisco Arribas and his companion 'got lost despite having two compasses with them, and they failed to locate the bridge they were told existed over the River Cabrillas; exhausted by hunger and tiredness they turned up at a mill where, after eating, they fell into a deep sleep, thus giving the miller the chance to notify the Nationalist soldiers on watch duty nearby'.[98]

During his mission, Antonio Conejos, a 31-year-old from Teruel, fell asleep and when he woke up, he realized his companions had vanished. He then decided to go and visit his parents but 'seeing he was on his own and didn't know the way to his village [Formiche Alto] …, he decided to go back to Segorbe (in Castellón province)'. As he was unfamiliar with the lie of the land, he lost his bearings and 'lacking in cunning and intelligence he gave himself away by mistake to a barman who then reported him'.[99] In Bernardo Ballesteros's case, mentioned above, it was hunger that gave him away. After two days without eating, he went into the nearest village to buy some provisions. He was intercepted by a patrol when he became confused and happened on the enemy's barbed wire; they ordered him to halt and when he failed to respond, they shot him. He managed to flee but a patrol later arrested him.[100] In the rush to escape some spies even managed to lose their pistol or threw their cap away in which compromising documents were hidden.[101]

On other occasions the spy made no mistake but the informer either betrayed him or let him down. Rafael Santamaría, a student from Granada, waited for two hours without anyone on the other side responding to his password.[102] Some agents 'were given orders to link up with people who turned out to be unreliable, and in one case one of them turned in the Red agent'.[103] This is what happened to Salvador Gordo and two other spies who 'thought that among their resident agents in Granada they had two spies who were really working for [a] Captain Pelayo' loyal to the Nationalist side.[104]

Finally, it could also happen that spies fell into traps prepared by *agents provocateurs*. In the case of Sebastián Callejo a stranger encouraged him to provide certain information in the presence of two other men, at which point Sebastián 'told him to keep his mouth shut and said under his breath, "These people aren't on our side"'.[105] José María Palomeque, a 44-year-old baker, was arrested and taken to prison in Móstoles in Madrid province. After he was put in a cell, a pro-Franco agent 'pretending to be a Red gained his trust and realized that from what he came out with he was very Red and the only thing that stopped him fleeing to the Red zone … was that he possessed substantial wealth which he couldn't move, and he expressed his regret that his lack of experience in matters of spying had got him caught up in such an ugly business'.[106]

The End of the Venture

Missions were tough and could end badly. Rufat recognizes that in the last six months of the war 'returning from enemy territory became increasingly dangerous'.[107] Although all agents had to sign the pledge to 'FIGHT TO THE DEATH',[108] in reality many chose in the end to give themselves in. The number of desertions increased in the last months of the war and cynicism gave way to survival.[109]

'After carrying out several espionage missions and after his network had been uncovered', Andrés Martín 'voluntarily handed himself over' to the enemy.[110] Sotero Fernández and his companion, Pedro, received the news that they were being pursued. Sotero suggested to Pedro that 'they should turn themselves over to the Nationalist authorities, a proposal that led them to argue and as a result of Pedro's refusal, Sotero picked up his pistol and shot him dead'; he then turned himself in to the Nationalist espionage service (known by the acronym SIPM). There he declared that 'he had given himself up, not because they were uncovered and located, but because he had family in the village of Guijosa, and because he was keen to serve Franco and his cause; he handed over two pistols, two hand grenades and another two of Italian make, and a note which gave instructions about his spying assignment'. Pedro's body was later found in a shepherd's hut in Torrevaldealmendras in Guadalajara province whereas Sotero went on to work for the pro-Franco espionage services.[111] In other cases, agents would try to escape when they were uncovered instead of turning themselves in, and would often be killed in flight.[112]

If in the end spies were caught alive, they would undergo an interrogation. Agents knew in advance that in theory they would be tortured and were expected to do everything not to betray their companions. In most cases spies had given a promise in writing linking them contractually to espionage work and the Republican cause; they had also guaranteed they would 'never in any circumstances reveal any aspect of the set-up of the espionage service', nor the specific work they had undertaken, on pain of 'expulsion from the espionage service'; and furthermore, if they did so, they could expect to be tried 'with the full rigour of military law in accordance with the Code of Military Justice in force at the time for the crime of high treason against the Republic and fatherland [the *Patria*]'.[113] In other cases spies signed a similar document in which they committed themselves 'not to reveal anything about the espionage service in the event of capture, on the understanding that if they failed to keep their promise, they would be put to death by other Red agents'.[114]

There were some who kept their word and remained as tight-lipped as they could. In this sense the best spies were the more experienced ones, those who had enlisted voluntarily at the start of the war and whose loyalty to the Republican cause was sincere and unwavering. José López, a 35-year-old socialist volunteer, was one of these, and in his interrogation he came across as contemptuous, according to his Nationalist captors.[115]

Nevertheless, partly as a result of a lack of an esprit de corps within the SIEP,[116] most of the captured agents quickly 'spilled the beans [*cantaban*]'; for example, Antonio Cuenca who 'has given all sorts of information and cooperation from the moment he was detained';[117] the young man, Domicilio Fuertes, who revealed the identity of all his informers;[118] Francisco Torres Bou, who handed over the instructions about his mission to the enemy, and also Fulgencio Martín and Pedro Antonio Álvaro who gave 'names of local informers in various villages' which led to the dismantling of a network of some sixty people.[119] A desire to survive often and understandably quickly took precedence over their previous loyalties, and many spies hoped that their willingness to collaborate during their interrogations would allow them to escape death, albeit with little honour.

The Nationalist Code of Military Justice stated that crimes of espionage incurred 'a penalty of long-term imprisonment or the death sentence'.[120] Although there are some isolated cases of spies being executed following interrogation,[121] in practice most agents were imprisoned after the death sentence had been handed down. However, Ramón Rufat admitted in his memoirs and later in an interview that 'those of us involved in espionage all got off. By that time, any information we had gathered was no longer important.'[122] With the war over, the top priority of Francoist justice was to execute the most dangerous members of the *Servicio de Investigación Militar* (SIM), or Military Investigation Service, a Republican agency dedicated to counterespionage,[123] whereas 'guerrillas and spies were left to rot in the Conde Toreno prison' in the province of Madrid.[124] A bitter ending, but at least many survived to tell the tale.

Conclusions

Republican military espionage developed amateurishly, making use of civilians up until the summer of 1937, and from then on training new agents in specialized schools and creating the dedicated SIEP. Throughout the conflict the Republicans relied more on goodwill than on advanced techniques, and although the agents, soldiers, and civilian informers did their best, successes were few and far between: at best they succeeded in unearthing the strength of the enemy but not its concrete plans. Bravery and determination abounded but there was a lack of means, money, and support from the officers and government. In short, the Republican forces were not successful in setting up a professional espionage network. Some agents signed up as volunteers with the aim of supporting the government cause as fully as possible. In contrast, others became spies because of close family ties and other contacts in the Nationalist zone or by the promise of receiving a better wage. It was also an opportunity to distance themselves from front-line fighting. A lack of training and the inherent danger of the work caused most missions to fail, and during interrogations betrayals prevailed over loyalty, to the extent that, by the end of the war, agents' desire to live was usually stronger than their commitment to the Republic.

Further Reading

Cabrera, Francisco and Blasco, Domingo. *El frente invisible: Guerrilleros republicanos 1936-1939*. Guadalajara: Silente, 2013.

Pastor Petit, Domingo. *Los dossiers secretos de la guerra civil*. Barcelona: Argos, 1978.

Rodríguez Velasco, Hernán. *Una derrota prevista. El espionaje militar republicano en la Guerra Civil española* (1936-1939). Granada: Comares, 2012.

Rodríguez Velasco, Hernán. 'Las guerrillas en el Ejército Popular de la República (1936-1939)'. *Cuadernos de Historia Contemporánea* 33 (2011): 235–54.

Rodríguez Velasco, Hernán. 'Una historia del SIM: antecedentes, origen, estructura y reorganizaciones del contraespionaje republicano'. *Ayer* 81, no. 1 (2011): 207–39.

Rufat, Ramón. *Espions de la République. Memoires d'un agent secret pendant la guerre d'Espagne*. Paris: Éditions Allia, 1990.

Notes

1   Archivo General Militar de Ávila (AGMAV), Caja (Cj.) 2489, Carpeta (C.) 7/15.

2   The only existing monograph on Republican espionage is Hernán Rodríguez Velasco, *Una derrota prevista. El espionaje militar republicano en la Guerra Civil española (1936-1939)* (Granada: Comares, 2012). Domingo Pastor Petit had previously provided an overview of both sides in *Los dossiers secretos de la guerra civil* (Barcelona: Argos, 1978) and *Espionaje. (España 1936-1939)* (Barcelona: Bruguera, 1977). Other works on Spanish Civil War espionage include Morten Heiberg and Manuel Ros Agudo, *La trama oculta de la Guerra Civil. Los servicios secretos de Franco 1936-1945* (Barcelona: Crítica, 2006); Yannick Pech, *Les services secrets républicains espagnols en France* (Editions Loubatières, 2005); and José Ramón Soler Fuensanta and Javier López-Brea, *Soldados sin rostro. Los servicios de información, espionaje y criptografía en la Guerra Civil Española (1936-1939)* (Barcelona: Inèdita Editores, 2008).

3 Ramón Rufat, *Espions de la République. Memoires d'un agent secret pendant la guerre d'Espagne* (Paris: Éditions Allia, 1990), 5.
4 Archivo Histórico del Partido Comunista de España (AHPCE), Fondo: Documentos militares de la Guerra Civil. Estado Mayor del Ejército soviético. Reel 6, 323.
5 Pastor Petit, *Los dossiers secretos*, 97.
6 Rufat, *Espions de la République*, 20–2.
7 The so-called Second Section of the general staff was responsible for military intelligence. Centro Documental de la Memoria Histórica (CDMH), Incorporados, 688, C. 1 and 2.
8 AGMAV, Armario (A.) 31, Legajo (L.) 7, Carpeta (C.) 12, Documento (D.) 1.
9 AGMAV, Cj.2490, C.21/3.
10 AGMAV, A.31, L.7, C.12, D.5/29.
11 AGMAV, Cj.2490, C.20/13.
12 AGMAV, A.31, L.7, C.12, D.6/32.
13 AGMAV, A.31, L.7, C.13, D.5/26.
14 AGMAV, Cj.2490, C.19/1.
15 AGMAV, A.31, L.7, C.13, D.6.
16 AGMAV, Cj.2490, C.20/3.
17 AGMAV, A.31, L.1, C.3, D.1.
18 AGMAV, A.31, L.7, C.13, D.3/10, 11, and 17.
19 AGMAV, Cj.2490, C.21/5.
20 AGMAV, Cj.2490, C.21/3.
21 AHPCE, Fondo: Documentos militares de la Guerra Civil. Estado Mayor del Ejército soviético. Reel 6, 323.
22 AGMAV, A.31, L.7, C.13, D.3/10.
23 Archivo Histórico Nacional (AHN), Archivo General Rojo, Caja 7/11.
24 AHPCE, Fondo: Documentos militares de la Guerra Civil. Estado Mayor del Ejército soviético. Reel 6, 326.
25 Rodríguez Velasco, *Una derrota prevista*, 37.
26 Ibid., 140.
27 AHPCE, Fondo: Documentos militares de la Guerra Civil. Estado Mayor del Ejército soviético. Reel 6, 324.
28 Ibid.
29 AGMAV, Cj.1971, C.3.
30 AGMAV, Cj.2499, C.27/7 and Cj.2510, C.18/13.
31 AGMAV, Cj.1750, C.2, D.5/3, 5, and 6.
32 AGMAV, Cj.2510, C.18/26.
33 AGMAV, Cj.2510, C.18/29.
34 AGMAV, Cj. 1968, C.11/35.
35 AGMAV, Cj.2510, C.18/29.
36 AGMAV, Cj.2489, C.16/3.
37 AGMAV, Cj.1971, C.3.
38 AGMAV, Cj.1970, C.7/24, 42, and 46.
39 AGMAV, Cj.1750, C. 2, d.2.
40 AGMAV, Cj.1971, C.3 and Cj.2499, C.27/7.
41 AGMAV, Cj.2510, C.18/30.
42 AGMAV, Cj.2490, C.22/28.
43 AGMAV, Cj.2489, C.7/8-10.
44 AGMAV, Cj.1968, C.7/1.

45 AGMAV, Cj.2499, C.22/5.

46 AGMAV, Cj.2489, C.16/11.

47 AGMAV, Cj.1971, C.3. Until the next footnote all quotes are from this same source.

48 AGMAV, Cj.1750, C.2, D.5/8-11; Cj.2499, C.27/9 and Cj.2490, C.22/40.

49 AGMAV, Cj.1750, C.2, D.5/8-11.

50 AGMAV, Cj.1970, C.7/25, 47 and 48.

51 AGMAV, Cj.2490, C.20/20.

52 AGMAV, Cj.2499, C.27/8.

53 AGMAV, Cj.2490, C.22/10.

54 AGMAV, Cj.2510, C.18/14.

55 AGMAV, Cj.2489, C.16/3.

56 AGMAV, Cj.2490, C.22/28.

57 AGMAV, Cj.2510, C.18/13.

58 AGMAV, Cj.1750, C.2, D.2/1 and 2.

59 AGMAV, Cj.2489, C.7/8-10.

60 For examples, see: AGMAV, Cj.1971, C.11/96 and Cj.2490, C.22/7.

61 Rufat, *Espions*, 176, 177 and 249.

62 Rodríguez, *Una derrota prevista*, 142–3.

63 AGMAV, Cj.1971, C.3/38.

64 AGMAV, Cj.2490, C.20/16.

65 AGMAV, Cj.2489, C.8/7.

66 In one round-up out of seventeen arrests only two were women. See: AGMAV, Cj.2489, C.8/9.

67 AGMAV, Cj.2490, C.21/51.

68 AGMAV, Cj.2510, C.18/13.

69 AGMAV, Cj.2489, C.9/1 and Cj.1971, C.13.

70 AGMAV, Cj.2490, C.20/4 and 10.

71 AGMAV, Cj.2489, C.7/14.

72 AGMAV, Cj.2489, C.7/5.

73 AGMAV, Cj.2490, C.21/49.

74 AGMAV, Cj.2489, C.9/1 and Cj.1971, C.13.

75 Rufat, *Espions,* 20–2.

76 AGMAV, Cj.2489, C.13/6.

77 AGMAV, Cj.2489, C.12/3.

78 AGMAV, Cj.2490, C.19/7.

79 AGMAV, Cj.2490, C.19/13.

80 AGMAV, Cj.2490, C.19/14.

81 AGMAV, Cj.2489, C.9/1 and Cj.1971, C.13.

82 AGMAV, Cj.2490, C.21/7 and 10.

83 AGMAV, Cj.2490, C.21/35.

84 AGMAV, Cj.2489, C.12/14.

85 AGMAV, A.31, L.7, C.12, D.3/17.

86 AGMAV, Cj.2489, C. 7/12.

87 AGMAV, Cj.2489, C.9/1 and 9/2.

88 AGMAV, Cj.2499, C.27/9.

89 For more on this topic, see: Hernán Rodríguez Velasco, 'Las guerrillas en el Ejército Popular de la República (1936-1939)', *Cuadernos de Historia Contemporánea* 33 (2011): 235–54; and Francisco Cabrera and Domingo Blasco, *El frente invisible. Guerrilleros republicanos 1936-1939* (Guadalajara: Silente, 2013).

90 AGMAV, Cj.2489, C.16/12.
91 CDMH, Incorporados, 674, Cp.1.
92 AGMAV, Cj.2510, C.18.
93 AGMAV, Cj.2490, C.22/30.
94 AGMAV, Cj.2490, C.22/17 and 18.
95 AGMAV, Cj.2490, C.22/24.
96 AGMAV, Cj.2489, C.16/12.
97 Ibid.
98 AGMAV, Cj. 2489, C.7/8-10.
99 AGMAV, Cj.1750, C.2, D. 5/8-11.
100 AGMAV, Cj.1750, C.2, D.2.
101 AGMAV, Cj.2490, C.22/35 and Cj.1971, C.5/49.
102 AGMAV, Cj.1970, C.5/28.
103 AGMAV, Cj.2499, C.27/9.
104 AGMAV, Cj.2490, C.22/38.
105 AGMAV, Cj.1971, C.5/51.
106 AGMAV, Cj.1971, C.5/3.
107 Rufat, *Espions*, 223.
108 AGMAV, C.2490, Cp.22/40.
109 Michael Seidman, *Republic of Egos: A Social History of the Spanish Civil War* (Madison, WI: University of Wisconsin Press, 2002), chapters 3 and 4.
110 AGMAV, Cj.2489, C.7/12.
111 AGMAV, Cj.2490, C.22/6 and 7.
112 AGMAV, Cj.2489, C.7/13.
113 AGMAV, Cj.2490, C.22/29.
114 AGMAV, Cj.2499, C.27/9.
115 AGMAV, Cj.1970, C.7/15.
116 Rufat, *Espions*, 243.
117 Ibid.
118 AGMAV, Cj.1750, C.2, D.5/5 and 6.
119 AGMAV, Cj.2490, C.22/10, 39, and 40.
120 AGMAV, Cj.1971, C.11.
121 AGMAV, Cj.2490, C.22/21.
122 Genoveva Crespo, 'Ramón Rufat. Un espía aragonés al servicio de la República', *El Heraldo de Aragón,* 18 August 1991: https://www.editions-allia.com/files/note_302 6_pdf.pdf
123 Hernán Rodríguez Velasco, 'Una historia del SIM: antecedentes, origen, estructura y reorganizaciones del contraespionaje republicano', *Ayer* 81, no. 1 (2011): 207–39.
124 Rufat, *Espions*, 295.

Part Three

REARGUARD AREAS AND ACTORS

Chapter 8

POLITICAL ECONOMIES AND MONETARY POLICIES DURING THE SPANISH CIVIL WAR

Michael Seidman

An exploration of the political economy and monetary policies of the two belligerents can help to explain the course and outcome of the Spanish Civil War and Revolution. The Nationalists maintained a relatively solid currency, which was able to gain and retain support from European and Spanish capitalists; whereas the Republicans possessed a progressively weaker peseta, which both foreign and domestic property owners distrusted. A stronger currency allowed the Nationalists to offer incentives to their peasants, workers, and soldiers, whereas the Republicans had more difficulty motivating the same groups because of a much higher rate of inflation. Given supply shortages that devaluation of the currency created and aggravated, Loyalist soldiers and civilians bartered and looted more than their enemies. These practices reinforced peasant hoarding and left the Republican army and its urban areas without sufficient nourishment. In sharp contrast, the wide acceptance of the Nationalist peseta permitted the provisioning of its soldiers and civilians. Furthermore, the authoritarian and centralized Francoists were much more effective raising revenue through taxation than their adversaries. In the Republican zone, militants who claimed to represent the working class collectivized much private property with the goal of creating a strong wartime economy through workers' control, but rank-and-file wage earners interpreted the revolution that accompanied the civil war as an opportunity to evade taxation and labour less. As the war continued, Republican soldiers' and workers' real wages declined. Republican transport and services had fewer vehicles and draught animals than their enemies. The healthier Nationalist political economy helped them win the war.

Property, Money and Taxes

The Republic's failure to convince owners that it could protect property rights plagued it internationally and domestically. Although the Republic sporadically attempted to protect foreign interests, owners of many nationalities stayed sceptical about its ability or desire to preserve private property. Unlike its Nationalist enemy, it could not float bonds attractive to domestic or foreign lenders.[1] British and American banks sabotaged its efforts to transfer funds to purchase desperately needed supplies, forcing it to turn to the Soviet banking system and its branches in America and Europe in order to overcome Western financial hostility.[2] In return for the Republic's gold supply, the fourth largest in the world, the Soviets provided firm diplomatic and political support, an irregular flow of supplies and approximately 3,000 military personnel. Conservatives used Russian intervention in the war to argue against aid to the revolutionary Republic.

Wealthy members of the Spanish bourgeoisie worked hard to help the Nationalists. They re-exported their capital, which they had invested abroad during the Republic, to aid the Nationalist cause.[3] The Burgos government provided them with loans and easy credit to reconstruct their enterprises, and hundreds re-established their businesses and lent their talents and capital to the *franquistas*.[4] For example, the loss of his factory in the Republican zone to revolutionary control did not diminish the entrepreneurial spirit of Francisco Luis Rivière who quickly restarted his Trefilerías Rivière in Pamplona.[5] Navarrese bankers and businessmen, such as José Fernández Rodríguez, donated hundreds of thousands of pesetas to the war effort in Navarre, the Basque country, and elsewhere.[6] The Navarre regional government, monarchist Carlists, fascist Falangists, and various charities all benefited from businesses' largesse.[7] The Spanish aristocracy was equally, if not more, supportive. Their financial holdings, jewels, and precious metals served as collateral for the loans that the London bank Kleinwort offered Juan March and the Nationalists.[8]

In contrast to their Russian and Chinese counterparts during their civil wars, the Spanish counter-revolutionaries managed to win international confidence in their currency, an achievement that general histories of the conflict have neglected to analyse sufficiently. Major domestic and foreign markets had faith in and a desire for a Nationalist victory. Fears of communist influence and practices in the Republican zone pushed sectors of the international bourgeoisie to help the insurgents. The assassinations and expropriations of Spanish colleagues in the Republican zone and relatively fresh memories of the Soviet precedent of elimination, confiscation, and exile during the previous decade led international financiers to distrust the Republic.[9] Bank managers and directors shared a world view that endorsed the Nationalist protection of property.[10] Wealthy conservatives – such as Francesc Cambó, Juan Ventosa i Calvell, and especially March – secured international financial support amounting to millions of dollars.[11]

The British, French, and Americans refused to advance substantial credits to the Republic; whereas, the Germans, Italians, Portuguese, and the Texas Oil Company generously offered them to the insurgents.[12] The Nationalists purchased 75 per cent of their petroleum products, often on credit, from US companies.[13] Credit was indispensable to Franco's victory and his construction of a national state. Credit compensated for the relative lack of Nationalist gold and precious metals. The insurgent triumph – like that of Parliament in the English Civil War or of the North in the US Civil War – rested upon healthier and more fortunate finances. Unlike the Republic, Franco's forces did not have to pay many of their main suppliers in precious metals or foreign currencies.[14]

From the beginning, Burgos – the official seat of the Nationalist government from October 1936 to the end of the war – forbade the export of foreign currency and fixed the peseta at its pre-war level. This helped to stabilize prices in the Nationalist zone at least until 1938–9. Republican attempts to freeze prices by decree were much less successful. Republican soldiers, who had initially been among the best paid in the world, became disappointed when inflation quickly devalued their 10 peseta daily salary.[15] They also were frustrated when the official rations could not be furnished. The successful defence of Madrid early in the conflict and the total failure of resistance to the Nationalist conquest of Barcelona at the end of the war showed the demoralizing effects of hunger and the growing desire for peace at any price in the Republican zone.[16] In starving Barcelona, the famished masses assaulted food stocks. Even communists recognized that their insistence on continuing the war at all costs made them unpopular in the Republican zone.[17] In contrast, Franco's rank-and-file soldiers received only 3 to 4 pesetas per day. Although their pay was initially lower than that of their Republican enemy, as the conflict endured the standard of living of the Nationalist soldiers quickly surpassed that of their foes. Higher salaries in solid currency incentivized soldiers to move up in rank.[18] Bravery and tenacity were rewarded with substantial bonuses.

In the Nationalist zone in November 1936, authorities made sure to record the amount of money by stamping circulating banknotes.[19] This measure and the lifting of restrictions on withdrawals, which had been imposed on 12 September 1936 or even earlier in certain provinces, forced savers to brave 'enormous queues' and 'great difficulties' and redeposit their holdings into bank accounts by the established deadlines.[20] However, it also restrained inflation through limitation on the issue of any new currency.[21] Likewise, financial authorities outlawed use of Republican currency in their zone.[22] In the spring of 1937, old script was withdrawn from circulation and replaced by a newly designed issue.[23] Nationalist ability to tax consumption and profits also restricted inflation.

The lack of hyperinflation in the Spanish Nationalist zone stands in stark contrast to the Republican zone. In the latter, the unilateral emission of all kinds of banknotes by local and municipal authorities made any accounting impossible. Furthermore the Republican peseta was not accepted throughout its own zone, and the trader or traveller had to show his safe-conduct pass to exchange money at banks or other institutions.[24] Savers ignored patriotic pleas from Popular Front newspapers and emptied their accounts even from financial institutions that had the solid backing of working-class organizations. The distrust of Republican currency spread to the military where some Republican soldiers resented being paid in 'paper money'.[25] Militiamen were threatened with severe punishment if they were caught in possession of 'fascist' banknotes.[26] By January 1937, Republican money could not buy everything. Some official organizations were reluctant to trade real goods for government paper. For example, the municipality of Altea (Alicante) forbade trading pork for Republican currency.[27]

Barter and not devalued Republican money was needed to obtain goods.[28] In the first year of the war, the Republican peseta lost approximately half of its value on foreign exchange markets. But this decline abroad was less important than the domestic loss of confidence. Prices in Catalonia rose 6 per cent to 7 per cent every month, and barter often had to be used to obtain desired items, including food (as explored in Chapter 11 of this volume). Collectives could and did exchange goods. The prohibition or absence of money in many towns has been portrayed as a socialist or libertarian measure since anarchist militants (of the *Confederación Nacional del Trabajo* (CNT), or National Confederation of Labour) were in theory against trading with 'individualists' [peasants] and the state.[29] While ideologically inoffensive, barter also enabled collectives to nominally adhere to the official price and thus not break the law. At the same time, barter allowed collectives to avoid the effects of devaluation of Republican currency. It was therefore a rational method of exchange among villages and collectivities.[30] Yet barter also meant a regression to a more primitive economy where the local took precedence over the regional and the national.[31] The money economy's more sophisticated and complex division of labour regressed to a simplified exchange of wares between producers. Those without direct access to real goods – in theory, workers in much of the secondary and tertiary sectors – were left out of the loop. Furthermore, the distrust of 'red money' also revealed the failure of the Republic to create a centralized state that 'is an important political correlate of a developed money economy'.[32]

As Republican military fortunes declined, so did their currency.[33] In June 1936 in the then-unified Spanish nation, 5,400,000 pesetas were in circulation. At the end of the war in the Republican zone alone more than 12,800,000,000 pesetas had been disseminated.[34] In 1938 for the first time in Spanish history, the Republic was obliged to print a 5,000-peseta bill. In the Republican zone so many different types of currency circulated that in January 1938 the government ordered that all script issued by regional and local organizations be withdrawn. Laurie Lee, a British poet who served in the International Brigades, reported that in the winter of 1937–8, recruits were given new 100-peseta notes. Lee, a Hispanophile who had travelled throughout the Iberian Peninsula, recalled that he could have lived for weeks on one such note before the war. By 1938 the Republican currency proved nearly useless since there was little to buy in the barracks town of Tarrazona de la Mancha. Lee and his mates ended up paying over 1,000 pesetas for three scrawny chickens.[35] Spanish smugglers of fugitives into France demanded either silver or *franquista* currency in return for their services.[36]

In contrast, the Nationalist peseta was universally accepted in its area of circulation. In this sense, the Nationalists created a nation, at least monetarily. Currency evasion to foreign destinations was less important in its zone than in Republican areas.[37] *The Times* of London attributed the strength of their peseta to 'the intelligent finances of the Nationalists that count among their supporters some of the best business and financial minds'.[38] Many historians have argued that it was the militarization of the Nationalist zone which led to its victory; however, advice and cooperation of civilian experts also contributed greatly to the Nationalist triumph. Their monetary conservatism continued the orthodox practices of the pre-war Republic. At the end of 1936 the Republican peseta had depreciated 19 per cent and the Nationalist 7 per cent; at the end of 1937 the Republican peseta had fallen 75 per cent and the Nationalist 17 per cent, and at the end of 1938 the Republican peseta had lost almost all value and the Nationalist only 27 per cent.[39] The steep currency devaluation prevented Republicans from purchasing desperately needed supplies from abroad – such as foodstuffs – which the Non-Intervention Committee had not prohibited. The Non-Intervention Agreement, brokered by Britain and France in the summer of 1936 to halt direct foreign involvement in the conflict, banned only military equipment and personnel, not what we would call today humanitarian aid.

Of course, the growing expectation that the Nationalists would win increased the value of their currency and reduced that of the 'reds'. Initially, many savers in the Nationalist zone were reluctant to put stamped or new money into banks and instead hoarded it at home.[40] Yet soon in Andalusia, money which had been withdrawn from banks in the first days of the conflict was re-deposited.[41] Burgos savings banks claimed that deposits rose rapidly in comparison to the wave of withdrawals that occurred after the electoral triumph of the Popular Front in February 1936.[42] In Pontevedra, in Galicia, the *Caja Provincial de Ahorros* saw a 64 per cent increase in deposits from 1936 to 1939.[43] Álava officials asserted that merchants' bank accounts grew rapidly.[44] With the major stock markets of Madrid and Barcelona closed during the war and that of Bilbao reopened only in 1938, investors left their savings in banks. Financial institutions paid relatively low rates of interest (1.25 per cent to 3.5 per cent) but paid them regularly.[45] Although private banks experienced intrusive state intervention, bankers made considerable profits.[46] Banks in the Nationalist zone absorbed a wealth of savings, and their deposits jumped from 1 billion pesetas before July 1936 to 3 billion two years later.[47] Andrés Amado, the Minister of Finance, assured a foreign reporter that Franco's zone accumulated 'enormous available funds' – often from war profits – which could be used to advance credit.[48] The confidence of savers, whose accumulated resources the state could tap, sustained the *franquistas*.

Savers bought farm animals or, more frequently, real estate, whose prices became inflated.[49] The inflation of both urban and rural real-estate values was yet another reason for landowners' support for Franco. In this context, it should be mentioned that tenants often paid their landlords in kind after the wheat harvest. Thus, rural landlords were securely protected from the relatively mild inflation in the Nationalist zone.[50] Rural landowners directly benefited from policies of higher agricultural prices which increased their earnings 25 per cent, especially compared to urban landlords and bond holders whose rent and interest payments remained the same.[51] To compete with real-estate investments, municipalities eventually offered thirty-year bonds at 6 per cent.[52] In May 1938 the Burgos government re-established interest payments to holders of state bonds, a measure which reaffirmed domestic and foreign confidence in the Nationalist peseta.[53] Many large private companies which had floated loans prior to the war made good on their obligations.[54]

In mid-August 1936 the nascent Nationalist Junta prohibited the export of gold.[55] In March 1937 its Foreign Money Commission decreed that all Spanish citizens had one month to declare the amount of their gold holdings, foreign currencies, stocks, and bonds to the government, which compensated them at below (foreign) market exchange rates and reaped a harvest of millions of pounds, dollars, and other currencies.[56] The Nationalist government effectively controlled all foreign currency transactions, much to the dismay of importers and exporters throughout its zone.[57] The influx of foreign currencies and tax on exports bolstered the Nationalist treasury. All Spanish exports had to be paid in foreign currencies, preferably dollars and pounds, which were turned over to the militarized treasury, the *Delegación Militar de la Hacienda Pública*, within three days.[58] Only offices of the Bank of Spain were authorized to purchase foreign currencies.[59] In early 1938, Nationalists claimed to have a healthy trade surplus.[60]

Whereas Republican exports declined drastically, exports from the Nationalist zone probably remained stable during the conflict.[61] Early in the war the Republican government temporarily prohibited food and chemical exports to reserve their use for its own needs.[62] In contrast, Nationalist exports greatly helped finance their war effort.[63] In 1938, the Foreign Money Commission received 48 per cent of its foreign currencies from Spanish exports.[64] The percentage would have been higher if the Nationalist peseta had not been overvalued on foreign exchange markets. In the spring of 1937, the Nationalist peseta was worth nearly three times more than its Republican counterpart on the international market.[65] By the autumn of 1938, it was worth six times.[66]

Spanish farmers generally welcomed Nationalist currency as much as they rejected the Republican militias' promissory notes. Peasants who insisted upon selling their produce for the same sum in Nationalist currency that Republicans had paid were considered outrageous price gougers.[67] In November 1938 at the end of the Battle of the Ebro, a woman in Benisanet (Tarragona) demanded the Republican price of 200 pesetas for a pair of chickens from a *requeté* lieutenant. He offered her the going rate of 15 pesetas in Nationalist currency. She refused and found her chickens confiscated as 'prisoners of war'.[68] Peasants learnt to make quick calculations concerning the value of various currencies circulating during the conflict.[69] After the conquest of major towns and cities, personnel of the Bank of Spain facilitated in marketplaces and later in banks the exchange of Republican currency for legal Nationalist script.[70]

The *franquistas* seem to have depended on regular collection of taxes, thereby providing soldiers with steady pay rather than unpredictable plunder. It is often forgotten that pay is a powerful incentive not only for mercenaries but also for the most ideologically committed soldiers.[71] The Nationalist treasury took several significant measures to finance the war. While successfully insisting on payment of previous obligations, it created five major new taxes, usually direct and indirect taxes on urban residents, and it delayed interest payments on the state's debt to its own citizens (decree of 11 August 1936).[72] It is estimated that taxes allowed the treasury to finance at least 30 per cent of its expenses. The remaining 70 per cent came from loans offered by the Bank of Spain (9,000–10,000 million pesetas) plus

Italian aid and a smaller amount of German assistance. During the conflict, the Nationalist treasury received revenues of 3,700 million pesetas and spent 12,000 million pesetas, leaving a deficit of 8,300 million pesetas.[73] The Bank of Spain financed the deficit through loans and credits.

The considerable financial support of Germany and especially Italy can be seen as a variety of 'matching grants', common in American philanthropy, whereby large donors match the sums of small donors who demonstrate to the former that more modest contributors are dedicated to the cause both emotionally and financially. The fascist powers, foreign banks in Lisbon and London, and American multinationals believed the Nationalists to be good risks because they were able to finance a substantial part of their purchases by themselves.[74] For example, at the end of December 1936, General Dávila ordered the state petroleum company CAMPSA to pay 200,000 dollars to the Texas Oil Company.[75] The latter firm had supplied gasoline to CAMPSA prior to the conflict and continued to fuel Franco's needs during the civil war, even if local shortages occurred.[76] In other words, the initial impulse of international capitalists and financiers to aid the insurgents was confirmed by the latter's ability to sacrifice their money and blood. In sum, Burgos was able to amass in credits from foreign states and banks roughly 700 million dollars, which was approximately equivalent to the sale of the gold of the Bank of Spain by Republican authorities.[77] Yet if the numbers were similar, the effort was not. Generally, Nationalists either had to export or to appear to be winning to receive credits; the Republicans, the official government of Spain, were fortunate to inherit a treasure of precious metals and currencies. The Francoist state was able to pay off both the German and Italian loans on very favourable terms.[78]

At the end of the war, Minister of Finance Amado earned a 'Great Cross of the Order of Isabella the Catholic' because of his success in increasing tax revenues.[79] His treasury claimed that its collections jumped 410 million pesetas from 1937 to 1938; 118 million pesetas in extra revenue was obtained from newly 'liberated' territories, and 292 million pesetas more from increased collections.[80] The only type of taxation which declined was that from customs which the autarkic policies of the regime reduced.[81] As many have noted, the conquest of the north gave the Nationalists the wide variety of financial, industrial, and demographic resources that they needed to win a war of attrition. For example, in newly liberated Oviedo, local authorities insisted that all owed taxes be paid. Evaders were subject to late fees as well as to the accusation of being disloyal to the regime.[82] Oviedo tax revenues recovered rather quickly in 1938.[83] Mine owners were publicly urged to pay their contribution or face the loss of their concessions.[84]

The stability of private property in the Nationalist zone provided a tax base which its enemies lacked. Fiscal policies and practices sharply separated the Nationalist zone from its Republican counterpart since the latter found it impossible to collect direct taxes.[85] In effect, no longer did property owners – whose ranks were greatly diminished by collectivization, confiscation, and flight – pay taxes on their belongings or earnings. Government revenue agents were reluctant to levy charges on salaries for fear of being labelled exploiters. By the end of 1937, the Republican treasury had lost nearly all capacity of collection.

The Generalitat performed fiscally somewhat better, but the Republican attempt to sell bonds in 1938 to finance the war effort was an unmitigated failure.[86] This was hardly surprising since not only did the Republic appear to be losing the war but also its cities had reneged on their obligations to bondholders.[87] Tax collections fell dramatically in the Republican zone as inflation soared. In contrast, in the Nationalist zone relatively heavy taxation helped to prevent an inflationary spiral.

Inflation contributed to rampant corruption in the Republican zone where the black market formed 'with unprecedented speed' and continued throughout the entire conflict.[88] Functionaries – such as postal workers – were not able to live on their official salaries and felt compelled to supplement their inadequate income with illicit gains. Drivers, who were supposed to transport mail, as well as mailmen themselves, would give priority to those who bribed them with food and money.[89] Postal workers were tempted to convert for their own personal use what they were conveying, and by the spring of 1937 the service had won a 'public and notorious reputation for disorder'.[90] In the fall of 1937 a mailman was convicted of stealing.[91] Throughout the war, drivers were reputed for their selfishness.[92] The 'dirty business' of chauffeurs and their agents created 'scandals worthy of fascists'.[93] Chauffeurs refused to permit accompanying postmen to take a change of clothes or even stamped packages. Instead, they filled the available space with their own highly priced merchandise.

The poor performance of the Republican post office had a profoundly depressing effect on the morale of the Popular Army. In contrast, Nationalist troops could rely on their postal service for packages of food, tobacco, and even money sent by family and friends.[94] In the Popular Army the situation was reversed. Republican soldiers sent more goods and money to the destitute home front than they received. Nationalist families also collected a subsidy if they provided a husband or son to the military. Families often forwarded to their soldiers at least part of the funds, which built morale by assuring the men that authorities supported and appreciated their own sacrifice and that of their families. Another morale booster was correspondence with *madrinas de guerra* (literally war godmothers: female pen pals) that the Nationalists used much more effectively given their more efficient post office and their greater confidence in their soldiers' morale. Republican officials worried – quite rationally – that their men would use the opportunity to complain and spread defeatism.[95]

Work and Production

Despite the anarchosyndicalist slogan, 'whoever doesn't work is a fascist', wage earners in the Republican zone took advantage of the revolution to avoid work.[96] In this most profound workers' revolution in European history, anarchists, communists, socialists, and their allied trade unionists assumed that wage earners would labour devotedly in their newly collectivized farms, factories, and workshops. The militants soon became disappointed since workers resisted work under the revolutionary political and trade union leaderships that had instituted various forms of democratic workers' control. Many wage earners continued to demand more pay and persisted in their attempts to avoid the constraints of factory space and time. The anarchosyndicalists of the CNT and the socialists and communists of the *Unión General de Trabajadores* (UGT), or General Union of Workers, opposed many of the workers' desires that they had once supported before the revolution and civil war. Instead, the activists called for more work and sacrifice. Rank-and-file workers frequently ignored these appeals and acted as though the union militants were the new ruling elite. Wage earners returned to their jobs at the end of July only 'little by little'.[97] Some decided to engage in only morning labour and use the afternoon to 'stroll around Barcelona'.[98] Women, who were the majority in the textile industry, received special criticism since they used the factory not merely as a workplace but also as a social space. One CNT militant complained, 'It is not rare that many women come to work, gossip too much, and do not produce enough. If the lack of raw materials is added to this, the collapse of production is considerable'.[99] The sexist male leaders of the peasant collective *Adelante*, or Forward, of Lérida concluded that 'the problem of women is similar in all the collectives. It is a result of egotism and lack of spirit of sacrifice. Unfortunately, there are few that are conscientious collectivists. Female comrades must do certain jobs, such as cleaning and washing.' A veteran militant, who was one of the most active and respected of the collectivists, proposed that 'we expel the gypsies. They are very young and have many children.'[100] Gypsies, of course, never adopted the productivist lifestyle propagated by activists of various modern 'isms'. As George Orwell noted, they continued to beg on the streets of Barcelona during the apex of the revolution.[101] Wage earners' direct and indirect refusals to work conflicted with the militants' urgent need for greater production of clothing and weapons. To make workers work and to reduce resistances, the urban revolutionary elite implemented piecework, elimination of holidays, medical inspections, and dismissals.

In sharp contrast, industrial production jumped in the 'liberated' regions where Nationalists militarized the workforce, taxed its overtime hours, and forced it to deliver fixed quotas.[102] The production of steel, used to make artillery and other weapons for the *franquistas*, recovered 'tremendously'.[103] Steel and iron production at least doubled under Nationalist control.[104] The Mieres metallurgical plant in Asturias had employed 580 workers who manufactured 2,596 tons during the 'leftist period', but by July 1938 1,082 workers produced 7,870 tons.[105] Output of steel and other types of metal increased tenfold. In mid-1938 each worker produced on the average 3.7 times more than during 'red domination'. Wages remained stable; therefore, workers were much more productive but not fully compensated for their gains. The *Fábrica de Metales de Lugones* experienced similar increases of output and productivity. Copper and brass production climbed respectively five- and sevenfold during 1938 compared to the year of Republican control. The Moreda factory saw an eightfold augmentation of tonnage with a workforce reduced from 837 to 779. Its wire production – including the barbed variety used on the extensive fronts – jumped almost four times.

In Asturias, coal production had fallen from 1,780,394 tons in 1936 to 245,368 in 1937, and then under Nationalist control climbed to 3,537,859 tons in 1938.[106] The insurgents ended regulations which limited working hours during holidays and permitted vacations: 'Employers, employees, and workers are reminded that any failure to fulfil an obligation is a crime.'[107] In Vizcaya, 1.4 million tons of ore were produced in 1936; only 0.7 in 1937, when the mines were mostly under 'red' control, and 1.8 million in 1938 under the Nationalists.[108] The production of the copper mines of Huelva, whose output was badly needed to earn foreign currencies, quadrupled during the war.[109] The jump in productivity was also true for miners and workers who laboured in areas – such as León and Cordoba – which had never been conquered by the 'reds'.[110] An official inspection by experts of the provincial government in the quarries of Valdeasores (Cordoba) belonging to Asland demonstrated that after the election of the Popular Front in February 1936 daily output had dropped 47 per cent. 'The [Nationalist] government cannot tolerate these abuses', and 'will not hesitate to establish production quotas if necessary'.[111] Production gains should not be attributed exclusively to terror since in no other industry in this period was the correlation between labour productivity and calorific input more direct than in mining.[112] The Republic which held the heavy industry of the Basque country for the first year of the war and Catalonia for the entire conflict never managed to equal the Nationalist arms industry of Seville, Plasencia, Oviedo, La Coruña, and the Basque industry during the final year of the conflict.[113]

Nationalists similarly exceeded Republicans in agriculture and animal husbandry. Burgos authorities adopted and propagated the slogan, 'The harvest is sacred'.[114] In Cordoba, where the white terror had eliminated thousands of leftists, workers' output increased after the plunge produced during the Popular Front, and harvest output returned to 'normal'.[115] The civil war created what may have been the first significant manpower scarcity in the history of modern Spanish agriculture. By early 1937 the Nationalist zone developed a labour shortage of farm workers which raised wages in some regions. In Cordoba province, an 'illicit' bidding war over wage workers between cereal and olive farmers ensued, a struggle which the governor attempted to halt by decree.[116] He recognized 'the lack of hands' had encouraged 'the professional vagrants, who live almost exclusively in the capital, who prefer leisure to productive labour, and who survive on the wages of the weaker sex'.[117] He told the Civil Guard to register the names of those who refused wage labour, whom he would provide with employment. In Galicia and Castile, some proposed hiring Portuguese labourers; others enlisting Falange youth (the *Flechas*, or Arrows, between fifteen and eighteen years old) to work the fields.[118] Zamora province reported a shortage of 1,485 skilled and semi-skilled harvesters and an excess of 268 female and child labourers.[119] The latter – legally and illegally – were common throughout urban and especially rural Spain.[120] The elderly also had to be mobilized for the sowing season.[121] The dominant political perspective on the civil war, which has focused nearly exclusively on the repression of left-wing parties and unions, has ignored full employment and the consequent rise in the cost of wage labour. These two factors greatly contributed to relative labour passivity in the Nationalist zone.

In the countryside, those who suffered the most economic distress in the Franco zone were not the labouring proletariat – except for those labelled as 'reds' who had been killed, jailed, or exiled – but rather non-producers, such as invalids, children, and the elderly who were without subsidies or pensions and thus depended upon charity (a topic examined in Chapter 9).[122] The Nationalists did provide pensions to widows and family members of their soldiers who were killed in action.[123] Of course, Republican children and widows were not as fortunate, and a good number of the latter had to prostitute themselves to survive.[124] *Franquistas* put into effect, in their own nasty way, the Pauline paraphrase, 'Those who don't work, don't eat.'

In the Republican zone, a labour shortage also arose. Many men had been conscripted into the army; others were attracted to urban areas because of higher salaries and greater opportunities in certain trades, such as chauffeurs, who had ample occasions to engage in potentially profitable petty entrepreneurship.[125] According to male trade unionists, women of the Infantes district (Ciudad Real) 'held such deep prejudices' against wage labour that an active campaign by female militants was necessary to get them into unions and working the fields.[126] Collectives established severe controls to ensure that females performed fieldwork.[127] By early 1938 the female presence was dominant in many villages. Unions maintained discrimination against women by paying them less.

The theme of collectivization has fascinated analysts of the Republican zone, but it must be remembered that although total confiscation may have amounted to approximately one-third of arable land, only 18.5 per cent of the land in the Republican zone was collectivized.[128] Thus individualists on the land remained overwhelmingly dominant. Even in Aragon, supposedly the most revolutionary and anarchist of regions, where the CNT was often the most powerful organization, most of the land was not collectivized. Notwithstanding the presence of militias who encouraged it, only 40 per cent of the land of the region was expropriated. Whether as individuals or collectivists, peasants were reluctant not only to trade their goods for Republican script but also to provide authorities with information. Agrarians continued to feel that the political economy of the Republic discriminated against them by setting maximums on agricultural but not on industrial products. The price controls of the Republic favoured the urban masses, who had defended it when the military rebelled and remained its firmest basis of support. In contrast, the more flexible price controls of the Nationalists, which allowed farmers larger profits by assuring them that the state would purchase their wheat crop at a reasonable price, reflected their peasant base, especially in Castile. Moreover, industrial goods in the Republican zone were largely unregulated and sharply increased in price. However, the loyalty of many urban workers declined as government controls were unable to prevent the de facto rise of food costs. In June 1937, in Alicante, 'people scatter through the surrounding orchards in search of some tomatoes, some eggplants, or even cabbage. Don't even mention potatoes. Meat and eggs do not seem to exist'[129] (see Figure 8.1).

Figure 8.1 Women hoe in the Republican rearguard. AGMAV, F.45, 50/50.

Nationalist journalists boasted that their supplies of working animals greatly surpassed those of their enemy, who, they claimed, ate their beasts, including mules and horses.[130] Although repeated *ad nauseum*, the charge was quite plausible. In the Republican zone peasants often preferred to consume their quadrupeds rather than have them 'purchased' by the 'red' militias or the Popular Army in exchange for useless vouchers (*vales*). Nationalists claimed – with much validity – that the 'Marxists' had slaughtered 'thousands and thousands of head of livestock' in the first few months of the war.[131] The *Junta Provincial Reguladora de Abastecimientos de Carne of Vizcaya*, an organization that controlled meat supply, reported that the number of cattle fell during Republican rule from 100,334 in July 1936 to 36,304 in July 1937.[132] Under Nationalist control, it recovered to 89,306 head. Similarly, the number of sheep declined from 97,150 before the war to 10,509 under Republican control and then rose to 97,159 under the Nationalists.

Conclusions

In sum, the Nationalists adopted pragmatic, if orthodox, monetary policies, which limited the money supply and kept inflation in check. A solid currency incentivized workers, farmers, and savers. This stability increased 'voluntary' donations and allowed heavier taxation. The Nationalists centralized political power under military control, although provincial authorities maintained considerable ability to collect revenue. The economically interventionist *franquistas* even won the cooperation of small businessmen and international capitalists. Ironically, at the end of the conflict as the Nationalists conquered the major cities, their appetite for sacrifice diminished, and they adopted less flexible price controls and counter-productive economic regulations which led to corruption and economic dysfunction reminiscent of the Republican zone.

The Republicans engaged in revolutionary anti-capitalism which alienated wealthy foreign and domestic businessmen. Many proletarians interpreted the revolution as liberation from taxes and labour. The Republic's tolerance of regional and local autonomy allowed many local and regional governments to print and mint countless amounts of currencies of different varieties. They stimulated hyperinflation and discouraged agricultural production and animal husbandry for the market. Republican governments were either unable or unwilling to tax. Their soldiers and public servants often lacked monetary incentives and proper nourishment. The different political economies help to explain the outcome of the conflict.

Further Reading

Corral, Pedro. *Desertores: La Guerra Civil que nadie quiere contar*. Barcelona: Debate, 2006.

Garzón Pareja, Manuel. *Historia de la Hacienda de España*. 2 vols. Madrid: Instituto de Estudios Fiscales, Ministerio de Economía y Hacienda, 1984.

Martín Aceña, Pablo and Elena Martínez Ruiz, eds. *La economía de la guerra civil*. Madrid: Marcial Pons, 2006.

Nonell Bru, Salvador. *El Laureado Tercio de Requetés de Nuestra Señora de Montserrat*. Madrid: Comunión Tradicionalista Carlista, 1992.

Sánchez Asiaín, José Ángel. *La financiación de la guerra civil española*. Barcelona: Crítica, 2012.

Sánchez Recio, Glicerio and Julio Tascón Fernández, eds. *Los empresarios de Franco: Política y economía en España, 1936-1957*. Barcelona: Crítica, 2003.

Serrallonga, Joan, Manuel Santirso, and Just Casa. *Vivir en Guerra: La zona leal a la República (1936-1939)*. Barcelona: Edicions UAB, 2013.

Notes

1   Memoria, Ávila, August 1938, 44/2790, Archivo General de la Administración [hereafter AGA].

2   Angel Viñas, *El oro de Moscú: Alfa y omega de un mito franquista* (Barcelona: Grijalbo, 1979), 218–27.

3   John R. Hubbard, 'How Franco Financed His War', *The Journal of Modern History* 25, no. 4. (December 1953): 394.

4   Pablo Martín Aceña, 'La quiebra del sistema financiero', in *La economía de la guerra civil*, ed. Pablo Martín Aceña and Elena Martínez Ruiz (Madrid: Marcial Pons, 2006), 402.

5   Eugenio Torres Villanueva, 'Los empresarios: entre la revolución y colaboración', in Aceña and Martínez, *La economía*, 448.

6   Torres Villanueva, 'Los empresarios', 437–9.

7   José Ángel Sánchez Asiaín, *La financiación de la guerra civil española* (Barcelona: Crítica, 2012), 121.

8   Torres Villanueva, 'Los empresarios', 436; Nicolás Salas, *Sevilla fue la clave: República, Alzamiento, Guerra Civil (1931-39)*, 2 vols. (Seville: Castillejo, 1992), 729.

9   Juan Velarde Fuertes, 'Algunos aspectos económicos de la guerra civil', in *Revisión de la guerra civil española*, ed. Alfonso Bullón de Mendoza and Luis Eugenio Togores (Madrid: Actas, 2002), 949; Hugh Thomas, *The Spanish Civil War* (New York: Harper and Row, 1961), 273.

10 Sánchez Asiaín, *Economía*, 256.

11 Torres Villanueva, 'Los empresarios', 440.

12 Guy Hermet, *La guerre d'Espagne* (Paris: Seuil, 1989), 184.

13 Hubbard, 'How Franco Financed His War', 404.

14 Fernando Eguidazu, *Intervención monetaria y control de cambios en España, 1900-1977* (Madrid: Heroes, 1978), 157.

15 Pedro Corral, *Desertores: La Guerra Civil que nadie quiere contar* (Barcelona: Debate, 2006), 86–7.

16 Joaquín Aisa Raluy, *Diario de un miliciano republicano (1936-1939)* (Barcelona: Base, 2010), 191.

17 Antonio Elorza and Marta Bizcarrondo, *Queridos Camaradas: La Internacional Comunista y España* (Barcelona: Planeta, 1999), 443.

18 José Llordés Badía, *Al dejar el fusil: Memorias de un soldado raso en la Guerra de España* (Barcelona: Ariel, 1968), 182, 216.

19 Sánchez Asiaín, *Economía*, 17, 44, 154; *ABC Sevilla*, 18 November 1936.

20 Manuel Garzón Pareja, *Historia de la Hacienda de España*, 2 vols. (Madrid: Instituto de Estudios Fiscales, 1984), 2:1155; *El Pueblo Gallego*, 22 September 1936; *El Correo de Zamora*, 17 September 1936; *La Provincia*, 31 July 1936; Sánchez Asiaín, *Economía*, 145, 155, 156; Garzón Pareja, *Historia de la Hacienda*, 2:1156; *ABC Sevilla*, 27 March 1937; *El Pueblo Gallego*, 15 May 1937.

21 Sánchez Asiaín, *Economía*, 152.

22 Martín Aceña, 'La quiebra', in Martín Aceña, *La economía*, 411.

23 Sánchez Asiaín, *Economía*, 108, 164.

24 Miguel Martorell Linares, 'Una Guerra, Dos Pesetas', in Martín Aceña, *La economía*, 334.

25 Archivo General Militar Ávila (AGMAV), Zona Nacional (ZN), Armario (A.) 42, Legajo (L.) 2, Carpeta (C.) 2, 23 División, 3 January 1937.

26 AGMAV, Zona Roja [*sic*] (ZR), A.75, L.1,200, C.11, Orden, 9 December 1936.

27 Jose Miguel Santacreu Soler, *La crisis monetaria española de 1937* (Alicante: Universidad de Alicante, 1986), 67.

28 AGMAV, ZR, A.90, L.760, C.12, Conforme, 18 February 1937.

29 Miguel Celma, *La collectivité de Calanda, 1936-1938*, (Paris: CNT Région parisienne, 1997), 64.

30 Gaston Leval, *Collectives in the Spanish Revolution*, trans. Vernon Richards (London: Freedom, 1975), 141–2; Agustin Souchy Bauer, *With the Peasants of Aragon*, trans. Abe Bluestein (Orkney: Cienfuegos, 1982), 55, 84.

31 Georg Simmel, 'Money in Modern Culture', *Theory, Culture, and Society* 8, no. 3 (August 1991), 18.

32 Gianfranco Poggi, *Money and the Modern Mind* (Berkeley: University of California Press, 1993), 152.

33 AGMAV, ZR, reel 93, Las operaciones de Teruel, 25 February 1938; Manuel Azaña, *Obras completas*, 4 vols., (Madrid, 1990), 3:520; Juan Sardá, 'El Banco de España (1931-1962)', in *El Banco de España: Una historia económica*, ed. Alfonso Moreno Redondo (Madrid: Banco de España, 1970), 448.

34 Banco de España, *Los billetes del Banco de España, 1782-1979* (Madrid: Banco de España, 1979), 298.

35 Laurie Lee, *A Moment of War: A Memoir of the Spanish Civil War* (London: Penguin, 1991), 85–115.

36 Salvador Nonell Bru, *El Laureado Tercio de Requetés de Nuestra Señora de Montserrat* (Barcelona: Comunión Tradicionalista Carlista, 1992), 106.

37 Sánchez Asiaín, *Economía*, 146.

38 *The Times* quoted in Gabriel Tortella and José Luis García Ruiz, 'Banca y política durante el primer franquismo', in *Los empresarios de Franco: Política y economía en España, 1936-1957*, ed. Glicerio Sánchez Recio and Julio Tascón Fernández (Barcelona: Crítica, 2003), 68.

39 Sánchez Asiaín, *Economía*, 90, 175.

40 Informe colectivo, la banca privada y cajas de ahorro, Burgos, August 1938, 44/2790, AGA.

41 Ricardo de la Cierva, *Historia ilustrada de la Guerra civil española* (Barcelona: Danae, 1977), 2 vols. 2:10; Antonio Olmedo Delgado and José Cuesta Monereo, *General Queipo de Llano: Aventura y audacia*, (Barcelona: AHR, 1957), 138; Ian Gibson, *Queipo de Llano: Sevilla, verano de 1936 (Con las charlas radiofónicas completas)*, (Barcelona: Grijalbo, 1986), 378.

42 Informe colectivo, la banca privada y cajas de ahorro, Burgos, August 1938, 44/2790, AGA.

43 Memoria, Pontevedra, 1939, 44/3122, AGA.

44 Memoria, Álava, 1938, 44/2790, AGA.

45 *El Pueblo Gallego*, 8 November 1936; Informe colectivo, la banca privada y cajas de ahorro, Burgos, August 1938, 44/2790, AGA.

46 Sánchez Asiaín, *Economía*, 242, 246, 288. On industrial price controls, see Jordi Catalan, 'Guerra e industria en las dos Españas, 1936-1939', in Martín Aceña, *La economía*, 191.

47 *ABC Sevilla*, 24 June 1938.

48 Ibid., 26 March 1938; *El Pueblo Gallego*, 2 April 1939.

49 *ABC Sevilla*, 24 June 1938, 24 August 1938.

50 SNT, Palencia, 27 October 1938, 61/13502, AGA.

51 SNT, Jefatura Provincial, León, 28 October 1938, Interior, 61/13500, AGA.

52 *El Pueblo Gallego*, 30 August 1938.

53 *ABC Sevilla*, 18 May 1938, 20 [?] June 1938.

54 Ibid., 10 May 1938.

55 Sánchez Asiaín, *Economía*, 149, 253.

56 Ibid., 149; Elena Martínez Ruiz, 'Las relaciones económicas internacionales: Guerra, política y negocios', in Martín Aceña, *La economía*, 300; Hubbard, 'How Franco Financed His War', 394; Borja de Riquer i Permanyer, *L'últim Cambó (1936-1947): La dreta catalanista davant la guerra civil i el primer franquismo* (Vic: Eumo, 1996), 182; Garzón Pareja, *Historia de la Hacienda*, 2:1152.

57 *La Provincia,* 10 April 1937.

58 *ABC Sevilla*, 25 August 1936.

59 Ibid., 9 October 1937.

60 Ibid., 13 January 1938.
61 Sánchez Asiaín, *Economía*, 95.
62 Martínez Ruiz, 'Las relaciones económicas internacionales', in Martín Aceña, *La economía*, 280.
63 Ibid., 279, 302; Hubbard, 'How Franco Financed His War', 398.
64 Martínez Ruiz, 'Las relaciones económicas internacionales', in Martín Aceña, *La economía*, 303.
65 *ABC Sevilla*, 21 March 1937.
66 Ibid., 27 October 1938; Hugo García, *Mentiras necesarias: La batalla por la opinión británica durante la Guerra Civil* (Madrid: Biblioteca Nueva, 2008), 14.
67 Nonell Bru, *El Laureado Tercio*, 539.
68 Ibid.
69 See Sánchez Asiaín, *Economía*, 136.
70 Ibid., 167.
71 Frank Thomas, *Brother against Brother: Experiences of a British Volunteer in the Spanish Civil War*, ed. Robert Stradling (Phoenix Mill: Sutton, 1998), 104.
72 Garzón Pareja, *Historia de la Hacienda*, 2:1148-9; Hubbard, 'How Franco Financed His War', 393; Martorell Linares, 'Una Guerra', 378; Velarde Fuertes, 'Algunos aspectos', 957; Michael Seidman, *The Victorious Counterrevolution: The Nationalist Effort in the Spanish Civil War* (Madison, WI: University of Wisconsin Press, 2011), 122-36.
73 Garzón Pareja, *Historia de la Hacienda*, 2:1151-53; Velarde Fuertes, 'Algunos aspectos', 956-9.
74 Martínez Ruiz, 'Las relaciones económicas internacionales', 274; Gabriel Cardona and Juan Carlos Losada, *Aunque me tires el puente: Memoria oral de la Batalla del Ebro* (Madrid: Aguilar, 2004), 332; Martorell Linares, 'Una Guerra', 382.
75 Garzón Pareja, *Historia de la Hacienda*, 2:1163.
76 Torres Villanueva, 'Los empresarios', 440; *ABC Sevilla*, 15 December 1936; Ángel Viñas, *La Soledad de la República: El abandono de las democracias y el viraje hacia la Unión Soviética* (Barcelona: Crítica, 2006), 135.
77 Martorell Linares, 'Una Guerra', 382.
78 Velarde Fuertes, 'Algunos aspectos', 961-3.
79 *El Pueblo Gallego*, 2 April 1939; *El Correo de Zamora*, 18 June 1939.
80 *El Correo de Zamora*, 29 February 1939; *La Provincia*, 7 March 1939.
81 *El Pueblo Gallego*, 2 March 1939.
82 *La Nueva España*, 30 November 1937.
83 Ibid., 11 December 1938.
84 Ibid., 16 December 1937.
85 Martorell Linares, 'Una Guerra', 358-61; Javier Cervera Gil, *Ya sabes mi paradero: La guerra civil a través de las cartas de los que vivieron* (Barcelona: Planeta, 2005), 305; Memoria, Granada, 1938, 44/2791, AGA.
86 Garzón Pareja, *Historia de la Hacienda*, 2:1133.
87 *ABC Sevilla*, 15 February 1939.
88 Joan Serrallonga, Manuel Santirso, and Just Casa, *Vivir en Guerra: La zona leal a la República (1936-1939)* (Barcelona: Edicions UAB, 2013), 43, 67.
89 CNT carteros, 26 February 1938, Madrid 2321, Archivo Histórico Nacional-Sección Guerra Civil, [hereafter AHN-SGC].
90 *Claridad*, 15 March 1937.
91 CNT carteros, 4 January 1938, Madrid 2321, AHN-SGC.

92   Acta, Comités de control de *El Liberal y Heraldo de Madrid*, 16 August 1937, Madrid 834, AHN-SGC.

93   CNT carteros, 29 April 1938, Madrid 2321, AHN-SGC.

94   James Matthews, *Reluctant Warriors: Republican Popular Army and Nationalist Army Conscripts in the Spanish Civil War, 1936-1939* (Oxford: Oxford University Press, 2012), 117.

95   Matthews, *Reluctant Warriors*, 123.

96   Cited in Enrique Moradiellos, *1936: Los mitos de la Guerra Civil* (Barcelona: Península, 2004), 127.

97   Raluy, *Diario*, 29.

98   Ibid., 30.

99   *Hoy*, January 1938.

100 Actas, 26 December 1937, PS Madrid 2467, AHN-SGC; Actas, 26 December 1937, PS Madrid 2467, AHN-SGC.

101 George Orwell, *Homage to Catalonia* (New York: Harcourt Brace Jovanovich, 1980), 6.

102 Sánchez Asiaín, *Economía*, 77; Catalan, 'Guerra e industria', 198; Velarde Fuertes, 'Algunos aspectos', 957.

103 Catalan, 'Guerra e industria', 199.

104 *ABC Sevilla*, 21 and 29 December 1938.

105 The following is based on Oviedo, 1938, 44/2791, AGA.

106 Sánchez Asiaín, *Economía*, 85; *ABC Sevilla*, 14 and 19 January 1938.

107 *La Nueva España*, 28 October 1937.

108 Sánchez Asiaín, *Economía*, 83. *ABC Sevilla*, 23 June 1938, gives different figures: Iron ore production in Vizcaya rose from 30,000 tons during the final months of Republican control to 137,000 tons in December 1937 and then to 170,000 tons in the spring of 1938.

109 Sánchez Asiaín, *Economía*, 84.

110 Gobierno Civil de León, Memoria, August 1938, 44/2791, AGA.

111 *ABC Sevilla*, 25 August 1936.

112 Adam Tooze, *The Wages of Destruction: The Making and Breaking of the Nazi Economy* (New York: Viking, 2006), 418.

113 Gabriel Cardona, *Historia militar de una guerra civil: Estrategia y tácticas de la guerra de España* (Barcelona: Flor de Viento, 2006), 246.

114 *El Correo de Zamora*, 26 May 1937.

115 *ABC Sevilla*, 28 November 1936.

116 Ibid., 30 November 1937.

117 Ibid., 3 December 1937.

118 *El Pueblo Gallego*, 10 June 1937.

119 *El Correo de Zamora*, 5 June 1937.

120 *La Provincia*, 5 February 1938.

121 *El Correo de Zamora*, 12 November 1937.

122 For the post-war period, see Óscar J. Rodríguez Barreira, *Migas con miedo: Practicas de resistencia el primer franquismo. Almería, 1939-1953* (Almeria: Ediciones Universidad de Almería, 2008), 203.

123 *La Provincia,* 20 October 1938.

124 Mirta Núñez Díaz-Balart, *Mujeres Caídas: Prostitutas legales y clandestinas en el franquismo* (Madrid: Oberon, 2003), 198.

125 Acta, 13 September 1937, PS Madrid 2467, AHN-SGC.

126 Informe, nd, Madrid 2467, AHN-SGC.

127 Leval, *Collectives*, 115.
128 Stanley Payne, *The Spanish Revolution* (New York: Norton, 1970), 240–1; Luis
     Garrido González, 'Producción agraria y guerra civil', in *El sueño igualitario:*
     Campesinado y colectivización en la España republicana, ed. Julián Casanova
     (Saragossa: Instituto Fernando el Católico, 1988), 100.
129 Serrallonga, *Vivir*, 93.
130 *El Correo de Zamora*, 12 and 15 November 1937; *La Provincia*, 18 May 1938.
131 *ABC Sevilla*, 16 January and 3 September 1937; *La Nueva España*, 29 April 1937 and
     12 July 1938; Bernabe Copado, *Con la columna Redondo: Combates y conquistas,*
     crónica de guerra (Seville: Imprenta de la Gavidia, 1937), 90; Excelentísimo Señor, 5
     June 1938, Interior, 61/13500, AGA; Gobierno Civil de León, Memoria, August 1938,
     44/2791, AGA; Huesca, Memoria, 1938, 44/2791, AGA.
132 *ABC Sevilla*, 21 December 1938.

Chapter 9

SOCIAL WORK IN THE SPANISH CIVIL WAR*

Ángela Cenarro
Translated by Stephanie Wright

The Spanish Civil War sparked one of the prominent social crises of the twentieth century in the Western world. Rearguard killings, which accounted for more than 100,000 civilian victims in the rebel zone and 55,000 in Republican territory, left a trail of widows and orphans in a precarious position. Bombings, particularly those carried out by the German and Italian air forces on Republican civilians in cities such as Madrid, Guernica, and Lérida, left approximately 11,000 dead or wounded. Images of these dramatic scenes were sent around the world to draw international attention to the suffering of civilians. Their vulnerability prompted the Republican government to organize mass evacuations, either abroad or to safer locations within Spain. In addition to the bombings, fear of the approaching enemy army triggered an exodus of men, women, and children who became refugees in areas away from the front line. The fact that the rebel army generally advanced at a faster rate into areas controlled by the Republic than vice versa meant that the dire circumstances of refugees were most evident in the main cities of the loyalist rearguard, such as Madrid, Barcelona, Valencia, or Almeria.

The depth of social crisis was not equally felt by both sides. The Republic was at an advantage when the military rebels rose up on 17 July 1936. However, two factors changed this situation in a matter of weeks: the unequal military support received from international powers and the degradation of state structures, caused by the collapse of the army and state security forces at the time of the coup. Furthermore, through their control of Spain's agricultural regions, the rebels were better able to supply soldiers and civilian populations with basic commodities. The scarcity of food, combined with difficulties in transporting and distributing supplies throughout the fragmented Republican zone, only deepened the initial imbalance between both sides. It seems clear, then, that the Republican state faced much greater challenges than the rebels in terms of organization and military manpower, given the more acute social crisis in the loyalist zone and its more limited resources for tackling such issues. As will be argued in this chapter, this unequal experience of 'total war' serves to question traditional narratives of the civil war, which pit the fragmented Republic against the better-coordinated Francoist militarized state.

Rather, in both cases, the state's authority established itself progressively while demanding more and more involvement from mobilized civil society, via political organizations, trade unions, associations, juntas, or committees.

At the beginning of the Spanish Civil War international humanitarian agencies mobilized to react to the conflict. The most established agencies with prior experience of responding to armed conflicts offered their assistance to both sides. This was the case for the International Committee of the Red Cross,[1] which instituted delegations in both zones, as well as Save the Children, and the Quaker organizations.[2] Other groups emerged in support of the Republic, such as the National Joint Committee for Spanish Relief (NJCSR), which served as an umbrella organization for the manifold committees which sprang up in Britain towards the end of 1936.[3] Later on, the *Comité Internacional de Coordinación e Información para la Ayuda a la España Republicana*, or International Information and Aid Coordination Committee for the Spanish Republic, was also established to coordinate the efforts of those linked to the anti-fascist movement around the world.[4] In addition, medical aid channelled through the International Brigades facilitated the use of innovations, including blood transfusions, at the front.[5] Some initiatives supported the rebel cause, such as the Catholic, British Committee for the Relief of Spanish Distress, founded in September 1936 under the leadership of Archbishop Hinsley. The General Relief Fund for the Distressed Women and Children of Spain, established in late 1936 under the patronage of Princess Beatrice of Saxe Coburg and Gotha – first cousin of Alfonso XIII of Spain – was also clearly Francoist, despite its claim to be impartial. Much aid reached Spain via the personal connections of pro-Franco aristocrats and elites. Support also arrived via the delegations of the 'external Falange' or contact with fascist organizations in Europe. Today, it is impossible to fully weigh up the humanitarian aid received on both sides from abroad. But perceptions of the Republic's relative military weakness and political isolation generated a wave of international and inter-class solidarity, mobilized through a worldwide network of local and national aid committees which did not exist for the other side.

This chapter adopts a comparative approach in its analysis of wartime social work in the Republican and Nationalist zones. It also discusses how the two sides' social support bases engaged with attempts to provide sustenance to soldiers and civilians. As will be seen, organization of the war effort, and particularly social work, depended on the different contexts in both zones – described above – in the aftermath of the coup and the early battles. It is also important to consider the particular characteristics of the civil war's competing political projects. The need to tend to soldiers, mothers, children, and refugees opened up a space in which different actors could put forward utopian visions for the construction of the New Spain, which spoke to the ideals of the competing political cultures on the left and right of Spanish politics.

Consequently, while responding to the daily demands of soldiers or civilians suffering on the front and in the rearguard, the two sides developed medical and aid projects intended to last beyond the conflict. Paradoxically, despite communicating different political messages, many of these proposals were identical or similar on both sides. This can be explained by their common belief in the importance of state intervention in social matters.[6] And it was a response to the crisis of liberalism, as well as a characteristic of modernizing trends within Western states since the beginning of the twentieth century. The men and women who put these projects in motion in 1930s Spain, be they democrats, revolutionaries, or reactionaries, operated within this conceptual framework.

'There is No Vanguard or Rearguard in Civil War':[7] The Organization of Social Work on Both Sides

Where the military uprising triumphed, the mechanisms for providing material and spiritual aid to soldiers were set up immediately. Individual and local initiatives rapidly proliferated under the auspices of the declaration of a state of war, and therefore also the authority of the rebellious military forces, and within months evolved into institutions at the service of the emerging Francoist state. In Seville, General Queipo de Llano quickly organized these initiatives to support the needs of the army, and his contacts among the Andalusian aristocracy and upper middle classes ensured their success.[8] In other cities, such as Salamanca or Saragossa, civil juntas were created to serve the military authorities, whose members clearly had political or social links to local, anti-Republican rightist groups.[9] In every province, the rebel generals, and later the new local powers, organized various fundraising drives to finance the troops. The press published lists of donors, identified by their full names and the quantity donated to the 'national cause'. An order from the National Defence Junta dispatched on 19 August regularized the hitherto disparate income collected by 'centres, juntas and commissions', which would subsequently be collated within an open account which in January 1937 became the *Suscripción Nacional*, or 'National Donation Fund'.[10]

Social policy remained in the hands of local administrations, or private and civic initiatives. In October 1936, Franco's nascent administration, the *Junta Técnica del Estado*, or Technical State Junta, pushed a process of centralization and regularization from above and took on the function of 'collecting taxes for charitable purposes'.[11] In practice, this first implied launching a series of special contributions to support demand for aid; second, the reorganization of the provincial social welfare juntas which were presided over by the new civil governors;[12] last, the creation of a fledgling welfare administration, *Beneficencia del Gobierno del Estado Español*, or Welfare of the Spanish State Government (also known as War Welfare), led by José María Martínez Ortega, Count of Argillo. The Francoist initiatives followed on from this, such as the Charitable-Social Welfare Fund, which was financed by collections from the *Día del Plato Único*, or the One-Course Meal Day – a tax levied on restaurants from the end of October – the *Subsidio Pro-Combatiente*, or Combatants' Subsidy, which taxed certain purchases, and the *Ficha Azul*, or Blue Token, a nominally voluntary donation but which individuals often felt forced to pay given its conception as a way of demonstrating one's support for the rebel authorities. In its first collection alone, in May 1937, the scheme raised the considerable sum of more than 264,000 pesetas.[13]

Other initiatives developed alongside the emerging rebel government's bureaucracy, but were quickly subsumed by it. This was the case of *Auxilio Social*, or Social Aid, the welfare organization established by Falange. Inspired by the Nazi Winterhilfe, the scheme emerged from the most radical Falangist wing, known as *jonsism* (from Juntas de Ofensiva Nacional Sindicalista; see below), thanks to the leadership of Javier Martínez de Bedoya and Mercedes Sanz Bachiller. The latter was the provincial head of the *Sección Femenina*, or Women's Section of the Falange, and had already spent months organizing clothing and food supplies in the Francoist stronghold of Valladolid. Following a targeted collection, the pair opened a soup kitchen for children called *Auxilio de Invierno*, or 'Winter Relief', on 30 October 1936, and one for adults a few weeks later. The project's success and impact as an instrument of propaganda were factors which allowed this embryonic aid organization to gain increasing prominence.

Indeed, the Falange's dominant role during the first months of the conflict was one of the main factors which led to its prominent position within the new single party, the *Falange Española Tradicionalista y de las Juntas de Ofensiva Nacional Sindicalista* (FET y de las JONS), or Traditionalist Spanish Falange of the Committees of the National Syndicalist Offensive, under the leadership of General Franco, and created via decree on 19 April 1937. The new political entity, which became the foundational block of the Francoist 'New State', acquired semi-official functions, which helped to consolidate its political elites. This process, conceptualized by Falangist revolutionary rhetoric as 'conquering the State', in practice meant the presence of party men in key posts within the Francoist state administration. The case of *Auxilio Social* was paradigmatic. First, as the *Auxilio de Invierno*, the government privileged the organization by authorizing it to collect donations and to use these funds for its activities 'as an advance [from the state]'. In May 1937, after the Unification Decree, the organization was accredited as a national delegation of FET-JONS under the leadership of Sanz Bachiller. The following year, in February 1938, the naming of its national secretary, Martínez de Bedoya, as director general of Welfare, guaranteed the rise of *Auxilio Social* through the state administration. Martínez de Bedoya was able to secure funding for *Auxilio Social* from the *Fondo de Protección Benéfico Social*, or Social Welfare Protection Fund, create a new *Consejo Superior de Beneficencia*, or Board for Welfare, dominated by Falangists, and, finally, launch the *Servicio de Auxilio a Poblaciones Liberadas*, or Aid Service for Liberated Populations to carry out 'distributions of emergency rations' while the rebel army advanced through Republican territory.[14]

Local initiatives were therefore promptly reorganized and placed under the control of the fledgling structures of Franco's nascent government: the Technical State Junta. When a state of war was declared across rebel-held territory in late July 1936, the supreme authority of the army was formalized, which paved the way for an increasingly centralized and 'top-down' management of welfare. But the need to secure support from civilians and the population at large meant that the efforts of ordinary men and women – and the latter in particular – were channelled into certain welfare activities which will be discussed in greater detail below.

The authorities in areas where the military coup failed – notably Barcelona, Madrid, the north, and the Levante – started on an altogether different footing. Here, the divisions within the military and the forces of law and order prevented the Republican government from organizing a centralized form of resistance. The Republic's authority collapsed under such impotence. The crumbling of the main pillars of the state administration caused a power vacuum which was occupied by the workers' organizations, especially the socialist and anarchist trade unions. Their leaders and members soon formed militias and committees, which became new anti-establishment organizations capable of controlling loyalist territory. Their activities included the fast-track training of militias for the front, the organization of transport and supplies in town centres, as well as the persecution of military rebels and their social support bases. They also organized a basic welfare infrastructure, which aimed to meet the needs of the militias.

Despite this initial dispersal of efforts and the Republic's loss of authority, the state soon made up for lost ground. In a decree on 12 August 1936, the government of the Republican José Giral seized control of the welfare institutions and, following a subsequent decree on 28 August, granted anti-fascist women a monopoly over welfare efforts in the rearguard.[15] The leader of the new executive, the socialist Largo Caballero, reorganized social and medical aid through the creation of a ministry occupied from November 1936 by the anarchist leader Federica Montseny. The minister described her work as a 'reformist project in a revolutionary sense',[16] a clear example of how even the most radically anti-establishment sectors understood the need for a centralized war effort, controlled 'from above'. Although these relatively autonomous committees continued throughout the first year of war, the state was recognized as the primary organizational force behind all projects.

A *Comité Nacional de Refugiados*, or National Committee of Refugees, had been in operation since the government of Giral. This body assisted the first evacuations, especially in the Madrid area. In February 1937, given the gravity of the problem, the committee became the *Oficina Central de Evacuación y Asistencia a Refugiados* (OCEAR), or Central Office for the Evacuation and Welfare of Refugees, under the auspices of the Ministry for Health and Social Welfare. Thus, the OCEAR became a state institution charged with tackling the massive displacement of civilian populations fleeing the advancing rebel army. More specifically, it was established to deal with the exceptional situation caused by the rebel attacks on Malaga. The city's occupation in February triggered a mass exodus of inhabitants trying to escape the advancing rebel army, supported by the Italian expeditionary corps and Moroccan *Regulares* troops. As they escaped via the Almeria road, men, women, and children were subjected to bombardments from the air and from ships waiting just off the coast. More than 60,000 evacuees managed to escape, which doubled the usual population of Almeria.[17] Other provincial capitals, such as Madrid and Barcelona, also received significant numbers of refugees. Before the battle of Madrid, the population of this city had increased by 30 per cent thanks to the arrival of troops and refugees, swelling to 1,300,000 inhabitants.[18] On the eve of the 'May Days', Barcelona was home to 300,000 refugees from the north, Levant, and Andalusia. In Teruel, 12,000 people were evacuated to Valencia and Castellón following the city's occupation by Republican forces in December 1937. One year before the city's iconic battle in the winter of 1937/8, the three Levant provinces already housed 274,000 refugees[19] (see Figure 9.1).

In its first year, OCEAR came to the assistance of three million refugees. The body provided medical care, distributed clothes, created a database to help reunite separated families, and organized the transportation of children to Russia, France, and Mexico. It had at its disposal staging posts, soup kitchens, hospitals, and maternity units. The organization established a relatively decentralized structure, based around the refugee committees. This enabled it to side-step the jurisdiction of the municipal councils (the highest local authority), and thus the difficulties of dealing with local populations hostile to the arrival of refugees. News even spread of the inadequate treatment of girl refugees, who were sometimes forced to work as maids or nannies. In February 1938, the office became the *Dirección General de Evacuados y Refugiados*, or Directorate General for Evacuees and Refugees, which was presented as another step in the stable Republican government's centralizing project, and undertaken in order to meet the 'scale of the problems it faces'.[20]

The same logic applied for other entities. *Socorro Rojo*, or Red Aid, founded in Spain in 1923 as part of the international network of the same name, grew considerably following the support it provided to those persecuted after the 1934 October revolution. Its organizational flexibility, which centred on local committees, and its anti-fascist and inter-class nature, which dovetailed with the

Figure 9.1 Refugees arrive in Barcelona after fleeing from the fighting. Comisariado de Propaganda de la Generalitat de Cataluña. Biblioteca Nacional de España, Madrid, GC-TP/7.

strategy of the Popular Front, facilitated its expansion into the middle and working classes. It grew exponentially between 1935 and 1937, during which time it went from 22,000 members to 278,529 during the northern military campaign. It went on to become a fundamental pillar of the Republican military health system, for which it built 275 field hospitals complete with stretchers, ambulances, and X-ray machines.[21] Its compassionate activities were conceived as the product of 'widespread popular mobilization', in which 'workers, peasants, women, children, and soldiers' took part through rallies, membership, lectures, and assemblies. The language of anti-fascism helped to develop a discourse of unity surrounding the Republic and its administration, which was able to attract considerable support from abroad, thanks to the Coordination Committee referenced above and the *Comité Internacional de Mujeres contra la Guerra y el Fascismo*, or International Committee of Women against War and Fascism.[22]

The aid provided to soldiers and the civilian population fostered interactions between committees and organizations of different ideological ilk. Even so, the decision of anarchist *Confederación Nacional del Trabajo* (CNT), or National Confederation of Labour, to establish *Solidaridad Internacional Antifascista*, or International Antifascist Solidarity, in April 1937, reflects the persistence of rivalries within the sphere of welfare. Nonetheless, the fact that this organization and *Socorro Rojo* were able to form a joint committee to organize the 'Winter 1937 Campaign', positioned as 'the campaign of the entire Spanish population, in an active expression of national solidarity',[23] underscores how the challenges posed by 'total war' occasionally transcended the irreconcilable political divisions within the Spanish left.

'Nobody Cares for the Sick Better Than a Woman': Women and Gender Identities in Rearguard Work

Throughout the civil war, thousands of Spanish women took a leading role in the management and execution of a broad range of welfare activities. This was nothing new on a European scale; during the First World War, women made a significant contribution to their respective national war efforts. After the Great War, the continent went through a period of marked exaltation of the nation-state, in part in order to overcome the trauma of the conflict, and the increasing presence of women in education, work, and formal politics was simultaneously accompanied by a return to traditional symbolism surrounding motherhood.[24] In Spain, the Second Republic, founded in 1931 recognized for the first time the equality of all citizens before the law irrespective of their gender, as well as women's right to vote. However, the nature of both the left and the right's mobilization of women drew on notions of gender identity constructed around a binary understanding of gender difference: domestic and maternal roles continued to underpin ideals of femininity during the 1930s.[25]

As a result, when the war began, the experiences of women on both sides were determined by certain understandings of femininity which were noticeably similar.[26] The maternal ideal encouraged the persistence of certain gender conventions which, in the context of war, were reframed and took on a new political dimension. The mobilization of women in the public sphere, though limited to roles as caregivers such as nurses or campaigners for social rights, eroded the traditional separation of public and private spheres.[27]

In the rebel zone, the *Sección Femenina* monopolized the mobilization of women. This organization emerged in June 1934 under the leadership of Pilar Primo de Rivera, sister of José Antonio, the founder of the Falange. At its inception, the aim of *Sección Femenina* was to support male Falangists who, as a result of their violent activism, had been arrested or imprisoned. Though the activities of the organization were limited to prison visits and supporting the families of those imprisoned, this experience sent significant numbers of women into the public and political realms. In the Republican zone, the *Comisión de Auxilio Femenino* (CAF), or Commission of Women's Aid, loosely represented female anti-fascists. The CAF was a delegation of the *Comité Nacional de Mujeres contra la Guerra y el Fascismo*, or National Committee of Women against the War and Fascism, given exclusive recognition by the Giral government to perform this task.[28] Among other activities, the CAF organized a clothes repository and a dressmaking workshop in Madrid during the summer of 1936.[29] This response to the civil war was presented as a continuation of the kind of work it had undertaken since its inception, notably supporting persecuted comrades, their families, and children who had been left orphaned or destitute following the repression of the 1934 October revolution in Asturias. The care provided from August 1936 in the *Hogar Pro Infancia Obrera*, or Home for the Children of Workers, which looked after the children and orphans of militiamen and soldiers in the former Madrid Orphanage, had been one of CAF's first activities. In this way, the archetype of female identity, which linked women to caregiving work, was soon resurrected in opposition to the idealized figure of the militiawoman, which had emerged as a symbol of the war and the revolution immediately after the military coup.[30]

During the summer and autumn of 1936, Pilar Primo de Rivera tried to coordinate and expand the work of her members to collect donations, search for support among local powerbrokers, produce clothing for the troops, and support the activities of *Auxilio de Invierno*. After the Unification Decree of April 1937, female management of social welfare was formalized. The *Sección Femenina* organized a division of washerwomen, as well as a corps of nurses, while managing 580,000 female members, more than half of which were mobilized in different services.[31] Out of these, 300,000 worked within *Auxilio Social*, under the leadership of Sanz Bachiller. Many others – though the figures are unclear – worked in the *Delegación de Asistencia a Frentes y Hospitales*, or Delegation for Assistance to the Fronts and Hospitals, the relatively autonomous Carlist initiative, led first by María Rosa Urraca Pastor, and, from July 1938, by Casilda Ampuero. *Frentes y Hospitales'* activities centred around care for soldiers, fundraising through charitable fairs, the distribution of food and clothing, as well as work within the military hospitals and *Hogares del Combatiente*, or 'Combatant Homes', where servicemen could rest if they had nowhere else to go. They also spread Catholic propaganda and, for example, coordinated the 'altar and worship service' so that military chaplains could hold mass while on campaign. The care which these 'selfless and brave *margaritas*' provided to soldiers was described in no uncertain terms: 'How many times have we seen amongst the bustle and cheers of locals and outsiders the moving sight of the combatant with the *margarita* by his side, sewing up those army uniforms, shabby from such hard battle!'[32]

In October 1937, the *Cuerpo de Damas Enfermeras Españolas*, or Corps of Spanish Nurses was created within the *Sección Femenina*, which sent 8,000 female volunteers into military hospitals after a fast-track specialist training course organized by the Falangist delegation for Health. The volunteers remained under the authority of the Inspectorate General for Female Hospital Services, managed by the nurse Mercedes Milá Nolla. The Inspectorate formed part of the Military Health infrastructure, in which 12,000 women participated as 'lady assistants'.[33] Around the same time, the junta in charge of *Auxilio Social* made a decision which would affect a great number of Spaniards: the creation of social service. This was a kind of female civilian service, in which all women between the ages of seventeen and thirty-five were obliged to undertake a period of unpaid social work. This ruling made it compulsory for thousands of women to support the war effort in hospitals, soup kitchens, centres for refugees from the 'red zone', and 'emergency' distributions of food in areas recently 'liberated' by the army.

Where the coup had failed, significant numbers of women had enrolled in the armed militias in the early stages of the war, a period defined by the crumbling of state structures and the territorial control of the workers' committees. But after a few weeks, the message communicated to Spaniards was 'men to the front, women to work'. This motto was shared by the government and by the main women's organizations, the *Agrupación de Mujeres Antifascistas* (AMA), or Association of Antifascist Women, and the anarchofeminist *Mujeres Libres*, or Free Women, who ensured that female contributions to the war effort fitted into hegemonic gender discourses for the defence of the Republic at war. The new feminine ideal was that of the working woman, who, through her activities in the factories, welfare centres, tailoring workshops, and hospitals, carried out work which was crucial to victory at the front. The training needed for such roles led to the establishment of different political initiatives. One such initiative was the *Casal de la Dona Treballadora*, or House of the Working Woman, set up by *Mujeres Libres* in Catalonia. Here a programme was established to train women for work in the war industries, as well as other centres, which attracted 911 students under the guidance of the anarchist doctor, and founder of the organization, *Amparo Poch i Gascón*.[34] In June 1938, the demands of the war effort led to the reorganization of the CAF and the intensification of its activities. These anti-fascist women took advantage of this change to 'ask for official support for women who work in the war industry, and their children'.[35]

Even workers' organizations lauded nurses, who embodied more than anyone the normative feminine ideal, as a model to aspire to.[36] As fighters at the front, they argued, women could carry out 'magnificent' work, but this was not what they should be doing: 'Nobody cares for the sick better than a woman; her exquisite delicateness and selflessness places her on a superior plane to the best male nurses in the world.'[37] High demand led to the organization of training courses, some of which were in collaboration with the AMA. Similarly, the government facilitated official recognition of women's qualifications through the army's distribution of certificates which were considered equivalent to those emitted by the Ministry of Public Education's centres.[38] During the National Conference of *Mujeres Libres*, which took place in spring 1938, delegates insisted on the need to mobilize several teams of nurses to the hospitals in the front and rearguard.[39]

The feminine contribution to the war effort had certain social and cultural implications. Although it is possible to presume that all cases of work in the public sphere empowered women, the meaning of such work differed on either side of the front. This was due to the different natures of both political projects, and the different social profiles of the women who were mobilized. The way in which these women perceived themselves depended, in large part, on their class identities. In the rebel zone, many upper-class women worked in front-line hospitals, such as the Larios sisters, who worked as nurses during the battle of Brunete,[40] or María Rosa Urraca Pastor, on the Somosierra front, even though they frequently painted the 'front lines' as a symbolically masculine space.[41] Their activities were imbued with new ideas of sacrifice, selflessness, and service, which they shared with their male colleagues, given that these tropes were characteristic of Falangist rhetoric. Even the activities of nurses, a feminine ideal which epitomized gender normativity and service to the cause, became imbued with a form of 'heroism' which was typical of hegemonic masculine traits, such as bravery and courage. These connotations presented Falangists as exceptional women, which legitimized their privileged position within the Francoist New State.

In the Republican zone, the return to a conventional understandings of gender was compatible with the demands of an active female citizenship. In the end – as was argued in rallies and publications – given that fascism used the submission of women to enslave the popular masses, women should help to defend democratic liberties. Such liberties were depicted as the only ones which would guarantee 'the defence of [your] interests and [your] children'.[42] The Republic at war crystallized a model of femininity which combined the complete incorporation of women into public life – through their participation in trade unions, education, and work – with a symbolic, maternal role. The communist leader Dolores Ibárruri, *Pasionaria*, embodied this new ideal, and extolled the virtues of women working in factories and workshops as much as those who worked in hospitals, who she conceptualized as 'the mothers of heroes'.[43] Calls for the mobilization of women continued throughout the war, because it was understood that the mobilization and training of women, as well as their work in the rearguard, was as imperative for the Republican victory as it was for the nurturing of a particular understanding of democratic citizenship.[44]

The Civil War and the Meanings of the New Spain

Social work provided a space in which to articulate a new vision for politics and society. The discourse and activities of social work organizations aimed to construct a new order, which meant they were closely linked to the competing sides' differing conceptualizations of the individual, society, and the nation. Although both sides instituted projects that were expected to last beyond the end of the fighting, only one of the two visions could endure beyond an eventual victory in the war.

For the Nationalists, the individual was conceptualized as part of a hierarchical national community. In contrast, on the Republican side, social welfare was linked to a humanistic and dignifying vision of human beings, which aimed to create a 'new man'. This idea descended from the rationalist enlightenment tradition, based on an understanding of the individual as a free subject which was essential to the construction of a new, more equal society. However, this notion of individual liberty was strongly linked to the perception that the Republic was in grave danger, and that it was necessary to defend and fortify it. The 'people' – the collective subject which underpinned the Republican political project – was invoked far more frequently than the individual, given that the latter could not be understood in isolation from the radically new community being created. Speeches insisted that caregiving was a way of dignifying human beings, and that welfare was the sphere in which it was most possible to show solidarity, and to carry out 'rehabilitating, … reconstructing and … moralizing work in favour of human relationships'. Welfare was the responsibility of 'all people, for the people', which could group together 'with its fertile work the whole, wide family of Spanish democracy, all good-hearted people no matter their inclination'.[45]

The proposals of both Republicans and Francoists drew on modernizing trends in the disciplines of health and social welfare, as well as preventative 'social medicine' from the 1930s conceived as a means to regenerate society.[46] This was the main driving force behind both sides' projects and activities, which shall now be addressed in greater detail.

It is undeniable that children were of particular concern in the loyalist zone. This was the group which, as a particularly vulnerable victim of fascist attacks, especially bombardments, embodied like no other the wickedness of the Republic's enemies. All measures taken to protect children must be understood within the context of child welfare developments during the preceding decades.[47] Very early on in the war, plans were made to evacuate children from Madrid to camps elsewhere in Spain or abroad. Organized by the Ministry for Public Education through the *Delegación Central de Colonias*, or Central Delegation of Colonies, created in March 1937, such camps were located in areas far from the front, and even in the south of France. A report written by Regina Lago, Delegate for Evacuated Children based in Paris, detailed the existence of 160 camps in Aragón, Levant, and Catalonia hosting 8,652 children.[48] Other regional governments also made their own arrangements, such as the Generalitat of Catalonia, which welcomed 6,000 children mainly from Madrid and Aragón through its organization *Ajut Infantil de Retaguarda*, or Rearguard Aid to Children.[49] Similarly, the Council of

Aragón established camps in the Pyrenees in the province of Huesca. Evacuations of children abroad were more controversial. Mainly managed by OCEAR, 33,000 children were evacuated to countries such as Great Britain, Mexico, France, Belgium, and the Soviet Union.[50]

Children were also the target of social hygiene and eugenic measures, developed in the preceding decades and closely linked to new understandings of motherhood. Women and children became the main focus of Republican social work projects during the war because both were 'the favourite target of the sadistic legions of the Spanish faction'.[51] Worthy of note were plans drawn up by the anarchists, whose understanding of the body, its relationship with nature, and free maternal and sexual desire formed an intrinsic part of their revolutionary project. Although the Generalitat of Catalonia legalized abortion and created specialist clinics, the practice went generally unregulated during the war. Abortion did not even occupy a central role within the wartime Republican project. Motherhood was, however, of concern to the Republic, as exemplified by the establishment of the Vélez-Málaga and Fuente Podrida houses in Cuenca as part of the measures taken to guarantee the health of mothers and children before, during, and after birth. Specialist courses were set up by the Pediatric School in Valencia,[52] which kept women up-to-date with the latest advancements in childcare and health. In the House of Maternity Centre in Barcelona, led by the anarchist Áurea Cuadrado, women were educated in 'psychobiology' in an attempt to tackle misconceptions, to prevent the abandonment of children 'raised without love and mother's milk', and to 'strengthen the foundations of the new society'.[53] In contrast to the anarchists, who worked towards a new social order, political Republican discourses underscored the importance of regeneration, and the reproduction of the nation, as well as the important role to be played by women as mothers. The raising of 'strong children', derived from the 'wellbeing of the nation', would forge 'a new generation in response to the sacrifice that we are making today'.[54] Women would acquire 'a sense of responsibility as women and as mothers ... [through] their role in the new order of things established socially by the Republican government'.[55]

The Republic's position on prostitution – abolished in 1935 – was particularly novel. The practice had been the subject of discreet debate in social hygiene and sexual reformist circles in the years leading up to the war. During her mandate, Federica Montseny attempted to establish a 'Liberators from Prostitution' project, led by the *Mujeres Libres* group, which aimed to morally and medically rehabilitate women through training and employment. But the difficult context in which the project passed through the Ministry of Health impeded its successful inauguration. The Republican government was more concerned with fighting venereal disease, which posed a threat to soldiers given the increased demand for prostitution in wartime. Consequently, the government's priority was to organize preventative campaigns using posters and pamphlets, and to treat the infected in hospitals and anti-venereal dispensaries.[56]

No such scheme existed on the Francoist side, where the realities of both abortion and prostitution were hushed up. After the war, prostitution was legalized and prostitutes were placed under the control of the Catholic Church via the *Patronato de Protección de la Mujer*, or Board for the Protection of Women. During the war, the rebels focused their attention on medical care for mothers and infants, which were key to the social work model of *Auxilio Social*. The foundations were laid for the establishment of a network of maternity and children's homes, which only became a reality in the immediate post-war period. In 1939, there were nearly 3,000 children's soup kitchens, more than 1,500 ordinary soup kitchens, and 25 homes which, in total, cared for over one million adults and children in need.[57] While producing children for the homeland was depicted as women's natural duty, the nascent Francoist state also promoted a form of 'conscious motherhood', which drew on the ideas of the liberal doctor, Gregorio Marañón. According to this concept, women should acquire the knowledge and lifestyle appropriate for the raising of children. As well as leaving their jobs – which were only suitable for unmarried women – mothers should be educated with regard to the correct forms of nutrition, education, and childcare. Professional maternity services provided channels through which motherhood could be rendered compatible with modernity in Francoist Spain. Convalescence camps for mothers, domestic help 'squads', and the promotion of breastfeeding were similar ways of achieving this aim. In a bid to reduce the reliance on wet nurses, plans were even made to create 'lactariums', in which mothers could sell their milk in exchange for a small sum of money. The 'social nurses' of the Falange, a form of nursing developed in the 1930s at the peak of social medicine, became agents of the state who advised women on health and nutritional matters. While not all of these projects came to fruition, they reflect the medico-care anxieties of the Francoists.[58]

As was to be expected for a state with imperial ambitions which emulated those of Fascist Italy and Germany, the rebel side soon expressed the need to reach 40 million Spaniards. The eugenicist concern of the Francoists to create a strong, healthy national community matched this objective. In this context, as in the early years of the post-war, pronatalism became a policy sanctioned by Catholic welfare initiatives, and entirely compatible with Falangist ambitions such as the Family Subsidy of 1938.

Conclusions

The military coup against the Republic presented an enormous welfare challenge, as pre-existing charitable-care structures were affected unequally in areas where the insurrection succeeded and failed. But on both sides, the context of 'total war' and deep social crisis created a demand for new welfare structures. In the summer of 1936, local juntas and committees met the population's most immediate needs. However, from autumn, the mechanisms of the state began to rebuild themselves, to regulate local initiatives, and to launch new ones of their own. Throughout the war, however, civil society continued to play an important role in welfare provision through committees, civil juntas, and political organizations, such as the Falange and Popular Front. The latter also channelled social work efforts through horizontal, anti-fascist solidarity networks. In this way, the tension between state control and civilian participation 'from below' mobilized by the war effort, continued in varying degrees throughout the conflict.

Social work was also a space for female empowerment within the confines of traditional gender roles, which linked women to care work. Women sustained the war effort with their work in soup kitchens, children's homes, refugee evacuations, and, most importantly, as nurses in front and rearguard hospitals. Such work, which conformed to conventional understandings of femininity, took on new meaning when carried out in support of their respective political projects. Social work either became the expression of Republican citizenship or epitomized the central role 'exceptional women' were to play in Francoism's 'New Spain'; in both cases their identity as women was recast by this collective experience in the public sphere.

Finally, pre-civil war debates on state intervention in social matters informed provisions put in place during the war for vulnerable groups, such as women, children, and refugees. All social work initiatives served to establish the foundations of a new social order. In the reconceptualization of the nation prompted by the civil war, motherhood and the protection of children – understood with reference to eugenicist and social medicine debates of previous decades – occupied a particularly central role.

Further Reading

Anderson, Peter. 'The Struggle over the Evacuation to the United Kingdom and Repatriation of Basque Refugee Children in the Spanish Civil War: Symbols and Souls'. *Journal of Contemporary History* 52, no. 1 (2017): 297–318.

Branciforte, Laura. *El Socorro Rojo Internacional (1923-1939). Relatos de la solidaridad antifascista*. Madrid: Biblioteca Nueva, 2011.

Cenarro, Ángela. *La sonrisa de Falange: Auxilio Social en la guerra civil y la posguerra*. Barcelona: Crítica, 2006.

El exilio de los niños, ed. Alicia Alted, Roger González and María Jesús Millán. Madrid: Ediciones Sinsentido, 2003.

Escrivá Moscardó, Cristina, and Rafael Maestre Marín. *De las negras bombas a las doradas naranjas. Colonias escolares* 1936-1939. Valencia: L'Eixam Edicions, 2011.

Graham, Helen. *The Spanish Republic at War*. Cambridge: Cambridge University Press, 2002.

Nash, Mary. *Defying Male Civilization*. Women in the Spanish Civil War. Denver, CO: Arden Press, 1995.

Notes

*   This work was undertaken with the Spanish government research project MINECO/ FEDER HAR2015-63624-P.
1   Juan Carlos Clemente, *Historia de la Cruz Roja Española* (Madrid: Cruz Roja Española, 1990), 155–69.

2   Gabriel Pretus, *La ayuda humanitaria en la Guerra Civil española (1936-1939)* (Granada: Comares, 2015).

3   Jim Fyrth, *The Signal was Spain. The Spanish Aid Movement in Britain, 1936-1939* (London: Lawrence and Wishart, 1986).

4   Coordination et d'Information pour l'Aide a l'Espagne républicaine, *Aidez l'Espagne! Conférence Internationale de Paris. 16-17 Janvier 1937. Pour l'aide aux blessés, aux veuves, aus orphelins, aux réfugiés de l'Espagne republicaine*, París, 1937. Ione Rodhes, 'Con la España republicana en el corazón', *Migraciones y Exilios* 5 (2004): 107–12.

5   Linda Palfreeman, *Spain Bleeds: The Development of Battlefield Blood Transfusion during the Civil War* (Brighton: Sussex, 2015).

6   *La ciudadanía social en España. Los orígenes históricos*, ed. Miguel Ángel Cabrera (Santander: Ediciones Universidad de Cantabria, 2013).

7   'Manifiesto a las mujeres españolas', *Mujeres. Portavoz de las mujeres antifascistas*, 30 September 1936.

8   Michael Seidman, *La victoria nacional. La eficacia contrarrevolucionaria en la Guerra Civil* (Madrid: Alianza, 2012), 151–2.

9   Ángel Alcalde Fernández, *Lazos de sangre. Los apoyos sociales a la sublevación militar en Zaragoza. La Junta Recaudatoria Civil (1936-1939)* (Saragossa: Institución Fernando el Católico, 2010).

10 Francisco Comín Comín and Miguel Martorell Linares, *La hacienda pública en el franquismo. La guerra y la autarquía (1936-1959)* (Madrid: Instituto de Estudios Fiscales, 2013), 44–7. During the war, the 'National Levy' amassed 120,000 million pesetas, in José Antonio Sánchez Asiaín, *La financiación de la Guerra Civil española. Una aproximación histórica* (Barcelona, Crítica, 2012), 719.

11 Comín Comín and Martorell Linares, *La hacienda pública*, 49 and 86.

12 Orden del Gobernador General, Francisco Fermoso, del 22 de octubre de 1936. *BOE*, 26-10-1936.

13 Comín Comín and Martorell Linares, *La hacienda pública*, 88–9. Ángela Cenarro, *La sonrisa de Falange. Auxilio Social en la guerra civil y la posguerra* (Barcelona: Crítica, 2006), 52.

14 Cenarro, *La sonrisa de Falange*, 1–13.

15 *Gaceta de Madrid*, 15 August 1936 and 29 August 1936 respectively.

16 Federica Montseny, *Mi experiencia en el Ministerio de Sanidad y Asistencia Social* (Valencia: Comisión de Propaganda y Prensa del Comité Nacional de la CNT, 1937), 13.

17 *Primer Congreso Popular de la Solidaridad. Celebrado los días 26 y 27 de Marzo de 1938* (Almeria: Secretaría de Agitación y Propaganda, 1938), 9.

18 Helen Graham, *La República española en guerra, 1936-1939* (Barcelona: Debate, 2006), 209.

19 Antonio Peiró Arroyo, *¡Evacuad Teruel! La odisea de 12.000 turolenses durante la Guerra Civil* (Saragossa: Editorial Comuniter, 2012), 215.

20 *OCEAR*, 2, 1 September 1937 and 8 (1938).

21 Laura Branciforte, *El Socorro Rojo Internacional (1923-1939). Relatos de la solidaridad antifascista* (Madrid: Biblioteca Nueva, 2011), 232.

22 The 'broad and popular mobilization' is from *Conferencia Nacional de la Solidaridad. 1 y 2 de noviembre de 1938. Normas para activistas* (Madrid, Socorro Rojo de España, 1938). The support of 'ten million antifascist women', from different European countries via the International Committee of Women against War and Fascism is from *¡Pueblos del mundo! Ayudar a España es ayudaros a vosotros mismos. Cuarto punto*

de la Conferencia Nacional de la Solidaridad, 1 y 2 de noviembre de 1938 (Madrid: Socorro Rojo de España, 1938).

23 *Memoria de la Campaña de Invierno* (Barcelona: Comisión Ejecutiva (SIA-SRI) de la Comisión Nacional Pro Campaña de Invierno, 1938), 6.

24 Karen Offen, *Feminismos europeos, 1700-1950. Una historia política* (Madrid: Akal, 2015), 357–69.

25 Mary Nash, 'Género y ciudadanía', *Ayer*, 20 (1995): 241–58.

26 Ángela Cenarro, 'Movilización femenina para la guerra total: un ejercicio comparativo', *Historia y Política* 16 (2006): 159–82.

27 This idea has been developed in Mary Nash, *Rojas. Las mujeres republicanas en la Guerra Civil* (Madrid: Taurus, 1999).

28 Encarnación Fuyola, *Mujeres antifascistas, su trabajo y su organización* (s. l.: Ediciones de las Mujeres Antifascistas, 1936), 6.

29 *Mujeres: Portavoz de las Mujeres Antifascistas*, 10, 15/10/1936, and 11, 22/10/1936.

30 Nash, *Rojas*, 90–9.

31 *Historia y Misión* (Madrid: Sección Femenina de FET-JONS, 1951), 20.

32 *Delegación Provincial de Asistencia al Frente y Hospitales. Navarra* (no author, 1939), 22.

33 Mercedes Milá Nolla, 'La mujer en la Guerra: enfermeras', *Los médicos y la medicina en la Guerra Civil española* (Madrid: Saned, 1986), 303–8.

34 *Mujeres Libres*, 12, mayo de 1938.

35 *Comisión de Auxilio Femenino del Ministerio de Defensa Nacional de la República Española* (Barcelona: Comité Nacional de Mujeres Antifascistas, 1938). Nash underlines its small influence in official circles and the secondary nature of its activities. Nash, *Rojas*, 118–22.

36 Miren Llona, 'From Militia Woman to *Emakume*: Myths regarding femininity during the Civil War in the Basque Country', in *Memory and Cultural History of the Spanish Civil War. Realms of Oblivion*, ed. Aurora Morcillo (Koninklijke: Brill, 2014), 179–212.

37 *Consejo Nacional de Educación Física, Cultural y Sanitaria de la Juventud. Consejería Femenina* (Valencia: Ed. Alerta, 1937), 14.

38 *Gaceta de la República*, 6 January 1937 and 1 April 1937 respectively.

39 *Mujeres Libres*, 12, mayo de 1938.

40 Carmen Werner, *Apuntes para una historia: las enfermeras de Brunete* (Madrid: s.n., 1965).

41 María Rosa Urraca Pastor, *Así empezamos (memorias de una enfermera)* (Bilbao: Editorial Vizcaína, 1940).

42 Fuyola, *Mujeres antifascistas*, 7.

43 Dolores Ibárruri, *¡A las mujeres madrileñas!* (Madrid: Partido Comunista Comité Provincial de Madrid, 1938), 6.

44 *Primer Congreso Popular de la Solidaridad*. Dolors Piera, *L'Aportació femenina a la guerra de la independencia* (Barcelona: Edicions del Departament d'Agitació i Propaganda del PSU, 1937).

45 Montseny, *Mi experiencia*, 27. The expression 'all people, for the people' is from W. Pieck, the president of International Red Aid. *Conferencia Nacional de la Solidaridad celebrada en Madrid los días 1 y 2 de noviembre de 1938. Documentos de Información* (Madrid: Socorro Rojo Internacional España, 1938).

46 *Ciencia y sanidad en la Valencia capital de la República* ed. Josep Lluís Barona and Josep Bernabeu-Mestre (Valencia: Publicacions de la Universitat de València, 2007).

47 Peter Anderson, 'The Struggle over the Evacuation to the United Kingdom and Repatriation of Basque Refugee Children in the Spanish Civil War: Symbols and Souls', *Journal of Contemporary History* 52, no. 1 (2017): 297–318.
48 Cristina Escrivá Moscardó and Rafael Maestre Marín, *De las negras bombas a las doradas naranjas. Colonias escolares 1936-1939* (Valencia: L'Eixam Edicions, 2011), 43.
49 Piera, *L'Aportació femenina,* 4.
50 Alicia Alted, 'El exilio de los niños', in *El exilio de los niños,* ed. Alicia Alted, Roger González and María Jesús Millán (Madrid: Ediciones Sinsentido, 2003), 20. Anderson, 'The Struggle'.
51 *Ayuda a la mujer* (Madrid: Ministerio de Trabajo y Asistencia Social, 1936?).
52 Montseny, *Mi experiencia,* 24.
53 *Mujeres Libres,* 7, marzo de 1937.
54 *Consejo Nacional de Educación Física, Cultural y Sanitaria de la Juventud. Consejería Femenina* (Valencia: Ed. Alerta, 1937), 7.
55 *Ayuda a la Mujer.*
56 Nash, *Rojas,* 219–33.
57 Pedro Cantero Cuadrado, *Doce años de asistencia social en España. Labor del Estado español (1936-1948)* (Madrid: Oficina Informativa Española, 1948), 48–9.
58 Cenarro, *La sonrisa de Falange,* 109–29.

Chapter 10

A LOST GENERATION? CHILDREN AND THE SPANISH CIVIL WAR

Verónica Sierra Blas*
Translated by Alan Matthews

For Rose

War and Childhood

It was the summer of 1936. It was a blue July, stained with explosive colours of gold. It was the time of year for harvesting and going for swims in the river. … I remember the weather was hot. … Suddenly one morning catastrophe was unleashed all around us. The world collapsed. Everything began to fall apart and we terrified children witnessed the end of our childhood. … [Our] questions, full of uncertainties and fears, remained unanswered for many years.[1]

In the words of Josefina Rodríguez Aldecoa the world fell apart when the Spanish Civil War broke out in July of 1936. She was ten years old at the time and, like other 'war children', her experiences of the conflict inevitably marked her character, as well as shaping the way she approached and understood things, wrote and taught. 'You remember your life as a sequence of haphazard events' is what Gabriela López Pardo declares on the first page of the first chapter of her *Historia de una maestra (Life Story of a Primary School Teacher).*[2] Haphazardly is how those children who saw their world turned upside down that summer of 1936 have remembered, and indeed still remember, what the war meant to them. Although every one of them experienced the war in different ways, it robbed them all of their childhood. Some people have maintained that Spanish children who were victims of the conflict ended up becoming a 'lost generation'. However, others view it differently: that all these children became the only hope for a country ravaged by war and bitterly divided in two.

This chapter aims to explore what day-to-day life was like for Spanish children during the civil war. It principally makes use of the writings of children who suffered the direct consequences of the conflict, as well as the objects and messages to which they were exposed to at the time. These documents offer the opportunity to analyse first-hand how these children lived and what they made of the conflict, and subsequently challenge the traditional historiographical views on children in a wartime context. Indeed, their testimonies demonstrate that far from being mere passive victims of the conflict, the children played an active role in it, even if it was a role that was sometimes orchestrated and instrumentalized by adults. This makes them legitimate witnesses and narrators of events and turns them into important actors in history.[3]

This research underscores the need and importance for historians to include the voices of children in their discourse. Documents originating from children have for too long been considered 'lacking in weight', difficult to believe, easily manipulated, and excessively 'sensitive',[4] but many historians have shown how the narratives of 'war children' can and indeed must help us to build a more comprehensive and more inclusive history, and also to offer new perspectives and ways of thinking, to help us understand and explain historical events which affected the lives of millions of people.

In order to offer the widest ranging overview, this chapter is divided into two parts. The first will deal with children who lived the Spanish Civil War 'from within', that is, inside the country. They, in particular, experienced the process of wartime cultural mobilization that both sides deployed during the conflict; a process which transformed their daily lives and left no room for a neutral stance with respect to the conflict. The second focuses on the other group of children who were evacuated abroad, who lived the war 'from the outside' and whose experience was characterized by upheaval and separation from their loved ones. The chapter concentrates on explaining how these evacuations of children to other countries took place and what importance they had in the midst of the war, and briefly considers the problem of repatriating the children, an issue regarded by both sides as an affair of state.[5]

The Civil War 'from Within' Spain

To write about the daily lives of children in the Spanish Civil War is to write about a succession of catastrophes that turned their lives into a veritable hell and from the very start made them aware of its disastrous consequences: bombs, sirens, and shelters; the desperate fighting of their fathers on the front line and the sacrifices of their worn-out mothers in the rear; the destruction or closing of schools; curfews and deserted streets; hunger and illness; those who were evacuated or who fled; those killed or wounded in action; those who disappeared or were murdered. For the children it was not a 'miniature war' but a war every bit as cruel and devastating for them as for the adults.

The figures are revealing although they vary considerably depending on the sources consulted. Whereas the statistics put out by the winning side claim that some 140,000 children died between 1936 and 1939,[6] historians such as Ramón Salas Larrazábal, Eduardo Pons Prades, Santos Juliá, or Julián Casanova put the figure of child deaths directly caused by the war as considerably higher, although they include the number of births that did not occur because of the conflict (around 380,000) and that indicate the dramatic drop in the country's birth rate in the war years.[7] Whatever the truth, it has been calculated that Spain lost a significant proportion of its child population during the conflict, the main causes of their deaths being bombardments and infectious diseases.[8]

As well as the tough living conditions and the real threat of death, children were exposed to a process of cultural mobilization inherent to the 'culture of war' of contemporary conflicts.[9] Both the rebels and the Republicans aimed to mobilize children and compel them to contribute to the war. Both sides saw the future generations as the natural heirs of the principles for which they were fighting on the battlefields; therefore, children were expected, insofar as they were able, to make a contribution to the final victory and, when the time came, to pick up the baton of their elders.

Propaganda was key to carrying out a successful programme of cultural mobilization of children. The recurring theme seen in posters and leaflets of abandoned, sick, wounded, or dead children was a powerful weapon to stir up hatred of the enemy and to create the image of 'child victims' who should learn to defend themselves and whom it was necessary to protect.[10] The production of such propaganda was generally linked to campaigns aimed at helping children, but occasionally the materials were printed and disseminated following a significant act of war in which the other side had particularly targeted minors.

There are numerous examples, but perhaps the most well-known is of the Nationalist bombing of Getafe in the province of Madrid on 30 October 1936; the Republican Ministry of Propaganda employed Rafael Pérez Contel to design a poster which was seen the world over and which – despite its harshness in depicting graphic images of the corpses of children – was used on the front pages of many international newspapers and magazines.[11] There was also the bombing of the Basque town of Guernica on 26 April 1937 about which the Ministry of War published a pamphlet called 'The Crime of Guernica'; the images shown were no less harsh than the poster cited above and they were disseminated just as far and wide. This is illustrated in the writing of María Álvarez del Vayo, a girl who had fled to Prague together with her family thanks to her father – the brother of foreign minister and later Commissar General Julio Álvarez del Vayo – being offered a job there.

One day after coming home from a walk with her mother along the banks of the Vitava river, María spotted this pamphlet on the desk in her father's office, and it made a strong impression on her. Although she knew she was not allowed to read 'adult things', when she saw it was to do with some Basque children, her curiosity got the better of her. She opened the pamphlet and came across lots of photos of 'slaughtered children, their clothes ripped to pieces, laid out in rows alongside each other, with their eyes closed and an identification tag round their necks'. As María relates in her memoirs, for the rest of the afternoon she was unable to play, holding back her tears, until when she was about to go to bed she told her mother what she had seen and could not get out of her mind:

> At bedtime I was overwhelmed by not having told anyone. These children, just like me, what were they doing lying on the ground with a name tag round their

necks? 'They are in heaven', my mother explained, but she did not tell me off. For some time afterwards I thought that these children needed to wear a name tag in order to get into heaven, to let them in just in case their names were not known.[12]

There are many 'war children' who vividly still remember those posters and pamphlets which were constantly in their sight, scattered on the ground, stuck up on walls, published in the press, exhibited in newspaper kiosks, and posted on notice boards of public buildings. However, in contrast with this image of passive 'child victims' created by the propaganda machines and which impacted the children so greatly, their games and toys promoted the image of an actively belligerent youth. In their unstructured games, children frequently reproduced on a small scale the war being fought by their elders, as is reflected in the testimonies of Julia Gutiérrez and Luis Garrido, among others:

> More than anything we used to play 'ration queues'. My sister would say, 'Go and join the queue', and I would go like a fool to the very long corridor at home, stand still and then every so often take a step forward.[13]

> Some of the boys would play football, [others] would pretend to give training, others played at giving speeches and there were some who would fight their own personal wars with stones and balls of paper shot with catapults.[14]

However, this small-scale imitation of the actual war, derived from what the children would see and hear every day, was not always something spontaneous but was influenced, and often heavily so, by the type of toys that were available at the time, regardless of whether these were aimed at boys or girls. They were mainly toys manufactured specifically for wartime, such as militia puppets which, as Susana del Castillo remembered, were on sale in the Madrid metro;[15] or the famous so-called 'special rifles' advertised in some children's magazines;[16] or lead soldiers and nurses, and tanks and airplanes made out of iron or cardboard. Alongside these specifically 'military' toys, traditional ones continued to exist, such as stickers, cards, dice, ludo, snakes and ladders, toy kitchens and sewing kits, and others all infused with war-related themes. All these toys were clearly intended to turn children into symbolic mini-combatants in their own right and have them play a role instrumentalized by adults for indoctrination purposes and, at least in some cases, a desire for profit.

A similar ambition drove the different political parties and unions to organize paramilitary activities for children and teenagers.[17] The Falangist 'Arrows', the Carlist 'Pelayos', or the Communist 'Pioneers' would march through the streets in their uniforms, waving their flags to celebrate the recapture of a town or village; their presence was widely applauded at charity and cultural events as well as at political rallies; they would even visit the front lines in the same way as local authorities, foreign journalists, and a significant number of well-known writers would do; the children also corresponded with the soldiers and played the part of 'war godparents', sending them encouraging and consoling letters and the occasional gift;[18] and the older ones regularly helped out in the rearguard by fortifying strategic positions or lending a hand in military hospitals or in the supply services. The underlying message was that children could play an important role in the war effort, as a part of the population at large encouraged to do so in a context of 'total war', although it was an effort appropriate for their age, abilities, and means.

Children on both sides of the war, wearing red or blue uniforms accordingly, thus demonstrated their commitment to the cause with small but symbolically important actions, as can be seen in this letter sent by a girl during the Defence of Madrid to Joaquín Arderíus, the president of *Socorro Rojo Internacional* (SRI), or International Red Aid, a left-wing relief society. And because of the good example it set, the text was published by the centrist and moderate Republican newspaper, *Ahora* (*Now*):

> I have read in *Ahora* that blood was needed for the wounded and although I'm only a girl of not yet ten years of age but in full health, I want to give my blood to a workman who has a daughter (like me). I haven't asked my mother for permission and she doesn't know I'm writing this to you, but as she's such a good person, she won't tell me off. ... [What's more] I've heard her say that she too would give blood to a wounded person. Long live the Republic and the brave people defending it![19]

Another strategy employed to make the cultural mobilization project successful leads us into the field of literature for children and teenagers. In fact, the world of children's and teenagers' publishing was completely transformed at this time: first, by the ideological instrumentalization of school books, as well as novels, short stories, and magazines; second, by the provision of these publications free of charge or for a much reduced price in order to guarantee their adoption and thus the transmission of the ideas, values, and speeches they contained; and finally by the new importance the war accorded to the child reader whose image changed from someone to be educated and entertained into a target audience for partisan messages.[20]

Although the two sides had quite different editorial approaches, their publications shared similar aims, namely to present an explanation and historical justification of the conflict and to create a series of model behaviours to hold up to junior readers and thus contribute to their present and future education in support of the ideals represented by each side.[21] A few examples will illustrate this.

In the first number of *Pionero Rojo* (*Red Pioneer*) dated 9 April 1937, a weekly magazine for working-class and country children and published in Barcelona by the Iberian Communist Youth, children of Republican families were 'spurred on to fight against their masters'; whereas in the magazine *Flecha* (*Arrow*) of 7 February of the same year, published in San Sebastian by the Press and Propaganda Organism of Falange, children of rebel families were 'exhorted to fight on behalf of the Empire'.[22] Similarly, Francoist comics like *El miliciano Remigio pa la guerra es un prodigio* (*Militiaman Remigio is a prodigy at waging war*)[23] and *El flecha Edmundo vence siempre a todo el mundo* (*Edmundo the 'Arrow' always beats everyone*)[24] sang the praises of their own soldiers and made fun of the Republican combatants; on sale on newspaper stands and in bookshops were stories such as *Las aventuras de Juanillo* (*The adventures of little Juan*)[25] or *Un héroe de diez años o ¡Arriba España!* (*A ten-year-old hero or Long live Spain!*),[26] starring children who were turned into big heroes of the war effort.

Republican illustrated posters drawn by Lola Anglada i Sarriera about the *Auça del noi catalá antifeixista i humá* (*Life of an Altruistic, Antifascist Catalan Boy*)[27] had similar objectives and were hugely popular. Their main character was a boy from a 'humble but honourable family' who volunteered to join the ranks of the Popular Army. The serialized publications recounting the adventures of the good-natured and antifascist *Sidrín*[28] were devoured by young readers and the illustrated series by José Bardasano y Baos, 'Cuentos para los Niños Antifascistas de España' ('Stories for Antifascist Spanish Children'), published in 1936 by the Ministry of Education, were distributed free of charge throughout schools and shelters. In the preface they included declarations such as this:

To Spanish children,

While the fascist murderers drop bombs on you and kill your little brothers and sisters, the Ministry of Education of the Popular Front gives you toys and stories and looks after your education so that tomorrow you will become productive adults in our new society.[29]

Although propaganda messages, games and toys, paramilitary activities, and children's literature all played an essential part in the process of wartime acculturation and in the mobilization of youth, there is no doubt that what had most influence on the children was their schooling. Schools in the Republican zone continued to defend the values on which the Republic was founded when it came to power: a Republican school had to be state-run and anti-fascist, and based on the twin pillars of being coeducational and secular; at the same time, it had to be 'innovative', and devise and implement 'revolutionary' teaching methods.[30] In marked contrast, schools in the rebel zone imposed a traditional, Catholic, patriotic, and militaristic approach, similar to that crystallized during Franco's years in power.[31] Nevertheless, despite the ideological and pedagogical differences separating them, both types of schools placed the war at the heart of children's education. The subject of war dominated and transformed their schooling, and this is well documented in surviving exercise books. These give a clear account of how the war was ever-present in the classroom regardless of the subject being taught and with the dual objective of motivating the young to participate in the war effort and create a new generation of Republicans or Francoists.[32]

This can be seen in the letter that José Vila wrote to his sister from his Republican school in Hostafranchs (Lérida) on 10 November 1936:

My dear sister,

I'm sorry about the way things have turned out so badly in the first four months of the war, especially that the fascists have stained Spain with blood by unleashing a civil war, which no one knows when it will end. From what you say, you already know what it is to suffer: your husband is away in the army fighting to defend the Republic and the loyalist government elected by the people. You need to put up with all this with patience, and with a strong spirit, and by toiling on the front lines and toiling in the rearguard, we will win the final victory and root out fascism from Spanish soil. Greetings to you and long live the Republic![33]

As it happened, on this occasion the school did not send José's letter although we know that sometimes pages containing these exercises were torn out of the notebooks and sent off, or copied out neatly on pre-stamped postcards provided free of charge to the schools to encourage the exchange between children and their families.[34] This was especially important if any of the children were a long way from home due to the conflict, or if the parents were engaged themselves in the fighting, such as the father of Manuel Ángel Arce, a soldier in the 3rd Company of the 131st Battalion of the Republican Army of the North, who received these lines from his son on 19 April 1937 reporting among other things on his school progress:

Dear Dad,

It will make me very happy to know that when you receive this you're in good health; we are doing fine here. Dad, I'm keeping track and writing every day in my notebook just as you told me to do. Yesterday I went with Mum to Oruña [near the city of Santander] to see our cousins and I played a lot with them. Goodbye for now and lots of love.[35]

The schools on a war footing insisted that the teachers explained to their pupils their respective sides' justification for war and kept them up-to-date with military actions and political developments. In this way schools became yet another contested front in the war, in which the two contrasting educational models were at loggerheads with each other.[36] However, schools did not always prove to be stable fronts; although some did stay open throughout the war and often provided the children with stability and continuity, many others were forced to close down because they were destroyed by bombings, or because the teachers were called up, purged, or murdered, as Marcelo García remembered in his memoirs:

At the start of the civil war the school was not closed down. … The teacher managed to turn the school into a sanctuary from the horrors of the news emanating from the front and from extreme hunger. I was about to turn seven when the Nationalist troops and the Falangists arrived. … But on that morning the teacher was not at school. We sat waiting … at our desks, our hearts in our mouths. At midday the news arrived: the body of Don Manuel had turned up on the banks of the river.

In 1938 we returned to school. The new teacher was a nasty-looking ex-soldier with a scar running down his cheek. … On the first day he read aloud from the primer [and] made it perfectly clear that the first thing we had to do when we entered the classroom was to stand in front of Franco's portrait, raise our arm in a fascist salute and say with conviction 'Long live Spain!'[37]

This grim account underscores the reality that for many Spanish children the civil war not only meant forsaking a portion of their childhood, but also their access to education.

The Civil War 'from Outside' Spain

Writing about children's experiences of the war 'from within' Spain highlighted the devastating effects the conflict had on children and revealed the lines along which both sides self-interestedly pushed their campaigns of wartime social mobilization with this target audience in mind. Writing about children's experiences of the war 'from the outside' now leads us to consider a phenomenon which irrevocably changed the lives of thousands of minors: the evacuations.

The exodus of children as a result of the Spanish Civil War has been interpreted by many historians as the most significant in the whole of the first half of the twentieth century.[38] Although the figures generally put forward are in need of a thorough re-evaluation, it is calculated that between 30,000 and 50,000 children left Spain between 1936 and 1939.[39] Needless to say this figure does not include those minors who crossed the border into France in January and February 1939 following the fall of Catalonia, and who were interned in French concentration camps such as Rivesaltes. This camp received the largest number of children in all of south-eastern France: around 3,000 children lived in its huts, which are still standing today.[40]

The origins of the evacuation of children can be traced back to the first months of the war, when the Republican government put in place a plan which gave priority to those children 'at risk': the wounded, the sick, orphans, soldiers' children, those living dangerously close to the front lines. The first evacuations were to so-called *colonias escolares* (school colonies) located in peaceful areas such as Valencia and Catalonia provinces. They were run by the *Comité Nacional de Refugiados de Guerra* (CNRG), or National Committee for War Refugees, and later, as from 1 March 1937, they were taken over by the *Delegación Central de Colonias* (DCC), or Central Delegation for Colonies, under the umbrella of the Ministry of Education.[41]

These colonies were an early and common destination for evacuated Spanish children.[42] Reports from the DCC describe how many were set up as the war raged on, and their statistics include those from the pre-war period that were revamped for this purpose. According to Regina Lago, the head of this organization, in 1937 alone there already existed 564 such colonies catering for over 45,000 children. They included 158 colonies working on a collective basis, a boarding school of sorts where the inmates were looked after by teams of professionals, and 406 working on a family basis, in which children were adopted by families who temporarily took charge of their education, maintenance, and care.[43]

As the war went on many of these colonies had to close down or move abroad, to those countries that offered the Republic assistance in caring for Spanish children. A new organization, the *Consejo Nacional de la Infancia Evacuada* (CNIE), or National Council for Evacuated Children, was set up with its headquarters in Paris to supervise these international evacuations, and it continued its work until January 1939.[44] Some of the countries to take in evacuated Spanish children were: France (20,000), Belgium (5,000), United Kingdom (4,000), USSR (2,895), Mexico (456), Switzerland (430), and Denmark (100). There were other countries as well, such as Norway and Sweden, which although hardly received any children, donated a generous amount of resources and provided personnel to help support colonies in Spain and in other countries.[45]

The first evacuations to other countries took place during the fighting on the Northern Front. It was after one of the heaviest bombing raids on Bilbao, on 4 January 1937, that the Basque government led by José Antonio de Aguirre decided to evacuate the first contingent of children abroad: 239 boys and 211 girls left the port of Bermeo on 20 March 1937 en route to France.[46] This pioneering experience was written up in detail in one of the first autobiographical novels written by a 'war child', *El otro árbol de Guernica* (*Guernica's Other Tree*). Its author, Luis de Castresana, adopts the name of Santiago Celaya, an 11-year-old boy from Ugarte, a small village near Baracaldo, in Bilbao, who is evacuated with his sister, Begoña. Castresana points out in the preface that his novel is 'a tribute, an authentic document [in which] all the events and characters [who appear] are absolutely authentic', and he adds: 'I know that everything I relate here has been lived and is not invented, and I know why these children fought and how they won their own personal war ..., an unheard, little war, unheralded, heroic, difficult ..., because I was one of them.'[47] The following extract gives us an inkling of how those Basque children must have felt as part of the first expedition abroad, many of whom had never left their hometowns before, and seeing themselves now on board an ocean-going destroyer like the *Campbell*:

> Those were proper ships ... warships, with huge cannons. ... When the children were going on board, in Bermeo, Santi had fixed his attention on the ship's name painted in large, black lettering: 'H.M.S. Campbell'. ... The weather was pleasant and the sea was calm but Santi felt a little upset. ... Some ladies from the Red Cross ... went round offering sandwiches and biscuits ... and glasses of milk and lemonade. ... The time passed slowly. ... It was getting colder and colder and everyone was keen to reach dry land. The lights from the shore were getting closer. All the children leant over the rail to have a look. ... And they could hear voices, shouts and noises from the port. It suddenly seemed most strange to Santi that those lights did not belong to Spain but to another country.[48]

The testimonies of children who took part shed considerable light on what the life of these war refugees was like following the first pilot initiative to move the vulnerable abroad. In addition to the memoirs and the autobiographical novels based on reality in which many of the children look back as adults to when they left Spain behind, the drawings they made in the colonies are a true reflection of their experience of evacuation and a valuable historical source.[49] It had already been demonstrated during the First World War that drawing was an effective way of combatting trauma,[50] and for this reason those responsible for the Spanish children during the civil war encouraged artwork, turning it into one of their favourite activities.[51]

The drawing reproduced here is an example of 'art as therapy' in this context and was done in 1937 by 12-year-old Rosita Corral in the Bayonne colony (in France).[52] She called it 'Evacuation by boat' and on the back she wrote, 'In this drawing you can see how we were evacuated from Gijón and left Santander for France.'[53] In the foreground Rosita drew other children who, like her, were about to board, and others who were accompanied by their mothers, the larger-sized figures. The little girl drew suitcases and bundles strewn over the dockside; they were about to be loaded into the hold and on them Rosita had written their owners' first names. The boat flies the Republican flag, both in the prow and in the stern, and one can make out the cabins through the portholes: it was about to set off and smoke was pouring out of the funnels and Rosita and other children are waving their handkerchiefs saying goodbye to their families. That the little girl used pastel-coloured pencils is possibly significant. The soft and pleasant tone, as well as being pale and delicate, enabled her to record in her drawing two feelings she probably felt at the moment of her evacuation: on the one hand, the sadness at having to part from her loved ones, and on the other, the hope of being able to depart and leave behind the dangers of war (see Figure 10.1).

As well as the children's drawings, the articles many of them wrote in their colonies' newspapers prove to be a useful source by which their daily lives away from home can be reconstructed. The CNIE recommended that the teachers set up a newspaper in which the children not only related 'what was happening in the life of their colony' but also recorded 'the most significant political and military events' of the war to help them assimilate and better understand what was happening back in Spain. It also served to connect them to the Republican cause and ensure the continuity of the children's political indoctrination.[54] For instance, in the Cambria House colony in Caerleon, in South Wales, the children wrote a monthly newsletter, which they would sell in town to earn some pocket money. The *Cambria House Journal* was much looked forward to by the people living there, and also by other Spanish children in colonies nearby with whom they exchanged letters and this type of school material.[55] Here is an article that one of the children wrote for the July 1939 edition and which gives a summary of the two years these little evacuees spent in the colony after arriving in the United Kingdom in May 1937:

On 10 July 1937 we arrived at 'Cambria House' where we have been so well treated. It is here that we have learnt all the English we know. On May 20th 1937, we set sail for England. After three days on the sea … we arrived at Southampton where we lived for two months in tents. … Then … they brought us here to Cambria House. … It is here that the football team was organized that played

Figure 10.1 'Evacuation by boat'. Rosita Corral, aged twelve. Bayonne colony (France), 1937. Biblioteca Nacional de España, Madrid, Departamento de Bellas Artes y Cartografía, Colección 'Dibujos Infantiles de la Guerra Civil', 19/1/844. Original in colour.

successfully. … It is here too, that the concert party was organized, that gave a number of concerts. … The money that is raised through these football matches and concerts goes towards the maintenance of the home. … The *Cambria House Journal* was founded, and such was the interest shown in the articles it contained, that it became popular throughout Wales, and a part of England.[56]

Crossing the Atlantic to Mexico, it is possible to track down documents about the so-called 'Children of Morelia' and find testimonies shedding light on their story as well. Among the 456 children who embarked in Bordeaux on the *Mexique* in May 1937 was Maruja Rodríguez. Like most of her companions Maruja was assigned to the Spanish-Mexican Industrial School in Morelia in the state of Michoacán, which was run and maintained by the *Comité de Ayuda a los Niños del Pueblo Español*, or Committee for Assistance to the Children of the Spanish People, an organization founded by President Lázaro Cárdenas in October 1936.[57] Soon after arriving in Morelia, in early June 1937, Maruja started to write a diary, which she kept up until 1943, the year in which the teaching centre closed. As well as jotting down the things she was doing, and also keeping herself occupied in her spare time, her intention was to be able to give it to her parents one day. On 23 September 1937 this is how Maruja described a typical day at her school in Morelia:

I'm writing [this diary] convinced that one day it will be read by my parents. …
I get up at 7, go to the bathroom to wash …, then we have … our first class; at 8
I have my breakfast of white coffee and bread, we finish at half past and then we
go out to play or do whatever we want until 9 when we're called in for lessons. …
We continue until 11 when we go out in the playground for 30 minutes, then
return to the classroom but finish the morning at 1 o'clock. At half past one the
bugle and drum band calls us in to eat. We each go to the table we've been told to
sit at, we eat three big courses as well as pudding. … When we've finished eating
we go out into the playground to play or rest until 3 o'clock when we're called
into the workshops … where we stay until half past six when … [we go back]
to the girls' school for dinner at 7. After eating dinner we go into the library …;
at half past eight we leave the library and go to the dormitory, at 9 it's lights out
and silence until the following morning when the minders come to wake us up.[58]

In addition to drawing, writing their colony newspapers, or scribbling diaries
there was one other activity that evacuated Spanish children regularly carried
out, and that was writing letters. This was an important psychological support
for these young children and they would often write home almost every day.
Before the children left, their parents would have stressed the importance of
maintaining regular written contact with the family, as the only means of keeping
them connected at a distance. Whatever else might happen, it was crucial that this
lifeline was not cut and so the children, realizing how important it was, frequently
made every effort to carry out this task.[59]

From the 2,895 children evacuated to the USSR, only about 200 letters have
survived. The majority of them were written by children who took part in the
second and third expeditions – there were four in total – which the Republican
government organized to what was then Leningrad (today Saint Petersburg), in
June and September 1937 from Bilbao and Gijón. Practically all these letters were
sent home as soon as the children disembarked, and in them they tell their parents
of their safe arrival before they were dispatched to the sixteen state-run care
homes organized by the *Narkompros* (the People's Commissariat for Education) in
different parts of the Russian Federation and Ukraine.[60] The letters were therefore
more like 'on board diaries' and they allow the reconstruction of the details of their
journey and the welcome they were afforded by the Soviet people.[61]

This letter written from Leningrad by Alfonso Ibáñez, a 10-year-old Basque
boy, to his parents on 23 June 1937, is a good example. What stands out in the letter
is the constant reference he makes to food, which even before the end of the first
year of conflict was already in short supply in many parts of Republican Spain (as
examined in Chapter 8 of this volume). It is a vivid reminder that children suffered
the acute shortages too and often more so than adults because of their ongoing
physical development. Alfonso explains that on board the *Habana*, the ship that
took the mission from the port of Pauillac in Bordeaux, the food was rather poor;
but it improved somewhat on the *Sontay*, the vessel they were transferred on to
and which took them to the USSR; and how it was even better after they arrived.

Most of these children came from very poor backgrounds so they were amazed at the lavish welcome they were given:

> My dear parents,
>
> I hope you are well, and wonder how the war is going. … We arrived safely [in Leningrad], there were loads of people to greet us, lots of flags and a white bear. We've been given underpants, a shirt and sandals and socks. We were taken in buses. They gave me a toothbrush and powder [to clean teeth] and soap. … On the first day … they gave us soup and afterwards … chicken, [and] they gave us some cakes. On the boat *Habana* … we had to queue up and for lunch [they gave us] coffee and black bread. We ate some beans but they were hard. At night [once again] coffee. But on the other boat [*Sontay*] we were better off because they gave us potatoes and they were well cooked, and they gave us white bread. For dinner [rice] and star pasta soup with cabbage.[62]

In addition to these early letters sent home by the so-called 'Russian Children' a smaller volume of later correspondence has also survived. These missives not only document the young refugees' daily lives, but they also reveal the significant ideological influence exerted on them by their schools, state-run care homes, and the Communist Party, in addition to that by different Soviet youth organizations, such as the Pioneers' movement.[63] As the Republic lost ground in the war the frequency of this epistolary exchange diminished, and many children lost contact with their parents for months and even years. Many, however, were persistent in their attempts to re-establish links and, for example, sent letters to the boards of *Asistencia Social*, or Republican Social Assistance, begging for help to locate their relatives. The following letter was written by Ignacio Ruano on 5 February 1938 from his state-run care home in Kharkov and ends with strong support for the Republic and its prominent communist leaders:

> Dear comrade Joaquín Bustos [the representative of the Basque branch of *Asistencia Social* in Barcelona],
>
> This letter is to tell you that [I am] a Spanish boy who finds himself in Russia as a result of the war in Spain. … We have spent a year in Russia, [during which time] I haven't been able to discover the whereabouts of my parents, and [I trust] that you can find them. My mother is called Magdalena Pajares. My father is called Daniel Ruano and [I also] have a 16-year-old brother, Alejandro Ruano. Please find at least one of them.
>
> In this country we are extremely happy. We are generously provided for and they look after us extremely well. We [children] are split up among various cities. We are in the city of Kharkov.
>
> With nothing else to add, farewell from a Spanish student who doesn't forget Spain.

Ignacio Ruano.

LONG LIVE Red Spain! LONG LIVE Dolores Ibárruri! LONG LIVE José Díaz![64]

After analysing these testimonies and acquiring an understanding of how the children lived the war from outside Spain, it is pertinent to end this section with a brief consideration of the question of repatriations. Although it is true that the Republic managed to create a favourable international atmosphere towards evacuating the children and also convinced many parents that the only way to save their children's lives was to send them off to other countries, it is equally true that, from the moment the children began to leave the country, Franco made every effort to undermine the authority the Republicans had over these children in the middle of a civil war, and to question the procedures the government adopted to execute the evacuation programme.

For the caudillo, it became a matter of priority to repatriate all those children 'stolen from Spain'. In the early days it was the responsibility of the *Junta de Protección de Menores*, or the Junta for the Protection of Minors, to locate the children and organize their return, but from July 1938 onwards Franco set up the *Delegación Extraordinaria de Repatriación de Menores* (DERM), or Special Delegation for the Repatriation of Minors, to take sole control of this matter. The delegation worked initially under the Ministry of Foreign Affairs but from June 1941 onwards it came under the Falange's Foreign Service Delegation, and demonstrated how much political importance the dictator gave to the repatriation of these children.[65]

Despite the protectionist laws of the different welcoming countries, despite the opposition of the people running the colonies and that of the adoptive families themselves, and despite the almost unanimous refusal of the biological parents to complete the official request form in their own handwriting as was required to negotiate the return of their children (and which also involved a thorough and potentially high-risk investigation into their lives), in the end Franco got his own way.

Many of the children evacuated between 1937 and 1938 were repatriated to Spain before the end of the war or immediately afterwards, and another large batch of them on the outbreak of the Second World War. According to statistics from the DERM, by 1949 between 20,000 and 25,000 children had been repatriated to Spain.[66] Only two countries, the USSR and Mexico, resisted this 'return policy' as neither Stalin nor Cárdenas recognized the legitimacy of Franco's government. Of the 456 child refugees in Mexico only sixty-one returned before the dictator's death, although it has to be said that many managed to be reunited with their parents in Mexico itself. Of the 2,895 children sent to the USSR fewer than a third returned, and these, with very few exceptions, had to wait for more than two decades, until after Stalin died in 1953; before then they were unable to obtain a return ticket permitting them to return to Spain without being accused of treason or putting their lives or those of their families at risk.[67]

However, this is not the most emotionally charged story of all, even taking into account those children who were never able to return to Spain. The most distressing outcome was that of children who were repatriated but not handed back to their parents. Only if there were no negative reports about the parents – in other words that they were considered fit to raise their children in accordance with the principles of the New State – were the children returned to their original homes. Otherwise, it fell to the provincial boards of the *Junta de Protección de Menores* in the district of the children's birthplace to take responsibility for them and to decide on their futures, which often involved institutionalization in state-run centres. An important role in deciding the fate of these minors was also played by the *Obra Nacional de Protección a los Huérfanos de la Revolución y la Guerra*, or National Organization for the Protection of Orphans of the Revolution and War, established in 1940, as well as the most important charitable organization of the dictatorship years, *Auxilio Social*, or Social Aid (and which is considered in Chapter 9 of this volume).[68]

Experiencing War 'through the Eyes of Children'

The first news Spanish children had of the civil war was often of bombardments, deaths, and people fleeing. From one day to the next the world they knew, the world in which they lived, was utterly shattered and many of their families were torn apart. The experience of war was very different for those who spent the three years in Spain and for those, on the other hand, who were evacuated to other countries. The first group was subjected to a constant barrage of information that both presented them as victims of the conflict, but also urged them to take sides, make an appropriate contribution to the war effort and absorb the messages that the two versions of Spain emphasized through their concerted propaganda campaigns. The second group had different experiences depending on the place and timing of their evacuation, but were united by the process of separation from their families, a discovery of new countries, often for the first time, and a desire to record their transitions.

However, none of the children who suffered the war emerged unscathed. Indeed, for many it was impossible to heal the traumas they were forced to endure throughout their lives. The generation of 'war children' is also referred to in Spanish historiography as the 'generation of memory', because many of them, in the words of Josefina Rodríguez Aldecoa, with whom this chapter opened, 'felt the need to describe [their experiences]'.[69] Writing about their lives was also frequently a healing process. Thanks to these wartime stories later narrated in the first person as adults and the preservation of their actual childhood writings in public and private archives – either haphazardly, or for repressive purposes, or as an act of memory by the authors – historians have been able to reconstruct the civil war through the eyes of children. In doing so, they have added a different dimension to one of the key events in contemporary Spanish history.

Further Reading

A pesar de todo dibujan. La Guerra Civil vista por los niños. Catálogo de la Exposición. Madrid: Biblioteca Nacional de España, Fundación Winterthur, 2006.

El exilio de los niños. Catálogo de la exposición, ed. Alicia Alted, Roger González and María José Millán. Madrid: Fundación Pablo Iglesias, Fundación Francisco Largo Caballero, 2003.

Enfants de la Guerre Civile espagnole. Vécus et représentations de la génération née entre 1925 et 1940. Paris: L'Harmattan, Fondation Nationale des Sciences Politiques, Centre d´Histoire de l´Europe du Vingtième Siècle, 1999.

Fernández Soria, Juan Manuel. *Educación y cultura en la Guerra Civil (1936-39).* Valencia: Nau Llibres, 1984.

Pons Prades, Eduardo. *Los niños republicanos en la guerra de España.* Madrid: Oberón, 2004.

Sierra Blas, Verónica. *Palabras huérfanas. Los niños y la Guerra Civil.* Madrid: Taurus, 2009.

Notes

*   Research undertaken with the following grant: *'Scripta in itinere'. Discursos, formas y apropiaciones de la cultura escrita en espacios públicos desde la primera Edad Moderna hasta nuestros días* (HAR2014-51883-P).

1   Josefina Rodríguez Aldecoa, 'Los niños del destierro', *El País Semanal,* 11 August 1996. See also Eduardo Pons Prades, *Los niños republicanos en la guerra de España* (Madrid: Oberón, 2004), 38–9. The transcriptions and subsequent translations in this chapter have been done according to modern-day orthography and syntax usage to facilitate their reading.

2   Josefina Rodríguez Aldecoa, *Historia de una maestra* (Madrid: Anagrama, 1990), 13.

3   Antonio Gibelli, *Il popolo bambino. Infanzia e nazione dalla Grande Guerra a Salò* (Turin: Einaudi, 2005), and Nicholas Stargardt, *Witnesses of War. Children's Lives under the Nazis* (New York: Alfred A. Knopf, 2006).

4   Dominique Julià, 'I documenti della scrittura infantile in Francia', *Materiali di Lavoro. Rivista di studi storici* 2, no. 3 (1992): 34; and Verónica Sierra Blas, '"En busca del eslabón perdido". Algunas reflexiones sobre las escrituras infantiles', in *The Written Memory of Childhood,* ed. Verónica Sierra Blas, Juri Meda and Antonio Castillo Gómez, *History of Education & Children's Literature* VII, no. 1 (2012): 21–42.

5   The children studied in this chapter ranged between 2–3 and 15–16 years old during the Spanish Civil War. This excludes older teenage boys who volunteered as combatants or who were later called up by the government's Popular Army in 1938–9 (known as the 'feeding bottle' reserve class) because a study of their experience would require a significantly difference analytical lens. See Emma Aixalà i Mateu, *La Quinta del biberó: els anys perduts* (Barcelona: Proa, 2004). On the figure of the child combatant in general, see *L'enfant-soldat, XIXe-XXIe siécle,* ed. Manon Pignot (Paris: Armand Colin, 2012) and the special issue 'Engagements adolescents en guerres mondiales', ed. Manon Pignot, *Le Mouvement Social* 261 (2017): 3–106.

6   Luis S. Granjel, 'La medicina en la guerra', *Historia 16* 14 (1987): 98.

7   Ramón Salas Larrazábal, *Pérdidas de la guerra* (Barcelona: Planeta, 1977), 52 and 426.

8 Tomás Vidal and Joaquín Recaño, 'Demografía y Guerra Civil', *Historia 16* 14, (1987): 68.

9 Stéphane Audoin-Rouzeau, *La guerre des enfants, 1914-1918* (Paris: Armand Colin, 2004), 33.

10 Tomás Pérez Delgado, 'La infancia en la cartelística republicana de guerra', *Historia de la Educación. Revista interuniversitaria* 6 (1987): 376.

11 Rafael Pérez Contel, *¡Asesinos! ¿Quién al ver esto no empuña un fusil para aplastar al fascismo destructor? Niños muertos en Madrid por las bombas facciosas. Víctimas inocentes de esta horrible guerra desatada por los enemigos de España* (Madrid, Valencia: Ministerio de la Propaganda, Gráficas Valencia, 1936). Biblioteca Histórica de la Universidad de Valencia, Fondo Antiguo, 'Carteles de la Guerra Civil', 1.245.

12 María Álvarez del Vayo, *Los últimos días. Recuerdos y reflexiones de una niña del exilio* (Madrid: Fundación Pablo Iglesias, 2003), 35.

13 Cfr. Juana Salabert, *Hijas de la ira. Vidas rotas por la Guerra Civil* (Barcelona: Plaza & Janés, 2005), 68.

14 Luis Garrido, *Los niños que perdimos la guerra* (Madrid: Libro-Hobby-Club, 2005), 25.

15 Salabert, *Hijas de la ira*, 191–2.

16 Teresa Pàmies, *Los niños de la guerra* (Barcelona: Bruguera, 1977), 87.

17 Juan Manuel Fernández Soria, *Educación y cultura en la Guerra Civil (1936-39)* (Valencia: Nau Llibres, 1984), 288–9.

18 Verónica Sierra Blas, 'Escribir en campaña. Cartas de soldados desde el frente', *Cultura Escrita & Sociedad* 4 (2003): 95–116.

19 Rafael Abella, *La vida cotidiana durante la Guerra Civil. La España republicana* (Barcelona: Planeta, 2004), 191–2.

20 César Sánchez Ortiz and Pedro César Cerrillo Torremocha, 'Literatura infantil y juvenil en la Guerra Civil española', in *Lectura, infancia y escuela: 25 años de libro escolar en España, 1931-1956*, ed. Pedro César Cerrillo Torremocha and Carlos Julián Martínez Soria (Ciudad Real: Universidad de Castilla-La Mancha, 2009), 89–99.

21 Fernando Cendán Pazos, *Medio siglo de libros infantiles y juveniles en España (1935-1985)* (Salamanca: Fundación Germán Sánchez Ruipérez, 1986), and Jaime García Padrino, *Libros y literatura para niños en la España contemporánea* (Madrid: Fundación Germán Sánchez Ruipérez, 1992).

22 Pàmies, *Los niños de la guerra*, 135 and 140; and Antonio Martín Martínez, *Historia del cómic español: 1875-1939* (Barcelona: Gustavo Gili, 1978), 156–228.

23 Joaquín Pérez Madrigal, *El Miliciano Remigio pa la guerra es un prodigio* (Ávila: Sigiriano Díaz, 1937).

24 Avelino de Aróztegui, *El flecha Edmundo vence siempre a todo el mundo* (San Sebastian: Talleres de Nerekán, 1937).

25 Carmen Martell, *Aventuras de Juanillo* (Madrid, Cádiz: Cerón, Librería Cervantes, 1941). The first edition was published during the conflict, probably in 1938 or 1939.

26 Manuel Barberán Castrillo, *Un héroe de diez años o ¡Arriba España! Lecturas patrióticas para niños* (Vitoria: J. Marquínez, 1938).

27 Joseph Obiols, *Auça del noi català antifeixista i humá* (Barcelona: Comisariado de Propaganda, Generalitat de Catalunya, [1937]).

28 The series, authored by Antonio Joaquín Robles Soler ('Antoniorrobles') and illustrated by Francisca Bartolozzi ('Pitti'), consisted of six fascicles, all of them published by Estrella in Valencia throughout 1938.

29 García Padrino, *Libros y literatura para niños*, 403 and 432–3.

30 Antonio Molero Pintado, *La educación durante la Segunda República y la Guerra Civil (1931-1939)* (Madrid: Ministerio de Educación y Ciencia, 1991).

31 Manuel de Puelles Benítez, *Educación e ideología en la España contemporánea* (Barcelona: Labor, 1991).

32 María del Mar del Pozo Andrés and Sara Ramos Zamora, 'Ir a la escuela en la guerra: el reflejo de la cotidianeidad en los cuadernos escolares', *Cultura Escrita & Sociedad* 4 (2007): 129–70.

33 Archivo General de la Administración, Alcalá de Henares (Madrid), Ministerio de Educación, 235/49.800.

34 See, for example, Francisco Aracil, *La Guerra Civil en la Historia Postal* (Madrid, Barcelona: Edifil, 1996), 112–13.

35 Centro Documental de la Memoria Histórica, Salamanca, Político-Social (PS) Santander, serie A, 235-7/7.

36 Alejandro Mayordomo and Juan Manuel Fernández Soria, *Vencer y convencer: Educación y política. España, 1936-1945* (Valencia: Universitat de València, 1993).

37 See, for example, Jaime Izquierdo, *Marcelo. Los otros niños de la guerra* (Madrid: Oberón, 2004), 36, 41–2 and 52–7.

38 Alicia Alted, *La voz de los vencidos. El exilio republicano de 1939* (Madrid: Aguilar, 2005).

39 Jesús J. Alonso Carballés, *1937. Los niños vascos evacuados a Francia y a Bélgica. Historia y memoria de un éxodo infantil, 1936-1940* (Bilbao: Asociación de Niños Evacuados el 37, 1998).

40 Pierre Marques, *Les enfants espagnols réfugiés en France (1936-1939)* (Paris: Author's edition, 1993), 170.

41 Alicia Alted, 'El exilio de los niños', in *El exilio de los niños. Catálogo de la exposición*, ed. Alicia Alted, Roger González and María José Millán (Madrid: Fundación Pablo Iglesias, Fundación Francisco Largo Caballero, 2003), 19–20.

42 Cristina Escrivá Moscardó and Rafael Maestre Marín, *De las negras bombas a las doradas naranjas. Colonias escolares, 1936-1939* (Valencia: l'Eixam, 2011).

43 Ramón Safón, *La educación en la España revolucionaria* (Madrid: La Piqueta, 1978), 110.

44 Alicia Alted, Encarna Nicolás Marín and Roger González Martell, *Los niños de la guerra de España en la Unión Soviética. De la evacuación al retorno (1937-1999)* (Madrid: Fundación Francisco Largo Caballero, 1999), 34–8.

45 Alted, González and Millán, *El exilio de los niños*.

46 Dorothy Legarreta, *The Guernica Generation: Basque Refugee Children of the Spanish Civil War* (Reno: University of Nevada Press, 1984), 39.

47 Luis de Castresana, *El otro árbol de Guernica* (Barcelona: Círculo de Lectores, 1968), 5–6.

48 Ibid., 29–37.

49 *A pesar de todo dibujan. La Guerra Civil vista por los niños. Catálogo de la Exposición* (Madrid: Biblioteca Nacional de España, Fundación Winterthur, 2006).

50 Manon Pignot, *La guerre des crayons. Quand les petits parisiens dessinaient la Grande Guerre* (Paris: Parigramme, 2004), 7.

51 Rose Duroux and Catherine Milkovitch-Rioux, *J'ai dessiné la guerre. Le regard de Françoise et Alfred Brauner* (Clermont-Ferrand: Presses Universitaires Blaise Pascal, 2011).

52 For a definition of 'art as therapy', see *Art as Therapy: An Introduction to the Use of Art as a Therapeutic Technique*, ed. Tessa Dalley (London: Routledge, 1984). For the case of the Spanish Civil War, an early and influential study was undertaken in Alfred and Françoise Brauner, *Dessins d'enfants de la Guerre d'Espagne* (Saint-Mandé: Expansion Scientifique Française, 1976).

53 Biblioteca Nacional de España, Madrid, Departamento de Bellas Artes y Cartografía, Colección 'Dibujos Infantiles de la Guerra Civil', 19/1/844.

54 *Children's Colonies. Spanish Republic. Ministry of Public Education. International Council for Evacuated Children* (Paris: La Productrice, 1937).

55 Mariano González-Arnao Conde-Luque, 'Los niños vascos refugiados en el Reino Unido (1937)', *Historia 16* XIX, no. 224 (1994): 25.

56 Newport Public Library (Wales) [http://www.caerleon.net/cambria/basque/page9 .html].

57 Dolores Pla Brugat, *Los niños de Morelia* (Mexico City: Instituto Nacional de Antropología e Historia, 1985), and Verónica Sierra Blas, 'Con el corazón en la mano. Cultura escrita, exilio y vida cotidiana en las cartas de los padres de los Niños de Morelia', in *Mis primeros pasos. Alfabetización, escuela y usos cotidianos de la escritura (siglos XIX y XX),* ed. Antonio Castillo Gómez and Verónica Sierra Blas (Gijón: Trea, 2008), 415–58.

58 Archivo General de la Nación de México, México D. F., Presidencias, Lázaro Cárdenas, 939-550/84.

59 Verónica Sierra Blas, *Palabras huérfanas. Los niños y la Guerra Civil* (Madrid: Taurus, 2009), 259–89.

60 Alted, Marín and González Martell, *Los niños de la guerra de España en la Unión Soviética.*

61 Verónica Sierra Blas, 'Las cartas de los Niños de Rusia. Diarios de a bordo de un exilio sin retorno', *Revista Brasileira de Pesquisa (Auto)Biográfica* 2, no. 5 (2017): 268–89.

62 CDMH, PS Bilbao, 5-12/71.

63 For this ideological influence, see Verónica Sierra Blas, '"Reconstructing Silences". On the Study and Edition of the Private Letters of Spanish Children Evacuated to Russia during the Spanish Civil War', *Variants: The Journal of the European Society for Textual Scholarship* 8 (2012): 95–109.

64 CDMH, PS Bilbao, 205/8-19.

65 Alicia Alted, 'Le retour en Espagne des enfants évacués pendant la Guerre Civile espagnole: la Délégation extraordinaire au repatriement des mineurs (1938-1954)', in *Enfants de la Guerre Civile espagnole. Vécus et représentations de la génération née entre 1925 et 1940* (Paris: L´Harmattan, Fondation Nationale des Sciences Politiques, Centre d´Histoire de l´Europe du Vingtième Siècle, 1999), 47–59.

66 Jesús J. Alonso Carballés and Miguel Mayoral Guíu, 'La repatriación de "los niños del exilio": un intento de afirmación del régimen franquista, 1937-1939', in *El régimen de Franco. Política y relaciones exteriores,* ed. Javier Tusell, Susana Sueiro, José María Marín and Marina Casanova, (Madrid: Universidad Nacional de Educación a Distancia, 1993), I, 363.

67 Antonio Vilanova, *Los olvidados. Los exiliados españoles en la Segunda Guerra Mundial* (Paris: Ruedo Ibérico, 1969), 465.

68 Ángela Cenarro, *La sonrisa de Falange: Auxilio Social en la Guerra Civil y en la posguerra* (Barcelona: Crítica, 2006) and *Los niños del Auxilio Social* (Madrid: Espasa, 2009).

69 Josefina Rodríguez Aldecoa, *Los niños de la guerra* (Madrid: Anaya, 1983), 9–10.

Chapter 11

HOME-FRONT COOKING: EATING AND DAILY LIFE IN REPUBLICAN CITIES DURING THE SPANISH CIVIL WAR

Suzanne Dunai

The Spanish Civil War transformed every aspect of life for Spaniards on the home front, including how they cooked and ate with their families. The municipal authorities in Spain's largest Republican-held cities – Madrid and Barcelona – attempted to normalize civilian life by implementing food regulations, but these would ultimately lead to a food crisis in 1937. In the decades prior to the outbreak of war, city residents had enjoyed an increase in per capita income that provided many Spaniards with access to better quality and more nutritious foods.[1] Additionally, the peacetime Republican government had implemented quality-control regulations and authorized the constructions of new markets, leading Spaniards to have relatively high expectations for food access and quality.[2] So, if these expectations for relatively plentiful and quality food were not met, urban Spaniards considered themselves hungry, and held the Republican authorities responsible for their hunger. But how were categories such as hunger, appetite, and satiation defined in a period of cultural and social upheaval?

This chapter addresses both the material shortages caused by Republican wartime mobilization efforts, along with the ideological and cultural cues that determined acceptable eating for ordinary Spaniards on the urban home front. It is argued that one of the consequences of the war was the breakdown in the social definition of the Spanish meal, leading many Spaniards to redefine the worth of their everyday eating habits. The Popular Front bombarded the home front with ideological campaigns advocating for civilian sacrifice for the war effort while cities in the Republican zone, such as Madrid and Barcelona, faced outright food crises.[3] The cultural definitions of the Spanish meal, and its opposite, inadequate food and hunger, set the stage for how material consumption would be assessed during the Spanish Civil War.

Territorial divisions and the redirection of resources to the war effort greatly disrupted Spain's foodways – the transport and processing of food from farm to consumers' homes. Following the uprising, the Nationalists quickly took control of most of Spain's best agricultural lands, while Spain's largest cities remained loyal to the Republic, creating a significant burden for government authorities to provision both the front lines and the home front. Spaniards hoarded comestibles and sought extra-legal means to secure foodstuffs through the black market in fear of going hungry. Chronic irregularities in food distribution within the city seemed to validate their fears, leading to more hoarding and black marketeering. As the war progressed, Spaniards lost their trust in the Republican government's ability to meet their most basic needs, leading to a burgeoning food crisis and greater political apathy on the home front. Within Republican cities, there was not enough food to satisfy Spanish consumer expectations that remained entrenched in the pre-war urban food culture.

Recent scholarship on the Spanish Civil War has re-examined the role of the civilian food supply in influencing public opinion and support of the war effort. Michael Seidman has gone as far to claim that food was a major contributing factor in the Nationalists' military victory.[4] He argues that more than ideological or cultural reasons, civilian Spaniards were motivated by material conditions – such as food – in determining their attitudes towards the war. Similarly, innovative scholarship on the social consequences of the war – with case studies on Madrid and Barcelona – demonstrate the countless victims of the war who never stepped foot on the battlefield. Scholars such as María Isabel del Cura and Rafael Huertas have drawn connections between the severe suffering of the Spanish population with advances in nutrition and scientific knowledge for the urban medical elite. They have identified how several doctors documented the wartime situation with case studies of malnourished city dwellers.[5] Other researchers, such as Carmen and Laura Gutiérrez Rueda, have chronicled the paltry foodscape of Madrid under siege through pairing rationing information with oral histories.[6] Yet, material conditions of the war are only one approach in the study of the history of food, and academic considerations of the consequences of wartime cooking on food culture have only relatively recently been addressed by scholars such as Ismael Díaz Yubero. In his work, he identifies how scarcity, rationing, and commodity substitution became written into the recipes of the civil war and Franco dictatorship.[7] This chapter combines both lines of investigation – the material and cultural significance of food – in order to glean a deeper understanding of the social and cultural consequences of the Spanish Civil War.

Within food studies, scholars have diverged into two lines of investigation: cuisine, which addresses the cultural representations of food within a society, or diet, which explores the physical consumption of food and its biological consequences.[8] Likewise, the absence of food, or hunger, can be characterized as both a biological response to the absence of food and an emotional appetite that reflects cultural cravings and abstentions. Historian James Vernon pioneered the combination of cultural and physical aspects of hunger in his work on nineteenth-century Britain, in which he claims that hunger, although rooted in a biological phenomenon, adopted a new cultural meaning with industrialization, modernization, and the emergence of the welfare state. Vernon goes as far as to argue that hunger, the most material of conditions, is shaped by culture.[9] Therefore, when this theory is applied to the Spanish Civil War, both a cultural and social historical analysis of the food situation is needed to understand how the war was experienced by ordinary people, which in turn further elucidates the politics of how the war unfolded on the home front.

From the context of the urban wartime situation, we can begin to understand the mentality of scarcity, monotony, and hunger that plagued the civil war period and how the social meaning of hunger reflected political ideas of distrust, disillusionment, or dissatisfaction with the Republican government. Anthropologist Mary Douglas developed a method for interpreting the meaning of a meal within certain cultural contexts. She hypothesizes that dishes are assigned value by the consuming population,[10] meaning that social groups look for particular cultural cues in their dishes to signal if eating food is considered a meal or snack, satisfying or lacking. She describes that how food is prepared, its ingredients mixed in proportions, and the plates or utensils used to consume the food all provide clues for how individuals interpret a menu, meal, course, helping, or mouthful.[11] Her theory can be summarized as follows: on the one hand, physical food provisioning levels might fluctuate among a population, but consumers will still feel generally satisfied with the food and consider it a meal given the correct cultural cues that define a meal. On the other hand, food provisioning levels can remain consistent, or the body can be adequately nourished, but the cultural meaning of the food's preparation or service indicates to the consumer that the quantity or quality is subpar.[12] Connecting this to Vernon's work, a government can then be held responsible for not meeting these cultural cues of a meal – failing to adapt the definition of hunger to that of the society it governs. In the case of the Spanish Civil War, we can see that the Republic attempted to maintain a balancing act through propaganda to reduce the food consumption in the home front as much as possible while still meeting the minimum cultural and physical needs of the civilian population. This chapter parses out the fluctuation in the physical provisioning of food to Republican cities during the war and its cultural impact. Food became politicized as daily cooking incorporated ideology that brought the front lines to the home front in the face of very real shortages. The fracturing between Nationalist and Republican sympathizers, as well as divisions within the Popular Front, acted to further rupture the meaning of the Spanish meal and hunger. Thus, understanding the fluctuation in the meaning of the Spanish meal can provide a lens into understanding tensions and divisions at multiple levels within the war itself.

The Spanish Civil War brought changes to the country's cooking and eating habits regardless of class, politics, or location. Madrid and Barcelona had very different food situations during the war – Madrid was under siege and evacuated by those who could flee, while Barcelona was well-connected to supply lines, but received a myriad of refugees from across Spain – yet both cities suffered irregularities in food provisioning. The food crisis strained the relationship between the state and its citizens. As available food dwindled in supply, civilian apathy increased with hunger, despite the efforts of Republican authorities to guarantee that the population was adequately fed.[13] To ease the shock of the war for the civilian population, the Popular Front attempted to normalize scarcity through an extensive propaganda campaign of home-front sacrifice to the war effort, with demands that became ever more drastic as the war raged on. Spanish families could aid the war efforts by cutting back on their consumption habits and making the most of the food that was available. While well-managed food provisioning for civilians meant better organization for materials and supplies to be sent to the battlefront, public morale and support for the war effort depended on the absence of food cravings.[14] But staving off hunger alone in Republican cities was not considered sufficient government provisioning by many Spaniards. They also expected modern levels of gastronomic diversity that had become standard in large cities across Europe in the early twentieth century, and they demanded an ease in shopping that was only possible with a sophisticated foodscape. Without these additional urban attributes, many Spaniards – and particularly the middle classes – would consider themselves hungry.

Propaganda efforts from both sides perpetuated food ideologies to civilians living in their respective zones, and the messages communicated regarding the food situation depended on military strategy and public morale.[15] In the case of Republican cities, it was crucial for authorities to redefine Spanish meals on the home front so that supplies could be redirected to the battlefront without civilians losing public approval for the war effort. Propaganda of the time – including posters, magazines, pamphlets, and nutritional guides – urged Spaniards within the Republican zone to alter their eating habits in support of prioritizing the provisioning of troops. Municipal authorities, unions, and associations distributed recipes and cooking instructions in an effort to redefine the Spanish daily meal according to the demands of wartime scarcity. Communists and anarchists, for example, had to balance their food objectives with Republican food policy, which often led to internal conflict within Republican cities. Communist trade union members, for example, feuded over whether or not to advocate for better wages and working conditions for food workers or sacrificing these social benefits for the war effort.[16] Anarchist vegetarian naturalists – an admittedly minority group – supported the war effort, but struggled to receive adequate rations and accommodations for their dietary restrictions. One anarchist column even protested the Republic's apathy for their dietary constraints by pouring out their wine rations.[17]

Additionally, the inefficiency of Republican resources further divided urban society in the Republican zone as food policy changed quickly and often as authorities scrambled to provision both the war and the home front. In the case of Madrid, the municipality founded the *Comisión Popular de Abastos*, or Popular Food Provisioning Committee, that was so bureaucratic that its secretary, Pedro Bautista, claimed that it was practically useless.[18] Although Madrid created a single entity to centralize Republican food distribution in the city on 23 April 1937, there were still union-led cooperatives, food stalls, and collective dining halls managed by non-governmental entities.[19] And although food distribution through dining halls, restaurants, and bars fell under the jurisdiction of the Republican municipal authorities, the workers in these facilities were often members of trade unions, who had their own rules and policies for who received food, the quantity of food to distribute, and the price for buying and selling foodstuffs.[20] Ideologically, the Popular Front tried to unify its base through the broad objective of food policy, and they advocated that civilian sacrifice through food abstention was a moral obligation of the citizenry, and that a new home-front diet would promote better physical and civic health.[21] But as noted before, this was only one voice contributing to the food dialogue in Madrid and Barcelona, as high-level politics clashed with the daily politics of the neighbourhoods and municipalities.

As the war dragged on and the situation for the Republic became more drastic, Spanish food habits for most civilians in Republican cities became increasingly irregular, paltry, and monotonous.[22] The haphazard nature of Republican wartime foodways led Spaniards to characterize their daily food acquisition and consumption as a food crisis. Despite the efforts of municipal leaders and Republican authorities to assure the population that their culinary sacrifices were essential to winning the war, ordinary Spaniards felt hungry. Taken together, this chapter will connect the war's repercussions on the food supply to its impact on Spanish cuisine. The first section explains how diet became political during the Spanish Civil War. Food was more than daily sustenance: it was ideologically charged as a form of mobilization for the home front. The second section connects the politicization of everyday eating to changes in the social meaning of the Spanish meal. As sacrifice and scarcity became ingrained in the urban food culture, Spaniards found themselves hungrier for peace and an end to the war.

Home-Front Meals

A food crisis occurred in Madrid by the first winter of the war, but was slower to form in Barcelona. As the war continued and daily sacrifice was sustained month after month, Spaniards became despondent with their daily diet. Through intense propaganda of the ideology-fuelled conflict, traditional Spanish foods were no longer daily meals of sustenance, but were politicized through the war to symbolize support or sabotage to the Republican effort. One dish of chickpea stew, a concoction of staple ingredients that had long been essential in the Mediterranean diet, was renamed during the war to demonstrate its politicization in popular culture. *Cocido de guerra*, or wartime stew, as it became called, symbolized scarcity and wartime resistance, and eventually, the people of Madrid became tired of the monotony:

> This was wartime stew (a dish eaten by the suffering and miserable in Madrid for almost three years), a soup of cooked chickpeas without any of the fixings of a traditional hearty stew of meat and bacon. But this stew of oil, tomato, onion, chickpeas, and some vegetables coloured with a little saffron or paprika transformed into a small dish of passive resistance with some bread. With vegetable proteins, bean starches and fat from the oil, the stew temporarily provided consumers economical energies that, when well-managed, could withstand the hardships, deprivations, and sufferings of war.[23]

The dish was considered a form of passive resistance because civilians – the women and children who stayed on the home front – were able to support the war effort through their everyday eating habits. And along with the monotony of chickpeas, Spaniards relied heavily on lentils to sustain their daily meals. Indeed, lentils were the cornerstone of Madrid's wartime diet, and eventually become known as 'resistance pills' or 'Dr Negrin's pills', after the Republican prime minister, who was also a medical doctor. Yet the quality of lentils deteriorated as the war progressed, and were often mixed with grit or even insects.[24] Legume consumption, whether chickpea or lentil, was tethered to Republican war efforts and thus highly politicized. By sacrificing taste and culinary diversity, ordinary civilians did their part in helping the Republic. But one consequence of these recipes and their monotony was that many ordinary Spaniards eventually decided they had had enough wartime stew and resistance pills, and particularly the urban classes hungered for the potential food options that peace would bring. The conditions of the war, as much of the ingredients of their stew, were no longer enough to sustain their everyday lives.

One of the biggest challenges for Spaniards was to negotiate the dwindling foodscape of the wartime cities. With many supplies being diverted to the front, civilians were left to find food in the city or the surrounding areas. In Barcelona, civilians struggled to shop for their families and often had to rely on an extensive network of connections in order to acquire all the ingredients necessary for meals.[25] Market hours were reduced, prices were set by authorities, and quantities of staple foodstuffs were limited through rationing. In Madrid, the municipal authorities attempted crowd control by regulating when lines were allowed to form outside stores and dining halls.[26] Madrid women were desperate to secure the food necessary to feed their family at all cost. In one account, a mother refused to get out of line even when bombing started. As women with weaker constitutions left the line to seek cover, she advanced further in the queue.[27] As the war progressed, the effects of the food crisis on the civilian population became more acute. The National Institute of Hygiene in Madrid observed average caloric consumption by civilians decrease from 1,514 calories per day in August 1937 to a desperate 852 calories per day by February 1939.[28] Chronic food shortages in Spanish cities clearly took a toll on the civilian population as each month of inadequate eating made the population more susceptible to life-threatening disease and vitamin-deficiency health conditions (see Figure 11.1).

Yet in both Barcelona and Madrid, the major disruption to the food supply was competing policies enacted by various authorities that obscured normal food supply practices.[29] In Madrid, the *Comisión Nacional de Abastecimientos*, or National Provisioning Commission, was created on 3 October 1936 to regulate rationing in the city, but the system was later controlled by the *Comisión Provincial de Abastecimientos*, or Provincial Provisioning Commission, created on 24 October 1936 to replace the municipal entity *Comisión Popular*, or People's Commission.[30] Later, on 9 November 1936, the Provincial Commission became the Council of Provisioning with the formation of the *Junta de Defensa de Madrid*, or Madrid Defence Council. Within the short time span of two months, the food provisioning

Figure 11.1 Civilians in Madrid queue for aid packages distributed by *Socorro Rojo Internacional* (International Red Aid). Archivo Regional de Madrid, 30941-012.

authority to the capital city changed four times, making it difficult for civilians to maintain correct documentation and rationing information during their food acquisition. Branches of the *Unión General de Trabajdores* (UGT), or General Union of Workers, and the *Confederación Nacional del Trabajo* (CNT), or National Confederation of Labour, the socialist and anarchist unions respectively, controlled all functioning hotels, bars, and restaurants in Madrid during the war, and by August 1936, the unions had repurposed 200 restaurants in Madrid to service the food supply of soldiers and their families.[31] With more food sites exclusively dedicated to Republican troops and their dependents, ordinary Spaniards without any connection to the front lines found themselves with fewer eating options within the city. Furthermore, even though food was available through the syndicate-operated dining halls, the sites themselves were highly political. Among waiters who were members of the UGT[32] there were often conflicts in meetings between supporting the austerity measures of the war effort and pushing for the much-desired labour reform.[33] In Barcelona, ideologies of various wings of the political left fuelled miscommunication and mismanagement of resources. Anarchists attempted to artificially lower food prices through seizure of *El Born* wholesale market, but their efforts ultimately failed to curb rampant inflation and chronic food shortages.[34]

Price variation was a chronic problem for people in the city, despite the intervention of municipal authorities that standardized prices for essential goods. Spaniards relied on staple foodstuffs in their everyday diet, yet the scarcity of goods drove up prices on everyday consumer commodities such as oil, bread, meat, and eggs. Whereas authorities tried to keep market prices down on commodities, some

Spaniards would buy goods at any price that vendors asked.[35] The newspaper *ABC* denounced the black market in an opinion piece published on 1 November 1937: 'Whoever grabs one peseta of groceries [on the black market] is a traitor to Spain; an enemy of freedom who might as well shoot a rifle against the soldiers of the people.'[36] In this article, food choices on the home front were equated with military actions on the battlefield. Spanish housewives could sabotage war efforts merely by indulging in food luxuries, and their support for the troops was measured in the amount of food that they abstained from in their daily meals. But historians have concluded that the hunger and starvation, and therefore also disease, would have been worse without the black market, and that extra-legal food gave individuals access to dietary essentials otherwise simply not available.[37]

As the war progressed, the elevated prices for staple foodstuffs fluctuated wildly in the official and unofficial economy and from one vendor or area of the city to the next, but the overall shortage of food in the cities hindered daily meals for many families. Barcelona's *Comissariat de Propaganda*, or Propaganda Commission, reported that in March 1937 the official prices of regulated foodstuff were sufficient for Spanish diet and health. The commission urged that it only took a little planning to maximize nutrition while saving money.[38] They claimed that with 1 peseta, a refugee or citizen of Barcelona could buy 2,500 calories of bread, 2,025 calories of oil, 1,312 calories of sugar, 1,300 calories of peanuts, 825 calories of dried beans, 540 calories of butter, 198 calories of beef, 680 calories of milk, 124 calories of eggs, or 240 calories of cheese.[39] Yet outside reports presented a much bleaker of the price situation in Barcelona. One source reported that the price of eggs increased from 3 pesetas per dozen to 9.50 pesetas. Sugar almost doubled in price from 1.40 to 2.50 per kilogram. Potatoes and meat prices doubled from July 1936 to July 1937, with prices per kilo rising from 0.35 pesetas to 0.70 pesetas and 7.50 pesetas to 15 pesetas, respectively.[40] A food critic noticed that one restaurant that had sold a hearty stew for 90 cents before the war increased the price to 7.50 pesetas in the first few months of 1938 as a consequence of scarcity and inflation.[41] Even daily prices in the markets would change based on the shopper's relationship with the vendor or the legality of the product sold. The price of a chicken in Barcelona varied from 25 pesetas to 50 pesetas based on who was willing to pay which price.[42] Coupled with the obstacle of inflating prices, many Spaniards lost confidence in Republican money (as argued in Chapter 8 of this volume), making it difficult to even carry out simple transactions for foodstuffs.[43] Some food vendors were benevolent and extended credit to those they trusted,[44] while for others, shopping for food became a major endeavour.

Although Madrid and Barcelona both experienced verifiable food crises by the end of 1937, the two cities experienced them in different ways. Many residents of Madrid fled their homes during the war, leaving their ration or coupon cards behind for neighbours or friends to redeem as a strategy of survival.[45] In contrast, Barcelona received refugees from all over the country. In October 1937, one volunteer British doctor recounted that the influx of refugees would deplete the city's food supply by the end of the year. Furthermore, the doctor observed that many of the refugees from rural areas in Spain knew little of how to live in a metropolis and lacked modern hygiene education.[46] Whereas Madrid suffered greatly in the transport of seafood – an important source of protein – to the city during the siege, Barcelona benefited from its close proximity to the Mediterranean and the French border. As the siege of Madrid continued into 1938, flocks of birds were nowhere to be found in the city parks, and family cats and dogs were captured and sold on the black market as food.[47] By the end of the war, much of the food that Madrid civilians ate did not come from the municipal authorities or the rationing system. Madrid's wealthy also suffered the shortages of luxury items and seafood supply dropped from its pre-war levels of seventy to eighty loads per day to one truck per day, leading to the saying 'he who eats shellfish eats gold'.[48]

In both cities, residents left the city for the surrounding rural areas in order to acquire food, and the everyday practice of food acquisition relied less and less on Republican provisioning. This survival strategy further proved that Republican cities had a food crisis – a failure of the government to adequately control and provision its population – rather than a famine. In Madrid, Spanish housewives travelled with their children to nearby villages that were accessible in the Republican zone. But despite their resilient efforts to secure food for their families, Republican authorities in Madrid prohibited civilians from returning to the city with more than 15 kilograms of foodstuffs. Spaniards responded to the food acquisition restrictions by renaming the train to Arganda, south of the capital, as the 'hunger train' and hid food in their sleeves or coats to avoid detection.[49] Spaniards showed passive discontent for the food situation, equating the long shopping commute on the train to hunger. In Barcelona, Spaniards relied on connections between the city centre and the rural hinterland in a sophisticated labyrinth of social networks that allowed women to buy, sell, and exchange foods.[50] Food scarcity and hunger had lasting effects on ordinary Spaniards living in both cities. The food crisis in Barcelona during the war made its legacy in the award-winning comedy *La Fam (Hunger)*[51] while malnutrition suffered by Madrid's working class became documented in medicine as 'Madrid syndrome'.[52]

Food and its counterpart of hunger were thoroughly integrated into the politics of the Spanish Civil War. Propaganda from the time implied that every ingredient that a consumer bought, the size of their meal, and the price that they paid for food all had ramifications for the Republican war effort. While Spaniards might have pledged loyalty to the Republic with their words, their food choices began to tell a different story as the war progressed. Discontent with the 'passive resistance' offered by wartime stew and daily grumblings against food provisioning to cities signalled a decline in public support and effort for the sacrifices needed to sustain the war. While it was necessary that food was politicized in order to prioritize Republican resources for the troops, it also meant that discontent with the Republic's food policy also inevitably meant discontent with the Republic's war.

Urban Food Culture during the Spanish Civil War

Food privations left their mark on Republican cities, but what did hunger mean to ordinary Spaniards? The propaganda circulated in the Republican zone emphasized the importance of civilian sacrifice for the war effort, and contemporary cooking literature followed the same theme. The cookbooks, recipe collections, and nutrition manuals produced by the Popular Front, municipal authorities, and Republican sympathizers embraced the narrative of sacrifice, substitution, and scarcity to meet wartime demands on the food supply. Some cooking literature co-opted aspects of nutrition science to justify wartime levels of food provisioning to the urban population and to defend the efforts of municipal authorities in food provisioning. Home economists and cookbook authors instructed Spanish housewives in how to implement culinary creativity in the kitchen to win the food battle on the home front.

The food culture of the Spanish Civil War as it was written into recipes suggested that little sacrifices cooked into everyday dishes would greatly help the troops in the trenches. The cookbook *Menús de Guerra* (*Wartime Dinners*) introduced its collection of recipes with 'ingredients that aren't abundant on the home front, but aren't scarce either.'[53] The booklet claimed, 'It's no sacrifice at all to go with a little less on the table: the extras. [Basic dishes] are quite enough when one takes into account that visual appetite satisfies the belly.'[54] What the author meant by removing the 'extras' was cutting back on garnishes and sauces, but it also alluded to cutting back on one of the main ingredients of the Spanish middle classes: meat. Some of the featured recipes from the collection did not include any meat at all: oven-cooked spinach, lettuce in its own juice, and salted potatoes[55] were just some of the examples of meatless dishes featured in the cookbook. Of the twenty-four recipes, fourteen called for a form of animal protein, but only two featured meat as the main ingredient in the dish by weight in comparison to the other ingredients, and only one recipe for stew required two different meats. The simplistic recipes suggested that meat should be used sparingly in the home-front cooking of Spanish housewives. By sticking to the basics – downplaying expensive and scarce meat in meals and only eating one type of meat per dish – civilians could cut back on their consumption levels and allow for foodstuffs to be rerouted to the front lines.

Consumption of animal protein had increased in Spanish cities during the early twentieth century, and the demand for meat grew along with family income in the cities.[56] In Barcelona, municipal records indicate that from 1914 until 1933, consumption increased per person for poultry, fish, eggs, milk, and cured meat.[57] For city dwellers, eating meat became a daily habit and was incorporated into the cultural meaning of a meal. It was a common belief that meat was needed in order for food to be considered a 'hearty meal'.[58] Yet, meat and its excellent quantities of fats and proteins were needed at the battlefront, so municipal authorities urged civilians to sacrifice their meat consumption for the war effort. The social value that Spaniards assigned to meat was transferred to the troops, albeit not always successfully, leaving middle-class Spaniards of Republican cities without this key ingredient. Without meat on the menu, Spaniards were likely to feel dissatisfied with their dinners, and they developed a hunger for meat to return to their meals.

To help curb the cultural demand for meat, the Popular Front used nutrition science to validate meatless meals for civilians. Nutrition science developed in the late nineteenth century as a social science to improve worker production and public health.[59] From its inception, the study of food nutrition was political and closely tied to public policy. Wartime propaganda attempted to justify consumer sacrifice according to scientific calculations, providing important information to Spaniards on how to eat less but remain healthy. They stressed that the health benefits of diminished caloric intake among the population and citing medical findings to justify contractions in the urban food supply. Dispelling the theory multiple times that poor diet causes susceptibility to diseases, or that eating large meals would help to maintain good health, Dr Noguer-Moré instead highlighted the health benefits of eating less. He wrote: 'The custom of eating a lot ... often more than what is necessary, normalizing the appearance of the majority of what are called nutritional diseases (obesity, gout, diabetes, etc.). ... The "full" feeling that one gets at the end of a large meal does not promote health, but proves that one has eaten excessively.'[60] Contrary to popular belief that Spaniards should feel full at the end of a meal, Dr Noguer-Moré warned that eating large meals could cause serious health problems. What the propaganda aimed to promote was that smaller meal sizes were not a sign of hunger, but rather better public health.

To further justify the allocation of the Republican food supply to the front lines and away from the home front, Dr Noguer-Moré made the following claim: sedentary or moderately active people only needed 2,000 to 2,300 calories each day. Factory workers on the home front, despite the intensity of their jobs, only needed 2,500 to 2,800 calories. It was the soldiers on the front lines who needed 3,000 to 3,200 calories each day.[61] From this interpretation, caloric need was measured in an individual's relationship to the war, and not conventionally by their age, sex, occupation, or metabolism. And just like *Wartime Dinners*, the nutrition manual urged Spaniards to cut back on their meat consumption. It balked at the popular belief that meat was necessary to make a filling and nutritious meal and instead promoted almonds, walnuts, hazelnuts, oil, and cheeses as viable meat-replacements for Spanish meals. He wrote, 'We invite the reader to consider caloric equivalencies of foods so that they can convince themselves that those [meat substitutes] are not more or less nutritious than meat.'[62] The ideal meal of nutrition science was created for calories, not taste, texture, or cultural symbolism. Meat, it was implied, was unimportant to Spaniards if the calories were substituted through another ingredient. Cooking literature for meat substitutes then spread throughout Republican cities during the war to accommodate the very real meat shortages in the civilian food supply.

Identifying and promoting alternatives to meat was crucial for municipal authorities who were in charge of provisioning food to Republican cities. For example, the *Comissariat de Propaganda* in Barcelona published leaflets in Spanish and Catalan with diagrams of substitutes: 'Did you know that just two walnuts have the protein value of 30g of meat?'[63] Dr Noguer-Moré echoed this sentiment. '[Some say] walnuts are snack foods and do not count as a food. ... It cannot be emphasized enough that nuts are a food with great nutritional value, one of the most nutritional foods known.'[64] Nuts had long been seen as a substitute for meat by vegetarian cooks, but how the substitute was presented suggested limited food choice. Along with abstaining from meat, Spaniards were encouraged to use animal products more than slaughtered animals for their protein intake. Milk, cheese, and eggs were all promoted as meat substitutes. Republican propaganda, nutrition experts, and vegetarians attempted to dispel the 'popular myth' that meat was an essential part of the Spanish meal, but their efforts largely fell on deaf ears. Spaniards maintained the saying, 'bread, wine, and meat make healthy blood'[65] along with 'bacon makes the meal, man makes the public life, and woman makes the home'.[66] Many Spaniards rejected outright the notion that food could be meatless and still constitute a satiating meal, and thus days without animal flesh generated a hunger for better food in Republican cities.

Sacrifice was generally measured in meat, but another objective of the wartime propaganda was to reprioritize foods that had previously been culturally marginalized in Spanish food culture. Sardines are one example of a food that Spaniards were urged to re-evaluate during the civil war. *Platos de Guerra: Cuaderno 1, Sardinas* (*War Dishes: Part 1, Sardines*), was authored by an 'anonymous home-front cook' and provided useful information on how to preserve and prepare sardines. The author wrote of the fish: 'The sardine is, without a doubt, the sea fish whose boom has reached even the popular classes, making the fish very cheap despite its tasty, delicate, and nutritious meat.'[67] Sardines were not a preferred fish like hake, or a large fish like tuna. Yet, the small blue fish was a suitable form of animal protein for the Republican civilian population as more prized meats were sent to the front. In the book, the author instructed Spanish women on how to preserve the fish by salting, smoking, canning in oil, and pickling.[68] Of the sixty-four recipes that ranged from stews, rice-based stews, roasts, and fried dishes, sardines were the main ingredient and only form of animal protein in the dishes. The publication contrasts sharply with the other cooking literature of the time in that it promoted the consumption of an animal protein rather than discouraging it. Yet, the publication still fits within the trend of cookbooks to emphasize the importance of civilian sacrifice as well as how to cope with chronic food shortages. The cookbook addressed monotony, but instead of criticizing monotony for its boring tastes and risk of poor nutrition, it celebrated creative ways that ordinary housewives could embellish a meal without diversifying the ingredients. Similar to the wartime stew, monotonous consumption of sardines was encouraged as a way to support the Republic. As the cookbook explained: 'War brings shortages and sacrifices, of which food is the most conspicuous. But it is our patriotic duty to carry on making cooking as easy as possible in hard times.'[69] For the home-front cook who wrote the recipes and the housewives who read them, the monotony of eating sardines was a form of sacrifice and patriotism.

As the Republic's situation became increasingly desperate and the food crises of the cities became more acute, more and more ingredients gained food value for propagandists and ordinary Spaniards. Olives, for example, were consumed in Spanish cities as a snack, garnish, or pressed into cooking oil prior to the outbreak of war, but they gained new food value as the war progressed. The publication *Alimentación en Tiempos de Guerra* (*Food in Wartime*), reported that 'olives, a snack food taken for granted in everyday life, in times of scarcity provide important nutritional value in that just 100g of olives contains over 200 calories.'[70] The publication urged Spaniards to consider the value of olives in caloric terms rather than a meaningless snack. Olive oil was re-branded as a food as well. Prior to the war, olive oil was not considered a food, but an additive to foods (such as a dressing for salad or fish) or as a means of frying. Its purpose changed during the food crisis in Madrid and Barcelona. As the Propaganda Commission of Barcelona wrote, 'Many daily meals leave their plates with oil remaining, and that is a travesty. When oil is placed on salad or vegetables for flavour, it not only gives the dish a good taste, but provides more calories than the rest of the salad.'[71] According to evidence, olives and olive oil did increase in importance and symbolic value in the practice of daily life of urban civilians. Municipal authorities made sure that olive oil consumption was limited within their cities through rationing,[72] and restaurants stopped putting jars of oil on tables for seasoning due to customers using excessive amounts on their plates or siphoning it from the bottles to take home.[73] Whether they wanted it or not, Spaniards had to begin to re-conceptualize their meals to be meatless and to re-evaluate previously marginal parts of the meal.

The cultural meaning of Spanish meals continued to unravel as the food crises grew. Shifts in edibility transpired, further demonstrating how much fluctuation had occurred in the meaning of a meal. Chef Doménech recalled a few recipes from Barcelona during the war that devolved cultural norms of edibility: omelettes made without eggs, coffee made from peanut shells, pastries made from carob pods, and propaganda posters used as cooking fuel for the oven.[74] This last measure – burning leaflets or posters to sustain a fire in the familial hearth – suggested a growing level of disillusionment that civilians had for the war effort. The countless posters, circulars, and pamphlets became, in practice, more valuable to ordinary Spaniards as fuel to burn in their household oven than for the ideology that they promoted.

So although urban Spaniards experienced shortages and irregularities in the food provisioning of Madrid and Barcelona by municipal authorities, there was no shortage of propaganda. Within the Republican zone, civilians were expected to sacrifice their comforts and food for the war effort by adopting new ways of eating meals. Through recipes, Spanish housewives were taught to devalue meat in their meals and prioritize other foods like vegetables, nuts, and olives. Nutritionists contributed their expertise by justifying the scarcity as public health measures. Science was used to promote eating less as a health benefit, not as a health risk. Chefs and cooks contributed their knowledge of gastronomy to suggest innovative ways to thwart monotonous taste or poor quality ingredients. Overall, a shift in the definition of edibility occurred, along with a shift in the meaning of the Spanish meal. With both of these categories blurred by the war, it markedly changed cooking and eating habits in Republican Spanish cities. Furthermore, ordinary Spaniards felt nostalgia for pre-war diet and desired to return to the society and meals of peace.

Conclusion: The War's End

With food clearly incorporated into the politics of the Spanish Civil War, ordinary Spaniards were encouraged to express their patriotism and support for the

Republican effort with every shopping trip that they made and every meal that they cooked. Little actions, such as what Spaniards bought in the market and how housewives prepared dinner, were correlated to significant consequences for the troops on the front lines. Spanish housewives who abstained from meat in their family meals or created their own cooking fuel meant that those essential supplies could be redirected to the battlefront. Municipal authorities in Madrid and Barcelona attempted to maximize home-front mobilization for the war effort by redefining cooking and eating through wartime propaganda. Science was used to validate and defend their food policies, and written propaganda and cooks were tasked with converting housewives to the new home-front food strategy.

Yet, Spaniards were largely unhappy with the change in the cultural meaning of the meal, and with the politicization of food, their discontent with the food situation equated to discontent with the war effort. Mismanagement of the supply ultimately caused public opinion to lose faith in the war. Eventually, ordinary Spaniards living in Republican cities lost the taste for the continuous sacrifice that was required to sustain the conflict. Apathy crept into public opinion as Spaniards grudgingly adopted a monotonous and restricted diet, and which became increasingly exacerbated as the Republic lost ground to its Nationalist enemies. Peace at any cost was considered cheaper than white bread at the time; and so many urban Spaniards eventually welcomed at least the material promises that Franco and the Nationalists made for 'Country, Justice, and Bread', as well as with the slogan: 'Not a single home without firewood or a Spaniard without bread'.[75] But Franco's provisionary promises would eventually fail to meet the dietary expectations of Spaniards as well. Scarcity and monotony continued in Madrid and Barcelona long after the war's end in a time remembered as 'the hunger years'. The food crisis persisted as Spaniards retained their distrust in the food supply and of vendors. Indeed, hoarding and the black market continued to be an integral part of Spanish cooking for at least another decade after the formal end of the Spanish Civil War.

Further Reading

Almodóvar, Miguel Ángel. *El hambre en España: una historia de la alimentación*. Madrid: Oberón, 2003.

Atkins, Peter J., Peter Lummel and Derek J. Oddy, eds. *Food and the City in Europe since 1800*. Burlington: Ashgate, 2007.

Barona Vilar, Josep. *La Medicalización del hambre. Economía política de la alimentación en Europa, 1918-1960*. Barcelona: Icaria Editorial, 2014.

Douglas, Mary. 'Deciphering a meal'. *Daedalus* 101 (1972), 1:61-81.

Medina, F. Xavier. *Food Culture in Spain*. Westpoint, CT: Greenwood Press, 2010.

Miller, Montserrat. *Feeding Barcelona, 1714-1975: Public Market Halls, Social Networks, and Consumer Culture*. Baton Rouge: Louisiana State University Press, 2015.

Vernon, James. *Hunger: A Modern History*. Cambridge, MA: Harvard University Press, 2007.

Notes

1 Roser Nicolau-Nos and Josep Pujol-Andreu, 'Urbanization and Dietary Change in Mediterranean Europe: Barcelona, 1870-1935', in *Food and the City in Europe Since 1800* ed. Peter J. Atkins, Peter Lummel and Derek J. Oddy (Burlington, VT: Ashgate Publishers, 2007), 39.

2 Montserrat Miller, *Feeding Barcelona, 1714-1975: Public Market Halls, Social Networks, and Consumer Culture* (Baton Rouge: Louisiana State University Press, 2015), 150.

3 'Food crisis' refers to the governing authority's mismanagement of resources that leads to a shortage of goods within a population. It is different from a famine, which is dependent on the countryside and often caused by environmental factors. Food crises are generally an urban phenomenon because residents are unable to secure their own food. For further reading, see: *Food and the City in Europe Since 1800*.

4 Michael Seidman, *Victorious Counterrevolution: The Nationalist Effort in the Spanish Civil War* (Madison, WI: University of Wisconsin Press, 2011), 6. Also see Chapter 8 of this volume.

5 María Isabel Del Cura, *Alimentación y enfermedad en tiempo de hambre: España, 1937-1947* (Madrid: Consejo Superior de Investigaciones Científicas, 2007).

6 Carmen Gutiérrez Rueda and Laura Gutiérrez Rueda, *El Hambre en el Madrid de la Guerra Civil, 1936-1939* (Madrid: Ediciones La Librería, 2003).

7 Ismael Díaz Yubero, 'El hambre y la gastronomía. De la guerra civil a la cartilla de racionamiento.' *Estudios sobre consumo* July: 66 (2003): 9–22.

8 Isabel González Turmo, *La comida de rico, la comida de pobre: Los hábitos alimenticios en el Occidente andaluz* (Seville: Universidad de Sevilla, 1995) 20.

9 Turmo, *La comida de rico, la comida de pobre*, viii.

10 Mary Douglas, 'Deciphering a Meal', *Daedalus* 101:1 (1972): 61–2.

11 Douglas, 'Deciphering a Meal', 63.

12 Ibid., 63–5.

13 Michael Seidman, *Republic of Egos: A Social History of the Spanish Civil War* (Madison, WI: University of Wisconsin Press, 2002), 7.

14 Jesus Noguer-Moré, *Nuestra alimentación en tiempos de escasez* (Barcelona: Biblioteca Higia, 1937), 6.

15 Seidman, *Victorious Counterrevolution*, 247.

16 'Del Frente: Los Sindicatos y la guerra' in *El Dependiente Rojo*, Año I, núm I, 2.

17 Josep María Roselló, *La vuelta a la naturaleza: El pensamiento naturista hispano (1890-2000): naturismo libertario, trofología, vegetarismo naturista, vegetarismo social y librecultura* (Bilbao: Virus Memoria, 2003), 130.

18 Gutiérrez Rueda, *El Hambre en el Madrid de la Guerra Civil*, 34.

19 Ibid., 36.

20 Ibid.

21 *Menús de Guerra* (Barcelona: Generalitat de Catalunya, 1936?), 2.

22 Díaz Yubero, *El hambre y la gastronomía*, 9.

23 Antonio Castillo de Lucas, *Refranillo de la alimentación: Divulgación de higiene de la misma, a través de los refranes y dichos populares* (Madrid: Graficas reunidas, 1940), 131.

24 Gutiérrez Rueda, *El hambre en el Madrid de la Guerra Civil*, 94.

25 Miller, *Feeding Barcelona*, 199.

26 Gutiérrez Rueda, *El Hambre en el Madrid de la Guerra Civil*, 50.

27 Ibid., 51.

28   Josep Barona Vilar, *La Medicalización del hambre. Economía política de la alimentación en Europa, 1918-1960* (Barcelona: Icaria Editorial, 2014), 116.

29   Miller, *Feeding Barcelona*, 193; Gutiérrez Rueda, *El Hambre en el Madrid de la Guerra Civil*, 38.

30   Gutiérrez Rueda, *El Hambre en el Madrid de la Guerra Civil*, 38.

31   Ibid., 40.

32   More specifically, *La Sociedad General de Dependientes de cafés, bares y cervecerías de Madrid*, UGT.

33   *El Dependiente Rojo*, Año I, núm I.

34   Miller, *Feeding Barcelona*, 194.

35   Ibid., 156.

36   Gutiérrez Rueda, *El Hambre en el Madrid de la Guerra Civil*, 41.

37   Miller, *Feeding Barcelona*, 199.

38   *La Alimentación en Tiempos de Guerra: Problemas de alimentación que plantea la guerra* (Barcelona: Comissariat de Propaganda, Generalitat de Catalunya, n.d.), 22.

39   Ibid.

40   'Observaciones medicas sobre el hambre en la España roja' (Santander: XV Congreso de la Asociación Española para el Progreso de las Ciencias, Agosto 1938), 3.

41   Ignacio Doménech, *Cocina de Recursos (Deseo Mi Comida)* (Barcelona: Quintilla, Cardona y C., S.L., 1940), 92–3.

42   Ibid.

43   Seidman, *Victorious Counterrevolution*, 93.

44   Miller, *Feeding Barcelona*, 200.

45   Gutiérrez Rueda, *El Hambre en el Madrid de la Guerra Civil*, 33, 48.

46   Richard White Bernard Ellis, *Famine Faces a Million in Spain/based on the Reports of two British Doctors Recently Returned from Investigation in Catalonia* (London: National Joint Committee for Spanish Relief, 1937), 7.

47   Ellis, *Famine Faces a Million in Spain*, 101.

48   Gutiérrez Rueda, *El Hambre en el Madrid de la Guerra Civil*, 40.

49   Ibid., 73, 67.

50   Miller, *Feeding Barcelona*, 197.

51   Joan Oliver, *La Fam* (Barcelona: Institució de les Lletres Catalanes, 1938).

52   Del Cura, *Alimentación y enfermedad*, 152.

53   *Menús de Guerra*, 2.

54   Ibid., 2.

55   Ibid., 2, 14, 26.

56   Nicolau-Nos and Pujol-Andreu, *Urbanization and Dietary Change*, 42–3.

57   Ibid., 46.

58   Noguer-Moré, *Nuestra Alimentación*, 22.

59   Vernon, *Hunger*, 84.

60   Ibid., 23.

61   Ibid., 14.

62   Ibid., 22.

63   *La Alimentación en Tiempos de Guerra,* 43.

64   Noguer-Moré, *Nuestra* alimentación, 25.

65   Castillo de Lucas, *Refranillo de la alimentación*, 83.

66   Ibid., 52.

67   Anónimo (Cocinero de Retaguardia), *Platos de guerra: Recetario completo para la conservación y condimento de la Sardina*. Primera edición. (s.l.: 1938), 5.

68 Ibid., 7–13.
69 Ibid., 3.
70 Noguer-Moré, *Nuestra alimentación*, 26.
71 *La Alimentación en Tiempos de Guerra*, 23.
72 Gutiérrez Rueda, *El hambre en el Madrid de la Guerra Civil*, 44–5.
73 Doménech, *Cocina de Recursos,* 293.
74 Ibid., title page, 16–17, 62–3.
75 *La Justicia Social en el Nuevo Estado Español* (Saragossa: El Noticiero, 1937).

Part Four

LEGACIES OF THE SPANISH CIVIL WAR, 1939–44

Chapter 12

THE DEMOBILIZATION OF FRANCOIST AND REPUBLICAN WAR VETERANS, 1939–44: A GREAT DIVERGENCE?*

Ángel Alcalde

The history of war veterans is a productive new field of analysis in military history[1] and one of the most suitable topics to be investigated from a 'war and society' approach. Since the First World War veterans have emerged as an influential albeit problematic social group.[2] Veterans were crucially important for the post-war process of cultural demobilization and for the construction of war memory.[3] As 'agents of memory',[4] veterans played a prominent role in remembrance commemorations, in particular performing rites of memory and mourning to the fallen soldiers. As political actors, veterans created associations that successfully lobbied governments. They often formed social movements which aimed to obtain better pensions and moral recognition, sometimes even adopting paramilitary tactics and aesthetics, for example, events such as the Bonus March in Washington in 1932 and the French veterans' demonstration of 6 *février* 1934 in Paris which challenged the authority of the state.[5] Veterans often claimed to be the best guarantors of international peace; they believed that their direct and traumatic experience of war provided them with a moral authority over the rest of society. As a result, some of them considered that they were the best means to secure friendly relations among nations.

Political activities of veterans in different countries that participated in the Great War made a significant mark on the history of the European continent during the interwar years. Most importantly, in the interwar period a crucial historical link existed between war veterans and fascism.[6] This was based on the transnational spread of myths and stereotypes about 'fascist veterans' who, it was widely believed at the time, had brought communism down in Italy during the early 1920s and seized political power to restore the 'politics of victory'. Indeed, Mussolini and Hitler were seen by many contemporaries as war veterans seeking to redeem their trench comrades. The *Duce* and the *Führer* had served in the military during the Great War, and many of their followers too.[7] However, at the same time, veterans also formed left-wing groups during the interwar period.[8] The Great War myth of the former combatant was also relevant for the European left during the

1930s.[9] This embellished narrative also had an impact in Spain during the civil war. For instance, it is significant that a battalion of German anti-fascist volunteers in the International Brigades was named after Ernst Thaelmann, a veteran of the Great War who had been leader of the communist combat organization *Rote Frontkämpferbund*, or Association of Red Front-Fighters, then became the president of the German Communist Party, the KPD, and later was imprisoned by the Nazis.[10] The commander of the Thaelmann brigade, Ludwig Renn, had also been a soldier in the Great War.[11] Historians soon realized the difficulty of associating veterans with any particular ideology or political grouping.[12] For decades a vast and diverse historiography has examined the multiple strands of veterans' history in the interwar period. The case of Spain, where no Great War veterans existed but millions of conscripts or volunteers were enlisted to fight in the civil war,[13] can be considered through this prism.

However, for a long time the history of the Spanish Civil War veterans was neglected. Innovative trends in social and cultural history of war arrived late to Spanish historiography and this partially explains this disregard.[14] Some recent contributions focusing on Spanish Civil War veterans have filled glaring gaps in our knowledge but further research is still needed. This chapter provides an overview of the processes of demobilization of civil war veterans and their reintegration between 1939 and approximately 1944. The stories of the 'return' of these veterans differed enormously depending on which side the men had fought. Furthermore, the experiences of ex-combatants in this period diverged widely, not only between victors and vanquished but also between certain veteran elite and the general mass of soldiers from the victorious Francoist army. However, this chapter will also stress a number of experiences that Republican and Francoist civil war veterans had in common.

War Mobilization and Veterans

As in the case of other countries that participated in the First World War, the history of Spanish Civil War veterans started many months before military operations had brought an end to the war. Veterans started to set up associations in the rearguard before the conflict ended. In a similar way to France and Italy in 1916–17, when French and Italian associations for the war wounded were established,[15] *mutilados de guerra*, or disabled veterans, were the focus of these first organizational projects. Scholars have not yet examined in detail the experiences of disabled veterans in the Republican and Francoist zones during the Spanish Civil War,[16] but it can be assumed that their problems were similar to those experienced by men wounded in the First World War. Advances in military medicine and surgery, as well as developments in the style of fighting and different weapons used by the warring parties, probably led to fewer incidences of severe limb mutilations among combatants in 1936–9 than in 1914–18.[17] However, the problems of rehabilitation of disabled veterans and their reintegration into the workforce back at home are analogous to those of the Great War. Yet there were significant differences in the experiences between the Republican and Francoist sides, as will now be explored in detail.

Republican Veterans

Disabled veterans from the Republican army enjoyed a certain degree of organizational autonomy, but their associations above all served the Republican government and the war effort. In May 1937 in Republican Madrid, the *Liga Nacional de Mutilados e Inválidos de Guerra* (LNMIG), or National League of War Wounded and Invalids, held its first assembly. The creation of this association was the first tangible outcome of the organizational efforts made by wounded Republican veterans. According to their provisional programme, their key concern was to remain 'useful' (*útiles*) to the war effort, and provide 'unconditional help to the government'. It was stated that the association should 'educate and re-educate the disabled veterans in physical and cultural terms'.[18] As a consequence of the efforts made by the LNMIG on behalf of disabled veterans, the government gave preference to the war wounded to fill vacant menial jobs such as janitors, messengers, and the like.[19] However, the activities of the organization and the articles in its official newspaper, *Mutilado*, had propagandistic objectives, and it is therefore difficult to be sure of its actual achievements in the field of re-education and rehabilitation.[20]

In August 1938, while the armies fought the Battle of the Ebro, the LNMIG held its first national congress in Valencia, the capital city of the Republic at that time. Some forty delegates attended the sessions, a significant number given the difficult economic situation in the Republican zone (as examined in Chapter 8 of this volume). One important decision taken at this congress was to open up the LNMIG to disabled veterans from the enemy army after the war came to an end.[21] The congress marked the high point of activity of the LNMIG during the civil war; nevertheless, other regional and local organizations also emerged to deal with veterans' issues in the ever-shrinking Republican zone. This fragmentation was a clear reflection of the splintering political power in the Second Republic after the coup d'état of July 1936, but also the democratic framework that allowed for the proliferation of associations. In December 1938 a number of representatives from different groups, including the LNMIG, its Basque counterpart, *Liga de Mutilados e Inválidos de Guerra de Euzkadi*, and the Catalan association, *Asociación de Mutilados e Inválidos de Guerra de Barcelona* among others, drew up a manifesto in favour of uniting the veterans' efforts and forming a single organization.[22] Not only were veterans divided between different organizations but the LNMIG also suffered from internal divisions and disputes among its political factions.[23] This complex situation probably prevented the LNMIG from being recognized as the official disabled veterans' organization by the Republican government.

After the Francoist army launched its final offensives to defeat the Second Republic in the early months of 1939, there would be insufficient time for Republican veterans to unite their separate associations. And during the last stages of the war, the level of disorganization in the Republican rearguard hampered the reintegration of disabled veterans into the total war effort. The most politicized veterans also complained that some disabled ex-soldiers had nothing more than their basic state pensions for sustenance.[24] LNMIG leaders called on disabled veterans to 'stand up' and do more to save the Republic,[25] but this exhortation never led to anything; it was prevented by the swift collapse of the Republican army in 1939.

Francoist Veterans

Veterans of the Francoist army had different experiences of the civil war to those of Republican ex-soldiers. This divergence was the result of the institutional and political practices of the two sides in the conflict. Fascist and totalitarian influence on the Nationalist war coalition – which went well beyond military and technical assistance from Hitler and Mussolini to the Francoist forces – had a profound impact on the political trajectory of veterans' organizations in the rebel zone.[26] For one thing, in the late 1930s Fascist Italy and Nazi Germany had transformed veterans' organization into instruments for their internal and foreign politics. At this time, fascist and Nazi veterans' associations were mere tools for totalitarian propaganda. The myth of the national-revolutionary potential of ex-combatants, one of the mobilizing strands of early fascist movements in their struggle for power, was a thing of the past. However, many right-wing and fascist Spaniards still believed that veterans, men allegedly transformed by the war experience into hardened individuals, would be agents of revolutionary change in the country. This contradiction caused tensions in the early Franco regime with regard to the appropriate political role of veterans. Whereas some leaders and rank-and-file members of Falange Española expected veterans to assume a prominent position in the regime after the destruction of the Second Republic, the military authorities, including Franco himself, envisioned a much more prosaic future for ex-soldiers of their army.[27]

Nothing illustrates better the restrictions imposed by the Francoist 'New State' on veterans than the case of the so-called *Agrupación Española de Excombatientes*, or Spanish Veterans' Association. This organization was created in Saragossa, one of the key provincial capital cities in Francoist territory. In October 1937, the president of this association submitted the organization's statutes to the authorities for approval. They represented no threat to the rigid political order imposed by the authorities in the Francoist zone, as the organization was based on the existing *Agrupación de Excombatientes de Ultramar*, or Association of Overseas Ex-combatants, created in November 1936 and representing veterans who fought in the nineteenth-century Cuban War.[28] Its members swore 'to serve Spain for ever' and to 'defend order and national integrity'; therefore no (left-wing) 'political propaganda' in the association would ever be tolerated. The organization was intended to help the authorities maintain order as and when requested. It would also function as a self-help society for veterans. The leaders of the *Agrupación* foresaw that veterans from the Moroccan war and other overseas campaigns would also join and together they would help crush any 'anti-Spanish' threat once peace had been restored. Despite this enthusiasm, however, in December 1937, the Francoist authorities dissolved the *Agrupación Española de Excombatientes*. Franco had taken the decision 'to constitute a single nationwide veterans' organization at a suitable moment'.[29]

The first officially sanctioned organization for war veterans in the Francoist zone was the *Benemérito Cuerpo de Mutilados de Guerra por la Patria* (BCMGP), or Distinguished Corps of Disabled in the War for the Fatherland. In January 1937 its managing body, the *Dirección de Mutilados*, was created and General José Millán-Astray, a personal friend of Franco since the creation of the Spanish Legion in Morocco and himself a war-wounded veteran, was appointed as its director.[30] The *Dirección de Mutilados* was tasked with radically transforming the old *Cuerpo de Inválidos*, the traditional military institution for disabled soldiers. The result was the creation of the BCMGP, which devised a new system for assessing war wounds and awarding pensions.[31] Because the BCMGP remained under the direct control of the military authorities, it cannot strictly be considered a veterans' association. It was not an organization created from the bottom-up by veterans sharing common interests and grievances; rather, it was a top-down hierarchical bureaucracy with the aim of maintaining control over veterans and providing them with limited compensation for their war-related health problems.

In practice, the BCMGP adopted a set of ideological premises that pushed the organization close to the totalitarian models first developed by Fascist Italy and later by Nazi Germany for the management of disabled veterans.[32] Yet the exclusion from the pension scheme of veterans suffering from mental disabilities was not something exclusive to fascist regimes: it was the norm in other warring First World War countries such as France.[33] It was a policy also adopted by the BCMGP. Nevertheless, the decision to make a more generous provision to veterans wounded by enemy fire had to do more with ideological prejudices. In line with the practice implemented by Fascist Italy since 1923,[34] disabilities caused by 'honourable' service at the front were looked on more favourably by the BCMGP. This preference was clearly following the same war culture as the Africanist military, officers who had spent much of their military careers fighting colonial wars in the Moroccan Protectorate, and this included Franco and Millán-Astray.[35] Furthermore, as in Fascist Italy and Nazi Germany, disabled veterans from the Francoist army received a set of symbolic rewards that contributed to the glorification of their war experience. In addition to receiving medals, they were called *Caballeros Mutilados*, or Disabled Gentlemen, and depicted as heroes. During the war, however, a key objective of the BCMGP was to ensure that disabled veterans did not become, in the language of the time, 'parasites', and that they continued to contribute to the total war effort.

In October 1937 the authorities of the Francoist zone drafted plans for the future demobilization of soldiers. Foreseeing that the return of men in uniform after the end of the war would cause economic disruption, a project for a *Servicio de Reincorporación de Excombatientes al Trabajo*, or Service for the Reintegration of Ex-combatants into the Workforce, was established. The plan was to give back to Francoist veterans their former jobs, or ones similar to those they had before the war. To enable this to happen, a complex and highly bureaucratic system was set up, in which representatives of the local Falange, military authorities, and local government were due to meet regularly in order to oversee the reintegration process. However, these commissions had no real authority to force employers to accept or re-accept veterans into their companies.[36] Furthermore, in most provinces they functioned very poorly. The key priority of the emerging Francoist dictatorship was political consolidation, and all the organizational efforts in veterans' affairs were shaped by this fundamental aim.

Veterans after the War

The year 1939 in Europe and particularly in Spain was turbulent. After 1 April 1939 the Spanish Second Republic could be considered militarily defunct. As from January onwards a massive flow of refugees from the Republican zone made their way towards France. While the Francoist army advanced victoriously, Republican soldiers faced bitter defeat. From this moment on, the experiences of Republican and Francoist veterans diverged dramatically.

Republican Veterans and Defeat

Republican veterans faced different but interconnected experiences after the end of the war. Their most common fate was imprisonment. During the civil war, the Francoist army had developed a system for managing the growing numbers of Republican prisoners. Many of these soldiers had been forced to fight for the Popular Army of the Republic and lacked any strong underlying ideological motivation (as examined in Chapter 4).[37] In similar fashion they were forced into the ranks of the Francoist army. Prisoners with political responsibilities, such as political commissars,[38] were often executed after a quick court martial. Others remained imprisoned in the growing network of concentration camps.

Massive surrenders of Republican soldiers in the last months of the war put even more pressure on the already overpopulated concentration camps throughout Francoist Spain. In the final Francoist offensive 177,000 Republican soldiers were taken prisoner. Under strain, the process of prisoners' classification grew and became faster, without becoming less harsh in its treatment of prisoners. In many Spanish villages and towns the Francoist authorities established concentration camps and prisons which varied widely in size and nature. Old buildings were re-fashioned into prisons. Areas demarcated with barbed wire served the same purpose. Some camps were home to just a few dozens of prisoners while others contained around 10,000 men. Living conditions in the camps were extremely poor, the key problem being overcrowding. Disease, death, hunger, maltreatment, lice, and filth marked the experiences of those Republican ex-soldiers in camps such as Albatera (Alicante), Castuera (Badajoz),[39] Miranda de Ebro (Burgos) and Porta Coeli (Valencia), to name but four of the most infamous. Towards the end of the war, the concentration camp system urgently needed more space to accommodate new prisoners. Former Republican soldiers who had turned themselves in voluntarily to the enemy were sent home, although some of them escaped again to the Republican zone. Thousands were compelled to join labour battalions (*batallones de trabajo*) and were then employed in different activities under the authority of the Francoist army. By the end of the war 87,500 Republican POWs were working in these units. In a number of camps there is also evidence of systematic extrajudicial killing of selected prisoners. According to official figures, in July 1939 the total number of POWs in the country was 156,789. As prisoners were either sent to labour battalions or liberated under certain conditions, in December 1939, the number of POWs dropped to 90,040. Yet a number of concentration camps continued to exist until 1947.[40] Today the history and memory of Francoist concentration camps is well known,[41] but a more exhaustive study of former Republican POWs after their release still needs to be undertaken.

Other soldiers of the defeated Republican army managed to escape from Spain as refugees, and France was the main destination. The arrival of Republican refugees, after crossing into France along the Pyrenean border, started mainly from January 1939 onwards as a consequence of the fall of Catalonia and Barcelona. Faced with this situation, the French government decided on 28 January 1939 to open the border to thousands of civilian Spanish refugees. On the night of 5 February 1939 disarmed ex-soldiers were also allowed to enter the country.[42] French authorities were always aware that in addition to civilians a great number of military personnel escaped from Spain, and this was just one of the reasons why the French political right were bitterly critical of the acceptance of Spanish refugees. Since July 1936, the Spanish Civil War had been a contentious and divisive issue in French politics and as a result the French government had adopted a strict control over Spanish exiles.[43] In total, almost 500,000 Republican refugees came into France in early 1939, although the figure decreased rapidly due to repatriations which amounted to a total of 173,000 in June of 1939[44] (see Figure 12.1).

The French approach to Spanish refugees had similarities with the Francoist treatment of POWs. Refugees were assembled in 'internment camps', which were at the time called 'concentration camps'. The camps at Argèles-sur-Mer and Saint Cyprien, both located in the Eastern Pyrenees *département*, were the most important. They were improvised zones for the concentration of refugees, situated on the beaches of these towns, under the surveillance of French colonial troops. Sanitary conditions were bad, and many cases of dysentery and scabies broke out. Some of the camps accommodated between 15,000 and 18,000 people, including many former soldiers.[45]

For a large number of Republican ex-soldiers the refugee experience in France was no more than a continuation of their Spanish war experience. They were first offered the chance to leave the French internment camps by joining the French military, in particular the Foreign Legion and later the *Régiments de Marche des Volontiers Étrangers* (RMVE). Created in 1939, these military units brought together Republican exiles, Jews who had fled the Third Reich and refugees from Central and Eastern Europe. Between 6,000 and 8,000 Spaniards, former Republican soldiers, joined these units and participated in the short campaign

Figure 12.1 A gendarme accompanies former Republican soldiers to the French border for repatriation to Spain after the end of the civil war. AGMAV, F.334, 12/12.

of 1939–40, the majority of them after the outbreak of the Second World War. Spanish soldiers made up 17 per cent of the RMVE forces, just behind the 18 per cent of Italians.[46] Historian Diego Gaspar Celaya has calculated that about 9 per cent of these Spanish combatants in the RMVE later joined the French Free Forces.[47] In total, for the duration of the Second World War, 1,182 Spanish volunteers were members of the French Free Forces. For them the Spanish Civil War and the Second World War formed a continuum of violence that ended in the victorious French Liberation of 1944. Some of these volunteers remained in the French army after 1945 and 90 per cent of them continued to reside in France, mainly in the Paris region.[48]

As we have seen, veterans from the Republican army faced long periods of imprisonment both in Spain and in exile. Thousands of soldiers and officers were court-martialled by the Francoist military authorities. In order to absolve their past in the eyes of the new regime, many Republican veterans were forced to spend years in military service in the Francoist army after the end of the civil war. Those who were allowed to return home faced marginalization, persecution, and fines imposed by the Francoist *Ley de Responsabilidades Políticas*, or Law of Political Responsibilities. Repression made it difficult for Republicans to organize resistance within Spain in the early 1940s. On some occasions the only option open to ex-combatants was to flee and hide out in mountainous areas. However, after 1943 some of these veterans in hiding (*los huidos*) managed to form an armed resistance movement. The Spanish Communist Party in exile became the leading force of an insurrectional movement. In mid-1944 the *Agrupación de Guerrilleros Españoles*, or Group of Spanish Guerrilla Forces, assembled between 8,000 and

9,000 armed men in Southern France and tried to invade Spain through the valley of Aran in the Pyrenees. This attempt turned out to be a military failure, but communist guerrillas in Spain continued to be active in different regions, such as Teruel and Eastern Andalusia.[49] The Spanish *maquis* was predominantly a rural movement with a high proportion of peasants among its members; however, it was also largely composed of former Republican combatants, held together by bonds of comradeship.[50] Most of the members of the guerrilla groups had been born between 1911 and 1920; for example, in Eastern Andalusia, 71 per cent of the *guerrilleros* would have been mobilized by the Republican army during the civil war.[51]

Francoist Veterans and the 'New State'

Shortly after the war was over, the Francoist authorities decreed the demobilization of several *quintas* or conscription reserve classes. The demobilization process took place in a wider European context of extreme international tension; it was slow and suffered interruptions.[52] The experiences of ex-soldiers from the victorious army were varied; while bourgeois officers often spent a most enjoyable, celebratory summer of 1939, thousands of low-ranking and barely literate soldiers returned to lives of extreme poverty. Discharged veterans had to return to their homes with little assistance from the authorities. They were given some clothes, and exceptionally they received some cash, or a *subsidio*, provided by the 'New State'.[53] This emergency aid did little to ease hunger and disease among veterans; many of them suffered from tuberculosis as a consequence of the war.[54] The demographic disruption caused by the end of the conflict was aggravated by the rapid migration of Francoist veterans from their rural villages into the cities they had visited as soldiers during the war and where naively they expected to find jobs.[55] The number of unemployed Francoist veterans was a long-lasting problem in every Spanish region, whereas former Republican soldiers and women were often expelled from their jobs.[56] The famous law of 25 August 1939, which reserved a substantial portion of civil servant positions for ex-combatants, was not enough to provide hundreds of thousands of veterans from the Francoist army with the employment they believed they deserved. These legal measures benefited only a portion of the great numbers of Francoist ex-soldiers and these laws and institutions in favour of veterans should be interpreted as a means of political consolidation.[57]

The creation of the *Delegación Nacional de Excombatientes* (DNE), or National Delegation of Ex-combatants, an organization of veterans affiliated to the single party *Falange Española Tradicionalista y de las JONS* (FET y de las JONS), or Traditionalist Spanish Falange of the Committees of the National Syndicalist Offensive, was a key political event in the process of Francoist veterans' demobilization.[58] The DNE was established in August 1939 and therefore at a time of the greatest fascist and national-syndicalist influence over the Franco regime. At the beginning of this month a new Spanish government had been formed. In this period Francoist governments were a mix of high-ranking military officers and Falangists who had participated in the war.[59] Thus, in August 1939,

Agustín Muñoz Grandes, a military officer, was appointed Secretary-General of FET-JONS. Franco's consolidation in power required a careful balance between conservative military officers and radical fascists from the Falange. Falangists, who were strongly loyal to Franco, such as the dictator's son-in-law Ramón Serrano Suñer, obtained positions of power. These factors led to the appointment of José Antonio Girón de Velasco, a young Falangist from Valladolid, to the position of *Delegado Nacional de Excombatientes*. He had fought with Falangist units during the war and attained the rank of Captain.[60]

Girón set up the political structures of the DNE during the months to follow. He appointed a number of old-guard Falangists (*camisas viejas*; literally 'old shirts') who had been made officers during the war to be in charge of the provincial branches (*delegaciones provinciales*) of the DNE. Some of these Falangists believed in the revolutionary national-syndicalist principles and thought that veterans should play a prominent political role; others accepted the position of veterans' delegate without much enthusiasm. The DNE was a veterans' organization deliberately set up from above, and it lacked the energy and power of genuine representation of other European veterans' movements. In the repressive context of the early Franco regime, it is not surprising that the DNE lacked a press organ. Francoist veterans had no possibility of reading any newspaper or journal on veterans' affairs and this contrasts sharply with the many publishing initiatives taken by veterans in other countries, including Fascist Italy and Nazi Germany.[61]

The main characteristics of Francoist veteran politics in 1939–40 were, however, in line with the totalitarian turn of veteran affairs in Fascist Italy and the Third Reich at that time. Italian and German veterans' organizations had gone through radical processes of 'fascistization' and 'Nazification' which, by 1938–9, had come to a head. With veterans' journals turned into propaganda organs, veteran politics in both totalitarian countries fundamentally served the interests of the state. The Fascist Party in Italy and the NSDAP in Germany had absolute control over veterans' associations. Francoist Spain followed the same pattern. It is significant that, in December 1939, both Fascist Italy and Francoist Spain reached the same political decision almost at the same time: namely, to offer to all veterans the chance of becoming members of the party simply by virtue of having participated in the war. Most probably, visits of Spanish Falangists, such as Girón and Millán-Astray, to Fascist Italy, as well as the existence of fascist networks operating in Spain,[62] helped to align Francoist veteran politics with the fascist model. The fascist glorification of the experience of war was shared by all fascist regimes, including Franco's Spain, and led to the instrumentalization of veterans to shore up the different dictatorships.[63]

Thus, the early Franco regime can be seen as a militaristic and fascist-inspired dictatorship in which veterans enjoyed a prominent position. As in Fascist Italy, veterans were not only an 'entitlement group', but a 'privilege group'.[64] Benefits offered to Francoist veterans were so attractive that they acted as an important motivation for some volunteers to join the Spanish Blue Division, the military unit organized in June 1941 by FET-JONS and the Spanish army to join Hitler's forces in the invasion of the Soviet Union (as examined in Chapter 13).[65] In this division young Spaniards, who for various reasons had not fought in the Francoist army during the civil war, were able to obtain the coveted status of ex-combatants.[66] Between 1939 and 1944 veteran status was a decisive factor for an individual to be selected as a member of local and provincial government structures. Especially in small villages and towns, local ex-combatants, who had become mayors or administration officials, played a crucial role in consolidating pervasive Francoist power at the local level.[67] In 1939–40, there were plans to reinforce Falangist Militia units with veterans. More successful was the incorporation of hundreds of former NCOs into the Civil Guard, the militarized police in charge of fighting the anti-Francoist guerrillas during the 1940s. As part of the priority given to veterans, many obtained positions in the civil service, for example, working in Francoist prisons as guards. Most importantly, hundreds of junior officers (*alféreces provisionales*), who had been quickly trained during the war by the Francoist army, turned into professional military men and became the backbone of the dictatorship's armed forces. Silently but steadily veterans permeated all the structures of the 'New State' during the first half of the 1940s.

At the same time, however, rigid hierarchies and sharp class inequalities existed among the allegedly unified community of Francoist veterans. Analysis of correspondence between the DNE national and provincial leaders and Francoist veterans reveals that ex-soldiers suffered problems of unemployment, poor health, lack of money, and adequate housing until at least the mid-1950s. For instance, in August 1943 the DNE sent a message to the FET-JONS Women's Organization asking that ex-combatant Emilio Morodo be provided with 'a shirt, trousers, handkerchiefs and a pair of shoes' as he was 'in a considerably needy condition'.[68] Messages of this nature were commonplace. As late as 1954 veterans were still writing bitter letters to the new National Delegate, a former officer of the Spanish Blue Division, Tomás García Rebull, complaining of their poverty.[69] These Francoist veterans from the lower ranks were supposedly victorious members of the so-called national community, yet their social class actually transformed them into the vanquished of the Spanish Civil War. The system devised by the Franco regime to deal with veterans and maintain their political loyalty is reminiscent of authoritarian regimes elsewhere, and not only in Fascist Italy and the Third Reich: in the Soviet Union and communist China, veterans who were publicly honoured as heroes were also victims of systems that impoverished them.[70]

Epilogue: A Period of Convergence

On 18 July 1986, fifty years after the outbreak of the Spanish Civil War and roughly a decade after the death of Franco, a Spanish public television channel featured an interview with two former combatants of the civil war.[71] The veterans, two ageing but lively men, sat on a couch and talked to the journalist José Antonio Martínez Soler on the occasion of the fiftieth anniversary of the conflict. The differences in their clothing, gestures, and eloquence revealed quite clearly that these veterans did not share a similar social and professional background. Indeed, they were veterans from opposite sides of the conflict: a former Republican soldier and a veteran from the Francoist army. However, they were on a television programme as representatives of the same movement of Spanish Civil War veterans. They maintained the same political stance, arguing that veterans from both sides of the conflict should receive equal compensation for the sufferings of the war, and that Republican veterans should be given the recognition denied to them for fifty years.

In reality, a common social movement composed of former soldiers from both the Francoist and Republican armies was started well before 1986. In Madrid in March 1977, a large group of former veterans of the Spanish Civil War founded the *Unión de Excombatientes de la Guerra de España* (UNEX), or Union of Ex-combatants of the Spanish War. This association favoured 'reconciliation' and in their founding manifesto, written a month before the first free elections held in Spain after Franco's death and a few weeks before the legalization of the Spanish Communist Party, the veterans explicitly rejected war and violence as a means to resolve differences; they also denounced the violent actions of groups that clung to 'civil war mentalities' and sought to derail the process of transition to democracy. The veterans did not renounce their different political views but they aspired to live together in peace, democracy, and liberty; in short, their organization was at the service of peace.[72] The logo UNEX displayed a handshake between former ex-enemy soldiers (see Figure 12.2).

Former ex-enemy veterans were seemingly transcending the profound divisions decades of dictatorship had imposed on them. In June 1977 the Francoist *Confederación Nacional de Combatientes*, founded years earlier by Girón as a platform for the most radical Falangist veterans, decided to dissolve their organization and initiate discussions to create a new Veterans' Confederation open to all Spaniards who fought in the 'tragic civil war', 'regardless of ideologies

Figure 12.2 *Unión de Excombatientes de la Guerra de España* (UNEX), 1977.

or sides'.[73] In July 1977 the leaders of the Francoist BCMGP and the Republican disabled veterans embraced each other at a joint meeting.[74]

In part the emergence of a reconciliatory movement of civil war veterans was a product of the overall political context of the late 1970s. While influential groups of Francoist veterans played a conspicuous part in the hard-line political 'bunker' aiming to prevent the transition to democracy,[75] it is not entirely unsurprising that Republican veterans and mixed groups of veterans from both sides stepped onto the turbulent political stage in favour of reconciliation.

Conclusions

Veterans from both sides of the conflict had very different post-war experiences. Indeed, Republican and Francoist soldiers' experiences diverged even during the years of the Spanish Civil War, when the authorities on each side developed distinct veteran politics and policies. On the Francoist side, veterans' groups were subjected to the authority of fascist-inspired structures and organizations; whereas Republican veterans enjoyed more liberty to create their own, largely autonomous and representative, associations. After the dramatic end of the civil war, the experiences of Republican and Francoist veterans became even more dissimilar, as defeat or victory played a large part in shaping their fate. Most Francoist veterans were sent home after going through a physical demobilization process. Yet, no 'cultural demobilization' really took place: the discourses, practices, and representations of the Francoist war culture persisted.[76] In the case of Republican veterans, historians cannot strictly talk about 'demobilization': experiences of imprisonment, concentration camps, hiding, resisting, and continued fighting during the Second World War formed a continuum of violence that marked their lives. It is more apt to consider their final reintegration into Spanish society as a 'return' rather than as 'demobilization'.

However, beyond the marked divergences, the history of the Spanish transition to democracy produced opportunities for a re-convergence of veterans from both sides of the Spanish Civil War. This reality encourages a re-examination of the shared experiences of Republican and Francoist veterans during the civil war. Beyond the profound ideological and political differences, on both sides of the conflict, veterans became agents of mobilization in a context of total war. Within both zones, the key political and social role of veterans in the rearguard was to continue their contribution to the war effort as far as their injuries allowed. After the end of the war veterans became historical actors in the context of an all-out, pan-European confrontation between fascism and anti-fascism. In Spain, Francoist veterans were organized within totalitarian political structures and subjected to stark hierarchies of power imposed with the help of Fascist Italy and Nazi Germany; while some groups of Republican veterans who escaped both repression and imprisonment continued the fight against the new regime. In exile, Republicans also joined the struggle against the fascist powers. During the first half of the 1940s, repression, death, disease, and hunger were part of the everyday lives of many ex-combatants of the Spanish Civil War, regardless of which side they had fought on. The divide between victors and vanquished was the most important, but not the only, defining historical reality. Thus, decades after the 'demobilization' and 'return' of civil war veterans, a common legacy of historical experiences shared by ex-combatants from both sides of the conflict allowed for the formation of an active social movement that contributed to democratizing Spain and the development of a culture of peace.

Further Reading

Aguilar, Paloma. 'Agents of Memory: Spanish Civil War Veterans and Disabled Soldiers'. In *War and Remembrance in the Twentieth Century*, edited by Jay Winter and Emmanuel Sivan, 84–103. Cambridge: Cambridge University Press, 1999.

Alcalde, Ángel. *War Veterans and Fascism in Interwar Europe*. Cambridge: Cambridge University Press, 2017.

Alcalde, Ángel. 'Francoist Veterans and the "New State": Social Benefits and the Consolidation of the Franco Regime (1938-1945)'. In *New Political Ideas in the Aftermath of the Great War*, edited by Alessandro Salvador and Anders G. Kjøstvedt, 219–39. Basingstoke: Palgrave Macmillan, 2017.

Alcalde, Ángel. 'War Veterans and Fascism during the Franco Dictatorship in Spain'. *European History Quarterly* 47, no. 1 (2017): 78–98.

Gaspar Celaya, Diego. *La guerra continúa. Voluntarios españoles al servicio de la Francia libre (1940-1945)*. Madrid: Marcial Pons, 2015.

Marco, Jorge. *Guerrilleros and Neighbours in Arms: Identities and Cultures of Anti-fascist Resistance in Spain*. Brighton: Sussex University Press, 2016.

Soo, Scott. *The Routes to Exile: France and the Spanish Civil War refugees, 1939-2009*. Manchester and New York: Manchester University Press, 2013.

Notes

*   I would like to thank Alan Matthews for his thorough language revision of this text.
1   For a historiographical overview of the field see Ángel Alcalde, 'Historias del retorno: la historiografía internacional sobre veteranos de guerra', *Ayer* 111 (2018): 109–31.
2   Antoine Prost, *Les Anciens Combattants et la Societé Française 1914-1939*, 3 vols. (Paris : Presses de la Fondation Nationale des Sciences Politiques, 1977); *The Great War and Veterans' Internationalism*, ed. Julia Eichenberg and John Paul Newman (New York: Palgrave, 2013).
3   John Horne, 'Démobilisations culturelles après la Grande Guerre', *14-18 Aujourd'hui, Today, Heute*, 5 (2002); Marco Mondini and Guri Schwarz, *Dalla guerra alla pace. Retoriche e pratiche della smobilitazione nell'Italia del Novecento* (Verona: Cierre edizioni/Istrevi, 2007).
4   Paloma Aguilar, 'Agents of Memory: Spanish Civil War Veterans and Disabled Soldiers', in *War and Remembrance in the Twentieth Century*, ed. Jay Winter and Emmanuel Sivan (Cambridge: Cambridge University Press, 1999), 84–103.

5   Stephen R. Ortiz, *Beyond the Bonus March and GI Bill: How Veteran Politics Shaped the New Deal Era* (New York: New York University Press, 2010); Chris Millington, 'February 6, 1934. The Veterans' Riot', *French Historical Studies* 33, no. 4 (2010): 545–72.

6   Ángel Alcalde, *War Veterans and Fascism in Interwar Europe* (Cambridge: Cambridge University Press, 2017).

7   Michael Mann, *Fascists* (Cambridge: Cambridge University Press, 2004).

8   Benjamin Ziemann, *Contested Commemorations, Republican War Veterans and Weimar Political Culture* (Cambridge: Cambridge University Press, 2013); Kurt G. P. Schuster, *Der Rote Frontkämpferbund 1924-1929* (Düsseldorf: Droste Verlag, 1975); Chris Millington, 'Communist Veterans and Paramilitarism in 1920s France: The Association Républicaine des Anciens Combattants', *Journal of War and Culture Studies* 8, no. 4 (2015): 300–14; Eros Francescangeli, 'De "caballeros de la muerte" a la "lucha por la vida". Los arditi italianos, de la guerra a la militancia antifascista', *Pasado y Memoria*, 15 (2016): 73–97.

9   George L. Mosse, *Fallen Soldiers. Reshaping the Memory of the World Wars* (Oxford: Oxford University Press, 1991).

10   Armin Fuhrer, *Ernst Thälmann: Soldat des Proletariats* (Munich: Olzog, 2011).

11   Arnold Krammer, 'Germans against Hitler: The Thaelmann Brigade', *Journal of Contemporary History* 4, no. 2 (1969): 65–83.

12   *The War Generation: Veterans of the First World War*, ed. Stephen R. Ward (Port Washington, NY and London: Kennikat Press, 1975).

13   It is widely accepted that the Republican and Francoist armies recruited circa 1 million soldiers each. For recruitment numbers see Chapter 4 of this volume.

14   Eduardo González Calleja, 'La cultura de guerra como propuesta historiográfica; una reflexión general desde el contemporaneísmo español', *Historia Social* 61 (2008): 69–87; on the tardy reception of George L. Mosse's work see Ángel Alcalde, 'Soldados caídos: un estudio introductorio', in *Soldados Caídos. La transformación de la memoria de las guerras mundiales*, ed. George L. Mosse (Saragossa: Prensas de la Universidad de Zaragoza, 2016).

15   Antoine Prost, *Les Anciens Combattants*, vol. 1, 7–45; Giovanni Sabbatucci, *I combattenti nel primo dopoguerra* (Bari: Laterza, 1974), 43–61.

16   For the Francoist disabled veterans see Stephanie Wright, 'Los mutilados de Franco: el Benemérito Cuerpo y la política social en la España franquista', *Revista Universitaria de Historia Militar* 5, no. 9 (2016): 75–92.

17   While in the First World War a great portion of casualties was caused by artillery fire, statistics available for the Spanish Civil War suggest that until 1938 the predominant cause of injury for combatants were bullets; see Cruz Roja Española (Asamblea Provincial de Zaragoza), *Actuación de la Cruz Roja durante la campaña 18 julio 1936, 1 abril 1939. Memoria*, Zaragoza, 1939.

18   Pedro Vega, *Historia de la Liga de Mutilados* (Madrid: 1981), 28.

19   *La Vanguardia* (Barcelona), 27 October 1937, 3–4.

20   Paloma Aguilar, 'Agents of Memory', 88–9.

21   Antonio Sánchez-Bravo y Antonio Tellado Vázquez, *Los Mutilados del Ejército de la República* (Madrid: 1976), 27; Pedro Vega, *Historia*, 28.

22   'Un manifiesto de los mutilados de guerra', *La Vanguardia*, 25 December 1938.

23   See 'Nuestro peor enemigo es la desunión de los mutilados', in: *Mutilado* (Madrid), 19 November 1938.

24   *Mutilado*, 19 November 1938.

25 'Mutilados: todos en pie para salvar la independencia de España', in *Mutilado*, 22 January 1939.

26 Javier Rodrigo, 'On Fascistization: Mussolini's Political Project for Franco's Spain, 1937–1939', *Journal of Modern Italian Studies* 22, no. 4 (2017): 469–87.

27 Ángel Alcalde, *Los excombatientes franquistas. La cultura de guerra del fascismo español y la Delegación Nacional de Excombatientes (1936-1965)* (Saragossa: Prensas de la Universidad de Zaragoza, 2017), 106–38.

28 Estatutos y Reglamento de la Agrupación Española de Excombatientes, Zaragoza: 1937, in: Archivo General Militar de Ávila (AGMAV), Caja (Cj.) 2317, Legajo (L.) 34, Carpeta (C.) 70. On the creation of the Agrupación de Excombatientes de Ultramar, see *Amanecer* (*Dawn*), Saragossa, 8 November 1936.

29 AGMAV, Cj. 2317, L. 34, C. 68–9.

30 Alcalde, *Los excombatientes franquistas*, 117–18.

31 Stephanie Wright, 'Los mutilados de Franco', 78.

32 On the Third Reich see Deborah Cohen, *The War Come Home. Disabled veterans in Britain and Germany, 1914-1939* (Berkeley: University of California Press, 2001), and Nils Löffelbein, *Ehrenbürger der Nation. Die Kriegsbeschädigten des Ersten Weltkriegs in Politik und Propaganda des Nationalsozialismus* (Essen, Klartext, 2013). On Italy see Pierluigi Pironti, *Kriegsopfer und Staat. Sozialpolitik für Invaliden, Witwen und Waisen des Ersten Weltkriegs in Deutschland und Italien (1914-1924)* (Köln, Böhlau, 2015), Barbara Bracco, *La patria ferita. I corpi dei soldati italiani e la Grande guerra* (Firenze, Giunti, 2011).

33 Stephanie Wright, 'Los mutilados de Franco', 80.

34 Alcalde, *War Veterans and Fascism in Interwar Europe*, 118–22.

35 Alfonso Iglesias Amorín, 'La cultura africanista en el ejército español (1909-1975)', *Pasado y Memoria*, no. 15 (2016): 99–122.

36 Alcalde, *Los excombatientes franquistas*, 137.

37 James Matthews, *Reluctant Warriors. Republican Popular Army and Nationalist Army Conscripts in the Spanish Civil War, 1936-1939* (Oxford: Oxford University Press, 2012).

38 James Matthews, 'Comisarios y capellanes en la Guerra Civil española, 1936-1939: una mirada comparativa', *Ayer*, no. 94 (2014): 175–99.

39 José Ramón González Cortés, 'Prisioneros del miedo y control social: El campo de concentración de Castuera', *Hispania Nova*, no. 6 (2006) http://hispanianova.rediris.es/6/dossier/6d004.pdf

40 Javier Rodrigo, *Cautivos. Campos de concentración en la España franquista, 1936-1947* (Barcelona: Crítica, 2005), 183–200.

41 Javier Rodrigo, *Los campos de concentración franquistas. Entre la historia y la memoria* (Madrid: Siete Mares, 2003).

42 Geneviève Dreyfus-Armand, *El exilio de los republicanos españoles en Francia* (Barcelona: Crítica, 2000). See also Scott Soo, *The Routes to Exile. France and the Spanish Civil War Refugees, 1939-2009* (Manchester and New York: Manchester University Press, 2013).

43 David Wingeate Pike, *France Divided: The French and the Civil War in Spain* (Brighton: Sussex Academic Press, 2011).

44 Diego Gaspar Celaya, *La guerra continúa. Voluntarios españoles al servicio de la Francia libre (1940-1945)* (Madrid: Marcial Pons, 2015), 128.

45 Gaspar Celaya, *La guerra continúa*, 115.

46 Stéphane Leroy, 'Les exilés républicains espagnols des Régiments de Marche des Volontaires Étrangers. Engagement, présence et formation militaire (janvier 1939-mai 1940)', *Cahiers de civilisation espagnole contemporaine*, no. 6 (2010) http://ccec.revues.org/3285

47 Diego Gaspar Celaya, *La guerra continúa*, 155–84.

48 Ibid., 449–60.

49 Mercedes Yusta, *La guerra de los vencidos. El maquis en el Mestrazgo turolense, 1940-1950* (Saragossa: Institución Fernando el Católico, 1999).

50 Jorge Marco, *Guerrilleros y vecinos en armas. Identidades y culturas de la resistencia antifranquista* (Granada, Comares, 2012), 18–25.

51 Marco, *Guerrilleros y vecinos en armas*, 64.

52 Ángel Alcalde, 'Los orígenes de la Delegación Nacional de Excombatientes de FET-JONS: la desmovilización del ejército franquista y la Europa de 1939', *Ayer*, no. 97 (2015): 169–94.

53 *Boletín Oficial del Estado*, 18 May, 11 October, and 22 December 1939.

54 Report 'Excombatientes tuberculosos' (1940), Archivo General de la Administración (AGA), Presidencia, Delegación Nacional de Excombatientes (DNE), C. 52/2289.

55 AGMAV, Cj. 3044, C. 19, 'Gobierno Militar de Zaragoza'; AGA, Delegación Nacional de Provincias, C. 51/20542, Correspondencia Zaragoza.

56 Alcalde, *Los excombatientes franquistas*, 132–9.

57 Ángel Alcalde, 'Francoist Veterans and the 'New State': Social Benefits and the Consolidation of the Franco Regime (1938-1945)', in *New Political Ideas in the Aftermath of the Great War*, ed. Alessandro Salvador and Anders G. Kjøstvedt (Basingstoke: Palgrave Macmillan, 2017), 219–39.

58 Ángel Alcalde, 'Los orígenes de la Delegación Nacional de Excombatientes de FET-JONS'. See also Francisco Sevillano, 'La política del 'combatismo' en el 'Nuevo Estado': discurso, protección y encuadramiento del excombatiente en la posguerra española (1939-1941), *Historia Social*, no. 74 (2012): 43–63.

59 Borja de Riquer, *La dictadura de Franco* (Barcelona: Crítica/Marcial Pons, 2010), 25.

60 Alcalde, *Los excombatientes franquistas*, 140.

61 Ángel Alcalde, 'War Veterans and Fascism during the Franco Dictatorship in Spain', *European History Quarterly* 47, no. 1 (2017): 78–98.

62 Matteo Albanese and Pablo del Hierro, *Transnational Fascism in the Twentieth Century. Spain, Italy and the Global Neo-Fascist Network* (Bloomsbury Academic: London, 2016), Chapters 1 and 2.

63 Alcalde, *War Veterans and Fascism in Interwar Europe*, 257–65.

64 On this conceptual distinction, see Martin Crotty and Mark Edele, 'Total War and Entitlement: Towards a Global History of Veteran Privilege', *Australian Journal of Politics and History* 59, no. 1 (2013): 15–32.

65 Xosé M. Núñez Seixas, *Camarada Invierno. Experiencia y memoria de la División Azul (1941-1945)* (Barcelona: Crítica, 2016).

66 Ángel Alcalde Fernández, 'Cultura de guerra y excombatientes para la implantación del franquismo en Albacete (1939-1945)', *Al-Basit*, no. 57 (2012): 37–69.

67 Miguel Ángel del Arco, '"Hombres nuevos". El personal político del primer franquismo en el mundo rural del sureste español (1936-1951)', *Ayer*, no. 65 (2007): 237–67; Ángel Alcalde Fernández, 'Excombatientes en los poderes locales del primer franquismo: experiencia de guerra e interpretación del apoyo social a la dictadura (Zaragoza 1939-1945)', in *Nuevos horizontes del pasado. Culturas políticas, identidades y formas de representación: Actas del X Congreso de la Asociación de Historia*

Contemporánea, ed. Angeles Barrio Alonso, Jorge de Hoyos Puente and Rebeca Saavedra Arias (Santander: Ediciones de la Universidad de Cantabria, 2011).

68 AGA, DNE, C. 52/2316, Correspondencia. Vicesecretaría General del Movimiento, 1942–4.

69 Alcalde, *Los excombatientes franquistas*, 268–78.

70 Mark Edele, *Soviet Veterans of the Second World War. A Popular Movement in an Authoritarian Society, 1941-1991* (Oxford: Oxford University Press, 2008); Beate Fieseler, 'De la "génération perdue" aux bénéficiaires de la politique sociale? Les invalides de guerre en URSS, 1945-1964', in *Retour à l'intime au sortir de la guerre*, ed. Bruno Cabanes and Guillaume Piketty (Paris: Tallandier, 2009), 133–48; Neil J. Diamant, *Embattled Glory: Veterans, Military Families and the Politics of Patriotism in China, 1949-2007* (Lanham: Rowman & Littlefield, 2009).

71 http://www.rtve.es/alacarta/videos/80-anos-de-la-guerra-civil/dos-ex-combatiente s-guerra-civil-charlan-50-anos-despues/1145852/ (accessed, 30 September 2017).

72 Archivo Histórico Provincial de Albacete, box 23075, file Correspondencia 1979– 2000.

73 *ABC* (Madrid), 5 June 1977.

74 Aguilar, 'Agents of Memory', 102.

75 Carlos Fernández, 'Llanto por el franquismo perdido', *Historia 16*, no. 119 (1986): 63–8.

76 Alcalde, *Los excombatientes franquistas*; Claudio Hernández Burgos, *Granada azul. La construcción de la 'Cultura de la Victoria' en el primer franquismo* (Granada, Comares, 2011); Francisco Sevillano, *La cultura de guerra del 'nuevo Estado' franquista: enemigos, héroes y caídos por España* (Madrid, Biblioteca Nueva, 2017).

Chapter 13

A SPANISH EXCEPTION IN A WAR OF EXTERMINATION? THE 'BLUE DIVISION' ON THE EASTERN FRONT, 1941–4

Xosé M. Núñez Seixas

The *División Española de Voluntarios*, or Spanish Division of Volunteers, was set up by the Franco regime in early summer 1941 to take part in the Russian campaign as a unit integrated into the German Wehrmacht. From 24 June through the first week of July 1941, hundreds of volunteers joined what would become known as the *División Azul*: the 'Blue Division', which was initially composed of around 17,000 infantry soldiers, including officers and NCOs, and without heavy equipment. They were recruited by both the Spanish Fascist Party (the *Falange Española Tradicionalista y de las JONS*, FET y de las JONS, or Traditionalist Spanish Falange of the Committees of the National Syndicalist Offensive), which provided most of the rank-and-file soldiers and the Spanish army, which supplied the officers and two thirds of the non-commissioned officers, as well as the first commander-in-chief of the expeditionary corps, General Agustín Muñoz Grandes, who was sympathetic towards the Falange and had earlier been general secretary of the single party for a short period. To these, a small air squad – composed of seventeen pilots, but no airplanes – was added. Subsequent replacements sent to Russia between March 1942 and October 1943 totalled some 30,000 additional men. Those who remained in the Blue Legion following the withdrawal of the Blue Division in the late autumn of 1943 hardly numbered 2,300 men; and barely a few hundred Spanish combatants continued to fight in the ranks of two Wehrmacht companies and some Waffen SS units between mid-1944 and May 1945. Almost 5,000 soldiers died, and around 450 became prisoners of the Soviet Red Army. The Spaniards were deployed in the northern area of the Eastern Front, first on the Volkhov Front (October 1941–August 1942), and later at the southern corner of the siege of Leningrad (until March 1944).

The Blue Division has received significant historiographical, literary, and testimonial attention. Most studies have addressed concrete aspects of this unit's participation in the German war of extermination on the Eastern Front (1941–5), from detailed narratives of the battles in which they fought to their role in diplomatic relations between Nazi Germany and Francoist Spain. From the summer of 1941, Spanish Falangist and Catholic volunteers fought alongside professional army officers and NCOs as part of the military operations in the East. Spaniards largely experienced a static front line and a trench warfare behind defensive positions, interspersed with some moments of offensive combat. While the military operations have attracted most attention from historians in Spain and beyond, until recently relatively little consideration has been paid to events behind the front lines. The occupation practices of the Spanish troops and their treatment of civilians, partisans, and Jews have largely been ignored. Most scholars have also neglected to explore the soldiers' perceptions of the enemy, their motivations for enlisting, and their possible role in the darkest facets of the war in the East.[1] This also relates to the scarcity of transnational and/or comparative histories of the experience and memory of non-German and German soldiers on the Eastern Front. Moreover, most historical approaches in Spain have openly ignored the progress made by German and Anglo-American (and to some extent also Russian) historians in the analysis of the Soviet-German conflict as an unprecedented war of extermination.[2] On the contrary, they have mostly presented the history of Spaniards on the Eastern Front from an exclusively national angle, as an epilogue of the Spanish Civil War. Until recently, most of these studies have ignored new currents in war history, from military history 'from below' to cultural approaches to the history of warfare and violence, and attempted to purely national answers to specifically national research questions. A transnational outlook,[3] which is mandatory for understanding a multifaceted topic such as the Eastern Front, has mostly been absent from that literature.

Moreover, far-right revisionist stances have had an overwhelming influence on historical approaches to the Spanish participation on the Eastern Front. Consequently, narratives had often neglected 'uncomfortable' issues such as the Holocaust and anti-partisan warfare. Traditional military history, dealing with operations and tactics, has largely dominated the field. Moreover, a soft legend of the Spanish behaviour in the German-Soviet war still persists to this day. This interpretation was systematically crafted in the immediate post-war historical culture by dozens of memoirs, novels, and films.

Spanish and German Experiences on the Eastern Front

To what extent was the experience of Germans and Spaniards on the Eastern Front comparable from a historical point of view? At first sight, there are almost as many similarities as differences between the two cases. While Germans were deployed everywhere along the front line, the Blue Division was ascribed to German Army Group North, and was first deployed on the Volkhov Front between October 1941 and August 1942. The Division was later stationed on the southern flank of the siege of Leningrad between August 1942 and November 1943. Spaniards fought alongside Flemish, Dutch, and Norwegian legionnaires and Waffen SS volunteers, and with whom they established a brotherhood of arms.[4]

Non-German units were a relatively small part of the Axis war effort in the East. German troops – composed both of Reich Germans and ethnic Germans from East-Central Europe – always constituted more than 70 per cent of all invading soldiers in the Soviet Union between 1941 and 1944. However, on several sectors of the Eastern Front, non-German units may have accounted for almost half of the occupying forces.[5] The participation of a Spanish contingent in the German war against the Soviet Union, alongside Finnish, Romanian, Italian, Hungarian, Slovak, and Croatian regular army units, as well as Western European and Scandinavian volunteers, had been useful for Nazi Germany to legitimize its war aims, expressed in the propagandistic slogan of the 'European Crusade against bolshevism'.[6]

The view from West Germany in the post-war period was peculiar, and was heavily influenced by pre-existing stereotypes regarding Spain. In general, the portrait was more positive for Spaniards than for Romanians and Italians. The Spanish volunteers always benefited from a persistent romantic image that dated from the nineteenth century or even earlier and depicted Spaniards as proud and brave – *stolze Spanier* – but undisciplined. Nostalgic military culture, as expressed in the popular novels of the series *Der Landser*, emphasized the image of the brave and romantic Spanish soldiers, who spoke a pidgin language made up of Italian and Spanish words.[7] In the Germans' eyes, Spaniards and Italians shared common stereotypes, but they were assigned very different degrees of heroism and masculinity. For example, Wolfgang Menge, scriptwriter of the popular TV series *Ein Herz und eine Seele* (*Birds of a feather*, 1973–4), recreated in its third episode a conversation between two Eastern Front veterans at a bar. One of them recalled Spaniards assaulting Soviet trenches with knives between their teeth, crying 'Avanti! Arriba! [*sic*]', while Italians were blamed for running away.[8]

What were the main differences that can be established, for comparative purposes, between the Spanish and the whole of the Wehrmacht's war experiences on the Eastern Front? These can be divided into three categories.

First, Blue Division and later Blue Legion volunteers were stationed on relatively quiet front areas, where they performed defensive tasks for most of their stay, and experienced just a few weeks of very intense combat (Volkhov offensive, October–December 1941; Volkhov pocket, June 1942; battle of Krasny Bor, February 1943, as well as several minor engagements), which did not affect the whole of the Division, but just some battalions and companies. The bulk of the Spanish Division was withdrawn before the start of the first massive Soviet counter-attacks on the Leningrad front in January 1944, followed by the great Bagration offensive in May that year, which caused high casualties within the German Army Group North. The Blue Legion was involved briefly in a few early battles but was subsequently forced to withdraw. It was then sent to Estonia for retraining before being repatriated a short time later, in March 1944, as a consequence of the increasing pressure exerted by the Allies on the Franco government, which abandoned its policy of non-belligerency and adopted a strict neutrality.[9]

Therefore, the survival rate of Spaniards was quite high in comparison to the overall figures of the German army and its allies on the Eastern Front. The Spanish units registered just more than 5,000 dead (approximately 11 per cent of all servicemen), with most casualties concentrated in two short periods: the Volkhov offensive and battle of Krasny Bor. This percentage is considerably lower than that of the German Army of the East (*Ostheer*) between 1941 and 1945, which is calculated as between 25 per cent and 27 per cent.[10] There were also relatively few Spanish prisoners of war, and their death rate was not particularly high in comparison with that of Germans, Italians, and Romanians in the ensuing years in Soviet prison camps: there were just 452 Spanish captives, of which 70 died in captivity. This amounted to around 15 per cent of all inmates.[11] Although the fate of Spanish prisoners of war in the Soviet Union until their return in April 1954 was a relevant theme within post-war politics of memory under the Francoist regime, this never became the key topic of subsequent narratives on the Blue Division. These focused instead on the military 'heroic deeds' of the Spanish volunteers.[12]

A second difference related to the social and political composition of the Spanish and German, Italian, Romanian, and Hungarian contingent. At least in theory, all Spanish combatants in the Blue Division were volunteers. A relevant proportion (around 25 per cent to 30 per cent) were staunch fascists, as well as radical Catholics and Francoist war veterans from the Spanish Civil War. Catholic-inspired anti-communism constituted their common label, and many were also motivated by the desire to see Spain joining the European 'New Order' from an advantageous position. Certainly, for many Spanish volunteers there was a defined continuity between the Civil War of 1936–9 and the campaign carried out on the Eastern Front against the same enemy ('Russian' communism). The Spanish troops were a heterogeneous mix of career officers, non-commissioned officers with little training, enthusiastic fascist volunteers from middle-class backgrounds – including a high percentage of university students – mercenary legionnaires, drafted soldiers who had been persuaded – and, in many cases, cajoled by their officers – to enrol in the replacements for Russia, adventurers and, finally, unemployed or non-skilled workers seeking a living. For many of them, the war culture inherited from the Spanish Civil War was an important factor for joining the Blue Division: the same war against communism was now waged on another, distant front.

Falangist volunteers, who expected Operation Barbarossa to be short and dreamed of a triumphal return after having paraded through Moscow's Red Square, were more abundant in the first contingent dispatched to Russia in July 1941. In contrast, drafted soldiers and workers increased their number in the replacements arrived in Russia from March 1942 on. Idealist volunteers coexisted with adventurers and 'materialist' volunteers, alongside a minority of Republicans and leftists who intended to defect to the Red Army once they were at the front, and the social composition of the volunteers also varied from province to province. While the number of Falangist students was higher in Madrid, Murcia, and Valencia, most volunteers from Badajoz, Huelva, and Aragon were day labourers, unemployed and non-skilled workers, as a sample of 3,056 civilian volunteers from six provinces and the region of Aragon shows (see Table 13.1).[13]

In some respects, the social and ideological composition of the Blue Division and its subsequent units was not very different from that of Western European

Table 13.1 Social composition of civil volunteers of the Blue Division (%) 1941–3

	Toledo	Santander	Huelva	Badajoz	Aragon	Murcia	Álava
Farmers, agricultural labourers, sailors	9.0	5.9	44.44	41.14	28.38	9.04	14.38
Unskilled manual workers	26.12	35.0	14.5	12.6	3.96	3.75	30.93
Skilled manual workers, blue-collar workers	26.12	25.3	24.81	15.0	32.3	9.89	34.53
Artisans, shopkeepers	10.8	6.61	5.94	11.8	0.42	14.67	2.15
Clerks, civil servants (middle and lower strata)	18.0	18.43	9.2	10.45	1.30	27.98	7.91
University students	5.4	4.2	0.46	1.83	3.74	24.91	4.31
Liberal professionals, landlords, merchants, and industry owners	2.7	1.89	0.46	1.97	2.66	5.97	1.43
Others and unemployed	2.86	3.6	0.19	5.21	4	3.75	4.31
Total amount of the sample; (3056)	111	423	639	707	451	586	139

See: Núñez Seixas, *Camarada invierno*, 92; for Álava, Archivo General Militar, Ávila, Cajas (C.) 5453–5 (courtesy of Dr Virginia López de Maturana).

'Legions' and Waffen SS volunteers (French, Flemish, Danish, or Walloon), which also took part in the 'Crusade against bolshevism'.[14] Since the Francoist regime never declared war on the Soviet Union, the Blue Division was neither a national unit allied to the Wehrmacht nor a 'national legion' of volunteers or a Waffen SS unit. In fact, Spanish soldiers enjoyed an unusual legal status within the German armed forces: they officially belonged to the Wehrmacht as the 250th Infantry Division, and wore German uniforms with a national coat of arms in their right arm, yet, they were subject to the Spanish Code of Military Justice.

A third difference with the bulk of the German *Ostheer* concerned the nature of war experience. As expressed above, Spaniards were deployed in mostly quiet areas of the northern section of the Eastern Front, where there were relatively few moments of intense combat. This also included the rearguard: partisan warfare in the immediate rear of German Army Group North was not as merciless and active as it was in the central and southern regions of the Eastern Front.[15] Therefore, the specific context of the Volkhov and particularly the Leningrad front was less favourable to brutalization than in other sectors of the East.

Spanish Occupiers: Experience and Memory

The main differences between the Wehrmacht and the Blue Division lay in their policies of occupation in the East. Although there is much evidence that sustains that Spanish soldiers engaged in theft and plunder on the Volkhov and Leningrad fronts, they never were systematic killers. As far as the occupation practices are concerned, there is some research consensus in highlighting that they generally behaved better towards civilians and prisoners of war than their German, Romanian, and Hungarian counterparts. This did not, however, exclude individual reprisals, rapes, and plunder.[16]

The Spanish Division did not have enough personnel to establish a system of capillary occupation, which encompassed a compact and designated area under its exclusive responsibility. Therefore, Spaniards restricted themselves to implementing the German directives. Nevertheless, Spanish practices were characterized by their milder profile. Just three Spanish soldiers were declared war criminals by the Soviet post-war inquiry commissions, compared to 40,000 Germans and Austrians. The Spanish occupants' apparently good behaviour towards Soviet civilians was subsequently idealized by veterans' post-war accounts; the myth of the open-minded, benevolent, and pleasant Spanish soldiers was spread through novels, press articles, films, and memoirs. Contrary to the merciless, rude Germans, it was stressed that Spaniards were not racist towards Slavs and Jews, and that they treated children and women well. Their frequent flirtation with Soviet girls evidenced their lack of prejudice, and they were depicted as sympathetic to the Russian common people, to the point that many affirmed after the war that they had fought on the wrong side. Did this mean that Spaniards were unable to embrace racism, as the trench journal of the Blue Division affirmed in 1943?[17] Was this a consequence of the deep imprint of Catholic culture and religion on the

Spanish volunteers? Or simply because, as 'Southern' people, they felt attracted by a kind of exotic sentiment of cultural and peripheral affinity with Russians?[18]

Undoubtedly, racial indoctrination was weaker among Spanish combatants than among German conscripts raised under the Nazi regime. Yet, ego-documents and contemporary diaries and letters also confirm that many *divisionarios* – and not only the most fascist or 'fascistized' among them – experienced negative reactions as they first encountered Soviet soldiers, prisoners of war, and civilians. As in the case of German and Italian soldiers, the reactions of the first volunteers to set foot on Soviet soil coincided in reporting the most basic element: filth and poverty. Newly arrived *divisionarios* after 1942 expressed similar impressions in their letters. They described the Russians as a people lacking hygiene, whose saunas seemed a 'savage, primitive system', while Russians were 'unacquainted with lights, electricity, European-style clothing, plumbing; their huts are poorly constructed of wood and full of misery'.[19] 'Animalization' was another characteristic the Spanish occupants often perceived in the peasants: a private spoke of how he won the trust of a 'human cub' with chocolate; months later he also described how the Russian women deloused each other like monkeys.[20]

All of them saw Russia as a 'dirty' country, attributed the peasants' poverty to the negative effects of communism, and regarded the Russians as culturally inferior people. However, not only were the latter viewed as victims of the communist regime, but also as individuals who were unable to reach a stage of full civilization due to the harsh natural environment and the long history of despotism that had characterized Russia from the tsars to the Bolsheviks. This attitude may be accurately defined as cultural racism, and was not markedly different from the first reactions of many German soldiers upon meeting Soviet civilians. Dirty, crude, primitive, and uncivilized people, or simply physically unattractive people, were not in the same league as *European invaders*. German soldiers expressed in their letters from Russia how the frontier between cleanliness and order – which they associated with the Western world and masculinity – and dirtiness and disorder, now constituted the difference between civilization and barbarianism. The Spaniards were not substantially different in this respect. In fact, many officers of the Blue Division had experienced similar sensations among the Berber population during their years in Africa. José Luis Gómez-Tello, a Falangist journalist and volunteer, vividly described Russia as a smell of the *Orient*, accentuating humidity and putrefaction: 'Rotten potatoes, *kapuska*, human misery, manure, and all manner of fermentation in an atmosphere that has not been ventilated for ten months'.[21]

However, none of the Spanish occupiers shared the mid-term objectives of extermination and domination of the Slavic peoples, which were advocated by the Nazis, and to some extent also shared by Wehrmacht combatants. On the contrary, many a Spanish volunteer, like many German Catholic soldiers, framed their war motivation in terms of the re-christianization of Russia and the Russians: their conversion would also mean a return to European tradition. The idea of 'combatant Christendom' was crucial for Falangist volunteers, many professional officers and even conscripted soldiers.[22] In fact, during their time in Russia,

Spanish soldiers participated in local religious ceremonies, infant baptisms, or even orthodox funerals.[23]

Less certainty exists regarding other aspects, such as the treatment of prisoners and methods applied in anti-partisan warfare.[24] General benevolence towards Soviet captives from December 1941 onwards was evident among Spaniards, but there were also summary executions, sometimes following interrogations of prisoners in combat. Moreover, Iberians were not especially effective, zealous, or cruel in reprisals and in the fight against partisans. They sometimes did execute civilians accused of hiding partisans. However, no evidence has been found that indicates they engaged in collective killings or reprisals against entire villages. German reports hardly mentioned Spanish participation in these activities. They do, however, reveal a certain lack of trust in Spaniards to carry out rearguard population control and cleansing actions, given what they saw as the demonstrated inefficacy of the Iberians in this area. In early 1942, the German command decided to relieve the Blue Division of all sentry duties in the immediate rearguard, partly because the Spaniards had to cover a very broad section of the front.[25] Where they were responsible for these duties, evidence suggests that control of the civil population was less brutal and thorough than with the Germans and their 'security divisions' and 'protection teams' that operated in the rear. The Iberians maintained practices reminiscent of those used in the former colonial wars, rather than the brutalized and radical 'totalitarian counter-insurgency' methods of the Wehrmacht.[26] The few testimonies that mention retaliatory operations indicate that locals were frequently handed over to the Germans.[27] Few Blue Division internal reports mention explicit anti-partisan actions or their results, but the exceptions show that they did occur.[28] However, as the Germans repeatedly complained, Spanish efficacy in the anti-partisan fight was questionable.[29]

The Spanish Division's compliance with the order to kill Red Army political commissars on the spot after being captured and interrogated – the Commissar Order – also remains unclear, as there is no mention of summary executions of Soviet *politruks* in Spanish officers' and soldiers' memoirs, nor in the Blue Division files held in the military archives. This does not necessarily mean it was not obeyed, since that order would have been transmitted verbally to Wehrmacht combatants and did not leave a significant written record either.[30] Some indirect evidence suggests that the order was known by the Spanish commanders and officers, and just abolished in May 1942, on the eve of the harshest fighting at the Volkhov pocket.[31]

The attitudes of Spaniards towards civilians were ambivalent. As mentioned above, the contemporary image of Russia and the Russians that Spanish officers and volunteers had, or forged at the front, did not include racial hatred. This particular vision of the enemy might have incited commiseration and paternalism, but never prevented Russian civilians from suffering requisitions and theft. This was aggravated by organizational deficiencies and a lack of discipline among the Blue Division troops. Yet, Spanish soldiers were not routinely involved in the homicide of Russian peasants; they coexisted reasonably well, given their condition as invading troops. The complexity inherent in the presence of an occupying army among civilians led many Spanish soldiers who lodged in the *isbas* to function as protectors of Russian families, which were mainly composed of young or elderly women, children, and old men. The *divisionarios* would feed and protect them in exchange for services that ranged from laundry to sexual favours.[32] Contrary to Romanian and Hungarian troops, the Spaniards did not become involved in systematic reprisals or large-scale murders of civilians. They were, nonetheless, responsible for continual theft, requisitioning and pillaging, along with occasional sexual abuse. This was typical of the experiences of other occupying Axis armies during the Second World War, such as the relatively benign presence of Germans in Norway, Denmark, and the Netherlands.[33]

A distinctive element of the Spanish Blue Division was its contemporary image of the enemy. In general terms, personal sources reflect that Mediterranean combatants tended to regard Red Army soldiers as culturally inferior: they were also viewed as victims of the communist regime and slaves of the dehumanized 'mass instinct' imposed on them by the Bolsheviks, particularly by political commissars. Yet the enemy was not regarded as a biologically inferior subhuman. Soviet prisoners of war were generally better treated by Spaniards than by Germans. However, it is also true that most of the captives were handed over to the Germans shortly after apprehension. But contrary to their German partners, the Spanish commanders did not necessary feel that the extermination of a great part of the Slavic population was a necessity.

While the lesser influence or the lack of previous ideological indoctrination may have played a role in the Spaniards' attitudes towards Soviet civilians and soldiers, the particular dynamics of brutalization of the Blue Division appear to have been much more decisive in shaping its stance. Many Spanish officers, NCOs, and privates had already experienced brutal wars in the recent past. Yet, conditions along the Eastern Front were not always similar. In the northern sector, Spanish soldiers had fewer opportunities to experience a 'cumulative radicalization', which was less accentuated than in the areas covered by the Army Group Centre and South. The northern part of the Eastern Front was more stable, with less partisan activity. Spanish soldiers had not been fighting for months before they arrived on the front and stayed less time on average (10–12 months) than their German comrades. These factors decisively enhanced the brutalization of the various Wehrmacht units, as has been demonstrated for the 121st, 123rd, and 126th German Divisions of the Army Group North.[34] The absence of these factors therefore conditioned the lack of steady brutalization of the Spanish Division.

Attitudes towards the Jews constituted another difference. As they marched from Suwalki to Vitebsk during September of 1941, the first contingent of Spanish volunteers witnessed the early segregationist measures implemented by the Germans in towns with considerable Jewish presence, such as Hrodna/Grodno and Oszmyanhy. Spanish military hospitals operated in Vilnius and Riga when the local Jewish communities were deported and their ghettos filled with new Jewish families from Germany, which lasted through mid-1942. Spanish soldiers in the rearguard of the Reich also witnessed some effects of Nazi anti-Semitic policies.

The letters and war diaries of Blue Division members reflected this reality to a certain extent. However, memoirs after 1945 show that the veterans re-wrote their experiences, seeking to adopt the position of a neutral observer, describing Nazi anti-Semitic policies while trying to distance themselves from what they had seen. Spanish volunteers, particularly those combatants who adhered to fascist and/or strongly Catholic beliefs, shared a traditional anti-Semitism based on confessional stereotypes. Unlike Italians or Romanians, they were not acquainted with anti-Jewish measures in their country of origin. Most *divisionarios* had little sympathy for the Jews as a collective, but in their majority, however, they had never met a Jew before. Anti-Semitic tones were stronger among highly motivated fascist and Falangist volunteers; despite this, they were far from sharing a biologically based anti-Semitism aimed at the long-term uprooting of Jews, and were not always able to justify the segregationist measures undertaken by Germans in the occupied territories in the East.[35]

Spanish soldiers had few opportunities to witness the persecution (not least the deportation and killing) of Jews. Therefore, they also had few chances to protect Jewish civilians. They barely met any Jews at the sections of the front where they were deployed: the Leningrad/Volkhov Front had already been 'cleaned up' by *Einsatzgruppe A* before the arrival of the Blue Division.[36] Certainly, Spaniards had some encounters with Polish Jews in some cities and villages of Eastern Poland between August and September 1941, and again during their stays as convalescent soldiers at the military hospitals of Riga and Vilnius. Yet, they never participated at killing operations, although some passively witnessed massacres. In fact, some Jewish survivors from Grodno expressed positive judgements about the Spaniards in their memoirs. Alexandre Blumstein wrote that they were 'very strange "Germans", outgoing and sociable …, one could see these soldiers joking with Polish and Jewish girls'. And Felix Zandman stated that the Spaniards 'associated with the Jewish men without a sign of dislike or hatred. They went out with the Jewish girls.'[37] However, there is just indirect evidence of a couple of cases where Spanish soldiers were involved in protecting Jews. In general, the label of 'bystanders' could be applied to the soldiers of the Blue Division: they were neither perpetrators, nor protectors[38] (see Figure 13.1).

Therefore, the Spanish 250th Division never had a prominent role in the war of extermination unleashed by the Wehrmacht, nor are there indications that the Spanish commanders knew of the long-term occupation schemes of the Third Reich leaders, which were implemented by the military. Unlike Hungarian soldiers in the Ukraine and Romanian combatants in Bessarabia, Bukovina, and Transnistria, Spaniards did not participate systematically in the rearguard in collective reprisals against Russian, Polish, Byelorussian or Baltic civilians, or Jews. However, it must not be forgotten that the Blue Division effectively though indirectly aided a strategic action that served the mid-range war of extermination plans behind the invasion of the USSR: the sentencing of three million people to death by starvation.[39]

A further characteristic was that of portraying themselves as double victims. Spaniards maintained a somewhat ambivalent relationship to their German allies.

Figure 13.1 Two soldiers of the Spanish Blue Division pose in German uniforms. Xosé M. Núñez Seixas's personal archive.

In general, the German staff officers and commanders disdained the military efficiency of Iberian soldiers from the very beginning of their deployment at the front, as they did with Romanians, Italians, and Hungarians. In so doing, German officers usually appealed to deeply rooted stereotypes about the laziness, lack of military discipline, and deficient training of southern soldiers. Furthermore, they were unable to understand the most salient traits of Spanish military culture, which was impregnated with the hierarchical nature of the social structure of a Southern European society.[40] In this respect, German liaison officers usually played the role of cultural mediators between the German Army and Army Group general staff and the Spanish staff and commanders. While they complained about the lack of efficiency, care, and discipline of Iberian soldiers, they also attempted to emphasize their purported virtues, such as their ability to improvise, their individual bravery, and their tradition of guerrilla warfare.[41]

Nevertheless, attitudes held by ordinary German soldiers (*Landser*) towards their Spanish brothers in arms were more positive than those of their commanders. Spaniards were usually deployed close to positions held by German units, and who came into frequent contact at the front with them. German soldiers and front officers admired the Spanish combatants' purported recklessness at the front line, but also complained about their exotic comrades' lack of discipline, as well as their unpredictable behaviour.[42] In contrast, ordinary Spanish soldiers felt great admiration for the Wehrmacht's military efficiency, which preceded their deployment at the Eastern Front. Spanish combatants – who were part of the Wehrmacht and received similar treatment, supplies, and equipment to the Germans – were especially fascinated by German military organization. Falangist volunteers even viewed the Wehrmacht as a truly 'National-Socialist' army, where officers did not inflict physical punishment on their subordinates, and relations were purportedly less hierarchical than in the Spanish army. Spanish soldiers were also fascinated by the modernity, welfare, and social secularization of the German home front – which Falangist volunteers regarded as a model to be imitated in their homeland upon their return.[43]

Certainly, war veterans' memoirs and accounts after 1945 tended to detach themselves from their former brothers in arms, and emphasized some negative traits of German soldiers and officers, such as arrogance, superiority complexes, racism, and brutal behaviour towards the occupied populations. Spaniards portrayed themselves as double victims: of the Soviets and of the German allies. Falangist war veterans often presented their presence at the Russian front as the price to be paid by the Francoist regime to preserve non-belligerency during the war. They regarded themselves as the last idealist defenders of the 'national-syndicalist' revolution, who after 1945 had become inconvenient heroes, marginalized by the regime for the sake of its survival in the new context of the Cold War. This self-compassionate image coexisted with the persistent admiration for the German Wehrmacht and feelings of comradeship towards German soldiers. Thus, Spanish veterans' associations vehemently adhered to the legend of the 'clean Wehrmacht', and distanced the German conscript soldiers from the war crimes on the Eastern Front, which were exclusively attributed to the SS and the *Einsatzgruppen*.[44] The former *divisionarios* also argued that only those who had fought side by side with the German comrades against communism were legitimately qualified to chide them for what they had purportedly done. Ángel Ruiz Ayúcar expressed this point of view in 1954: 'Much has been said about the concentration camps in this sad and spiteful post-war period. … But we will not join in this stoning.'[45]

At the same time, Iberian veterans also insisted on presenting their performance and behaviour at the Eastern Front under a more positive light than that of the German army in general. They crafted a legend of the good Spaniards, who were even *cleaner* than the *clean* Wehrmacht.[46] This legend was consistently transmitted first by war veterans' memoirs and writings, and later by amateur and revisionist historians, either on the far right or simply emotionally linked to the veterans' associations.[47] A myth of Spanish exceptionalism on the Eastern Front emerged and consolidated itself in the Spanish public sphere. This reproduced many of the stereotypes and discursive strategies used by revisionist and amateur military historians in North America regarding the Wehrmacht.[48]

Unlike Italians and Western European Waffen SS volunteers, Spanish veterans returned to a country where a para-fascist dictatorship managed to survive under a Catholic and authoritarian cover. Therefore, in theory at least, there were no constraints to publicly remembering and commemorating the 'heroic deeds' of Spaniards in the East. Spanish involvement on the Eastern Front was now presented as an entirely anti-communist initiative, and veterans were portrayed sympathetically. This narrative also fitted extremely well in the corporative politics of memory of the Spanish army. In fact, the Russian campaign was (and still is) regarded by the Spanish military as a glorious chapter of their professional history, and parallels were conveniently traced to the new situation created by the Cold War. Therefore, the Spanish participation in the war of extermination was justified as a merely anti-communist endeavour, which was supposedly devoid of any racial, exterminatory, fascist, or imperial objectives.

The Cold War had confirmed to Spanish veterans of the Russian front that Soviet communism was the main enemy of *Western civilization, European culture,* and especially *Christian values.*[49] The fall of the Berlin Wall, and the full *conversion* of Russia and the other Eastern Bloc countries reinforced this line of argument. In their view, this constituted the Blue Division's posthumous victory. Some of them returned to visit their former battlegrounds, undertook initiatives to repatriate the remains of their fallen comrades, and portrayed in positive terms their re-encounters with Russian peasants. This pilgrimage served to reassess their past convictions, as well as their perception of being moral winners of history: 'eternal' Russia had re-emerged.[50]

Conclusions

The German war of extermination in the East was not only a conflict between Germany and the Soviet Union. Nor were its consequences restricted to the two main countries which participated at the hostilities. Thousands of northern, western, southern, and eastern Europeans also took part in the war; experienced the brutalization of the front to varying degrees; witnessed or participated in war atrocities, rapes, and murders; and in some cases were actively or passively involved in the Holocaust. The conduct of the different national units at the front and the rear was conditioned by situational and structural factors. While some of their members were strongly motivated by fascism, anti-communism and/or anti-Semitism, many others were simply conscripted soldiers, adventurers, or even non-enthusiastic warriors who had enlisted for different reasons. The type of war they conducted, as well as the different intensities of combat on the front line decisively conditioned their behaviour, their perceptions of the conquered land and the enemy, and may have contributed to the radicalization of their attitudes towards Soviet civilians and partisans. In this respect, the same interpretative framework which has been applied for the study of the German Wehrmacht in the East, and therefore similar research questions, can also be extended to its foreign allies and collaborators. Were Spaniards' divergent attitudes from the Wehrmacht an endorsement of the thesis that ideology and indoctrination of soldiers were the main prerequisite for their brutalization? Or were they a further example of how combat conditions and environment determined soldiers' behaviour?[51]

As explained above, evidence can be found to endorse both hypotheses. In contrast to Germans, Spaniards lacked strong racial-oriented ideological indoctrination; but many aspects of their behaviour did not reveal any substantial difference to ordinary German soldiers. However, the situationist hypothesis seems to better explain the differences that existed between Spaniards and Italians, who were also characterized by the lack of racial indoctrination, but had to fight in much worse conditions, and also carried out some violent repressive measures against civilians.[52] Despite what post-war literature and veterans' accounts have instilled in the Spanish public sphere, there was no specifically 'Mediterranean' pattern of war experience determined by an epicurean character, the peculiarity of their type of fascism and/or anti-communist creed, or the lack of racial prejudice towards Jews and Slavs. On the contrary, the bulk of the Blue Division was always composed of fascist and anti-communist volunteers, plus professional NCOs and army officers. Their ideological cohesion was stronger than that of Italian, Romanian, and Hungarian units on the Eastern Front, mostly made up of conscript soldiers. And, in many ways, this made the Blue Division more comparable to the ideological Western European volunteers in the Waffen SS.

Further Reading

Bowen, Wayne. *Spaniards and Nazi Germany: Collaboration in the New Order*. Columbia: Missouri University Press, 2000.

Kleinfeld, Gerald R. and Lewis A. Tambs, *Hitler's Spanish Legion: The Blue Division in Russia*. Carbondale, IL: Southern Illinois University Press, 1979.

Kovalev, Boris. *Dobrovol´cí na cyzoj voyne. Ocerki istorii golyboj divizii*. Veliki Novgorod: Novgorodskij gosydarstveii´j universitet, 2014.

Moreno Juliá, Xavier. *La División Azul: Sangre española en Rusia, 1941-1945*. Barcelona: Crítica, 2004.

Moreno Juliá, Xavier. *Legión Azul y Segunda Guerra Mundial. Hundimiento hispano-alemán en el frente del Este, 1941-1944*. Madrid: Actas, 2014.

Núñez Seixas, Xosé M. *Camarada invierno. Experiencia y memoria de la División Azul, 1941-1945*. Barcelona: Crítica, 2016; German ed.: Münster, Aschendorff, 2016.

Núñez Seixas, Xosé M. 'Russia and the Russians in the Eyes of the Spanish Blue Division Soldiers, 1941-4', *Journal of Contemporary History* 52, no. 2 (2017): 352–74.

Núñez Seixas, Xosé M. 'Good Invaders? The Occupation Policy of the Spanish Blue Division in Northwestern Russia, 1941–1944'. *War in History* 25, no. 3 (2018): 361–86.

Notes

1   To quote some general accounts, see Gerald R. Kleinfeld and Lewis A. Tambs, *Hitler's Spanish Legion: The Blue Division in Russia* (Carbondale, IL: Southern Illinois University Press, 1979), and Wayne Bowen, *Spaniards and Nazi German. Collaboration in the New Order* (Columbia: Missouri University Press, 2000). From a diplomatic and operational viewpoint, see also Xavier Moreno Juliá, *La División Azul: Sangre española en Rusia, 1941-1945* (Barcelona: Crítica, 2004). From

Russian historiography, see the contribution by Boris Kovalev, *Dobrovol´cí na cyzoj voyne. Ocerki istorii golyboj divizii* (Veliki Novgorod: Novgorodskij gosydarstveii´j universitet, 2014).

2   See some examples in Christian Hartmann, *Wehrmacht im Ostkrieg: Front und militärisches Hinterland 1941/42*, (Munich: Oldenbourg, 2009); Stephen Fritz, *Ostkrieg. Hitler's War of Extermination in the East*, (Lexington: University Press of Kentucky, 2011), and Christian Hartmann et al., *Der deutsche Krieg im Osten 1941–1944. Facetten einer Grenzüberschreitung* (Munich: Oldenbourg, 2009).

3   See, for example, *Transnational Soldiers. Foreign Military Enlistment in the Modern Era*, ed. Nir Arielli and Bruce Collins (Basingstoke: Palgrave, 2012), as well as *War Volunteering in Modern Times: From the French Revolution to the Second World War*, ed. Christine G. Krüger and Sonja Levsen (Basingstoke: Palgrave, 2010).

4   See, for example, *Schlacht am Wolchow* (Riga: Propaganda-Kompanie, 1942), and *Spaniens Freiwillige an der Ostfront: Los voluntarios españoles en el frente. Ein Bildbuch von der Blauen Division* (Kaunas: Propaganda-Kompanie der Armee Busch, 1942).

5   See figures in David Glantz, 'The Soviet-German War 1941-1945: Myths and Realities: A Survey Essay', Distinguished Lecture at the Strom Thurmond Institute of Government and Public Affairs, 22 October 2001, available at: http://sti.clemson.edu/publications-mainmenu-38/commentaries-mainmenu-211/cat_view/33-strom-thurmond-institute/153-sti-publications-by-subject-area/158-history.

6   For a general account, see Rolf-Dieter Müller, *The Unknown Eastern Front: The Wehrmacht and Hitler's Foreign* Soldiers (London: I. B. Tauris, 2012), as well as Jochen *The Waffen SS. A European History* ed. Böhler and Robert Gerwarth, (Oxford: Oxford University Press, 2016), and *Joining Hitler's Crusade* ed. David Stahel(Cambridge: Cambridge University Press, 2017).

7   See, for example, Fred Nemis, *Der Stützpunkt am Ilmensee*, Rastatt n. d. [Der Landser, 496]); Ibid., *Der Letzte der Legión*, Rastatt n. d. [Der Landser, 2594]).

8   *Ein Herz und eine Seele*. 1973. Episode 3, *Besuch aus der Ostzone* [Visit from the Eastern zone], first broadcast on 12 February 1973. Available at: http://www.youtube.com/watch?v=yUan2fGw_kE (Minutes 24:10–24:50). Last accessed 27 August 2017.

9   Exhaustively on this, see Xavier Moreno Julià, *Legión Azul y Segunda Guerra Mundial. Hundimiento hispano-alemán en el frente del Este, 1941-1944* (Madrid: Actas, 2014).

10 See Rüdiger Overmans, *Deutsche militärische Verluste im Zweiten Weltkrieg* (Munich: Oldenbourg, 2000, 228 and 313–23. More than half of all dead are concentrated in a relatively short period (the last twelve months of the war).

11 Data reproduced by Teresa Giusti, *I prigioneri italiani in Russia* (Bari: Laterza, 2003), 97.

12 See Valeria Possi, 'Idealismo e imaginario falangista en las primeras novelas de la División Azul', *Castilla. Estudios de Literatura* 8 (2017): 216–57. Yet, some memoirs of Spanish officers who returned from Soviet captivity, such as Captain Palacios, achieved great success: see Torcuato Luca de Tena and Teodoro Palacios Cueto, *Embajador en el infierno. Memorias del capitán Palacios: once años de cautiverio en Rusia* (Madrid: Kamerad, 1955), as well as the film by José M. Forqué *Embajadores en el infierno* (1956).

13 See for a comprehensive discussion, also based upon the comparison of several provinces, Xosé M. Núñez Seixas, *Camarada invierno. Experiencia y memoria de la División Azul, 1941-1945* (Barcelona: Crítica, 2016), 69–102.

14 See *The Waffen SS*, ed. Böhler and Gerwarth as well as *Die Waffen-SS. Neue Forschungen* ed. Jan-Erik Schulte, Peter Lieb and Bernd Wegner (Paderborn:

Schöningh, 2014), and David Alegre, 'Experiencia de guerra y colaboracionismo
político-militar: Bélgica, Francia y España bajo el Nuevo Orden (1941-1945)', Ph. D.
Thesis, Autonomous University of Barcelona, 2017.

15 See Jeff Rutherford, *Combat and Genocide on the Eastern Front: The German Infantry's
    War, 1941–1944* (Cambridge: Cambridge University Press, 2014), and Alexander Hill,
    *The War behind the Eastern Front: The Soviet Partisan Movement in North-West Russia
    1941-44* (London: Frank Cass, 2005).

16 Exhaustively on this, see Xosé M. Núñez Seixas, 'Good Invaders? The Occupation
    Policy of the Spanish Blue Division in Northwestern Russia, 1941–1944', *War in
    History* 25, no. 3 (2018): 361–86. The Russian historian Boris Kovalev (*Dobrovoltsy*,
    327–75) arrives to similar conclusions, based on testimonies collected among
    Russian peasants to Soviet party officials in 1944. For Hungarians and Romanians,
    see Krisztián Ungváry, 'Das Beispiel der ungarischen Armee. Ideologischer
    Vernichtungskrieg oder militärisches Kalkül?', in *Verbrechen der Wehrmacht. Bilanz
    einer Debatte*, ed. Christian Hartmann, Johannes Hürter and Ulrike Jureit (Munich:
    Beck, 2005), 98–106, and Armin Heinen, *Rumänien, der Holocaust und die Logik der
    Gewalt* (Munich: Oldenbourg, 2007), 109–49.

17 'La raza', *Hoja de Campaña* (10 October 1943).

18 This argument has been implicitly put forward by authors such as Moreno Juliá, *La
    División Azul*.

19 Vicente Rodríguez Vela to Lieutenant Colonel Leandro García González, 22 March
    1942 (Museo del Pueblo de Asturias, Gijón – Fondo Leandro García González).

20 'Diario de un voluntario. Notas de mi macuto', *Nueva Alcarria*, 20 December 1941;
    'División Azul. Cartas de un voluntario', *Nueva Alcarria*, 21 March 1942.

21 See Michaela Kipp, *Großreinemachen im Osten. Feindbilder in deutschen
    Feldpostbriefen im Zweiten Weltkrieg* (Frankfurt a. M./New York: Campus, 2014),
    47–110; José Luis Gómez-Tello, *Canción de invierno en el Este. Crónicas de la División
    Azul* (Barcelona: Luis de Caralt, 1945), 50.

22 See Xosé M. Núñez Seixas, 'Russia and the Russians in the Eyes of the Spanish Blue
    Division Soldiers, 1941-4', *Journal of Contemporary History* 52, no. 2 (2017): 352–74.
    For the contrast with German Catholic soldiers, see Nicholas Stargardt, *Der deutsche
    Krieg 1939–1945* (Frankfurt a. M.: Fischer, 2015), 207–8.

23 A. Andújar, 'Otra vez Katia', *Hoja de Campaña* (1 August 1943); 'Han matado a
    una niña', *Hoja de Campaña* (15 August 1943); Javier Sánchez Carrilero, *Crónicas
    de la División Azul* (Albacete: n. ed., 1993), 91–3; Fernando Torres, 'Rusos en la
    retaguardia', *Lucha* (15 July 1943).

24 Russian testimonies after 1944 only indicate that a Spanish lieutenant in Koritsko
    was responsible for some shootings of peasants suspected of collaborating with the
    partisans (Kovalev, *Dobrovoltsy*, 369).

25 Instruction of the High Command of the XXXVIII Army Corps, 5 January 1942
    (Bundesarchiv-Militärarchiv [BA-MA], Freiburg i. Br., RH.24-38/34).

26 For a comparative discussion, see Beatrice Heuser, *Rebellen-Partisanen-Guerilleros.
    Asymmetrische Kriege von der Antike bis heute* (Paderborn: Schöningh, 2013),
    142–215.

27 General Instruction 2023, 7 July 1942 (Archivo General Militar [AGM], Ávila,
    2006/1/1/7); Report from Abt. Ic, 1-22 November 1941 (BA-MA, RH 20-16/473).

28 Daily report of 250th Division to the XXXVIII Army Corps, 18 December 1941 (BA-
    MA, RH 24-38/171). Memoirs of Vladimir Kovalevskii, Russian interpreter of the
    Blue Division (Hoover Institution, Stanford).

29 See, for example, Army Corps L, Order dated 10 July 1943 (BA-MA, RH 24-50/66).
30 See Felix Römer, *Der Kommissarbefehl. Wehrmacht und NS-Verbrechen an der Ostfront 1941/42* (Paderborn: Schöningh, 2008).
31 General staff of BD, 2nd Section, Instruction 2,018, 12 May 1942 (AGM 2005/18/1/6).
32 More details in Núñez Seixas, 'Good Invaders?'.
33 See *Die deutsche Herrschaft in den 'germanischen' Ländern, 1940-1945*, ed. Robert Bohn (Stutgart: Franz Steiner Verlag, 1997); Jennifer L. Foray, 'The "Clean Wehrmacht" in the German-occupied Netherlands, 1940-1945', *Journal of Contemporary History* 45, no. 4 (2010): 768–87.
34 Rutherford, *Combat and Genocide*, 115–52 and 240–79.
35 See, for example, Dionisio Ridruejo, *Los Cuadernos de Rusia* (Barcelona: Planeta, 1978), 42–3, 53, 60–4, and 80–1. More radical in his anti-Semitism was Gómez Tello, *Canción de invierno*, 64–73.
36 See details in Yitzhak Arad, *The Holocaust in the Soviet Union* (Lincoln and Jerusalem: University of Nebraska Press/Yad Vashem, 2009).
37 Alexandre Blumstein, *A little house on Mont Carmel* (London: Valentine Mitchell, 2002), 71–3; Felix Zandman, *Never the Last Journey* (New York: Schocken Books, 1995), 42.
38 For more details, see Núñez Seixas, *Camarada invierno*, 296–318.
39 See Jörg Ganzenmüller, *Das belagerte Leningrad 1941-1944. Die Stadt in den Strategien von Angreifern und Verteidigern* (Paderborn: Schöningh, 2005).
40 See Richard L. Di Nardo, 'The Dysfunctional Coalition: The Axis Powers and the Eastern Front in World War II', *The Journal of Military History* 60, no. 4 (1996): 711–30.
41 See Núñez Seixas, *Camarada invierno*, 122–4.
42 See, for example, letters from corporal Otto M., 30 October 1941, and Captain Hermann Sch., 5 November 1941 (Bibliothek für Zeitgeschichte, Stuttgart – Sterz Collection).
43 Extensively on this, see Xosé M. Núñez Seixas, 'Wishful Thinking in Wartime? Spanish Blue Division's Soldiers and Their Views of Nazi Germany, 1941–44', *Journal of War and Culture Studies* 11, no. 2 (2018): 99–116.
44 On the legend of the 'clean Wehrmacht', see Detlef Bald, Johannes Klotz and Wolfram Wette, *Mythos Wehrmacht. Nachkriegsdebatten und Traditionspflege* (Berlin: Aufbau Taschenbuch, 2001).
45 Angel Ruiz Ayúcar, *La Rusia que yo conocí* (Madrid: Fuerza Nueva Ed., 1981 [1st. ed. 1954]), 156.
46 See Xosé M. Núñez Seixas, 'Russland war nicht schuldig: Die Ostfronterfahrung der spanischen Blauen Division in Selbstzeugnissen und Autobiographien, 1943-2004', in *Militärische Erinnerungskultur. Soldaten im Spiegel von Biographien, Memoiren und Selbstzeugnisse*, ed. Michael Epkenhans, Stig Förster and Karen Hagemann (Paderborn: Schöningh, 2006), 236–67, as well as Jesús Guzmán Mora, 'Visiones de Rusia en la narrativa española. El caso de la División Azul', Ph. D. Thesis, University of Salamanca, 2016.
47 See, for example, Pablo Sagarra, *Capellanes en la División Azul. Los últimos cruzados* (Madrid: Actas, 2012), as well as Gustavo Morales and Luis E. Togores, *La División Azul: las fotografías de una historia* (Madrid: La Esfera de los Libros, 2008).
48 Ronald Smelser and Edward J. Davies, *The Myth of the Eastern Front. The Nazi Soviet War in American Popular Culture* (Cambridge: Cambridge University Press, 2008).

49 See Possi, 'La narrativa'; Xosé M. Núñez Seixas, 'Unconvenient heroes? War veterans from the Eastern front in Franco's Spain (1942-1975)', in *War Veterans and the World after 1945. Cold War Politics, Decolonization, Memory*, ed. Ángel Alcalde and Xosé M. Núñez Seixas (London: Routledge, 2018), 187–202.

50 See Fernando Garrido Polonio and Miguel A. Garrido Polonio, *Nieve roja. Españoles desaparecidos en el frente ruso* (Madrid: Oberon, 2002).

51 For the 'situationist' argument, see Sönke Neitzel and Harald Welzer, *Soldaten. Protokolle von Kämpfen, Töten und Sterben* (Frankfurt a.M.: Fischer, 2011). For the structural-ideological argument, see Omer Bartov, *The Eastern Front, 1941–45, German Troops and the Barbarization of Warfare* (Houndmills and New York: Macmillan, 2001 [1985]). For a reappraisal of this thesis, see Felix Römer, *Kameraden. Die Wehrmacht von innen* (Munich and Zürich: Pieper, 2012).

52 See X. M. Núñez Seixas, 'Unable to hate? Some comparative remarks on the war experience of Spanish and Italian soldiers on the Eastern front, 1941-44', *Journal of Modern European History* 16, no. 2 (2018): 269–89.

Chapter 14

'BOYS INTO MEN': MARTIAL MASCULINITY AND SEXUAL BEHAVIOUR IN FRANCO'S ARMY, 1939–44

Ian Winchester

Masculinity as a gendered construction has great consequence in the military, where normative constructions of manhood and male sexuality are created, problematized, challenged, and resisted. Militaries are not hermetically sealed from society, and in modern history, militarized masculinities have been integral to conditioning general cultural and societal conceptions of masculinity. Franco's Spain provides such an example. The dictatorship and the Spanish armed forces consciously sought to use conscription in the gendered endeavour of forming Spanish men by creating and inculcating a normative Francoist martial masculinity. In other words, as part of the dictatorship's efforts to mould the Spanish nation in its own image following victory in the Spanish Civil War, it institutionalized a militarized masculinity in the armed forces that it intended to impose on Spanish men during their required two years of active duty.

The Francoist military formulated the tenets of its normative masculinity through discursive means. Generating a cohesive canon of military thought through the mediums of books, conferences, journals, magazines, and training manuals, military authors elaborated and promulgated a normative Francoist masculinity based on militarized values. Inculcating its idealized notion of manhood through compulsory military service for men, the Franco regime intended to create martial, masculine, and obedient members of the nation. This project began during the Spanish Civil War and accelerated afterwards. The Francoist military knowingly understood and then exploited its opportunity to reconstruct Spanish society following its victory. A militarized masculinity played a fundamental role in the construction of nationalism in Franco's Spain, as well as in the dictatorship's practices of repression and the entrenchment of its power. Examining processes of discourse creation and dissemination during those formative years, this chapter delineates the parameters of Francoist masculinity and demonstrates the ways in which Francoists imagined the military as an institution for the civic education and social regulation of men.

Most historians speak of the Francoist military's belief system in terms of morality, values, and spirit. Predating the Spanish Civil War and similar to European-wide nineteenth- and early twentieth-century notions of fighting spirit and élan, an important current of Spanish military thought (later dominant in Francoism) held that the human factor was more important in war than the technical.[1] The Spanish military inculcated this attitude in its academies, barracks, and training camps.[2] Francoist martial principles not only exalted memories of the civil war, but as historian Gabriel Cardona demonstrates, also combined them with 'the greatness of Spain during the *Siglo de Oro* [Spain's 16th and 17th century Golden Age], the moral values of which had been recuperated by the Crusade [the civil war], freeing [those values] from the poisons of the Enlightenment and Liberalism'.[3] In relation to both those martial and Catholic ideologies – or in other words, two codifying ingredients of Francoist normativity – the military disseminated and imposed norms. Mandatory service was the tip of the spear in that endeavour, and most scholars agree that the Francoist military served as an institution of social control.[4]

Within the armed forces, the *Apostolado Castrense* (Martial Apostolate; the chaplaincy within the armed forces) held great influence over the creation and dissemination of discourse about masculinity. The organization's genesis came from the right-wing lay Catholic group, *Acción Católica* (Catholic Action), which the Nationalist Army incorporated into its ranks during the first months of the Spanish Civil War. Following victory, *Acción Católica* developed a plan for a specific church entity within the Army, efforts that in 1944 resulted in the creation of the *Apostolado*, which then became independent from *Acción Católica*. The Catholic Church's organization in the military viewed itself as the agent of the spiritual transformation of the armed forces and of Spain.[5] Its major contribution to military discourse during the years covered by this chapter was the training manual ¡*Para ti... Soldado!* (*For you... Soldier!*), which is discussed in more detail below. The church had also been active in the wartime Nationalist Army via the military chaplaincy, which provided religious personnel for all Francoist units and aided the projection of the war as a crusade (as explored in Chapter 4 of this volume).

During the years 1939–44, and especially until the Nazis were forced onto the defensive in 1943, the Falange held significant sway in conceptions of Francoist ideology. Important in their own right, this chapter does not delve into Falangist conceptions of a Francoist masculinity. Within the military, Falangism took a back seat to Catholicism and conservatism and did not have significant influence on discourse. Importantly as well, with the Unification Decree of May 1937 that created a single political party in the rebel zone, the regime militarized the Falange, infusing it with the non-fascist values of the armed forces rather than the Falange exerting its influence within the military.

This chapter primarily utilizes the discursive sources of books, journals, magazines, and training manuals to inform its analysis of Francoist normative martial masculinity in its formative years from 1939 to 1944. It also incorporates courts-martial from the time period in analysing the practice of military justice in relationship to discursive impetuses. The *Apostolado's* training manual, *¡Para ti..., soldado!*, in particular provides a representative source for the discourse of normative masculinity during the first six years of the Franco regime. Targeted at teenage boys before their conscription, this manual was the *Apostolado's* most widely produced pamphlet.[6] Its publication by the Ministry of the Army as from 1944 demonstrates the influence of the *Apostolado* on the army as a whole; the pamphlet – as well as the ones mentioned below – can also be seen as a crystallization of official views and discourse that dated from the end of the civil war and the reintroduction of a Francoist peacetime military service. Another source published in the same year by order of the Ministry of the Army and also representative of early Francoist discourse is *Cartilla del soldado* (*Soldiers' Booklet*).[7] Especially important in sexual education, this chapter also uses the manual, *Reflexiones morales* (*Moral reflections*), published by the army in 1943.[8]

Underlying and buttressing the Francoist military's mission of educating the nation's male youth, military authors made clear that recruits could only become true men by learning how to be good soldiers, and vice versa. Good soldiers and ideal men were consubstantial and military authors frequently discussed the utility of military service for the inculcation of gendered military values. Understandings of the motivations behind obligatory military service in Francoist Spain should include this specifically gendered rationale underpinning the education and training of soldiers. Nearly all interest groups and ranks of soldiers in the military consciously and perspicuously strove for the symbiotic masculinization and militarization of Spain's male population. Rather explicitly, military discourse asserted that compulsory service would change the fabric of the nation by influencing generations of Spanish men's masculinity and rectifying the unmanliness that Francoists attributed to the Republic.

An influential historiographical school of thought about the nature of Francoist masculinity views it in the paradigm of the 'half monk, half soldier', in which ideal Spanish men were conceived as warriors engaged in or dying for a religious crusade. Mary Nash provides a summation of this understanding in her piece on morality, National-Catholicism, culture, and gender during Francoism:

> In the post-war years male gender models were those of outstanding soldiers and fighters, exceptional figures that transcended daily life. The image of the warrior-monk shaped around a combination of *conquistador* and the founder of the Jesuits, Saint Ignatius de Loyola, and combining courage, virility, religiosity, and military values, became the prototype of role models for young Spanish males.[9]

The priestly warrior trope certainly played an important part in particularly Catholic and Falangist imaginations of martial masculinity, but was only one portion of a complex whole. In its polyvalence, Francoist normative martial masculinity contained many important attributes that fall outside the strict purview of the soldier-monk.

Spanish men's membership in the nation was predicated upon their embodiment of certain broad militarized and gendered characteristics. The most important of these martial values, as authors frequently referred to them, included military morality, spirit, and virtues; chivalric honour; and the triad of discipline, obedience, and subordination. Military discourse gendered each of these values. Linked especially to honour, a heteronormative male sexuality based on morality and the reproduction of the family also played a prominent role in that masculinity, with homosexuality marking a punishable transgressive step away from Francoist martial norms.

Inculcating Gendered Martial Values

When discussing the type of training that would make soldiers into manly members of the nation, authors stressed the importance of military morality. Not surprisingly, religion influenced definitions of military morality. In the regime's third year of existence, Jorge Vigón – the most representative author on normative masculinity and a key figure in the *Apostolado* – wrote in the military's premier publication, *Ejército* (*Army*), that the religious component of morality was paramount in ensuring that soldiers possessed the correct motivations behind their actions.[10]

To create paradigmatic men, the armed forces also educated soldiers in military spirit, which, like morality, was considered to hold more importance than technical knowledge. Demonstrating the consubstantiality of all the components of normative martial Francoist masculinity, *Reflexiones morales* stipulated in 1943 that the three most important military virtues were order, discipline, and valour.[11] Further revealing military thinking following the Spanish Civil War and in conjunction with the purpose of mandatory service, this source informed troops that military virtues did not end when they finished their active duty, but would truly begin to bear fruit when they returned to their hometowns.[12]

Possessing martial spirit could only be achieved if coupled with military virtues. Bravery, for example, was a crucial military virtue connected to both morality and honour. An article in *Ejército*, published in 1941 and written by a lawyer and professor of philosophy with the rank of provisional lieutenant, posited bravery as the cornerstone of military morality. Valour was the primary quality of a soldier: 'The entirety of military morality is based on this primordial condition of a soldier. The two terms, military and bravery, are inseparable.'[13] Helping lay the foundation for these notions of military virtues, in 1945 a magazine for troops presented Franco both as the epitome of a man who possessed martial virtues and as a leader attempting to instil them in Spaniards:

The virtues necessary in all good soldiers – faith, valour, loyalty, discipline, morality, generosity, the sense of command and love for the *Patria* – are those that delimit and illuminate [*aureolar*] the figure of the Caudillo; the virtues that, from his seat of honour, he has sought to inculcate in the people day by day, in order to persuade them of their duties and [devote their lives] to the good of all.[14]

Turning boys into men and returning them to society where they would embody and perform the masculine traits instilled in them during their two years of active duty comprised a central aspect of the rationale underpinning gendered military educational initiatives.

Military publications made clear that discipline, obedience, and subordination were crucial not only in the armed forces but also, as gendered constructions, to the functioning of the economy and society. Presented in a military magazine in 1945 and indicating the regime's employment of military service to control post-civil war Spanish society, education in the barracks would teach discipline to previously rebellious workers.[15] *Reflexiones morales* posited that out of all the military virtues Spain was most in need of discipline: 'The country is in much need of these virtues, but principally discipline. A century of libertinism has habituated the Spanish to disobedience, criticism, gossip and partisanship.'[16] Explicitly working to eradicate the values of the Second Republic, such discourse used masculinity to create a Francoist male nationalism in soldiers that would be transferred from the barracks to society (see Figure 14.1).

These aspects of martial masculinity were intertwined with military morality, as *Cartilla de soldado* posited: '*Military discipline* is a truth, within which is enclosed all the morality of the soldier.'[17] Likewise, obedience constituted 'the most fundamental of the military virtues, without *obedience there is no discipline*'.[18] Discipline, obedience, and subordination themselves were consubstantial and frequently repeated. *Cartilla de soldado* stipulated that 'without subordination, obedience is impossible and, therefore, discipline and subordination are the

Figure 14.1 Peacetime conscripts from the 1942 reserve class parade and swear allegiance to the Spanish flag in Vizcaya in the Basque Country. AGMAV, F.364, 2, 23/23.

recognition of the superiority of that which commands you'.[19] These aspects of mandatory military education worked to instil in soldiers the fortitude expected for combat along with the equally important docility that the Franco regime wanted to infuse in its male citizens.

Military authors conceived of educational mandates in the context of masculinity, gendering these aspects of the identity that the military and regime sought to create in soldiers. Deploying, to use Michel Foucault's terms, 'this new distribution of power known as discipline, with its structures and hierarchies, its inspections, exercises and methods of training and conditioning',[20] the military attempted to establish and solidify the power of the Franco dictatorship. The armed forces made discipline consubstantial with the only 'true' form of masculinity a Spanish man could possess. Viewed through the lens of the Foucauldian 'obedient subject', this type of man and citizen allows authority to 'function automatically in him'.[21] The education and training received during their required time in the military would, in intent and on a systemic level, influence individual men to not only unquestioningly obey authority, but also unconsciously function according to Francoism's directives. Accordingly, the Franco dictatorship utilized conscription to reify its power over and within Spanish society, specifically through the attempted creation of disciplined and obedient men who knew and performed their subordinate positions in military, political, and social hierarchies.

Controlling Male Sexuality

The values of discipline, obedience, and subordination played a further role in conditioning men's sexuality, as they supposedly aided men in controlling their sexual urges. Notions of honour also played a crucial role in that process. Francoist military authors often maintained that honour comprised the normative behaviour military men should demonstrate. For instance, in 1944 a certain General Barrueco writing in *Ejército* stated that honour 'advises us on that which we should do and that from which we must abstain'.[22] In that sense, concepts of honour loomed especially large in, and provided the discursive bridge for, norms of male sexuality. As General Barrueco's statement indicates, the military held positions on when sex was positive, but also when it was negative, or what a man ought not to do in terms of sex and sexuality. On the one hand, the broader military had the attitude that male sexuality needed an outlet, and in that vein provided soldiers with practical sexual education, especially how to prevent sexually transmitted infections (STIs). Catholic interpretation of sexuality, on the other hand, posited chastity before and procreative sex within marriage as the only moral forms of sexual behaviour.

The *Apostolado* informed soldiers that chastity – a truly manly quality connected to Catholic morality – was the best way to avoid the dangers inherent in sexuality. To defend against other malicious influences that might lead a young soldier away from chastity, ¡*Para ti..., soldado!* warned in 1944 that anyone who argued that sexuality was natural, or who maintained that chastity was impossible, was actually attempting to justify their own depraved conduct.[23] These messages, dating to the 1940s, were not uniquely disseminated by the *Apostolado*. According to a non-*Apostolado* military instructional pamphlet from 1944, the Don Juan or womanizer was less of a man despite his litany of sexual conquests: 'Do not suppose that he is more of a man who goes with many women, on the contrary, [he is more of man] who guards his chastity.'[24] In this case, rather than the common societal conception of *donjuanismo* – in which the strength of a man's masculinity was tied to his sexual conquest of multiple women – this author proposed that the fewer times a man had sex, the greater his masculinity.[25]

According to military sources, and especially pronounced in *Apostolado* discourse, a man's purpose in life was to marry an honest woman and have children. The précis of the *Apostolado*'s attitude in this regard consisted of sex being healthy and natural only when it occurred between a man and a woman during marriage for the sole purpose of procreation.[26] Authors inside and outside the *Apostolado* often connected these notions to Catholicism and marriage. In 1944 *¡Para ti..., soldado!* stated that 'Jesus Christ has made marriage a Sacrament, a noble vocation, great and beautiful. Prepare yourself to lead an honest and glorious life in this sublime role as leader and head of a family.'[27] The same source described the purposes of sex in a combination of biological, heteronormative, and religious terms: 'God has created two different sexes, which are also equipped [*provistos*] with different organs, called genitals, so that, through the union of the man and the woman, the human species perpetuates itself.'[28] As pleasure accompanied the 'procreational act', *¡Para ti..., soldado!* notified soldiers that although it might be tempting to seek sex for the sake of gratification, in so doing a man avoided the 'end for which it was established'.[29] Accordingly, 'Each time that this act takes place outside of [a] marriage sanctified by the Sacrament, or within marriage [but] done trying to avoid the propagation of the species, one gravely sins'. *Reflexiones morales* stated in 1943 that chastity and procreative sex within marriage were 'the conditions of moral law. He errs, therefore, who joins with a women in order to have children, if that woman is not his legitimate [wife]. Those husbands err as well who use [certain] methods in order to have few or no children.'[30] Similarly, *Campaña premilitar* (*Premilitary campaign*), a training pamphlet, imparted the lesson that with sex, 'the law faithfully observed is a source of life and the abuse [of that law] is the abyss of death'.[31] This final word of advice demonstrates how the military in the 1940s established the imperative to make men obediently follow the sexual norms of the Franco regime.

Those norms included keeping one's body morally and hygienically pure. To maintain purity the *Apostolado* and military cautioned soldiers against STIs and the dangers of having sex with prostitutes. While Catholic-inspired sources like *Reflexiones morales* posited abstinence as the best way to avoid venereal disease,[32] the military published training manuals with practical advice for those soldiers who during their time in active duty would engage in sexual acts with women. A tension existed between these types of educational directives and more religious ideas about sex. *Reflexiones morales* informed soldiers that when first arriving in the barracks they would be given advice from a doctor about how to avoid venereal diseases, but that troops should not assume that those instructions were imparted with an attitude of permissiveness. Rather, such actions 'are prohibited because of morality and patriotism, the same as they were when you were a young man and when you lived as a youngster at home, and they will be for your whole life, because the law of good and of bad is the same everywhere and at all times.'[33] According to this source, STIs were a punishment from God, the negative consequences of which would carry over to a man's children: 'Blind, paralyzed, monstrous children, innocent victims of a sin they did not commit, will always be in front of the eyes of the father who remembers that he enjoyed himself at their expense in his youth.'[34] These sources indicate that the military was aware that soldiers were having sex outside of wedlock and provided sexual education that would help mitigate potential negative consequences from such behaviour. Such discourse used traditional Catholic morality and hinged on moral panic to try and make young men remain chaste during their time in the military.

Within a discourse that conceived of women as vectors of disease, men contracted STIs from immoral women in particular. As *Reflexiones morales* stated: 'The cheap prostitutes, who the depraved [*vicioso*] soldier tends to visit, are all infected. And, in general, you can consider as dangerous all *easy* women.'[35] In line with historiography about 'fallen women' in Franco's Spain,[36] Francoist military discourse presented prostitutes and women who engaged in sex outside of marriage or had subjective sexual desires as a threat to the healthy body politic because they spread disease and contaminated masculine morality. Military discourse contrasted such women to the pure body of the bride and wife.

Running counter to these strict discursive imperatives, less-Catholic military discourse regarded normative masculine sexuality as likely needing the outlet of the prostitute, such that spaces existed within Francoist martial mores wherein it was acceptable and normal for men to use the body of the prostitute for their sexual desires. Military education recognized this and provided advice that accepted the fact that soldiers had sex with prostitutes. Unlike *Reflexiones morales* and its lack of any advice beyond chastity, *Cartilla del soldado*, for example, taught soldiers more practical sexual education, warning soldiers to 'avoid kissing prostitutes'.[37] *Cartilla del soldado* taught that 'when this is not observed, practice coitus with a preservative, commonly called a condom. After urinating, wash with water and soap.' This type of pedagogy inspired more by health and hygiene than morality and religion comprised the larger focus of the military's sex education initiatives.[38] In general, the Catholic message of sex and sexuality conflicted with both that of the military and Spanish society. Sexual education for troops in training manuals like *Cartilla de soldado* or the talks *¡Para ti... soldado!* referenced reflected the reality that soldiers often had sex before and outside of marriage. The military did not encourage its troops to have sex with prostitutes, but accepted such conduct and provided soldiers a sexual education that taught them about prostitutes and gave them information on what to do if they contracted an STI.

Discourse on prostitutes presented a conundrum of conflicting messages. On the one hand, the *Apostolado* and the military informed soldiers that having sex with prostitutes was injurious to the *Patria*, personally emasculating, morally repugnant, and dangerously unhealthy. On the other hand, troops lived in the barracks (a site of socialization wherein sex was a popular topic of discussion), received practical sexual education, and had sex with prostitutes and outside of marriage. Although the Francoist military sought to control the kind of women with whom troops had sexual relations, it did not regulate prostitutes themselves or take strong measures to prevent soldiers from using prostitutes as sexual outlets. These opposing influences corresponded to and are explained by the discourse and practicalities of the Francoist military. A Catholicized message of chastity and morality held sway within certain segments of the armed forces, but it was not influential enough to overcome the reality that soldiers had sex out of wedlock. Neither could it surpass the prevalent cultural attitudes of male sexuality as needing an outlet and recourse to prostitution as an inevitable expression of robust masculine heterosexuality.

Further sexual behaviours that military discourse sought to eradicate included masturbation and pornography. Training manuals informed young men that masturbation was physically, mentally, and spiritually debilitating. *¡Para ti... soldado!* stated in 1944 that the 'solitary vice' would result in a litany of disasters. Madness, for example, resulted from such practices, with one's willpower debilitated to such an extent that a man would become 'a slave to sin', incapable of all higher and generous feelings, and would fall into egoism. According to this *Apostolado* source, masturbation was a path that easily led to 'a thousand other disorders', as well as misery, shame, and desperation. It dissipated a man's health, wasting away strong men. The direct consequence of sexual self-stimulation was that 'above all, he who has surrendered to impure vice has been lost as a son of God'.[39] Here, the *Apostolado* and the military engaged more in a discourse of health and morality than of masculinity: masturbating might not erode masculinity, but it would lead to physical and mental problems as well as forfeiture of one's relationship with God.[40]

An immoral practice that went hand-in-hand with masturbation, pornography also represented a threat to troops. *Reflexiones morales* sarcastically stated that before the Franco regime pornography had been 'one of the *benefits* of freedom of the press', but that 'today the State suppresses that liberty'.[41] As part of the surveillance initiative of soldiers reporting other soldiers for immoral behaviour, this training manual asked troops to inform their superiors if they saw anyone looking at pornography, even if doing so risked being called a bad *compañero*, or buddy. Pornography was a 'true moral leprosy that threatened dignity and the life of the spirit'.[42] As with education about masturbation, this type of discourse in training manuals established in the 1940s that true men did not engage in or look at material that facilitated onanism. Yet the existence of such advice throughout the Franco regime indicates the failure of its message and that soldiers masturbated and consumed pornography enthusiastically. As the years went by, this type of sexual education harped on about the perception that, rather than dissipating, the problems of pornography and masturbation were worsening.[43]

Creating and inculcating these mandates of normative male sexuality, the Spanish armed forces carried out the sexually repressive intentions and practices of Francoism in order to protect the nation from perceived social degeneracy. The heteronormative institution of the Francoist military imposed and maintained stringent regulations of male gender and sexual norms to create a specific type of Spanish man. Military authors intended these discursive initiates to make normative male sexuality align with a system that subordinated women to men, and both sexes to God and nation.

The ideal of the Don Juan referenced above provides a revealing example of this process. Content in military training manuals and print culture portrayed the model of the Don Juan as a negative other type of sexuality that soldiers should avoid if they aspired to become ideal husbands and fathers. The Don Juan's sexuality was based on sexual conquest rather than marriage and fatherhood. Linked to broader cultural discourses about *donjuanismo*, diatribes against the Don Juan represent a common current of thought within Francoist military discourse dating to the 1940s. In 1945, a colonel writing in the periodical for troops, *Yunque* (*Anvil*), described the Don Juan as a harmful and damaging 'chimerical fantasy', as well as a coward and delinquent.[44]

Military discourse viewed the Don Juan as dangerous because he conquered multiple women for sexual ends rather than respectfully courting one woman for the purposes of marriage. Placed within a Foucauldian conception of the modern world, such a man further jeopardized the regulation of sexuality: 'There were two great systems conceived by the West for governing sex: the law of marriage and the order of desires – and the life of Don Juan overturned them both.'[45] For Francoists, the sexuality of the Don Juan threatened to undermine their desire for a Spanish nation comprised of men who controlled their sexual urges, were chivalrous towards women, and submitted themselves to the institution of marriage. Replacing *donjuanismo* with Catholic norms of procreative sex within marriage better fit with the ultimate objective of constructing obedient members of the nation who conformed to the mandates of marriage and fatherhood.

While many Spanish men did get married and have children, military sources from the entirety of the Franco regime indicate that soldiers ignored the more strict directives of the military and the *Apostolado*, especially in terms of sexual behaviour. Military discourse in the form of training manuals, journals, and magazines provides evidence of this state of affairs when describing the sexually charged atmosphere of the barracks and the never-abating practices of soldiers having sex before marriage, visiting prostitutes, masturbating, and looking at pornography.[46] Courts-martial records further contain evidence of homosexual practices and identities within the military.[47] That many Spanish men married after their time in the military indicates some success in perpetuating those norms, but inculcating specific practices and understandings of sex and sexuality sheds light on the broader failure to impose a normative Francoist martial masculinity.

Such failure was part of the changes that affected Spain in the 1960s and 1970s as the nation's economic modernization brought with it sociocultural modernity. Regardless of its influence within the military and its sophisticated discursive appeals to masculinity, morality, and physical health, the regime ultimately failed to control and shape the sexuality of several generations of Spanish men. Although the *Apostolado* and official military discourse on sexuality show little change over time, the times themselves changed. Within the overall context of attempting to control sexuality during the Franco regime, the military's efforts paradoxically contributed to a sexual liberalization of the nation. The armed forces provided one of the few avenues of practical – if informal – sexual education in Spain and placed young men in an environment where they could discuss and explore their sexuality. These men created a culture of sexual licentiousness, if not experimentation, that superseded that of religious morality.

Homosexuality

An aspect of this culture was homosexuality, which represented an even greater threat than sexual impiety or the Don Juan to Francoist heteronormativity. The system of military justice both disciplined and punished men for transgressions against heteronormativity, and military jurisprudence put into practice discursive notions of a sexualized martial honour wherein that concept performed a regulatory function in preventing men from acting in certain ways. The *Código de Justicia Militar* (CJM), or Military Justice Code, legislated certain acts as constituting crimes against honour and punished men who transgressed those boundaries. Until 1954, with the passing of the *Ley de vagos y maleantes*, or Law of Vagrants and Miscreants,[48] the CJM was the only law in Franco's Spain that expressly punished homosexuals. This power was especially salient in cases of homosexuality, in which the Francoist system of military justice operated as a regime of discipline and system of power that sought out intimate knowledge about sexual acts to punish men who overstepped the boundaries of masculine heteronormativity.

Soldiers caught in homosexual acts appeared in judicial records during the years 1939–45.[49] Courts-martial reveal that a regime of discipline and the infliction of punishments worked towards both defining and controlling Spanish men's gendered identities and personal sexualities. During the early 1940s, for example, Sergeant Manuel M. O. and another man, Francisco G. R., took several vacations with one another, exchanged gifts, and were caught in bed together by Francisco G. R.'s mother. In 1944, a military tribunal sentenced Manuel M. O. to six years in military prison and discharged him from the armed forces for this crime against martial honour. His sexual relationship with another man earned him the maximum sentence and made him no longer worthy of serving in the military.[50]

In a case from 1941 a private named José B. O. serving in a Falangist unit was tried for a crime against honour. Two years earlier a male civilian had masturbated José B. O., who was at the time wearing his military uniform. The court found that these acts had taken place without 'violence, intimidation, or publicity'. Although admitting guilt, the defence asked for six-months-and-a-day of prison, making the argument that the act had only been attempted (*en grado tentativa*) and not actually carried out. The court gave José B. O. a sentence of one year in prison with the rest of his time in active duty to be spent in a disciplinary unit.[51]

A military court found that in 1945 two second-class artillery gunners, 22-year-old Juan R. P. and 33-year-old Pedro A. R., had (separately) participated in sodomy at the request of a 33-year-old sergeant named Manuel O. M. The court ruled that the artillery gunners had engaged in anal sex with the sergeant voluntarily, 'without opposition', and with no coercion or physical violence on the part of Manuel O. M.[52] For these repeated sexual offences (the sergeant had participated in anal sex with each of the defendants at least three different times), the court sentenced Manuel O. M. to six-months-and-a-day of military prison along with a discharge, and the other two soldiers to prison sentences of six-months-and-a-day but without discharges. The magistrates deemed the active pursuer of anal sex to be unworthy of remaining in the military and decided that the other two defendants required punishment but did not consider their actions to be worthy of a discharge.[53]

Conversely, when homosexuality constituted a key factor in an infraction the military would not necessarily bring charges of a crime against honour. In 1943 two corporals named Joaquín Ramón P. M. and Eusebio S. P. were charged with abuse of authority for attempting to make fellow soldiers commit homosexual acts. Knowing that two other soldiers of lower rank had previously engaged in 'dishonest' acts with each other, Joaquín Ramón P. M. and Eusebio S. P. ordered the two men to take off their trousers (apparently to humiliate them), an order with which they refused to comply. For this infraction, the military found Joaquín Ramón P. M. and Eusebio S. P. guilty of abuse of authority and sentenced them to two-months-and-a-day in prison.[54] Conceivably, the military did not invoke the specific charge of dishonest acts with a member of the same sex because the pair had not themselves engaged in homosexual behaviour. The performance of making other men carry out homosexual acts as a means to humiliate them did not contravene military honour. Rather, those homophobic actions helped reinforce heteronormative conceptions of male sexuality.

The punishments of prison sentences and discharges in these cases and the general anti-homosexual stances within the armed forces mirrored and reinforced Francoism outside the barracks. In accordance with definitions of normative masculinity and its importance to a healthy body politic, Francoism codified male homosexuality as dangerous and insidious. Consequently, the military, state, and society persecuted homosexual men.[55] In concert with the heteronormative boundaries of the regime's power, normative martial Francoist masculinity discursively mandated heterosexuality and pathologized homosexuality. As with the Spanish military during the twentieth century before and during the Spanish Civil War, the Francoist-controlled armed forces used its control over Spanish men to enforce these discursive mandates and punish individual men for transgressions against heteronormativity.

Conclusions

The Franco regime employed mandatory military service as a major technique of power to construct and maintain gender normativity for men. Michael Richards contends that the economic practice of autarky contained 'particular ideas of purity and nationalism [that] were the backdrop of sacrifice and social control, the basis of a kind of internal colonization which was the essential condition for Spain's resurgence during Francoism'.[56] Inculcating Francoist normative martial masculinity through conscription served similar functions for the regime.

The discursive polyvalence embedded in martial values and male sexuality allowed the Francoist military spaces in which to formulate, prescribe, and regulate soldiers' gender and sexuality. Military training manuals, print culture, and jurisprudence formed the support pillars in efforts to mould manly martial, obedient, and pious members of the nation and make them into heteronormative husbands and fathers. The specifically Francoist basis for such a male identity came out of the years 1939–44: having its antecedents in pre-civil war military, conservative, and Catholic thinking and forged in the historical conditions of the Spanish Civil War, this dominant archetype of masculinity was solidified at the beginning of Franco's rule.

Understanding that the Franco regime used mandatory military service not only for the purposes of war, but also for indoctrination and social control, clarifies how concern over masculinity in the Francoist armed forces was more about social reproduction and 'national regeneration' than military prowess or combat on the battlefield. In practice, however, Spanish men did not by any means always adhere to the regime's mores, especially as far as non-normative sexual practices were concerned, even if they did often obey the mandate to marriage and live acquiescently under the political power wielded by the Franco regime. This mixed outcome indicates the limits of conscription as a means of social control. Mandatory military service deluged soldiers with messages of Francoist normative masculinity and helped maintain Franco's power for the duration of his rule, but the ideal image that the regime had for Spanish men failed to fully define the gendered identity of the nation.

Further Reading

Losada Malvárez, Juan Carlos. *Ideología del Ejército franquista, 1939–1958*. Madrid: Istmo, S.A., 1990.

Morcillo Gómez, Aurora. *The Seduction of Modern Spain: The Female Body and the Francoist Body Politic*. Lewisburg: Bucknell University Press, 2010.

Nash, Mary. 'Towards a New Moral Order: National-Catholicism, Culture and Gender'. In *Spanish History since 1808*, edited by José Álvarez Junco and Adrian Shubert, 289–300. Oxford: Oxford University Press, 2000.

Vincent, Mary. 'The Martyrs and the Saints: Masculinity and the Construction of the Francoist Crusade'. *History Workshop Journal*, no. 47 (Spring 1999): 68–98.

Vincent, Mary. 'La reafirmación de la masculinidad en la cruzada franquista'. *Cuadernos de Historia Contenporánea* 28 (2006): 131–51.

Winchester, Ian. 'So[u]ldiers for Christ and Men for Spain: The *Apostolado Castrense*'s Role in the Creation and Dissemination of Francoist Martial Masculinity'. *Revista Universitaria de Historia Militar* 4, no. 8 (July–December 2015): 143–63.

Notes

1 See, for example, Juan Carlos Losada Malvárez, *Ideología del Ejército franquista, 1939–1958* (Madrid: Istmo, S.A., 1990), 50–1.

2 See, for example, Mariano Aguilar Olivencia, *El ejército español durante el franquismo: Un juicio desde dentro* (Madrid: Ediciones Akal, 1999), 296.

3 Gabriel Cardona, *El poder militar en el franquismo: Las bayonetas de papel* (Barcelona: Flor del Viento, 2008), 181.

4 The most comprehensive works are: Aguilar Olivencia, *El ejército español durante el franquismo*; Cardona, *El poder militar en el franquismo*; Losada Malvárez, *Ideología del Ejército franquista*; José Antonio Olmeda Gómez, *Las fuerzas armadas en el estado franquista* (Madrid: El Arquero, 1988); and Fernando Puell de la Villa, *Historia del Ejército en España* (Madrid: Alianza, 2005). Each of these works investigates issues pertaining to the history of the military, including the social makeup of the officer corps, the political power of the military within and vis-à-vis the state, the key players and important changes that occurred during the course of Franco's reign, and the successes and failures of the military during that time period.

5 For a full examination of the *Apostolado*'s influence on Francoist martial masculinity see: Ian Winchester, 'So[u]ldiers for Christ and Men for Spain: The *Apostolado Castrense*'s Role in the Creation and Dissemination of Francoist Martial Masculinity', *Revista Universitaria de Historia Militar* 4, no. 8 (July–December 2015): 143–63.

6 Aresio González de Vega, *¡Para ti..., soldado! (Manual del soldado) (Obra declarada de utilidad por el Ministerio del Ejército)* (Madrid: Ministerio del Ejército, 1944). For more on this pamphlet see Losada Malvárez, *Ideología del Ejército franquista*, 270.

7 Felipe Sesma Bengoechea, *Cartilla del soldado: De utilidad para los reclutas, individuos de las clases de tropa y subinstructores* (Barcelona: Simpar, S.A., 1944).

8 Ignacio de Otto y Torra, *Reflexiones morales (charlas para el soldado)* (Madrid: Ediciones Ejército, 1943).

9 Mary Nash, 'Towards a New Moral Order: National-Catholicism, Culture and Gender', in *Spanish History since 1808*, eds. José Álvarez Junco and Adrian Shubert (Oxford: Oxford University Press, 2000), 289–300. See also: Mary Vincent, 'The Martyrs and the Saints: Masculinity and the Construction of the Francoist Crusade', *History Workshop Journal*, no. 47 (Spring 1999): 68–98; and Mary Vincent, 'La reafirmación de la masculinidad en la cruzada franquista', *Cuadernos de Historia Contenporánea* 28 (2006): 131–51.

10 Jorge Vigón, 'Educación militar', *Ejército*, no. 26 (March 1942): 19–22.

11 Otto y Torra, *Reflexiones morales*, 40.

12 Ibid., 43.

13 Antonio Sánchez del Corral y del Río, 'En torno de la Moral Militar', *Ejército*, no. 12 (January 1941).

14 Jesús Vasallo, 'Franco, Caudillo de España: Virtudes militares en el caudillaje de Franco', *Yunque*, no. 4 (10 October 1945).

15 Francisco Vargas Borrego, 'Armas y Letras: Disciplina', *Yunque*, no. 6 (December 1945): 10.

16 Otto y Torra, *Reflexiones morales*, 43.

17 Sesma Bengoechea, *Cartilla del soldado*, 11. Original italics.

18 Ibid., 12.

19 Sesma Bengoechea, *Cartilla del soldado*, 13–14.

20 Michel Foucault, *Power/Knowledge: Selected Interviews and Other Writings, 1972–1977*, ed. Colin Gordon (New York: Vintage Books, 1980), 158.

21 Michel Foucault, *Discipline and Punish: The Birth of the Prison* (New York: Vintage Books, 1991), 128–9.

22 General Barrueco, 'El mando y la moral', *Ejército*, no. 55 (August 1944): 9–12.

23 González de Vega, *¡Para ti…, soldado!*, 67.

24 Sesma Bengoechea, *Cartilla del soldado*, 59.

25 More recent scholarship on masculinity in twentieth-century Spain has begun to explore the importance of counter-narratives to the macho Don Juan in constructions of normative masculinity. See especially, Narea Aresti, *Médicos, donjuanes y mujeres modernas: Los ideales de feminidad y masculinidad en el primer tercio del Siglo XX* (Bilbao: Universidad del País Vasco, 2001); and *¿La España Invertebrada? Masculinidad y nación a comienzos del siglo XX*, ed. Nerea Aresti et al. (Granada: Comares, 2016).

26 González de Vega, *¡Para ti…, soldado!*, 67.

27 Ibid., 75.

28 Ibid., 67.

29 Ibid.

30 Otto y Torra, *Reflexiones morales*, 72.

31 González de Vega, *¡Para ti…, soldado!*, 67.

32 Otto y Torra, *Reflexiones morales*, 77.

33 Ibid., 75.

34 Ibid., 73–5.

35 Ibid., 76.

36 See especially Mirta Nuñez Díaz-Balart, *Mujeres caídas: Prostitutas legales y clandestinas en el franquismo* (Madrid: Oberón, 2003); and Aurora Morcillo Gómez, *The Seduction of Modern Spain: The Female Body and the Francoist Body Politic* (Lewisburg: Bucknell University Press, 2010), 90–131.

37 Sesma Bengoechea, *Cartilla del soldado*, 58.

38 This type of advice remained consistent as the years progressed. See, for example: Serrano Expósito and Revilla Martínez, *Manual del recluta y del soldado de aviación*, 5th ed. (Saragossa: Gráficas Iris, 1962), 217; and Sinforiano Morón Izquierdo, *¡Vencer! Breviario del soldado y de los mandos inferiores*, 16th ed. (Barcelona: Ramón Sopena, S.A., 1969).

39 González de Vega, *¡Para ti…, soldado!*, 70–1.

40 Ibid.

41 Otto y Torra, *Reflexiones morales*, 128–9. Original italics.

42 Ibid., 129.

43 See, for example: Luis, Arzobispo de Sion, 'La pornografía va a los cuarteles', *Guías Información y Directivas del Apostolado Castrense*, año IV, no. 17 (September 1955).

44 Fr Coronel de Estambre, 'Lo que vale de "Don Juan Tenorio"', *Yunque*, no. 5 (10 November 1945).

45 Michel Foucault, *The History of Sexuality. Vol. 1: An Introduction* (New York: Vintage Books, 1990), 39–40.

46 See, for example: Arzobispo de Sion, 'La pornografía va a los cuarteles'; Gonzalo Muinelo Alarcón, 'Tony el recluta ye-yé', *Formación*, no. 163 (February 1967); Morón Izquierdo, *¡Vencer!*; and 'La pareja humana: Acotaciones biologicas', *Reconquista*, no. 261 (September 1971): 61–2.

47 See below.

48 For an overview of the *Ley de vagos y maleantes* see Jordi Terrasa Mateu, 'La legislación represiva', in *Una discriminación universal: La homosexualidad bajo el franquismo y la transición*, ed. Javier Ugarte Pérez (Barcelona: Editorial Egales, 2008), 79–107, 96–8.

49 However, as Javier Ugarte Pérez points out in the introduction to the volume he edited about discrimination towards homosexuals during Francoism and the transition to democracy, homosexual men could be charged and punished under other crimes under the Penal Code of 1944 such as dishonest abuses (*abusos deshonestos*), public scandal, and corruption of minors, for which, he argues, homosexuals received higher penalties than did heterosexuals for the same crimes. Javier Ugarte Pérez, ed., 'Introducción', in *Una discriminación universal*, 18.

50 Archivo General e Histórico de Defensa: Justicia Militar: Contra el Honor Militar: Sumario 1333, Legajo 321, Año 1960.

51 Archivo General Militar de Guadalajara: 4. Unidades, Centros y Organismos (UCOS): 4.1 Prisiones Militares: 4.1.11 Castillo de Santa Catalina (Cádiz), Expedientes Personales: Legajo 12, Sumario 777, Causa 1255/39 (hereafter: AGMG: CSC: 12/777, 1255/39).

52 AGMG: CSC: 82/5116, 8/46.

53 Juan R. P. and Pedro A. R. having been the parties who acquiesced rather than initiated the homosexual acts, might have played a mediating role in the verdict not cashiering them.

54 AGMG: CSC: 83/5167, 1072/43.

55 See, especially, Arturo Arnalte Barrera, *Redada de violetas: La represión de los homosexuales durante el franquismo* (Madrid: La Esfera de los Libros, 2003); and Alberto Mira Nouselles, *De Sodoma a Chueca: Una Historia cultural de la homosexualidad en España en el siglo XX* (Barcelona: Editorial Egales, 2004).

56 Michael Richards, *A Time of Silence: Civil War and Repression in Franco's Spain, 1936–1945* (Cambridge: Cambridge University Press, 1998), 4.

INDEX

Ingram Content Group UK Ltd.
Milton Keynes UK
UKHW021155040423
419514UK00003B/111

9 781350 030121